Bibliographic Checklist of African American Newspapers

Bibliographic Checklist of African American Newspapers

Barbara K. Henritze

DEDICATION

This book is dedicated to my husband, Philip Warren Zak, who never once asked why I was writing it, and always encouraged me onward, and also to my daughter, Katherine Armstrong Zak, whose arrival inadvertently delayed the book more than a year.

CONTENTS

ACKNOWLEDGMENTS

This book would not have been written if not for my friend Sandra Craighead, Editor of *Afro-American Historical and Genealogical Society, Inc., Cleveland Chapter Newsletter*. The book started out as an article and grew to an amazing length, as I discovered more and more newspapers and periodicals. With her support and encouragement, the article grew into a book.

The research for this book would not have been attempted before I had access to the wonderful resources and helpful staff at the Western Reserve Historical Society Library. The data would not have coalesced into a book without the never-ending encouragement, questions, and editing from Ronna Bryant, Sue Cook, Sandi Craighead, Birdie Holsclaw, Jeff Hoye, and Phil Zak.

Computer help (software, hardware, training, and even some data entry assistance) came from Peggy Bonnet, Birdie Holsclaw, Russ Holsclaw, Jeff Hoye, Ilona Major, Denise Tursic, Susan White, and WordPerfect Corp.

Special thanks go to Ellen Robertson, reference librarian at Norlin Library, Boulder, who helped immensely with the interlibrary loan process and untangled OCLC's FIRST SEARCH process; Frank Carroll at the Library of Congress; and Jim Danky at the State Historical Society of Wisconsin. Project encouragement came from Nudie E. Williams and Henry Suggs, professors and scholars interested in African American newspapers and their histories.

Librarians and research staffs at many repositories were very supportive, including Roger Torbert at the Birmingham Public Library; Stephen Gutgesell at the Ohio Historical Society in Columbus; Ann Jones at the Tennessee State Library and Archives; Harriett Robinson at Lincoln University, Jefferson City, Missouri; Randall Jelks at the Grand Rapids Public Library; Tony Wappel at the Mullins Library of the University of Arkansas in Conway; DeVita Mitchell at Tuskegee University Archives; and James Lynch at the American Baptist-Samuel Colgate Historical Library. Marli Vauss from Amalgamated Publishers Inc., Clarence Vinton from the *Asheville Advocate*, and Joseph Coley from the *Bakersfield News Observer* were helpful and informative.

Countless unknown librarians and staffs were cooperative and prompt including those from the U.S. Department of Commerce Library in Maryland, Vermont State Historical Society, Montana State Library, Idaho State Library, New Hampshire State Library, North and South Dakota State Libraries, Wyoming State Library, Maine Historical Society, four separate departments of the Denver Public Library, Hampton University Library, Chattanooga Afro-American Heritage Museum, Chicago Public Library, Albuquerque Public Library, Purdue University Library, Milwaukee Public Library, Clarksdale-Montgomery County Public Library, Shelby County Historical Society, Iowa State Historical Department, *The Communicator Newspaper*, *Mobile Beacon and Alabama Citizen*, and *Urban Spectrum*. As in all research projects, calls and letters to some repositories were not returned or answered.

Special accolades go to Mrs. Ada Treadwell, who, on her own, has collected and preserved the only known copies of many Waterloo, Iowa, black newspapers. I know there are more people like her in the world and hope they always have the space and inclination to collect and preserve.

Without a doubt, I have left out some individual or repository, which I regret. Prior to writing this book, I never understood why authors needed so much space for acknowledgments. Now I do. I could not have done it alone.

FOREWORD

In 1946 Warren Brown, professor of Sociology and Anthropology at Hunter College in New York City, compiled a list of 467 newspapers (*Checklist of Negro Newspapers in the United States [1827-1946]*). It was published by the School of Journalism at Lincoln University in Jefferson City, Missouri. Brown states it "attempts, with as much completeness as possible, to list all of the papers about which anything is known and that had more than temporary existence." There have been other bibliographies since then, building upon this early list. Now, almost fifty years later, aided by computerized electronic searches and sophisticated telecommunications Barbara Henritze has included over 5,000 newspaper titles in her bibliography. Little did anyone know in 1946 that Brown only identified one-tenth of the actual number of African American newspapers.

What started out as a small project by Ms. Henritze, to compile a list of the African American newspapers in Cleveland, Ohio, has emerged into a monumental effort. During this research, Ms. Henritze identified thousands of other African American newspapers published throughout the United States. Before this project, researchers would have had to consult dozens of publications to identify African American newspapers. In fact, Ms. Henritze has used one hundred seven sources, listed in Appendix A, to identify African American newspapers.

Ms. Henritze has, in effect, combined more than one hundred directories and bibliographies of African American newspapers into one publication. In the past, researchers have had to go to several directories to determine the existence of newspapers. Having one publication that combines all these directories is very useful and needed.

Newspapers have almost always been used by historians in researching past events. Much of the research in Arthur Ashe's three-volume set, *A Hard Road to Glory: A History of the African-American Athlete*, published by Warner Books in 1988, was based on information found in African American newspapers. Newspapers are a neglected but important source for genealogists. Unfortunately, genealogists almost always pass over sources that are not indexed. An unindexed source is as valuable, if not more valuable, than an indexed source; it's just more time-consuming to research. Indexed sources should be searched first, but unindexed sources should not be eliminated.

A lot of African American genealogists fail to realize there *are* several indexes to African American newspapers. James de T. Abajian compiled the three volume set, *Blacks in Selected Newspapers, Censuses and Other Sources: An Index to Names and Subjects* in 1977, published by G. K. Hall. A two volume supplement followed in 1985. Donald Jacobs indexed early African American newspapers in *Antebellum Black Newspapers: Indices to NY Freedom's Journal 1827-1929, The Rights of All 1829, Weekly Advocate 1837, and The Colored American 1837-1841*, which was published by Greenwood Press in Westport, Connecticut in 1976. Currently, the *Black Newspapers Index*, and its predecessor *Index to Black Newspapers*, has been published annually since 1977 by University Microfilms of Ann Arbor, Michigan.

Newspaper indexing is one of the last challenges for genealogists. More indexes need to be created, and hopefully this book will encourage genealogists and genealogical societies to seek out African American newspapers and index back issues.

Most newspapers contain a wealth of information but are almost virtually inaccessible because they are so voluminous and are unindexed. This book will assist in the process of identifying them, accessing them, and hopefully creating indexes to them.

The information contained in newspapers, such as obituaries; birth, death, and marriage notices; club news; social and fraternal events; catastrophes; and day-to-day news from a Black perspective, is usually a one-of-a-kind source for African American genealogists. It will be found nowhere else. Two articles published in 1895 in the small town newspaper of California, Pennsylvania solved one of my own longstanding family riddles.

The advertisements placed in African American newspapers following the Civil War are among the most valuable sources of information. Families were divided during slavery as a result of forced sale, escape, and enlistment into military service. Family members sometimes placed "Information Wanted" ads to search for their missing relatives. These ads often include family members' names, physical descriptions, residences during slavery, and sometimes the names of slaveowners and plantations.* These ads are invaluable for African American genealogists. Oftentimes, the newspaper is the only source of this information.

Ms. Henritze's illustrations of the problems in cataloguing names of titles of newspapers will assist many readers in locating missing issues. Many researchers have been frustrated trying to locate existing papers because the titles could be listed several different ways in the card catalogue or computer catalogue. They could be listed under the title of the papers, the city or state in which it was published, the frequency of publication, or variations of the three. Ms. Henritze gives excellent examples of these variations.

I have recently learned that items in closed stack libraries and archives can often be difficult to retrieve, even though the items are in the collection. This problem not only frustrates researchers, but also reference librarians, who can't locate items in their own collection because they do not know how the cataloguer listed the items in the computer.

We want to commend Ms. Henritze for this monumental work. Something like this has been needed for a long time. Hopefully, it will renew efforts for searches for defunct publications. As Ms. Henritze discovered, there are issues of rare newspapers still in people's bookcases, basements, attics, and closets. She even gives suggestions on where researchers can go to

---

* For examples, see Sandra Craighead's article transcribing such ads in *Abstracts from the Colored Tennessean: 1865-1867*, Journal of the Afro-American Historical and Genealogical Society, Vol. 12, nos. 3 & 4 (Fall and Winter 1991), 168-170; and Lori Husband's *Lost Kinsman*, Park Forest, IL, self published in 1993, which transcribes similar ads in the *Chicago Defender* from 1925 to 1935.

preserve these valuable papers. Hopefully this book will stimulate genealogists to venture into these neglected but valuable resources. The genealogical and historical community will be eternally grateful to Barbara Henritze for compiling this bibliography.

Tony Burroughs

August 13, 1994

INTRODUCTION

This book contains a checklist of African American newspapers identified in more than one hundred resources. These sources include not only newspaper annual advertising directories, union lists, and finding aids, but also African American bibliographies, yearbooks, and several specifically African American newspaper sources. This book is not a union list of newspapers, which lists *available* issues (long runs or individual issues) of specific papers and the repositories that house them. Although the source codes may give clues to repositories, the search for specific individual issues is left to the researcher.

Listed within are 5,539 newspapers and assorted periodicals that have served Americans of African descent. Non-newspapers are found in the checklist because many sources used did not exclude them. Thus a publication such as *Ebony*, known to be a magazine, will be found in the checklist. These newspapers have been owned, published, edited, and/or read predominantly by African Americans and have been identified in forty-four states and the District of Columbia. The states with the largest number of black newspapers are New York, Mississippi, Georgia, Alabama, and Texas. Fewer than ten newspapers were found in each of the states of Alaska, Hawaii, Maine, Montana, Nevada, New Mexico, and Utah. No newspapers were identified in six states: Idaho, New Hampshire, North Dakota, South Dakota, Vermont, and Wyoming. A numerical breakdown by state is shown in Table 1.

VALUE

Newspapers are one of the most overlooked historical resources. Daily and weekly newspapers, by definition, are ephemeral. Editors worry about getting the paper out, selling it, then preparing the next issue, not about the historical content or the preservation of previous issues. An anonymous writer in 1955 sums it up:

> Negro editors may not know it as a body, but it is one of the inescapable truths of our time that the Negro weeklies of today will be prized possessions of the future and will be religiously sought out for the record of the Negro's thinking, his movements in a flexible society, and his manner of encountering a rebuff...The editor may go unheralded and unrewarded in this hour but the perennial monument to his name is a carefully preserved...file of his daily labors.[*]

Despite recent journalistic trends, newspapers are a researcher's gold mine. Genealogists always want names, dates, and places, but also crave additional facts about events that can flesh out a bare-bones family history. Club news, county fair awards, out-of-town visitors, sports, outlying district news — a newspaper gives the flavor of a neighborhood and defines an area.

---

[*]Roland E. Wolseley. *The Black Press, U.S.A.* (Ames, Iowa: Iowa State University Press, 1971), p. 92. (Ellipses by Wolseley.)

Whether you are black or white, it is important to read newspapers written from all viewpoints in order to get the full context of the community. For example, compare a white mainstream daily's coverage of King's "I have a dream" speech with that of a black weekly. In order to see the true and clear picture, it must be viewed from all angles. A vivid comparison of black and white views on one subject is depicted in Susan Tucker's *Telling Memories among Southern Women*. Researchers of *all* races should examine *all* the available newspapers from a specific community in order to set the scene.

Religious communities and their respective newspapers and periodicals are often underused in historical and genealogical research. Many black religious periodicals have been published, preserved, and made available for research. Theological libraries and denominational archives may have years of religious periodicals and newspapers from various denominations. These newspapers, especially obituaries of their church members, can be used for "standard" genealogical research. However, they can also be used as a window on the issues of the times. Issues raised in current religious periodicals — such as gay rights within the church, worldwide human rights, environmental and ecological stewardship of the planet, child abuse by persons of religious authority, and the ordination of women — are as much a reflection of our times as the issues of abolition, education, child labor, and temperance were of the nineteenth century.

White researchers should read African American newspapers to learn how both whites and blacks in a community were seen and portrayed by blacks. For all researchers of modern black history, accessibility to major black newspapers is facilitated by the *Index to Black Newspapers*, in which the contents of eleven of the largest of these newspapers are indexed. Currently, those newspapers are: the *Afro American* (national edition), *Amsterdam News* (N.Y.), *Argus* (St. Louis), *Bilalian News* or *American Muslim Journal* (Chicago), *Call & Post* (Cleveland), *Defender* (Chicago), *Daily World* (Atlanta), *Michigan Chronicle* (Detroit), *New Pittsburgh Courier* (Pittsburgh), *Sentinel* (Los Angeles), and *Journal & Guide* (Norfolk). Researchers should be aware that, regrettably, only obituaries which appear as news items are indexed. Local obituaries are not *all* included and this index does *not* include funeral notices or classified death notices.*

IDENTIFICATION

The checklist in this book can be used to identify African American newspapers published in the time period and geographical area needed for research. For each newspaper in the checklist, a code or codes indicates which sources identified that newspaper. These sources are listed alphabetically by code in Appendix A.

---

*The ten newspapers indexed in *Black Newspapers Index, Second Quarter, 1994* (Ann Arbor, Mich.: UMI, 1994), mentioned only 39 total deaths in that three-month period as follows: Deaths (28), Fatalities (1), Funerals (3), and Memorial Services (7).

Sometimes the checklist also indicates readily available extant copies as shown by the following codes. Many of these newspapers are available on interlibrary loan.

- OCLC — A microform or original copy of this newspaper has been catalogued on the OCLC network as an African American newspaper by at least one repository.

- Cam — Newspapers mentioned in G. Campbell's book, which exist in original or microform; and the issues described in her union list.

- NUC — Newspapers cited in the National Union Catalog.

- Lc83 — Newspapers mentioned in the Library of Congress, 1983 edition of *Newspapers in Microform*, including black and ethnic newspapers, with existing original or microform copies; repositories cited for each with dates available.

- Lc91 — African American newspapers available at the Library of Congress mentioned in Pluge's list published in 1991.

- Gr — At least one repository indicated to Winifred Gregory, compiler of the *Union List of Newspapers*, that it had an original or copy of this newspaper.

- HS — Issues of this newspaper are located at that historical society.

- PL — Issues of this newspaper are located at that public library.

If you know about a black newspaper not on this list, please let the compiler know the title, location, and any other publication data available. In order to preserve these valuable research tools, it is necessary to identify them. This newspaper may be the hometown paper from which your grandmother clipped articles and notices to send you while you were away at college, it may be listed in a city directory or mentioned in a county history, or it may be the newspaper piled at the bottom of your cellar steps at home.

REPOSITORIES

Since every state or county historical society, library, and archives in the country could not be contacted, some general guidelines are given here to assist the researcher. Newspapers are commonly deposited in the following types of repositories and/or are available through the following avenues:

- state library

- state archive

- state historical society library

- regional historical society library

- local public library

- local historical society

- local genealogical society

- university or college library

- newspaper library

- theological library

- denominational archive

- official or unofficial town historian's office

- microfilm through interlibrary loan

- microfilm through purchase

- microfilm through the LDS church

- newspaper publisher's office

Some newspapers may be available in many locations, some in only one location in newsprint with no microfilm, and some may not be available at all. A newspaper is most likely to be preserved at the state library, archive, or historical society. Next try the local library of the community in which it was published. Continue searching at a local college or university library and then a nearby historically black college.* A bibliography is contained in Appendix B to assist further research. Note all titles (or every issue of each series) listed in the bibliography were not used in compiling this checklist, only those listed as sources in Appendix A.

---

*Ruby D. Higgins, ed. *The Black Student's Guide to College Success*. (Westport, Conn.: Greenwood Press, 1993). This book contains a list of historically black colleges and universities.

Kansas, Tennessee, Wisconsin and Wyoming have excellent statewide collections of newspapers. The people responsible for funding and operating these programs are to be commended. Some repositories with countrywide collections of newspapers are the State Historical Society of Wisconsin, the American Antiquarian Society in Boston, Howard University Moorland Spingarn Research Center, the Schomburg collection at the New York Public Library, and the Library of Congress in Washington. All of these repositories, undoubtedly, need financial assistance to continue their preservation work.

The State Historical Society of Wisconsin has an excellent newspaper collection with coverage for the entire United States. There has been a special emphasis on collecting labor, Native American, and African American newspapers. The staff is currently using a National Endowment for the Humanities (NEH) grant to compile a union list of African American newspapers. When complete, this union list will be invaluable to researchers because, among other things, it will list specific issues available at specific repositories. The bibliography, edited by James P. Danky, Newspaper and Periodicals Librarian, and compiled by Maureen E. Hady, is expected to be a two-volume set detailing 3,600 to 4,000 extant publications. Any information regarding titles published in a specific area or an issue held in a specific repository should be sent to James P. Danky or Maureen E. Hady:

> State Historical Society of Wisconsin
> 816 State Street
> Madison, WI 53706-1488
> (608) 264-6532

An example of another regional repository with an African American collection, including newspapers, is the Western Reserve Historical Society Library in Cleveland.

PRESERVATION

Preserving newspapers is usually best left to professionals, since many old newspapers are extremely brittle and may be hard to safely handle more than once. An intensive, professional microfilming program may be the only realistic way to safeguard the information contained in the newspapers. If you come across an unusual newspaper or a missing set of issues (for instance, the *Kansas City Call*'s first six months in 1919 are missing, as are the first ten years of the *Cleveland Call*), keep in mind that historians, genealogists, researchers, librarians, and collectors may all be looking for these papers. They may not be monetarily valuable, but they are rare. Treat them with care. Deposit the newspapers at the local historical society, even if only one or two issues are located. While one issue by itself does not necessarily lend itself to study, it does begin a collection, it does name an editor, and it may contain a great-grandmother's maiden name. These papers all need to be preserved! If the local historical society or public library does not have a newspaper preservation program, find a county, state, regional, or national society or library that does.

State historical societies, libraries, and archives in Kansas, Tennessee, Wisconsin, and Wyoming have ongoing statewide microfilming projects (which is one reason why they also have excellent newspaper collections). Other states may also have preservation projects; however, they can't film newspapers they don't have. Donate, donate, donate. Repositories specializing in black newspapers may lack specific issues. Keep these repositories in mind if you locate a "singleton" that the local library or state archive is unwilling or unable to process, catalogue, and preserve.

Editors should be encouraged to keep two complete sets of files in separate places, and also add to their subscription lists two or three institutions likely to save and preserve their titles. Encourage collectors, researchers, genealogists, historians, and pack rats to donate their newspapers to a suitable repository or make provisions to do so in their wills. The closest repository to the publication city is generally the best place, followed by repositories at the county and state level. Some institutions, due to lack of interest, knowledge, or funding, may be inappropriate. In that case, an alternate choice is recommended, one with a collection policy that includes black newspapers.

TITLES

The first column in the checklist is for the title of the newspaper, listed alphabetically within the city and state. Leading articles (a, an, the) are not included in the title. Newspaper titles as found in directories, card catalogues, and bibliographies are a constant aggravation to experienced and beginning researchers alike, because they change ever so slightly from time to time. Assumptions and mistakes are made by cataloguers that result in slightly different title entries for the same newspaper. A recent check on OCLC lists the *United States Newspaper Project (USNP)*, 1993 edition, at least six different ways by professional cataloguers. The checklist in this book is a compilation of titles from many sources including many non-bibliographic sources; unless the newspapers mentioned were obviously identical, they are listed under each different title.

To illustrate with a simple imaginary case, *The New York Daily Press* is the masthead title of a newspaper. This title will definitely not be listed under T for "The." Your first choice in this book should be under N for "New York," the second choice should be under P for "Press," and the last choice should be under D for "Daily." Some bibliographic sources would place this under P, since New York is a location and Daily is an adjective describing frequency. However, the paper may have been referred to as the *Daily Press* in the first issue. A cataloguer generally lists papers under the first known title; so if the *Daily Press* was published in 1914 and changed to the *New York Daily Press* in 1915, it would be catalogued for both years under "Press," as long as the cataloguer is positive it is the same paper because of the same sequential volumes, address, and ownership. In a perfect world, there would be an additional entry in the card catalogue or computer data base under N. However, the cataloguer may not have used the Library of Congress cataloguing rules, may not have been trained as a cataloguer, or may not have noticed the name change; or the repository may have acquired the 1915 issue first, in which case the newspaper's main listing may be under *New York Daily Press*, rather than *Press*.

An exception to the indexing rule about dropping articles could be a newspaper published in The Colony, Texas, named *The Colony News*. The proper name of the town is "The Colony." In this case, the paper could be listed under T for "The" as the first part of a proper noun, under C for "Colony," or N for "News." The latest edition of the *Chicago Manual of Style* indicates this title should be indexed under C, while atlases by Rand McNally and the National Geographic Society have cities such as these indexed under T. This is an obvious style discrepancy. Awareness of style changes, understanding of human decisions and frailties, and creativity in the search process will increase your chance of finding the needed title in both this book and in other resources.

Catalogue update bulletins are continually published by the Library of Congress. These bulletins change the rules ever so slightly or tremendously. For instance, the subject heading for people of African American descent has changed from **Colored**, to **Negro**, to **Black**, to the current subject heading of **African American**. Several newspapers were also found listed under **Afro-American**. A slight variation, an added hyphen in **African-American,** alters the results of a computer catalogue search as will newspaper vs. newspaper<u>s</u>. Most writers, editors, and researchers have not been trained as cataloguers and do not appreciate the intricate minute differences. Cataloguing, while inherently subjective, is an increasingly precise technical endeavor. When done by volunteers or untrained paraprofessionals in a small local historical society or local library, it is a labor of love intended to give the public access to various materials. Don't expect all the titles to be cross-referenced perfectly; be grateful the newspapers are preserved. If a newspaper has changed its name officially or just in the masthead, look under all possible variations and then go one step further: substitute the state name for the city name. The *Birmingham Weekly Review* should be checked under the letters B, R, and W; however, it would also be prudent to check under the letter A for *Alabama Weekly Review*. It may or may not be the same paper.

CITIES

The second column in the checklist is for the publication city, arranged alphabetically within state. New York City has the largest number of identified African American newspapers, which is statistically reasonable given the population.

This state/city/title alphabetic arrangement follows that used in most newspaper guides, union lists, bibliographies, and annual newspaper advertising directories. One exception is Thompson's book on Mississippi black newspapers.* He arranged the newspapers alphabetically by county, which may be easier for genealogists, since many genealogically valuable records such as marriage and census records are created, divided, and stored by county. However, the format of

---

*Julius Eric Thompson. *The Black Press in Mississippi 1865-1985: A Directory.* (West Cornwall, Conn.: Locust Hill Press, 1988).

Thompson's book makes it more difficult to use in conjunction with other newspaper sources, which are arranged by state and then by cities, not counties.

In a book or card catalogue, the *Columbus Recorder* from Columbus, Georgia may be referenced under Columbus, Ohio or Columbus, Indiana. Typographical and other errors have been made since the first typesetting and are continually propagated in print.

If you think a paper was published in San Francisco, look under Berkeley and Oakland in catalogues as well. In metropolitan areas, a notation of "Tri-cities" or "Quad-cities" can refer to multiple sets of cities. In Alabama it means Sheffield, Anniston, and Birmingham; in Tennessee it means Bristol, Kingsport, and Johnson City; in New York it means New York City, Newark, and Stamford; while in Washington State it means Kennewick, Pasco, and Richland. People in eastern Iowa and western Illinois know the Quad-cities are Rockford, Moline, Davenport, and Muscatine, but a map may be necessary for those not from the area.

STATES

The postal abbreviations for each state and the District of Columbia are listed in the third column of the checklist. New York and Mississippi have the largest number of identified African American newspapers. As more and more books and theses are written about individual state collections of black newspapers, the proportions will change. States for which specific books or theses have been written and published, for example, Arkansas, Mississippi, Oklahoma, and Texas, have large numbers of identified newspapers. These states probably have a larger percentage of extant newspapers reported, since the newspapers have been rediscovered and identified by those authors. States that haven't had this type of research done, Alabama for instance, may actually have had more black newspapers published.

Kansas City, Missouri and Kansas City, Kansas are in different states, separated by the Missouri River. A newspaper office may have been moved back and forth due to rental rates and local tax codes. Bristol, Virginia and Bristol, Tennessee are the same city, separated by Main Street which is also the state line. Philadelphia, Pennsylvania and Camden, New Jersey may be considered sister cities by some, but are not easily distinguished and identified as such, since the name of the city changes as well as the name of the state. While the newspaper itself may not have changed publishers or editors, the state or city from which it was issued may be different from time to time, for example, the move of the *Broad Ax* from Salt Lake City to Chicago. The greater New York City area includes northern New Jersey and nearly all of the state of Connecticut.

In this book the District of Columbia is listed separately, as a state. Some papers published in Baltimore, Maryland or Arlington, Virginia are known as Washington, D.C. papers. It is possible a Washington, D.C. newspaper may be listed as a Washington State paper and vice versa.

FREQUENCY

A frequency code is listed in the fourth column of the checklist. Most newspapers in the checklist are local weeklies. Many of those that do not have a frequency identified were probably issued weekly with some irregularities. Sometimes so few copies exist that it is difficult to determine the frequency. Some of the titles may be black periodicals rather than newspapers in the traditional sense of the word. A monthly newsletter or quarterly journal may be included. Titles published more frequently than monthly are most apt to be newspapers. Conversely, titles published less frequently are apt to be magazines and journals. Without the opportunity to visually review each title, the decision was made to be inclusive rather than exclusive. The following codes identify the frequency of the corresponding newspaper:

d	=	daily
w	=	weekly
bw	=	bi-weekly
fn	=	fortnightly
sm	=	semi-monthly
m	=	monthly
bm	=	bi-monthly
q	=	quarterly
sa	=	semi-annually
ir	=	irregular
3xw	=	3 times a week (for instance)

DATES

Years of publication are listed in the fifth column of the checklist. Most of the dates listed for each newspaper will not be completely inclusive or fully accurate. If there was a reference that listed the paper as being published in 1912 and no further reference had dates, the only date listed in the checklist will be 1912. This is probably not the year the paper was founded, or the year publication ceased. It is simply the first year for which a reference for a specific paper was found. A plus (+) after 1991, 1992, 1993, or 1994 means there is no indication the newspaper has ceased publication. An end date without a plus signifies there is no indication the paper was published after this date.

The newspapers may have been launched earlier or lasted longer than previously known. In addition, there have definitely been typographical or other errors in the sources used to compile this book. Annual directory publication dates may not match; for example, the 1994-1995 edition of Gale's *Media Directory* was actually published in 1993. Since newspaper and periodical directories are compiled from information request forms provided by owners or publishers, a newspaper could be listed for several years after publication ceased. An Arizona newspaper continued to appear in the Gale directories for 7-10 years after publication ceased because a form was returned. Directories are only as good as the information supplied.

SOURCES

Source codes are listed in the last column of the checklist. More than one hundred sources were consulted to find and identify the 5,539 black newspapers and periodicals listed. Each source was given a code, which is explained in the alphabetical list of codes in the Source section in Appendix A. Several series were used:

> *N. W. Ayer's Newspaper Directory* 1880-1994
> *Rowell's Directories* from 1867-1912
> *Standard Periodical Index* from 1967-1994
> *Editor and Publisher Yearbook* from 1935-1993.

During the 1950s, black newspapers were not separately identified in the *Editor and Publisher Yearbook*. Newspaper sources vary; some are yearbook-style directories, some cover extant newspaper availability, and others cover defunct papers, some cover those on microfilm or in specific repositories.

Many newspapers — such as the Norfolk *Journal and Guide*, the *Afro-American* published in Baltimore, the Chicago *Defender*, and the *Atlanta World* — are mentioned in nearly every source. All years of each source or even all the sources could not possibly be listed in these cases. For those papers blessed with the largest circulation figures and extremely long runs, the sources listed are only the first and last years of the series sources; for example, "EP37,93" means the paper was first found in the 1937 issue of *Editor and Publisher Yearbook* and last found in the 1993 issue.

The sources most readily available to the largest number of researchers are:

1.   Winifred Gregory's *American Newspapers 1821-1936*, published in 1937, is a union list of newspapers.

2.   OCLC's *USNP National Union List*, 4th edition, microfiche, published in January 1993 is also a union list. This is a grand-scale newspaper cataloguing project with many states obtaining NEH grants to catalogue their newspapers. In 1985 the book had 25,000 titles; the current (1993) 4th edition on microfiche has more than 100,000 titles.

3.   *Newspapers in Microform*, published in 1983 by the Library of Congress, a three-volume set, is a union list of newspapers with the holdings delineated by original or microfilm copies. This edition updates the 1972 and 1977 editions.

4.   *N. W. Ayer and Son's Directories*, now published by Gale Research as *Gale Directory of Media Publications*, a series dating from 1880 to the present, is generally used for current advertising needs.

5.   *Editor and Publisher Yearbook*, a series published from 1935 to the present, is also used for current advertising needs.

Any discussion of newspaper research sources is incomplete without a mention of Clarence S. Brigham's *History and Bibliography of American Newspapers 1690-1820*, published in 1944. However, since the first black paper began publication in 1827, this checklist is outside the scope of Brigham's book.

The main body of work on black newspapers was begun by Dr. Armistead Scott Pride of the School of Journalism at Jefferson University, Missouri. This research was sponsored by the Committee on Negro Studies of the American Council of Learned Societies in 1947. Due to his help and encouragement, 232 Negro newspapers were collected and preserved on 192 reels of microfilm by the Library of Congress, entitled *Negro Newspapers on Microfilm*. In 1970, one of his students, Jennelle Barrens, rearranged his Ph.D. dissertation by beginning and ending publication dates, used as source "Ba" in this checklist.

LAST RESORTS

After you find a newspaper of interest in the checklist, check the logical repositories – the local public library, the state historical society, or state library and archive. However, it is possible that none of these will have a copy.

Then, check OCLC by using FIRSTSEARCH, an online subject search of the OCLC worldwide catalogue. This catalogue is continually updated, so the needed newspaper may have been recently catalogued. Widen your search to include all local and regional repositories. Use the latest editions of *American Library Directory, Directory of Historical Organizations in the United States and Canada,* and *Directory of Archives and Manuscript Repositories in the United States* to find additional likely repositories. Not all repositories have entered all of their newspapers onto OCLC. (Perhaps they ran out of money after entering 90 percent of their holdings, entered only those newspapers within the scope of their main collection, or entered only mainstream newspapers, leaving religious and other periodicals out of the OCLC network.)

Many smaller libraries, museums, or archives may not have plans to enter their holdings onto OCLC. Some libraries separate the periodical and newspaper catalogues and listings from the main catalogue. Some have separate notebooks of newspapers or periodicals. Perhaps the newspaper you need was identified as a periodical by the library holding copies, so it may not be listed or catalogued so you can find it. Perhaps the newspaper was just received, processed or catalogued. The publication you are looking for may be a religious newspaper; check the largest local churches to see if copies are held in the church office, the state church repository, national denominational church archives, and theological libraries. Check repositories in the surrounding cities, counties, regions, and states.

Research the family of the editor of the newspaper to find the last-known address of the editor, spouse, or a descendant. A good example is Edwin Fletcher Horn, the editor and publisher of several early black newspapers in Evansville, Indianapolis, Atlanta, and Chattanooga from 1878 to 1896. He died in Brooklyn in July 1939. His children and grandchildren are spread out across the country in California, Florida, Georgia, New York, Pennsylvania and Washington, D.C.[*]

Check with the State Historical Society of Wisconsin for any and all titles not found anywhere else. With their NEH grant for the five-year project of compiling a union list of black newspapers, they may have just recently located or received the newspaper or periodical needed.

Another possibility is to use a book search firm, sometimes listed in antiquarian booksellers association directories, or to advertise in *Collectible Newspapers,* the quarterly publication of the Newspaper Collectors Society.

The Newspaper Collectors Society prints a *Primer on Collecting Old and Historic Newspapers.* The 1993 edition of 24 pages is available for $1.00 with a #10 SASE. Several of the 300-plus members specialize in African American newspapers. Membership in the society is $18.00 per year, which entitles you to the membership roster, one year of the quarterly, *Collectible Newspapers*, and the ability to place classified ads for a nominal fee.

> Newspaper Collectors Society of America
> c/o Rick Brown
> Box 19134-A
> Lansing, MI 48901
> (517) 887-1255

The National Newspaper Publishers Association maintains a list of African American newspapers (190 newspapers in 1993), which is available for $15.00 prepaid. Membership lists from other years may be available. Some of the editors on this list may have more information about other newspapers and the location of extant copies.

> National Newspaper Publishers Association
> 3200 13th Street, NW
> Washington, DC 20010
> (202) 588-8764 FAX (202) 588-5029

---

[*]Gail Lumet Buckley. *The Hornes: an American Family.* (New York: Alfred A. Knopf, Inc., 1986), 262 pp. See pages 41, 43, 47 for references to newspapers and page 136 for a reference to his death. His children and grandchildren's various residences are mentioned throughout the book. The Horn name was changed to Horne during Edwin Horn's life.

There is a National Association of Black Journalists, established in 1975, whose members might be able to help locate files of newspapers.

National Association of Black Journalists
P. O. Box 17212
Washington, D.C. 20041
(703) 648-1270

Another association, established in 1979, whose membership may be of some assistance is:

Black Women in Publishing
P. O. Box 6275
FDR Station
New York, NY 10150
(212) 772-5951

Any city listed in the checklist once has a reasonable chance of having at least one other unidentified black newspaper. Although individual city directories and county histories were not generally consulted in the preparation of this checklist, these are often good sources for missing titles, some of which may not be known as black newspapers.

This book was written to facilitate research and to encourage identification and preservation of black newspapers. In order to study history effectively, sources from a variety of cultures must be saved, preserved, catalogued, and consulted. It is my hope that this book makes historical and genealogical research easier by identifying the titles of many African American newspapers.

Table 1

African American Newspapers Published by Individual States

Alphabetical by State		Total by State	
Alabama	319	New York	348
Alaska	3	Mississippi	337
Arizona	13	Georgia	336
Arkansas	217	Texas	325
California	258	Alabama	319
Colorado	58	Illinois	288
Connecticut	35	California	258
Delaware	28	North Carolina	255
Dist. of Columbia	121	Tennessee	230
Florida	202	Arkansas	217
Georgia	336	Ohio	203
Hawaii	3	Florida	202
Idaho	0	South Carolina	195
Illinois	288	Virginia	191
Indiana	74	Louisiana	182
Iowa	34	Pennsylvania	176
Kansas	140	Kansas	140
Kentucky	104	Missouri	137
Louisiana	182	Oklahoma	133
Maine	1	New Jersey	127
Maryland	67	Dist. of Columbia	121
Massachusetts	57	Michigan	107
Michigan	107	Kentucky	104
Minnesota	39	Indiana	74
Mississippi	337	Maryland	67
Missouri	137	Colorado	58
Montana	5	Massachusetts	57
Nebraska	16	Washington	46
Nevada	3	West Virginia	41
New Hampshire	0	Minnesota	39
New Jersey	127	Wisconsin	38
New Mexico	7	Iowa	34
New York	348	Connecticut	34
North Carolina	255	Delaware	28
North Dakota	0	Rhode Island	20
Ohio	203	Nebraska	16
Oklahoma	133	Oregon	13
Oregon	13	Arizona	12
Pennsylvania	176	New Mexico	7
Rhode Island	20	Utah	6
South Carolina	195	Montana	5
South Dakota	0	Alaska	3
Tennessee	230	Hawaii	3
Texas	325	Nevada	3
Utah	5	Maine	1
Vermont	0	Idaho	0
Virginia	191	New Hampshire	0
Washington	48	North Dakota	0
West Virginia	41	South Dakota	0
Wisconsin	38	Vermont	0
Wyoming	0	Wyoming	0
TOTAL	**5539**	**TOTAL**	**5539**

Bibliographic Checklist of African American Newspapers

CHECKLIST

TITLE	CITY	ST.	FREQ.	DATES	SOURCES
Alabama Time Piece	Aldrich	AL		1895-1898	Shelby Co. His. Soc.,Jcw
Tallapoosa News	Alexander City	AL		1902-1903	Ba
Vidette	Alexander City	AL		1888-1888	Ay1888,1889[nlb]
Anniston Observer	Anniston	AL		1922	NY22
Baptist Leader	Anniston	AL	w	1878-1981	Ba,Ay1906,1972,Oclc,Jcw[1900],Cam, Lt1907,Pr,Penn,Lb,Bp,Rh
Herald	Anniston	AL	w	1919-1922	Ba,Ay1920,1921
Herald of Mission & Patriotism	Anniston	AL	w	1918-1919	Ba,Ay1919
Mirror	Anniston	AL	w	1966-1970	Pr,EP67,73,Bp,Lb,SPD67
Reporter	Anniston	AL		1896-1897	Ba,Jcw[b1897]
Union Leader	Anniston	AL	w	1901-1904	Ba,Oclc
Union Ledger	Anniston	AL		1907-1910	Ba
Weekly Review	Anniston	AL	w	1897-1898	Ba
Array	Athens	AL	w	1898-1901	Ba,R1900
Guardian	Attalla	AL		1902-1903	Ba
American Banner	Bay Minette	AL	sm	1894-1904	R1898,1900,Cam,Jcw[1886]
American Progress	Bay Minette	AL	sm	1888-1891	Ba,Ay1890,1891,1889[Progress]
News	Belmont	AL		1902-1903	Ba
Plantation Missionary	Beloit	AL	bm	1890-1922	NY19,22,Jpd
Citizen	Bessemer	AL		1903-1904	Ba
Enterprise	Bessemer	AL	m/w	1917-1929	Ba,Ay1917,1929,NY26,Boris1
Industrial Enterprise	Bessemer	AL	w	1908-1916	Ba,Ay1911-1914,1916
Mirror	Bessemer	AL	w	1974	EP74
Tribune	Bessemer	AL	w	1906-1910	Ba,Ay1908,1909
Southern Star	Bethel	AL	w	1895-1900	Oclc,Jcw
Advance	Birmingham	AL		1876-1877	Ba
Afro-American Labor Sentinel	Birmingham	AL		1896-1897	Ba
Alabama Citizen	Birmingham	AL		1888-1890	Ba,Ay1889,1890
Alabama Clipper	Birmingham	AL		1912	NY12
Alabama Voice	Birmingham	AL		1946-1949	Ba,NH49
Alabama Weekly Review	Birmingham	AL	w	1947-1954	Ba,Ay1950,1954,EP49-51,NY52
American Bulletin	Birmingham	AL	w	1888-1891	Ba,Ay1891
American Press	Birmingham	AL	w	1888-1895	Ba,Br,Jcw
American Waiter	Birmingham	AL	w	1921-1923	Ba,Ay1921S
Baptist Leader	Birmingham	AL	w	1909-1992+	Ba,Ay1909,1970,Oclc,Nuc,ABSCHSL, Cam,EP37,76[1912],Jcw[1890-1964],EBA, EH,NH42,46,NY12,19,22,26,32,46,52, Dc41,44,Bir.CD1909,Lb,Mather
Birmingham American	Birmingham	AL	w	1911-1912	Oclc,NY12
Birmingham Blade	Birmingham	AL	w	1907-1909	Oclc,Rh,Bir.PL
Birmingham Era	Birmingham	AL		1888-1892	Ba,Penn,Jcw
Birmingham News	Birmingham	AL		1915-1915	Fleming [Adams, Oscar William]
Birmingham Observer	Birmingham	AL		1881-1881	Bir.PL

TITLE	CITY	ST.	FREQ.	DATES	SOURCES
Birmingham Times	Birmingham	AL	w	1964-1994+	Ga88,94,Pr,Oclc,EBA,EP67,93,BRG,Bp, EH,Bir.PL,WPN94,SPD67,70,74
Birmingham Voice	Birmingham	AL	w	1948-1949	EP48,49
Birmingham Weekly Review	Birmingham	AL	w	1933-1951	Ba,Ay1940,1950,Oclc,Br,EP37,51,NH44, 46,49,Rh,NY46,52,Dc41,44
Birmingham World	Birmingham	AL	w/2xw	1930-1994+	Ba,Ay1935,1975,Ga91,94,Oclc,WI,Lc83, EP35,93[1932],BRG,API94,EH[b1932], NH42,44,46,49,Rh,NY32,46,52,Dc41,44, SPD67,70,74,Bir.PL,Bl,Fleming
Broad Axe	Birmingham	AL	w	1891-1892	Ba,Ay1891,Bir.CD1891
Christian Era	Birmingham	AL		1887-1888	Ba,Penn,Jcw
Christian Hope	Birmingham	AL	w	1893-1915	Ba,Ay1906-1915,Jcw[e1911],NY12, Lt1907,Bir.CD1915
CPSB Newsletter	Birmingham	AL		1975	Unct
Eagle	Birmingham	AL	w	1902-1979	Ba,Ay1921,1937,Go,Br,Gr,Oclc,Lc83, NY22,26,NY32,Bir.CD1920,Boris2
Eye	Birmingham	AL	w	1906-1907	Ba,Rh,Lt1907
Fisherman	Birmingham	AL		1908	Bir.CD1908
Free Speech	Birmingham	AL	w	1901-1905	Ba,Ay1905,Oclc,Bir.CD1902
Golden House Digest	Birmingham	AL		1947	Ba
Harrison's Pet	Birmingham	AL	w	1892-1895	Ba,Ay1894,Eur94
Headlight	Birmingham	AL	w	1891-1892	Ba,Ay1891,Bir.CD1891
Hot Shots	Birmingham	AL	ir/w	1889-1913	Ba,Ay1911-1913,Oclc,Jcw,Bir.PL [1898-1911]
Informer	Birmingham	AL		1946	Ba
McConico's Monthly Magazine	Birmingham	AL	m	1910-1914	Ay1912,1913,1914,NY12
Messenger	Birmingham	AL	w	1908-1914	Ba,Ay1911-1914,Bir.CD1911,Rh
Metropolitan Journal	Birmingham	AL	w	1892-1895	Ba,Br
Mirror	Birmingham	AL	w	1946-1977	Ay1966,1977,Pr,Oclc,EBA,EP50,78 [b1949],EH[1948],NY52,Bp
Missionary Herald	Birmingham	AL	w	1895-1900	R1900
Mouth-piece	Birmingham	AL	w	1932	NY32
Negro American	Birmingham	AL	w	1885-1888	Ba,R1888,Penn,Oclc,Jcw,Bir.PL,DANB39
Negro Enterprise	Birmingham	AL	sm	1900-1907	Ba,Ay1905,1906,Rh
New Era Banner	Birmingham	AL	w	1918-1919	Oclc
New Man's Idea	Birmingham	AL		1909	Bir.CD1909
Newspic Magazine	Birmingham	AL	m	1945-1946	EP45,46,NY46
Pleiades	Birmingham	AL	w	1888	Oclc
Reporter	Birmingham	AL	w	1906-1950	Ay1908,1935,NY19,22,26,32,Rh, Bir.CD1907,Lt1907,Fleming
Searchlight	Birmingham	AL		1910-1914	Ay1914[nlb],Rh
Southern Broadaxe	Birmingham	AL	w	1894-1897	Ba,Ay1896
Southern Sentinel News	Birmingham	AL	w	1896-1903	Ba,Ay1898,Bir.CD1900,Br,Jcw[e1899]
Southwestern Christian Advocate	Birmingham	AL	w	pre 1928	Boris2 [Allen, Cleveland G.]
Sparks Magazine	Birmingham	AL	m	1911-1915	Ba,Ay1915,NY12,Mather
Times Plaindealer	Birmingham	AL	w	1919-1923	Ba,Ay1920,1921,Go,Oclc,Rh,Bir.CD1920

TITLE	CITY	ST.	FREQ.	DATES	SOURCES
Truth	Birmingham	AL	w	1903-1932	Ba,Ay1905-1916,Oclc,Cam,Rh,NY22,32, NY19[MS],Lt1907,Bir.CD1904
Voice of the People	Birmingham	AL	w	1913-1925	Ba,Ay1914,1921,1925,Go,Br,Oclc,NY19, Bir.CD1915
Weekly Pilot	Birmingham	AL	w	1883-1884	Oclc,Bir.PL
Wide Awake	Birmingham	AL	w	1888-1920	Ba,Ay1896,1920,R1900,Oclc,WI, Jcw[e1900],Eur94,NY12,Bir.PL,Lt1907,Rh
Wide Awake Bulletin	Birmingham	AL	w	1887-1920	Ba,Gr,Br,Cam,Oclc,Lc83
Workmen's Chronicle	Birmingham	AL	w	1918	Oclc,Bir.CD1918
World Order Magazine	Birmingham	AL		pre 1950	Fleming [Durr, Robert Driscoll]
Industrial	Boligee	AL	m	1907-1920	Ba,Ay1909,1911
Blade	Brewton	AL	w	1919-1922	Ba,Ay1921
Enterprise	Brewton	AL		1902-1903	Ba
Bibb County Sentinel	Centreville	AL	w	1895-1898	Boris1 [Davidson, Henry Damon]
Bibb Sentinel	Centreville	AL		1900-1902	Ba
Free Mission Pioneer	Claiborne	AL	w	1899	Jcw
Colored Voice	Columbiana	AL	sm	1902-1905	Ba,Ay1905
Advance	Decatur	AL	w	1910-1911	Ay1911 (see GA)
Decatur Tribune	Decatur	AL	w	1892	Jcw[1889?]
Enterprise	Decatur	AL		1898-1900	Ba
Guardian	Decatur	AL	m	1910-1917	Ba,Ay1912-1917,Cam
Light in the Valley	Decatur	AL		1896-1897	Ba
Plain Dealer	Decatur	AL	w	1895-1898	Ba,Ay1896,R1898
Speakin' Out News	Decatur	AL	w	1983	Oclc
Speakin' Out Weekly	Decatur	AL	w	1980-1993+	Oclc,EP86-93
Baptist Banner	Demopolis	AL	w	1908-1911	Ba,Ay1911
Christian Hope	Demopolis	AL	w	1893-1898	Ay1898,Jcw
Dothan Eagle	Dothan	AL		pre 1946	Rh,Lt1907[listed as Democratic], Ay1912[nlb]
Dothan Times	Dothan	AL	w	1975-1976	EP75,76
Southern Star	Dothan	AL	sm/w	1913-1931	Ba,Ay1919-1921,1931,Oclc,NY22
Star	Dothan	AL	sm	1913-1918	Ay1916-1918
Union Messenger	Dothan	AL	sm	1907-1913	Ba,Ay1909,1911,1912,1913
Voice of the Negro	Dothan	AL	w	1914-1925	Ba,Ay1925[b1922],Oclc,NY19,Go
Eufala Herald	Eufala	AL	w	1896	Jcw
Vindicator	Eufala	AL		1885-1890	Ba,Penn,Jcw[1890]
Blade	Eutaw	AL	w	1894-1901	Ba,Ay1896
Greene County Democrat	Eutaw	AL	w	1890-1994+	Ga88,94,Baid90,92,Ay1905[nlb],BRG, EP91,92[b1984],93
Western Guide	Eutaw	AL	sm	1905-1909	Ba,Ay1908,1909
Afro American Banner and Messenger	Evergreen	AL	w	1899-1900	R1900
Christian Monitor	Evergreen	AL	w	1881	Jcw
Ladies Will	Evergreen	AL	m	1907	Lt1907
Times	Evergreen	AL		1896-1897	Ba
Petal Paper	Fairhope	AL	m	1953-1974	SPD70,74

TITLE	CITY	ST.	FREQ.	DATES	SOURCES
Watchman	Fayette	AL		1902-1903	Ba
Advocate	Florence	AL	w	1905-1906	Ba,Ay1906
Republican State Sentinel	Florence	AL		1872	DANB514
Shoals News Leader	Florence	AL	w	1980-1994+	Ga88,94,Baid90,92,BRG,EP81,93,NA
Watcher	Florence	AL	w	1888-1889	Oclc,Jcw
Fort Deposit Vindicator	Fort Deposit	AL	w	1896-1900	Ba,Gr,Cam,R1900,Jcw[1894]
Gadsden Call	Gadsden	AL		1946	Rh
Gadsden Call Post	Gadsden	AL	w	1939-1945	Ba,Br,EP39,40,45,NH44
Gadsden Messenger	Gadsden	AL	w	1888-1896	Ay1894,1896
Negro Press	Gadsden	AL	w	1890	Jcw
Tri Cities Informer and Call Post	Gadsden	AL	w	1946-1949	Ba,Br,EP46,48,49
Wideawake	Gadsden	AL		1902-1907	Ba
Progressive Banner	Georgiana	AL	sm	1926-1929	Ba,Ay1927,1929
Temple Star	Georgiana	AL	sm	1908-1921	Ba,Ay1909,1921,NY19,22
Eastern Sunlight	Girard	AL	sm	1909-1914	Ba,Ay1911,1912,1913,NY12
Alabama Republican	Greensboro	AL		1899-1902	Ba
Ventilator	Greensboro	AL	w	1887-1888	Ba,Ay1888
Afro-American	Greenville	AL		1899-1902	Ba
Banner and Messenger	Greenville	AL	w	1890	Jcw
Saint Joseph Defender	Greenville	AL	sm	1906-1911	Ba,Ay1908,1909,1911
Southern Pride	Horse Creek	AL	w	1903-1906	Ay1905,1906
Bloom of Youth	Huntsville	AL	m	1891	Jcw
Colored Cumberland Presbyterian	Huntsville	AL		1891	Jcw
Cumberland Flag	Huntsville	AL	m	1915-1994+	SPD87,91,Ga94[nlb]
Eagle Eye	Huntsville	AL	m	1971-1973	Bp
Educator	Huntsville	AL	m	1899-1915	Ba,Ay1912-1915,R1900,Lc83 [1879-1894],NY12,Mather
Huntsville Gazette	Huntsville	AL	w	1879-1894	Ba,Ay1880,1894,Gr,Go,Br,Penn,Cam, Oclc,WI,Jcw,Eur94
Huntsville Herald	Huntsville	AL	w	1877-1884	Ba,Br,Oclc,Jcw,DANB138
Huntsville Journal	Huntsville	AL	w	1895-1912	Ay1896,1912,Gr,Br,Cam,R1898,Oclc,Jcw, Rh,NY12
Huntsville Mirror	Huntsville	AL	w	1952-1970	Pr,Oclc,EP67,72,Lb,SPD67,70,74
Huntsville News	Huntsville	AL	w	1917-1939	Ba,Ay1920,1921,Oclc,Br
Huntsville Star	Huntsville	AL	w	1900-1901	Ba,Gr,Br,Cam,Oclc,Lc83,WI
Huntsville Weekly News	Huntsville	AL	w/bw	1968-1983	Oclc,EH[b1969],EP72[b1969],83,Bp,Lb
Negro Fortune Teller	Huntsville	AL	w	1904-1912	Ba,Ay1912(b1910)
Normal Index	Huntsville	AL	w	1885-1896	Ay1887,1896,R1888,Jcw
Primitive Baptist Herald	Huntsville	AL	w	1908-1926	Ba,Ay1911-1913,NY12,19,22,26,Boris1
Speakin' Out News	Huntsville	AL	w	1980-1994+	Ga90,94,Baid90,Oclc,BRG,EP93,API94
Weekly Review	Huntsville	AL	w	1944	Ba
Sun	Jackson	AL		1900-1902	Ba
Walker County Mirror	Jasper	AL	w	1965-1972	EBA,EP71,72,73
Eagle	Kempsville	AL	sm	1899-1899	Oclc

TITLE	CITY	ST.	FREQ.	DATES	SOURCES
Eagle	Kempsville	AL	sm	1899-1902	Ay1889,Oclc,Jcw
Eagle	Lovan	AL	sm	1888-1891	Ay1890,1891,1894,Oclc
Sun	Madison Station	AL		1905-1907	Ba
Journal Reporter	Marion	AL	w	187?-1881	Oclc
Normal Reporter	Marion	AL	w/m	1880-1887	Ay1887,Jcw
Black Belt Missionary	Millers Ferry	AL	m	1912-1922	NY12,19,22
Ace	Mobile	AL		1975	Oclc
Adviser	Mobile	AL	w	1889-1891	Ba,Ay1890,1891
Alabama Citizen	Mobile	AL	w	1943-1955	EH,MBAL
American	Mobile	AL		1945	Ba
A.M.E. Zion Quarterly Review	Mobile	AL	q	1890-1916	Ay1914-1916,Mather
Baptist Banner	Mobile	AL	w	1907	Lt1907
Baptist Leader	Mobile	AL	w	1890-1908	Ba,Ay1908
Christian Weekly	Mobile	AL	w	1887-1889	Ba,Ay1888,1889,Jcw
Church Observer	Mobile	AL		1902-1904	Boris1 [Davenport, William Henry]
Delta News	Mobile	AL	w	1894-1895	Ba,Br,Jcw
Forum	Mobile	AL	w	1918-1931	Ba,Ay1919,1930,NY19,22,26,Go,Boris1
Gulf Informer	Mobile	AL	w	1942-1956	Ba,Ay1947,1956,Oclc,EP45,51,NH49,NY52,Rh
Herald	Mobile	AL		1918-1923	Ba
Informer Freeman	Mobile	AL	w	1950-1956	Ay1956
Inner City News	Mobile	AL	w	1976-1994+	Ay1983,Ga87,94,Baid90,92,BRG,EP80,92,API94
Magnet	Mobile	AL	sw	1881	Jcw
Methodist Vindicator	Mobile	AL		1888-1892	Ba,Penn
Mobile Beacon	Mobile	AL	w	1954-1955	Pr,Oclc,MBAL,SPD70[1944],74
Mobile Beacon & Alabama Citizen	Mobile	AL	w	1955-1994+	Ay1966,1983,Ga87,94,Pr,Oclc,EBA,EH,EP72,93,Baid90,API94
Mobile Nationalist	Mobile	AL	w	1865-1869	Oclc,Cantrell
Mobile Weekly Advocate	Mobile	AL	w	1911-1961	Ba,Ay1925,1961,Oclc,EP35,49,NH42,44,46,49,NY12,19,22,26,32,46,52,Dc41,44,Boris1,Rh
Mobile Weekly Press Forum [Sun]	Mobile	AL	w	1929-1943	Ba,Ay1935,1938,Oclc,NY32,Go,Br,Cam
New Times	Mobile	AL	w/bw	1981-1994+	Ga90,94,Baid90,Oclc,EP86-93,BRG,WPN94,API94
Press	Mobile	AL	w	1894-1929	Ba,Ay1896,1930,Oclc,Jcw,Br,Go,NY12,19,22,26,Lt1907,Rh,Boris1
Press-Forum Sun	Mobile	AL	w	1937-1944	EP37,38,41,42,44
Press-Forum Weekly	Mobile	AL	w	1935-1946	Ay1935,1940,EP35,46
Republican	Mobile	AL		1892	Jcw
Southern Watchman	Mobile	AL	w	1890-1907	Ba,Ay1894[b1893],1906,Oclc,Lt1907
State Republican	Mobile	AL	w	1890-1892	Ba,Ay1891
Sun	Mobile	AL	w	1931-1936	EP35,36,NY32
Times Forum	Mobile	AL	w	1921-1956	Ay1956
Watchman	Mobile	AL	w	1894	Eur94

TITLE	CITY	ST.	FREQ.	DATES	SOURCES
Weekly Sentinel	Mobile	AL	w	1893-1895	Jcw
Ledger	Montevallo	AL		1894-1895	Ba
Advance	Montgomery	AL	w	1877-1882	Ba,Go,Br,Oclc,Jcw[1881]
Alabama Enterprise	Montgomery	AL	w	1885-1886	Ba,Ay1886,Cam,Oclc,Jcw
Alabama Guide	Montgomery	AL	m	1884-1885	Ba,Cam
Alabama Republican	Montgomery	AL	w	1880	Oclc
Alabama Review	Montgomery	AL		1916-1918	Ba,Br,Jcw[pre1900]
Alabama Tribune	Montgomery	AL	w	1934-1967	Ba,Ay1940,1955,Pr,Br,EP37,67,Lb, Jcw[pre1900],NH42,44,46,49,NY46,52, Dc41,44,SPD67
Argus	Montgomery	AL	w	1890-1898	Ba,R1898,Br,Oclc,Jcw,Eur94
Baptist Leader	Montgomery	AL	w	1878-1895	Ba,Ay1888,Nuc
Colored Alabamian	Montgomery	AL	w	1907-1916	Ba,Ay1912,1915,Oclc,Lc83,Gr,ABSCHSL, Cam
Colored Citizen	Montgomery	AL	w	1884-1884	Oclc,Jcw
Emancipator	Montgomery	AL	w	1917-1930	Ba,Ay1888,Oclc,Lc83,NY19
Emancipator	Montgomery	AL	w	1898-1900	Ay1888,Go,Gr
Evening Appeal	Montgomery	AL	w	1886-1887	Oclc
Good Shepherd's Magazine	Montgomery	AL		1912-1922	NY12,19,22,Mather
Helping Hand	Montgomery	AL	w	1906-1922	Ba,Ay1911-1919,Cam,Oclc,NY12,19,22, Rh
Herald	Montgomery	AL	w	1886-1888	Ba,Ay1887,1888,Oclc,Cam,Penn,Jcw
Herald	Montgomery	AL	w	1902-1903	Ba
Hornet and Freshmore	Montgomery	AL	sm	1949-1960	Ay1960
Hornet Tribune	Montgomery	AL	w/m	1905-1977	Ay1966,1977,Bp
Josephite	Montgomery	AL	q	1919	NY19
Leader	Montgomery	AL	w	1894	Eur94
Mirror	Montgomery	AL	w	1955-1976	EBA,EP71-76,Bp
Monitor	Montgomery	AL	w	1881-1892	Ay1882,Jcw
Montgomery Enterprise	Montgomery	AL	w	1898-1901	Ba,Oclc,Lc83,WI,Gr,Cam
Montgomery/Tuskegee Times	Montgomery	AL	w	1975-1993+	Ga90,91,Baid90,Oclc,BRG,EP75-93
Musical Messenger	Montgomery	AL	w	1886-1887	Ba,Jcw
National Farmer's Review	Montgomery	AL		1890	Jcw
Negro Pilot	Montgomery	AL	w	1902-1905	Ba,Ay1905
Negro Watchman	Montgomery	AL		1874	Br
Odd Fellows Journal	Montgomery	AL	w/m	1885-1894	Ba,Ay1886-1888,1891,Jcw,Eur94
Saint John Herald	Montgomery	AL		1909-1911	Ba
Southern Courier	Montgomery	AL	w	1965-1970	Oclc,WI,EP72,SPD70
Southern Review	Montgomery	AL	w	1888-1894	Ba,Ay1889,1891,1894
Southern Voice	Montgomery	AL	w	1900-1905	Ba,Ay1905
Tribune	Montgomery	AL	w	1951-1967	EP51,62-65,67
Weekly Citizen	Montgomery	AL	w	1884	Oclc
Weekly Review	Montgomery	AL	w	1944-1949	Ba,NH49
World	Montgomery	AL	w	1932-1938	Ba,Ay1936,1937,EP35,38

TITLE	CITY	ST.	FREQ.	DATES	SOURCES
Twin City Record	New Decatur	AL	w	1901-1907	Ba,Ay1905,1906,Lt1907[Record]
Index	Normal	AL	m	1885-1922	Ay1906,1918,Eur94,NY12,19,22
Headlight	Opelika	AL		1898-1900	Ba
People's Choice	Opelika	AL	w	1894-1904	Ba,Ay1896,R1898,1900,Jcw,Br
Hopson City News	Oxford	AL		1900-1901	Ba
Pointer	Patton Junction	AL	w	1897-1904	Ba,Oclc
Messenger	Pell City	AL	m	1921-1923	Ba,Ay1921,NY22
Afro-American Journal	Pratt City	AL	2xm	1900-1905	Ba,Ay1905
Negro Search Light	Pushmataha	AL	sm	1903-1906	Ba,Ay1905,1906,Lt1907[w Searchlight]
American Star	Russellville	AL	sm	1901-1937	Ay1935,1937
Baptist Leader	Selma	AL	w	1878-1900	Ba,Ay1896,R1898,1900,Nuc
Baptist Lime Light	Selma	AL	w	1912-1926	NY12,19,22,26,Boris1
Baptist Pioneer	Selma	AL	m	1878-1883	Ba,Ay1882,AAE2,Cam,Oclc,Jcw
Baptist Women's Era	Selma	AL		1900-1901	ABSCHSL
Citizen	Selma	AL	w	1945-1951	Ba,EP48-51,NH49
Cyclone	Selma	AL	w	1886-1891	Ba,Ay1888-1891,Oclc,Lc83
Dallas Post	Selma	AL	w	1880-1891	Ba[b1887],Jcw,Ay1884[nlb]
Guiding Star	Selma	AL		1887	Jcw
Herald	Selma	AL		1887	Jcw
Independent	Selma	AL	w	1884-1889	Ba,Ay1888,1889,Oclc,Lc83
Mirror	Selma	AL	w	1935-1976	EP35,71,73-76,EBA,EH,Bp
Missionary Searchlight	Selma	AL	sm	1899-1908	Ba,Ay1905,1906,1908,R1900
New Idea	Selma	AL	w	1886-1901	Ba,Ay1894[1891],R1900,Br
News	Selma	AL	w	1888-1896	Ay1894,1896
People's Observer	Selma	AL	w	1904-1908	Ba,Ay1906,1908
Record	Selma	AL		1899-1904	Ba
Selma Sun Post	Selma	AL	w	1972-1976	EP73-76,EH,Lb
Southern Christian Recorder	Selma	AL	w	1886-1889	Ay1889,Rh
Southern Independent	Selma	AL	w	1884-1889	Ba,Ay1886,1887,Cam
State Republican	Selma	AL	w	1890-1892	Ba,Ay1890
American Star	Sheffield	AL	sm	1921-1929	Ba,Ay1921,1925[1901]
Tri Cities Mirror	Sheffield	AL	w	1966-1967	Pr,EP67,SPD67
Tri-Cities Weekly Review	Sheffield	AL	w	1945	Ba
Headlight	Shelby	AL	w	1910-1911	Ba,Ay1911
Ardis Times	Slocumb	AL	w	1909-1911	Ay1911 (see McComb MS)
Black Belt	Snow Hill	AL	m	1919-1922	NY19,22
Southern Sentinel	Talladega	AL	m	1877-1881	Oclc
Student	Talladega	AL	m	1893-1977	Ay1975,1977,NY46
Talladega Times	Talladega	AL	w	1984-1993+	EP87-93
Talladegan	Talladega	AL	bm	1912-1922	NY12,19,22
Eagle	Tincie	AL	sm	1888-1896	Ay1894,1896
Afro-American Advocate	Troy	AL		1901-1906	Ba
Afro-American Star	Troy	AL	w	1902-1904	Ba,Ay1905,1906

TITLE	CITY	ST.	FREQ.	DATES	SOURCES
Church Herald	Troy	AL	w	1894-1896	Ba,Ay1896
Pike County News and Record	Troy	AL	w	1919-1922	Ba,Ay1921
Southeast Baptist	Troy	AL	w	1896-1898	Ay1898,Jcw
Eagle	Tunnel Springs	AL	sm	1902-1920	Ay1906,1909,1911-1920,Oclc
Alabama Black Citizen	Tuscaloosa	AL	w	1945	EP45
Alabama Christian Index	Tuscaloosa	AL	w	1910-1914	Ay1914
Alabama Citizen	Tuscaloosa	AL	w	1946-1963	Ba,Ay1947,1963,Oclc,EP46,51,NH49, NY52
Alabama Citizen & Tuscaloosa Weekly Review	Tuscaloosa	AL	w	1943-1947	Ba,Ay1947,Oclc
Chronicle	Tuscaloosa	AL	w	1896-1899	Ba,Oclc,Cam
Colored American	Tuscaloosa	AL		1907-1916	Br
Courier	Tuscaloosa	AL	w	1980-1983	EP80-83,Lb
Christian Hope	Tuscaloosa	AL	w	1890-1895	Ba,Ay1894
American Star	Tuscumbia	AL	sm	1901-1920	Ba,Ay1905,1920,Cam
Tennessee Valley Reporter	Tuscumbia	AL		1899-1900	Ba
Campus Digest	Tuskegee	AL	w/bw	1931-1994+	Ay1950,1983,Ga88,94,EP50,51,NH42,46, 52,Dc41,44
Hawk's Cry	Tuskegee	AL	w	1944-1946	EP46,Dc44,Fleming
Herald	Tuskegee	AL	w	1949-1952	EP50,51,EP73,NY52
Journal of the National Medical Association	Tuskegee	AL	q	1908-1950	Ay1913,1916-1920,Yenser6
Messenger	Tuskegee	AL	w/m	1905-1981	Ba,Ay1908,1940,NY12,WI,NY32,Br,Rw, Cam,BJ[e1915]
National Association Notes	Tuskegee	AL	m	1912	NY12
National Negro School News	Tuskegee	AL	m	1910-1916	Ay1913-1916,NY12
Negro Business League Herald	Tuskegee	AL	m	1912	NY12
Negro Farmer	Tuskegee	AL	sm	1913-1951	Ba,Ay1915,1916,EP50,51,BJ[1914-1915], Mather
Negro Farmer and Messenger	Tuskegee	AL	bw	1913-1918	Ba,Ay1917,1918,Lc83,BJ[b1915]
News of Tuskegee Institute	Tuskegee	AL	m	1951	EP51
Rural Messenger	Tuskegee	AL		1922	NY22
Service	Tuskegee	AL	m	1936-1955	Ay1940,1955,EP39,40,NY46,Dc44
Southern Letter	Tuskegee	AL	m	1880-1925	NY12,19,22,WI,Jcw
Student Messenger	Tuskegee	AL		1926	NY26
Tuskegee News	Tuskegee	AL		1991-1992+	BRG,Ga94[nlb]
Tuskegee Progressive Times	Tuskegee	AL	w	1970-1971	Oclc,EP73,Lb
Tuskegee Student	Tuskegee	AL	bm/w	1884-1925	Ay1911,1925,WI[b1906?],NY12,19,22, Mather
Tuskegee Times	Tuskegee	AL	w	1974-1976	EP75,76
Tuskegeean	Tuskegee	AL	w	1966-1994+	Pr,EP,67,71,Lb,SPD94
Voice	Tuskegee	AL	w	1976-1977	Oclc,Lb
V. C. Endeavor and S. S. Headlight	Tuskegee	AL		1912	NY12
Headlight	Union Springs	AL	w	1906-1910	Ba,Ay1908,1909

TITLE	CITY	ST.	FREQ.	DATES	SOURCES
Negro Leader	Uniontown	AL	w	1909-1922	Ba,Ay1911-1917,Oclc,NY19,Gr,Go,Cam,Lc83
News	Uniontown	AL	w	1908-1917	Ba,Ay1916,1917[1908],Oclc
Observer	Wetumpka	AL	w	1910-1912	Ba,Ay1911,1912
Racial Endeavors	Yantley	AL		1906-1907	Ba
Tribune	York Station	AL	w	1888-1896	Ay1894,1896
Alaska Spotlight	Anchorage	AK	w	1952-1977	Ay1969,1977,Oclc,Sch,WI[e1968],EP67,78,Pr,Lb,SPD67
North Star Reporter	Anchorage	AK	sm	1982	Oclc
Tundra Times	Anchorage	AK	w	1962-1994+	Ga94[nlb],BRG
93rd Blue Helmet	Fort Huachuca	AZ	w	1942-1943	Oclc
Arizona Gleam	Phoenix	AZ	w	1935-1946	Ba,EP35-40
Arizona Informant	Phoenix	AZ	w	1971-1994+	Ay1983,Ga87,94,Oclc,EH,BRG,EP72,93,Baid92,API90,WPN94,SPD94
Arizona Informant	Phoenix	AZ	w	1958-1961	Oclc,EH
Arizona Sun	Phoenix	AZ	w	1940-1965	Ay1965,EP51[Sun],NY52
Arizona Tribune	Phoenix	AZ	w	1958-1979	Pr,EBA,EH,EP64,73,Lb,SPD67,70,74,79
Index	Phoenix	AZ	w	1936-1942	Ba,EP39-42
Phoenix Press Weekly	Phoenix	AZ	w	1981-1982	EP81-86,BRG
Tribune	Phoenix	AZ	w,m	1918-1941	Ba,Ay1921,1941,EP38,39,Gr,Go,NY19,22,26,32,Yenser4
Western Dispatch	Phoenix	AZ		1927-1929	Ba
Arizona Times	Tucson	AZ		1930-1934	Ba,NY32
Arizona's Negro Journal	Tucson	AZ	w	1941-1946	Ba,Lc91,NH44,46,Dc44
Inter-State Review	Tucson	AZ	w	1920-1935	Ba,NY22,26,32,Boris1
Arkansas African Methodist	Argenta	AR	w	1899-1920	Ba,Ay1911,1912,1915-1920,NY12
Voice of the Twentieth Century	Argenta	AR	w	1901-1922	Ba,Ay1906,1915,NY12,19,22,Go,Lt1907
Reporting Star	Arkadelphia	AR	sm	1900-1904	Ba,Saar
Free Lance	Augusta	AR	sm	1902-1903	Saar
Baxter Vidette	Baxter	AR	sm	1902	Oclc
Arkansas Survey-Journal	Camden	AR	w	1934-1955	Ba,Ay1945,1950,1955,Saar[1945-1955]
Camden News	Camden	AR	d	1940	EP40
Camden Weekly	Camden	AR	w	1961-1961	Saar
Courier	Camden	AR	w	1892-1893	Ba,Saar
Express	Camden	AR	w	1939	EP39
South Arkansas Journal	Camden	AR	w	1962	Saar
Southern Negro	Camden	AR	w	1907-1910	Ba,Ay1909,Saar
Arkansas Baptist Flashlight	Carlisle	AR	sm	1940-1946	Ba,Saar,NH42,46,Dc41,44
People's Intelligencer	Conway	AR	w	1923-1931	Ba,Ay1925[1924],1930,Saar
Watchman	Conway	AR	bm	1896-1897	Ba,Saar
Weekly Colored Tidings	Conway	AR	w	1927-1928	Ba,Saar
Weekly Colored Times	Conway	AR	w	1928-1929	Ba,Saar
News	Crossett	AR	w	1906-1907	Ba,Saar
Advocate	Dermott	AR	2xw	1895-1901	Ba,Saar

TITLE	CITY	ST.	FREQ.	DATES	SOURCES
Afro-American	Dermott	AR	w	1903	Saar
Fraternal World	Dermott	AR	w	1902-1904	Ba,Saar
Industrial Chronicle	Dermott	AR	w	1909-1921	Ba,Ay1911-1913,1915,1917-1921,Saar
South East Advocate	Dermott	AR	w	1907-1910	Ay1906,1908,Saar
South Eastern Baptist	Dermott	AR	w	1899-1906	Ba,Ay1906,Saar
Southern Afro-American	Dermott	AR	w	1896-1904	Ba,Saar
Messenger	Dumas	AR	w	1900-1901	Ba,Saar
Eastern Arkansas World	Earle	AR	w	1940	Saar
Dixie Appeal	El Dorado	AR	w	1904-1906	Ba,Ay1906,Saar
Washington Hi Bulletin	El Dorado	AR		1930	AHGM
New Era	Eudora	AR	w	1905-1912	Ay1909,1911,NY12,Saar
Herald	Eufaula	AR		1893-1899	Ba (see AL)
Bradley District Herald	Fordyce	AR		1913-1919	Ba,Saar,NY19
Evangel	Fordyce	AR	w	1900-1902	Ba,Saar
Negro Advocate	Fordyce	AR	m	1917-1922	Ba,Ay1920,NY19,22,Saar,Go
Star Messenger	Fordyce	AR	w	1900-1913	Ba,Ay1911,Saar[1910-1913]
Western Star	Fordyce	AR	sm	1900-1909	Ba,Ay1909,Saar
Advocate	Forrest City	AR	w	1886-1888	Ay1887,1888,Saar
Arkansas Baptist Flashlight	Forrest City	AR	sm	1939-1939	Saar
Enterprise	Forrest City	AR		1889-1890	Saar
Herald	Forrest City	AR	w/bw	1896-1903	Ba,Br,Saar,AHGM
Homeland	Forrest City	AR	m	1991-1994+	Oclc,AHGM
New Light	Forrest City	AR	sm	1899-1902	Ba,Br,Saar
Royal Messenger	Forrest City	AR	w	1915-1922	Ay1918-1920,Saar
Southern Liberator	Forrest City	AR	w	1936	Oclc
Appreciator	Fort Smith	AR	w	1898-1900	Saar,Lt1907
Appreciator-Union	Fort Smith	AR	w	1912-1922	Ba,Br,Go,Saar,NY12,19, Mather[1902-1911]
Arkansas Appreciator	Fort Smith	AR	w	1898-1912	Ba,Ay1905,1906,1908,1911,1912,Saar
Arkansas Baptist Flashlight	Fort Smith	AR	sm	1934-1946	Ba,Saar,NY46
Banner	Fort Smith	AR		1896-1897	Saar
Fraternal Union	Fort Smith	AR	w	1907-1914	Ba,Ay1909,1912,Lt1907,Saar,NY12
Golden Epoch	Fort Smith	AR	w	1888-1890	Saar
Informer	Fort Smith	AR		1912	Saar
Our Eastern Star	Fort Smith	AR	m	1899-1908	Ba,Saar[1899-1903]
People's Protector	Fort Smith	AR		1889-1892	Ba,Penn,Saar
Pythian Herald	Fort Smith	AR	w	1904-1908	Ba,Ay1905,1906,1908,Saar
Heber Springs Headlight	Heber Springs	AR	w	1907-1918	Ba,Ay1911,1912[nlb],Saar[e1911],Lc83
Arkansas Mule	Helena	AR	w	1890-1891	Ba,Ay1890,Saar
Arkansas Survey-Journal	Helena	AR	w	1934-1955	Ba,Ay1940,1955,Saar[b1941]
Baptist Reporter	Helena	AR	m/sm	1891-1907	Ay1906,Saar
Colored American	Helena	AR	w	1902-1903	Ba,Saar
Golden Epoch	Helena	AR	w	1881-1888	Saar
Informer	Helena	AR	w	1939	EP39

TITLE	CITY	ST.	FREQ.	DATES	SOURCES
Interstate Reporter	Helena	AR	w	1891-1934	Ba,Ay1908,1930,Saar,NY12,19,22,26,32, Go,Yenser6
Jacob's Friend	Helena	AR		1888-1890	Ba,Penn,Saar
New Era	Helena	AR	w	1888-1891	Ba,Ay1891,Saar
People's Friend	Helena	AR	2xw	1888-1890	Ba,Ay1890,Saar
Press	Helena	AR	w	1937-1938	EP37,38
Progress	Helena	AR	w	1880-1902	Ba,Ay1894,Go,Haley,Br,R1898,Saar
Reporter	Helena	AR	sm	1891-1901	Ba,Ay1896,1905,Saar,WI,AHGM[e1907], Cam,Oclc,Lc83
Royal Messenger	Helena	AR	w	1909-1922	Ba,Ay1921,Saar,NY19
Southern Mediator Journal	Helena	AR	w	1940	Saar
Southern Review	Helena	AR	w	1882-1890	Ba,Ay1889,1890,Saar
Times	Helena	AR	bm	1886-1886	Saar
World Picture	Helena	AR		1950	Saar
Arkansas Banner	Holly Grove	AR	w	1887-1890	Ba,Ay1890,Saar
Star	Holly Grove	AR	w	1887-1890	Ba,Ay1888,1889,Saar
Southwestern Outlook	Hope	AR	w	1901-1926	Ba,Ay1916-1921,1925,Saar
Arkansas Citizen	Hot Springs	AR	w/m	1962-1976	Saar,Oclc,Lb
Arkansas Mansion	Hot Springs	AR		1883	Saar
Arkansas Review	Hot Springs	AR	w	1898-1927	Ba,Ay1916,1925,Saar[1898-1922]
Arkansas Survey-Journal	Hot Springs	AR	w	1934-1955	Ay1950,1955,Saar[1949-1953]
Citizen	Hot Springs	AR	w	1958-1977	Oclc,EP72[e1972],Lb
Crusader Journal	Hot Springs	AR	w	1940-1947	Ba,Saar,EP43,44,45,NH42,44,Dc41,44
Crystal	Hot Springs	AR	w	1898-1899	Ba,Br,Saar
Hot Springs Echo	Hot Springs	AR	w	1898-1946	Ba,Ay1905,1915,R1900,Oclc,Saar [e1927?],NY12,19,22,26,32,Go,Br,Boris1
Sun	Hot Springs	AR		1885-1892	Ba,Penn,Saar
W. O. U. Messenger	Hot Springs	AR		1930-1933	Ba,Saar,NY32
Southern Mediator	Jacksonville	AR	w	1978-1979	Oclc
News	Jericho	AR	w	1901-1902	Saar
Progress	Kingsland	AR	sm	1900-1902	Saar
American Guide	Little Rock	AR	w	1889-1906	Ba,Ay1905,R1898,1900,Cam,Br,Lc83, Oclc,Saar,WI,AHGM[1869-1871]
Arkansas Banner	Little Rock	AR	w	1911-1926	Ba,Ay1915-1920,Saar,NY19,22,26,Go, Boris1
Arkansas Baptist	Little Rock	AR	w/sm	1882-1937	Ba,Ay1886,1912[b1881 nlb],R1888,1900, Saar[1896?]
Arkansas Baptist Flashlight	Little Rock	AR	sm	1935-1952	Saar,EP50,51,NY52,Br
Arkansas Carrier	Little Rock	AR	w	1975-1977	Saar,EP77
Arkansas Dispatch	Little Rock	AR	w	1880-1897	Ba,Br,Gr,Penn,Saar[1886-1897],Eur94
Arkansas Freeman	Little Rock	AR	w	1869-1871	Ba,Br,Gr,Cam,Oclc,Saar,WI,AHGM
Arkansas Herald	Little Rock	AR	w	1880-1884	Ba,Ay1884,Br,Cam,Penn,Saar
Arkansas Herald Mansion	Little Rock	AR	w	1884-1886	Ba,Br,Cam,Penn,Saar
Arkansas Journal and Advertiser	Little Rock	AR		1960-1960	Saar
Arkansas Monitor	Little Rock	AR		1911-1912	Saar

TITLE	CITY	ST.	FREQ.	DATES	SOURCES
Arkansas Review	Little Rock	AR		1883-1890	Ba,Saar
Arkansas State Press	Little Rock	AR	w	1941-1994+	Ba,Ay1959,Ga88,94,Oclc,Saar,WI [1931-1959],EP43,93,NH42,44,46,49,52, Dc41,44,AHGM[b1984]
Arkansas Survey	Little Rock	AR	w	1923-1935	Ba,Ay1930,1935,Oclc,Saar,NY26,32,Br
Arkansas Survey-Journal	Little Rock	AR	w	1931-1971	Ba,Ay1940,1950,Br,Oclc,Saar,EP36,51, NH42,44,46,49,NY46,52,Dc41,44
Arkansas Times	Little Rock	AR	w	1925-1933	Ba,Saar,NY26,32,Boris1
Arkansas Tribune	Little Rock	AR	w	1973-1973	Oclc
Arkansas Vanguard	Little Rock	AR		1940	Saar
Arkansas Voice	Little Rock	AR	ir	1965	AHGM
Arkansas Weekly Mansion	Little Rock	AR	w	1880-1886	Ba,Ay1882,1886,Lc91,Oclc[e1884],Saar, WI,AHGM[1880-1884],NWU,Mather
Arkansas Weekly Sentinel	Little Rock	AR	w	1978-1983	Oclc,EP80-83
Arkansas Wesleyan	Little Rock	AR		1892-1898	Saar
Arkansas World	Little Rock	AR	w	1940-1957	Ba,Ay1950,1956,Oclc,Saar,EP41,51,Br, NH42,44,49,NY46,52,Dc41,44,AHGM
Arkansas-Oklahoma African Methodist	Little Rock	AR	m	1949	Saar
Arkansaw Dispatch	Little Rock	AR	w	1886-1896	Ay1888,1889,1894,Saar[1886-1893],Gr
Baptist College News	Little Rock	AR	m	1912-1922	Saar,NY12,19,22
Baptist Vanguard	Little Rock	AR	sm/w	1882-1976	Ba,Ay1894,1953,Saar,ABSCHSL,Br,EP38, 51,NH42,46,NY12,19,22,26,32,46,52, Dc41,44,Mather[Helena AR],Lt1907,Penn, Fleming
Black Consumer	Little Rock	AR		1972-1973	Saar
College Advocate	Little Rock	AR	m	1910	Saar
College Messenger	Little Rock	AR		1911-1912	Saar
College Quarterly	Little Rock	AR		1913-1913	Saar
Colored Churchman	Little Rock	AR	m	1930-1939	Saar
Commercial Gazette	Little Rock	AR	m	1902-1903	Saar
Consumer	Little Rock	AR	w	1973-1994+	Saar,AHGM[1972-1994]
Enterprise	Little Rock	AR	w	1906-1907	Saar
Eulogizer	Little Rock	AR		1910-1911	Saar
Fulcrum	Little Rock	AR	w	1906-1912	Ba,Ay1908,1909,1911,Saar
Fulcrum's Weekly	Little Rock	AR	w	1907-1907	Saar
Fulton's Sun	Little Rock	AR		1884-1885	Ba,Saar
Herald Mansion	Little Rock	AR		1884-1886	Ba,Penn,Saar
Little Rock Sun	Little Rock	AR	w	1884-1890	Ba,Ay1888,1890,Saar,Penn
Mansion	Little Rock	AR		1886-1887	Penn
Minority Business Journal	Little Rock	AR	bm	1972-1973	Saar
Mosaic Guide	Little Rock	AR	w	1885-1886	Ba,Saar
Mosaic Guide	Little Rock	AR	w	1888-1926	Ba,Ay1906[b1889],1912,Saar,NY12,19,22, 26,Boris1[Helena],DANB83
National Democrat	Little Rock	AR	w	1890-1891	Ba,Ay1891,Saar
Observer	Little Rock	AR	w	1925-1927	Saar,NY26,Boris1

TITLE	CITY	ST.	FREQ.	DATES	SOURCES
Our Review	Little Rock	AR	m	1908-1920	Ba,Ay1915-1920,Saar,NY12,Mather
Panther Journal	Little Rock	AR	m/txm	1940-1946	Saar,NY46
People's Herald	Little Rock	AR	w	1900-1903	Ba,Saar,Mather
Reporter	Little Rock	AR	w	1901-1909	Ba,Ay1905,1909,Oclc[e1906],Saar,AHGM[1902-1906]
Shorter Bugle	Little Rock	AR		1952	AHGM
Southern Christian Recorder	Little Rock	AR	w	1886-1946	Ba,Oclc[b1930],Saar[b1932],EP38,40,NH46,Dc41,44,AHGM[b1885]
Southern Mediator	Little Rock	AR	w	1979-1987	Ay1979,1983,Ga87,Oclc,EP81,86
Southern Mediator Journal	Little Rock	AR	w	1938-1978	Ba,Ay1970,1978,Oclc,Saar,EBA,EH,EP67,78,AHGM,SPD67,70,74,79,Lb,Bp,Pr,Lc83
State Press	Little Rock	AR	w	1941-1959	Ay1950,EP67,83,NH46,49,NY46,52,Dc44
State Weekly News	Little Rock	AR	w	1976-1994+	Oclc,EP77,78,Lb,SPD87,94
Statewide Mediator	Little Rock	AR	w	1980-1983	EP80,NA83
Sun	Little Rock	AR	w	1884-1890	Ay1886,1887,Saar
Taborian Visitor	Little Rock	AR	m	1895-1917	Ba,Saar,EP37-41
Twin City Press	Little Rock	AR	w	1937-1940	Saar,AHGM,Oclc
Visitor	Little Rock	AR		1898	Saar
Voice of the Twentieth Century	Little Rock	AR		1898-1901	Ba
Western Review	Little Rock	AR	w	1919-1925	Ba,Saar,NY19,22,26,Go
Monitor	Malvern	AR	w	1902-1903	Ba,Saar
Elevator	Marianna	AR	w	1904-1905	Ba,Ay1905,Saar
Enterprise	Marianna	AR	w	1907-1908	Ba,Ay1908,Saar
Opinion-Enterprise	Marianna	AR	w	1907-1926	Ba,Ay1909,1919,Go,NY12,19,22,26,Boris1
Headlight	Marion	AR	w	1886-1888	Ba,Ay1888,Saar
Trumpet	Montrose	AR	w	1901-1906	Ba,Ay1905,Saar
Union Trumpet	Montrose	AR	w	1906-1910	Ba,Ay1906,Saar,NY12
Clarion	Morrilton	AR		1888,1890	Saar
Conway County Clarion	Morrilton	AR	w	1887-1888	Ba,Ay1888,Saar
Tribune	Morrilton	AR	w	1905-1909	Ba,Ay1908,1909,Saar
Voice	Morrilton	AR	m	1919-1924	Ba,Ay1920,1921,Saar,NY19,22
Zion Trumpet	Nashville	AR	m	1941-1946	Saar
Arkansas Progress	Newport	AR	w	1887-1888	Ba,Ay1888,Saar
Headlight	Newport	AR	w	1909-1914	Ba,Ay1911,1912,1913,Saar
White River Advance	Newport	AR	w	1913-1920	Ay1915,1917-1920,Saar
White River Advocate	Newport	AR	w	1913-1926	Ba,Saar,Go,NY19,22,26,Boris1
African Methodist	North Little Rock	AR		1919-1922	Saar
Arkansas African Methodist	North Little Rock	AR	w/bw	1921-1927	Ay1921,1925
Eastern Star	North Little Rock	AR	m	1898-1899	Saar
Our Eastern Star	North Little Rock	AR	m	1899-1905	Saar
University Herald	North Little Rock	AR	bw	1898-1906	Ba,Saar
Voice	North Little Rock	AR	w	1906-1907	Saar
Voice of the Twentieth Century	North Little Rock	AR	w	1898-1922	Saar

TITLE	CITY	ST.	FREQ.	DATES	SOURCES
Arkansas Advocate	Osceola	AR	sm	1895-1898	R1898
Plaindealer	Osceola	AR	w	1895-1897	Ba,Ay1896,Saar
Agricultural, Mechanical and Normal College Informer	Pine Bluff	AR	q	1940	AHGM
Arkansas American	Pine Bluff	AR	w	1925-1926	Saar,NY26,Boris1
Arkansas Baptist Flashlight	Pine Bluff	AR		1948-1949	EP48,49
Arkansas Colored Catholic	Pine Bluff	AR	m	1899-1902	Ba,Saar
Arkansas Dispatch	Pine Bluff	AR	w	1962,1975-1976	Saar,Oclc
Arkansas Masonic Monitor	Pine Bluff	AR		1917-1923	Saar
Arkansas Mirror	Pine Bluff	AR	w	1967-1970	Saar,EP71,Oclc
Arkansas Survey-Journal	Pine Bluff	AR	w	1934-1955	Ba,Ay1940,1950,Saar[1941-1956]
Arkansasyer	Pine Bluff	AR	m	1928-1940	Saar
Arkansawyer	Pine Bluff	AR	bm	1945-1973	Saar,Bp
Baptist Organ	Pine Bluff	AR	sm	1882-1883	Ba,Saar
Christian Educator	Pine Bluff	AR		pre 1950	Fleming [Reddick, D. M.]
Echo	Pine Bluff	AR	w	1889-1900	Ba,Ay1894,1896,Penn,Saar,Eur94
Echo-Progress	Pine Bluff	AR	w	1900	Saar
Hornet	Pine Bluff	AR	w	1889	Ay1889,Saar
Negro Spokesman	Pine Bluff	AR	w	1938-1958	Ba,Ay1950,Saar,EP43,51,NH42,44,49, NY52,Dc41
Pine Bluff Post	Pine Bluff	AR	w	1902-1908	Ay1908,Saar
Pine Bluff Press	Pine Bluff	AR	w	1937-1942	Saar,EP37,38,AHGM
Pine Bluff Weekly Herald	Pine Bluff	AR	w	1900-1907	Ba,Saar,WI,NY12,Gr,Cam,Oclc
Pine City News	Pine Bluff	AR	w	1910-1910	Saar
Republican	Pine Bluff	AR	w	1887-1888	Ba,Ay1888,Saar
Richard Allen Review	Pine Bluff	AR	w	1910-1910	Saar
True Reformer	Pine Bluff	AR	w	1885-1885	Saar
Arkansas School News	Stamps	AR	m	1915-1922	Saar,NY22
Reminder	Stamps	AR		1913-1913	Saar
Times	Stamps	AR		1911-1913	Saar
Appreciator-Union	Texarkana	AR	w	1915-1922	Ay1915-1921[b1898],Saar, Mather[1911-1915],Ba[TX]
Arkansas Appreciator	Texarkana	AR	w	1913-1915	Ay1913,Saar,Mather[b1896]
Fraternal Union	Texarkana	AR	w	1900-1906	Mather [Pettus, John Wilson]
Progressive Citizen	Texarkana	AR		1920-1922	Saar
Sun	Texarkana	AR		1885-1892	Ba,Saar[1888]
Universal Brotherhood	Texarkana	AR	w	1940	EP40
People's Protector	Van Buren	AR		1888-1888	Saar
School Herald	Warren	AR	w	1912-1923	Ba,Saar,NY19,22,Go,Mather
Arkansas World	West Memphis	AR	w	1958-1963	Ay1956,1963,Saar
Many Voices	West Memphis	AR	bw	1970-1972	Saar,Oclc
Life Line	Wynne	AR	sm	1906-1919	Ba,Ay1908,1909,1919,Saar
Pilot	Wynne	AR	w	1897-1919	Ba,Ay1906,1919,Saar

TITLE	CITY	ST.	FREQ.	DATES	SOURCES
Black Times	Albany	CA	m	1971-1973	Ay1972,Oclc,WI,EH,EP72,Lc77,Unct, SPD72,74
Pasadena Eagle	Altadena	CA	w	1968-1976	EH,EP72,73,75,76,Bp,Lb
Antelope Valley Metro Star	Bakersfield	CA	w	1975-1981	EP78,81
Bakersfield News	Bakersfield	CA	w	1955-1975	Oclc,EP71,72,75,EBA,EH,Lb
Bakersfield News Observer	Bakersfield	CA	w	1977-1994+	Ga88,94,Lb,Baid90,Oclc,BRG,EP80,93, EBA,WPN94
Colored Citizen	Bakersfield	CA		1913-1915	Ba,Cam
Metro Star	Bakersfield	CA	w	1975-1981	EP77,78,81,Lb
Outlook	Bakersfield	CA	w	1966-1970	Pr,EP67,69,70
San Fernando News Observer	Bakersfield	CA	w	1981-1994+	Coley,WPN94[b1978]
Call	Bell Gardens	CA	m	1972-1976	EP76
Ball and Chain Review	Berkeley	CA		1969-1970	WI,Unct
Bay Viewer	Berkeley	CA	m	1969-1979	SPD74,79
Black Politics: A Journal of Liberation	Berkeley	CA	m	1968-1968	WI,Unct
Black Thoughts Journal	Berkeley	CA	bm	1973-1983	Ay1975,1983
California Voice	Berkeley	CA	w	1919-1993+	Ba,Ay1983,Ga87,94,EP90-93,BRG
Campus Core-lator	Berkeley	CA	q	1964-1967	SPD67
Echo	Berkeley	CA		1881	Penn
Ivy Leaf	Berkeley	CA	q	1950	Ay1950
Seaside Post	Berkeley	CA	w	1963-1972	Ay1969(Post),EP72,EH
Carson Courier	Carson	CA		1980	EP80
Star News: The Voice	Chula Vista	CA		1970-1979	SPD70,74,79
Carson Bulletin	Compton	CA	w	1974-1994+	Ga90,Baid90,BRG,EP75,93,Bp
Compton Bulletin	Compton	CA	w	1975-1994+	Ga90,Baid90,EP75,92[b1970],93,BRG
Herald-American	Compton	CA	2xw	1935-1952	Ay1952
Metropolitan Gazette	Compton	CA	w	1966-1994+	Ay1969,1979,EH,EP72,75,Ga94, 92[Compton Gazette]
Western Advocate	Compton	CA	w	1966-1970	Pr,EP67,69,70
Crenshaw News	Culver City	CA	w	1975-1987	Ay1983,SPD87
Culver City Star	Culver City	CA	w	1980-1993+	Ga94[formerly Culver City Westchester Wave]
Peninsula Bulletin	East Palo Alto	CA	w	1967-1979	EP71,75,77-79
California Advocate	Fresno	CA	bm/w	1967-1994+	Ga90,94,WI[1975],EP71,93,EH,EBA, BRG,SPD79
Grapevine	Fresno	CA		1969-1979	WI
Journal of Pan African Studies	Fresno	CA	q	1987-1993+	Ga94
La Voz de Aztlan	Fresno	CA	w	1974-1982	Ay1981,1982
Uhuru Na Umoja	Fresno	CA	m	1974-1983	Ay1983
New Lady Magazine	Hayward	CA	m	1966-1974	Ay1970,EH,SPD70,74
Bronze America	Hollywood	CA	m/bm	1963-1974	SPD67,70,74
National Record	Hollywood	CA	w	1944-1994+	BRG,Ga94[nlb](see Record),SPD94
Record	Hollywood	CA	w	1944-1983	Ay1970,1983,Lb (see National Record)
Minority Business Enterprise	Inglewood	CA	6xy	1984-1994+	Ga88,94

TITLE	CITY	ST.	FREQ.	DATES	SOURCES
Inglewood Tribune	Inglewood/Compton	CA	w	1990-1994+	Ga90,94,Baid90,BRG
LA Bay News Observer	Inglewood	CA	w	1981-1994+	EP90,WPN94[b1977 Bakersfield]
News Advertiser	Inglewood	CA		1970	EP71,Lb
Long Beach Express	Long Beach	CA	w	1966-1994+	Ga92,94
Afro-Tempo	Los Angeles	CA	w	1940-1945	Ba,NH42,46,Dc41,44[susp.43]
American News	Los Angeles	CA	w	1930-1960	Ay1960
Black Lace	Los Angeles	CA	q	1993+	Ga94
Black Politician: A Quarterly Journal of Current Political Thought	Los Angeles	CA	q	1969-1974	BJ,SPD72,74
Bronzville News	Los Angeles	CA	w	1943-1944	Oclc
California Cactus	Los Angeles	CA		1912	NY12
California Eagle	Los Angeles	CA	w	1879-1981	Ba,Ay1921,1953,Go,Gr,Cam,Lc91,Oclc[1875-1966],EP37,75,NH42,44,46,49,NY12,19,22,26[Eagle],32,46,52,Dc41,44,Rw,Yenser3,Mather
California News	Los Angeles	CA		1926-1944	Ba,EP38,Yenser6
California Tribune	Los Angeles	CA		1947-1950	Fleming [Steward, Leon Walker] (See LA Tribune)
Central News	Los Angeles	CA	w	1953-1975	Ay1970,1975,Ga87,EBA,EP71-75 [b1966],Rw,WPN94[b1963]
Central News Wave Group	Los Angeles	CA	w	1938-1992+	EP80,93,EH,Ga90
Central Southwest News	Los Angeles	CA	w	1970	EP70
Central Star/Journal Wave	Los Angeles	CA	w	1919-1994+	Ga91,92,94,BRG
Citizens Advocate	Los Angeles	CA	w	1916-1923	Ba,Ay1921,NY19,22,Go
Citizens Voice	Los Angeles	CA	w	1964-1975	EH,EP75,Lb
Compton/Carson Wave	Los Angeles	CA	w	1919-1994+	Ga91,94 (see Compton),BRG
Courier	Los Angeles	CA	w	1954-1971	Ay1954,EP67,PR
Craftsman Aero News	Los Angeles	CA	m	1939-1940	EP39,40
Criterion	Los Angeles	CA	w	1942-1951	Ba,Ay1950,Br,NH49,NY52
Culver City/Westchester Wave	Los Angeles	CA	w	1919-1992	Ga91,92,BRG (see Culver City Star)
Defender	Los Angeles	CA		1916-1919	Ba,Ay1919
Eastside News	Los Angeles	CA		1936-1936	Ba
El Mundo	Los Angeles	CA		1993-1994+	API94
Enterprise	Los Angeles	CA	w	1907-1915	Ba,NY12,Lt1907
Femme	Los Angeles	CA	m	1954-1962	Ay1962
Firestone Park News/Southeast News Press	Los Angeles	CA	w	1916-1994+	Ga87,94,Baid90,BRG,EH[1916],EP62,93[b1924]
First Word	Los Angeles	CA		1943-1946	Ba
Graphic	Los Angeles	CA		1939	Ba
Happenings	Los Angeles	CA	w	1962-1977	EP77[1976],78[1962]
Harambee	Los Angeles	CA		1975	Oclc
Harambee	Los Angeles	CA		1967	Oclc
Hard Line	Los Angeles	CA		1967	Unct
Herald-Dispatch	Los Angeles	CA	w	1952-1994+	Ay1968,1983,Ga87,94,Oclc,Rw,EH,WI [b1950?],BRG,EBA,EP62,93,SPD67,70,74

TITLE	CITY	ST.	FREQ.	DATES	SOURCES
Illustrated Reflector	Los Angeles	CA		1939	Ba
Inglewood Hawthorne Wave	Los Angeles	CA	w	1972-1994+	Ga91,94[b1978],BRG,EP72,78,79
International Review of African American Art	Los Angeles	CA		1991	Ga91
Liberator	Los Angeles	CA	m/w	1900-1922	Ba,Ay1905,1917,NY12,19,22,26,Go, Mather
Los Angeles Evening Express	Los Angeles	CA		1913-1925	Boris2 [Thompson, Noah Davis]
Los Angeles News	Los Angeles	CA	w	1959-1980	Pr,EP67,80,EBA,EH,Lb
Los Angeles News Press	Los Angeles	CA	w	1962-1976	EH,EP73,75,76,Lb
Los Angeles Sentinel	Los Angeles	CA	w	1933-1994+	Ba,Ay1950,1975,Ga87,94,Lc91,Oclc,WI, EP38,75[b1934],93,EH,EBA,NH42,44,46, 49,NY46,52,Dc41,44,API94,Rw,Fleming
Los Angeles Tribune	Los Angeles	CA	w	1940-1963	Ba,Ay1953,1960,Br,Lc91,EP44,51,NH44, 46,49,NY46,52,Dc44
Lynwood Wave	Los Angeles	CA	w	1919-1994+	Ga91,94,BRG
Mesa Tribune Wave	Los Angeles	CA	w	1919-1994+	Ga91,94,BRG
Militant	Los Angeles	CA		1944-1946	Ba
National Herald	Los Angeles	CA		1976-1977	WI
Neighborhood News	Los Angeles	CA	w	1930-1955	Ba,Ay1945,1955,EP46,49,NH42,46,49, NY46,52,Dc41,44
New Age	Los Angeles	CA	w	1907-1926	Ba,Ay1912,1925,NY12,19,Go,Cam, DANB526,Mather
New Age Dispatch	Los Angeles	CA	w	1925-1948	Ba,Ay1927,1948,Sch,EP38,39,NH49, NY26,32,Gr,Cam,Boris1
New Age Negro	Los Angeles	CA		1904-1925	Ba,Cam
News	Los Angeles	CA		1944-1946	Ba
News Guardian	Los Angeles	CA	w	1937-1944	Ba,Ay1944,EP38,39,NH42,44,Dc41
Orange Star Review	Los Angeles	CA	w	1975-1976	EP75,76
Outlet	Los Angeles	CA		pre 1925	DANB590
Pacific Defender	Los Angeles	CA	w	1923-1938	Ba,Oclc[b1923],NY26,32
Players	Los Angeles	CA	w	1973-1994+	Ay1975,Ga87,94,SPD87,94
Quotable Karenga	Los Angeles	CA		1972-1974	SPD72,74
Record Newspapers	Los Angeles	CA	w	1943-1972	Ay1969,1970,EBA,EP71,72
Scoop	Los Angeles	CA	w	1966-1977	EP75-77
Searchlight	Los Angeles	CA	w	1893-1908	Ba,Ay1905,1908[1896],Cam
Sepia Hollywood	Los Angeles	CA	m	1944-1950	Ay1950
Silhouette Pictorial	Los Angeles	CA	m	1940-1950	Ay1940,1945,1950
Soul	Los Angeles	CA	w	1965-1982	Ay1970,1982,WI,Sch[b1966],EP75-77, SPD79
Soul Illustrated	Los Angeles	CA	bm	1968-1973	Ay1970,1973,EH
Southeast Wave Star	Los Angeles	CA	w	1938-1994+	Ay1968,1975,Ga87,92,EP71,79,SPD87,94
Southern California Guide	Los Angeles	CA		1891-1895	Ba,Ay1894
Southside Journal	Los Angeles	CA	w	1938-1994+	Ay1968,EP71-75,Ga87,92,WPN94 [b1963]
Southwest News	Los Angeles	CA	w	1953-1994+	Ay1970,1975,EP71-75[1966],SPD87,94
Southwest News Wave	Los Angeles	CA	w	1919-1994+	Ga87,94,Lb,Rw,EBA[b1953]

TITLE	CITY	ST.	FREQ.	DATES	SOURCES
Southwest Topics/Sun Wave	Los Angeles	CA	w	1922-1994+	Ay1975,Ga87,94,Lb,Go,Rw,BRG, EP71-75,SPD87,94
Southwest Wave	Los Angeles	CA	w	1921-1994+	Ay1930,1968,Ga87,BRG,EP71-75,Rw, SPD87,94
Southwestern Sun	Los Angeles	CA	w	1948-1994+	Ay1975,Ga92,EP71-79,SPD87,94
Spotlight	Los Angeles	CA	w	1944-1951	Ba,EP50,51,NH44,NY46,NY52
Star Review	Los Angeles	CA	w	1951-1952	EP51,NY52
Teller	Los Angeles	CA		1944-1946	Ba
United Pictorial Review	Los Angeles	CA	w	1965-1975	Ay1969,1975,EH,Pr,Rw
Watts Star Review	Los Angeles	CA	w	1975-1994+	Ga87,94,Lc91,WI,Baid92,EP71[1904],75, [1942],92[1968],93,EH[1929],BRG, EBA[1904]
Watts Times	Los Angeles	CA	w	1980	EP80
WCLC Newsletter	Los Angeles	CA	m	1965-1970	SPD70,74
Western Christian Recorder	Los Angeles	CA	sm	1900-1947	Ba,Ay1940,1945,EP38,NH42,Dc41
Western Dispatch	Los Angeles	CA	w	1921-1922	Ba,Oclc,NY22
Western Informant	Los Angeles	CA	m	1939-1940	EP39,40
Western News	Los Angeles	CA		pre 1893	DANB421
What's Going On	Los Angeles	CA	w	1975-1987	EP77,78,SPD87[TV Journal]
Lynwood Journal	Lynwood/Compton	CA	w	1919-1994+	Ga90-94,Baid90,BRG
Feeling' Good	Manhattan Beach	CA	6xy	1988-1993+	Ga94
Belmont Courier Bulletin	Menlo Park	CA	w	1978	EP78
Black Times Voices of the National Community	Menlo Park	CA	m	1971-1986	Ay1980,1986,SPD79[b1971]
Menlo Atherton Recorder	Menlo Park	CA	w	1978	EP78
Ravenswood Post	Menlo Park	CA	w	1953-1981	Ay1981,EP67,78,EBA,EH,Lb,Pr
San Carlos Enquirer	Menlo Park	CA	w	1978	EP78
Black Echo	Milpitas	CA		1969-1974	SPD72,74
Bayou Talk	Moreno Valley	CA	m	1992+	Baid92
Journal of Black Studies	Newbury Park	CA	q	1970-1994+	Ga90,94,WI,BJ[LA],SPD87
Auto Workers Focus: Rank & File Newspaper of the Black Panther Caucus	Oakland	CA		1970	Unct
Beacon	Oakland	CA		1945	Ba
Berkeley Tri-City Post	Oakland	CA	2xw	1963-1994+	Ay1970,1975,Ga87,94,EH,BRG,EP67,75, API90,94,WPN94[b1970]
Black Panther	Oakland	CA	w/fn	1965-1980	Oclc,Lb,WI,EH[1965],EP72,76[1967], SPD72,74,Gl
Black Scholar	Oakland	CA	6xy	1969-1994+	Ga91,94,WI,BJ[Sausalito],SPD72,74,87
Burning Spear	Oakland	CA	m	1968-1987	SPD87
California Voice	Oakland	CA	w	1919-1989	Ay1921,1983,Pr,EH,EBA,EP38,79,NH42, 44,46,49,NY22,26,32,46,52,Dc41,44, Boris1,SPD67,70,74,79
California World	Oakland	CA		1919	Ba
Herald	Oakland	CA	w	1943-1951	Ba,Ay1950,1951,EP49,NH49,NY46,NY52
Illustrated Guide	Oakland	CA	w	1892-1900	Ba,Ay1896

TITLE	CITY	ST.	FREQ.	DATES	SOURCES
Independent	Oakland	CA		1929-1936	Ba,Aba,EP35
Light	Oakland	CA	w	1944-1946	Ba,NY46
Newark Forum	Oakland	CA	w	1977	EP77
Night Edition News	Oakland	CA	w	1972-1978	EP78
Oakland Independent	Oakland	CA	w	1929-1935	Ay1935,Gr
Oakland New Day Informer	Oakland	CA		pre 1944	Yenser6 [Marsh, Vivian Osborne]
Oakland Post	Oakland	CA	2xw	1963-1994+	Ay1975,Ga91,94,API90,94,WI,BRG,EII, EP72,93,SPD87
Oakland Sunshine	Oakland	CA	w	1897-1922	Ba,Ay1905,1920,Lc91,Oclc,Aba,WI, NY19,Lt1907,Go,Cam
Oakland Times-Journal	Oakland	CA	w	1952-1987	Ay1981,SPD87
Pacific Times	Oakland	CA	w	1912	Oclc
Richmond Post	Oakland	CA	2xw	1963-1994+	Ay1975,Ga90,94,API90,94,Rw,BRG,EH, EP75,93,WPN94,SPD87
San Francisco Mundo Hispano	Oakland	CA	w	1975	Ay1975
San Francisco Post	Oakland	CA	w	1963-1994+	Ay1975,Ga94,API90,94,Oclc,WI,BRG,EH, EP72,93,WPN94
Seaside Post	Oakland	CA	w	1963-1994+	EP75,93,Ga94,SPD87
Times	Oakland	CA	w	1923-1924	Ba,Br,Oclc
Uhuru	Oakland	CA		1970	Gl
Unity	Oakland	CA	ir	1970-1994+	SPD87,94
Voice	Oakland	CA	w	1962-1970	EP62,70
Western American	Oakland	CA		1926-1929	Ba,Br,Aba,Gr
Black Unity	Oceanside	CA		1970	WI
Black World	Pacoima	CA		1970-1971	WI
San Fernando Gazette Express	Pacoima	CA	w	1966-1993+	Ga94
Black Times Voices of the National Community	Palo Alto	CA	m	1971-1978	Ay1975,1977,WI,EH,EP75-78,Lc77
Peninsula Bulletin	Palo Alto	CA	w	1966-1981	Ay1975,1981,EH,EBA,EP70,72,Lb
Los Angeles Metropolitan Gazette	Pasadena	CA	w	1966-1992+	Ga87,91,Bp,Baid90,BRG,EP80,81
Pasadena Gazette	Pasadena	CA	w	1966-1994+	Ay1983,Ga92,94,BRG
Pasadena Journal News	Pasadena	CA	w	1989-1993+	Oclc,EP91,92,93
Pomona Clarion	Pomona	CA	w	1970-1979	EH,EBA,EP71-73,Lb,SPD79
Antelope Valley Metro Star	Quartz Hill	CA	w	1980-1992+	Ga91,92,EP80,81,SPD87
Bakersfield Metro Star	Quartz Hill	CA	w	1980-1992+	Ga91,92,EP80,81,SPD87[b1975]
Los Angeles Metro Star	Quartz Hill	CA	w	1980-1992+	Ga91,92,EP80,81,90
Colored Citizen	Redlands	CA	m	1907	Lt1907
News	Richmond	CA		1945-1946	Ba
Black Voice News	Riverside	CA	w	1972-1994+	Ay1983,Ga87,94,Oclc,EP90-93[1973], BRG
Observer	Riverside	CA	w	1962-1976	EP75,76
American	Sacramento	CA	w	1944-1947	Ba,NY46
California Times	Sacramento	CA	d	1856-1857	Aba
Forum	Sacramento	CA		1906	Aba
Hollywood Happenings	Sacramento	CA	w	1994	WPN94

TITLE	CITY	ST.	FREQ.	DATES	SOURCES
Los Angeles Happenings	Sacramento	CA	w	1981-1983	EP81,NA83
Outlook	Sacramento	CA	w	1942-1967	Ay1967
Sacramento Observer	Sacramento	CA	w	1962-1994+	Ay1969,1975,Ga91,94,Baid90,Cam,WI, EBA,EH,BRG,EP67,81[b1963],93,SPD67, 70,87
Settlers and Miners Tribune	Sacramento	CA		1850	Aba
Western Outlook	Sacramento	CA	w	1981-1983	EP81,NA83
Western Review	Sacramento	CA	m	1914-1926	Ba,Ay1918,NY19,22,26,Go,Aba,Mather
American News	San Bernardino	CA	w	1969-1994+	Ay1970,1983,Ga87,94,EP69,93,BRG, WPN94
Precinct Reporter	San Bernardino	CA	w	1965-1994+	Ga87,94,Baid90,BRG,EH,EP73,93, WPN94,SPD87,94
Tri County Bulletin	San Bernardino	CA	w	1945-1952	Ba,Ay1950,1952,Br,EP46,49,NH49,NY46, 52
Comet	San Diego	CA	w	1946-1953	Ba,Ay1950,1953,EP48-51,NH49,NY52
Eagle	San Diego	CA	w	1922-1925	Ba,Ay1925,Aba
Informer	San Diego	CA	w	1937-1947	Ba,Ay1940,1948,EP38-40,NH42,44,NY46, Dc41
Lighthouse	San Diego	CA	w	1939-1975	Ba,Ay1969,1975,Pr,EP67,71,Lb,SPD67, 70,74
New Idea	San Diego	CA	w	1921-1926	Ba,Ay1925
San Diego Monitor	San Diego	CA	w	1988-1993+	EP91,92,93
San Diego Voice	San Diego	CA	w	1964-1974	EP64,65,67,69,SPD67,70,74
San Diego Voice & Viewpoint	San Diego	CA	w	1959-1994+	Ay1970,1975,Ga91,94,Baid90,EBA,BRG, EH,EP70,93[1961],API90,WPN94,SPD87
South California Informant	San Diego	CA		1889	Penn
Voice News	San Diego	CA	w	1961-1974	SPD70,74
San Fernando Gazette Express	San Fernando	CA	w	1966-1992+	Ga92 (see Pacioma)
Alto California	San Francisco	CA		1851	DANB258
Bay Area Report	San Francisco	CA	m	1987	SPD87
Bay Guardian	San Francisco	CA	w	1975-1976	EP75,76
Berkeley Metro Reporter	San Francisco	CA	w	1975-1994+	EP75,77-79,API90,94,BRG
Black Dialogue	San Francisco	CA	ir	1965-1979	WI,SPD79
Black Power	San Francisco	CA		1972-1974	SPD72,74
California Voice	San Francisco	CA	w	1923-1994+	BRG,EP78,WPN94,API94
Choice Magazine	San Francisco	CA	q	1981-1987	SPD87
Citizen	San Francisco	CA		1888-1890	Ba
Elevator	San Francisco	CA	w	1865-1904	Ba,Go,Cam,Oclc,Aba,WI,Lb,DANB39
Independent	San Francisco	CA	w	1966-1969	Pr,EP67,71,Lb,SPD67,70,74
Insurgent	San Francisco	CA		1965	WI
Journal of Black Poetry	San Francisco	CA	q	1966-1973	BJ
Labor Herald	San Francisco	CA	sm	1948-1951	EP48,49,51,NY52
Metro	San Francisco	CA	m	1972	EH
Mirror of the Times	San Francisco	CA	w	1855-1862	Ba[1853-1860],Penn,Lc91,Oclc[b1857], Aba,WI,NY12
New Bayview	San Francisco	CA	w	1976-1994+	Ga91,94,BRG,EP90,WPN94

TITLE	CITY	ST.	FREQ.	DATES	SOURCES
Oakland Metro Reporter	San Francisco	CA	w	1975-1994+	Ga91,BRG,EP73,91,API90
Observer	San Francisco	CA	w	1962-1981	Ay1980,1981,EP77,78
Pacific Appeal	San Francisco	CA	w	1862-1880	Ba,Penn,Cam,Lc91,Oclc,Aba,WI,DANB39
Pacific Coast Appeal	San Francisco	CA	m/sm	1901-1925	Ba,Ay1919,1925,Lt1907,Cam,Aba
Peninsula Metro Reporter	San Francisco	CA	w	1975	EP75
People's Advocate	San Francisco	CA	bm	1944	Oclc,Sch
Richmond Metro Reporter	San Francisco	CA.		1975-1994+	Ga91,BRG,EP75,77-79,API90,94
San Francisco Metro Reporter	San Francisco	CA	w	1973-1994+	Ga91,94,EP75,92[1975],93,BRG,API90, 94,WPN94
San Francisco Post	San Francisco	CA	w	1991-1994+	Ga91,94
San Francisco Reporter	San Francisco	CA	w	1943-1949	Ba,EP46,48,NH44,46,49,NY46,Dc44,Br
San Francisco Sentinel	San Francisco	CA		1889-1890	Cam,Penn,Br,DANB39
San Joaquin Metro Reporter	San Francisco	CA	w	1973-1994+	Ga91,94,EP75,API90,94
San Jose/Peninsula Metro Reporter	San Francisco	CA	w	1975-1994+	Ga91,94,BRG,EP75,78,API90,94
Sentinel	San Francisco	CA	w	1880-1890	Ba,Ay1891,Aba
Spokesman	San Francisco	CA	w	1966-1967	Pr,EP67
Spokesman	San Francisco	CA		1935-1938	Ba,EP35,36,Lb,Aba[1933-1935]
Sun	San Francisco	CA	w	1942-1949	Ba,Oclc,EP48,NH49
Sun Reporter	San Francisco	CA	w	1948-1994+	Ay1954,1980,Ga91,94,WI,EBA,BRG, EP49,92[1942],NY52,API90,94,Rw
Urban West	San Francisco	CA	sm/bm	1967-1973	Ay1969,1970,1973
Vallejo Metro Reporter	San Francisco	CA	w	1975-1994+	BRG,EP73,79,API90,94
Vindicator	San Francisco	CA	w	1884-1906	Ba,Ay1896,1906,Cam,Lc91,Oclc,Aba,WI, Br
Western Appeal	San Francisco	CA	sm	1918-1934	Ba,Ay1925,Gr,Oclc
Western Outlook	San Francisco	CA	w	1894-1928	Ba,Lc91,Oclc,WI
San Joaquin Progressor	San Joaquin	CA	w	1969-1972	EBA,Lb,EP71
Forum	San Jose	CA		1908	Aba
La Voz Latina	San Jose	CA		1993-1994+	API94
Afro-American Speaks	San Pedro	CA		1971	WI
Orange County Star Review	Santa Ana	CA	w	1971-1975	Lc91,EH,EP72,73,75,76,Lb
Bay Cities Informer	Santa Monica	CA		pre 1946	Ba,Br
Post News Sentinel	Seaside	CA	w	1947-1994+	Ga90,Baid90,API90,WPN94[b1946]
Guide	Stockton	CA	w	1944-1947	Ba,NY46[Sacramento]
Observer	Stockton	CA	w	1979-1984	EP84
Press	Stockton	CA		1944	Ba
San Joaquin Progressor	Stockton	CA	w	1969-1972	EP71,72,Lb
Soul	Watts	CA		1969-1979	SPD70,72,74,79
Wilmington Beacon	Wilmington	CA	w	1990-1994+	Ga90,91,94,BRG
Essence: The Magazine for Today's Black Woman	Boulder	CO	m	1970-1982+	BJ (see New York)
Colorado Advance	Colorado Springs	CO	w	1914-1917	Ba,Ay1916,1917,Oehco
Colorado Advocate	Colorado Springs	CO	w	1919-1926	Ba,Go,NY19,22,26
Colorado Advocate	Colorado Springs	CO	w	1892-1898	Ay1896,Oehco

TITLE	CITY	ST.	FREQ.	DATES	SOURCES
Colorado Springs Gazette	Colorado Springs	CO		pre 1915	Ay1912(b1872-1912 nlb),Mather [Embry, Julia A.]
Colorado Springs Sun	Colorado Springs	CO	w	1911	St
Colorado Voice	Colorado Springs	CO	w	1948	Oclc
Colored Dispatch	Colorado Springs	CO	w	1900-1901	Ba
Dispatch	Colorado Springs	CO	w	1906-1913	Ba,Ay1912,St,Oehco[e1909]
Eagle	Colorado Springs	CO	w	1910-1913	Ba,Oehco,Mather
Light	Colorado Springs	CO	w	1897-1912	Ay1912,Mather,DANB526
Voice of Colorado	Colorado Springs	CO		1912-1914	Ba,Br
Voice of Colorado	Colorado Springs	CO	w	1936	Oclc
Western Enterprise	Colorado Springs	CO	w	1892-1912	Ba,Ay1912,Oehco,Oclc[b1896],WI,St
Advocate	Denver	CO		1920-1922	Ba,Go
African Advocate	Denver	CO	w	1890-1891	Oclc,St
Afro-American	Denver	CO	w	1889-1890	Ba,Oehco,St
Argus	Denver	CO	w	1880-1881	St
Argus	Denver	CO	w	1886-1888	Ba,Ay1888,Oehco,St[e1887]
Body of Christ	Denver	CO		1993+	Urban Spectrum
Colorado Argus and Weekly Times	Denver	CO	w	1891-1891	St
Colorado Black Lifestyle	Denver	CO	m	1982-1987	SPD87
Colorado Exponent	Denver	CO	w	1892-1895	Ba,Ay1894,Oehco[1894-1895]
Colorado Journal	Denver	CO	w	1948	Oclc,St
Colorado Statesman	Denver	CO	w	1895-1961	Ay1912,1950,Cam,Oehco,Oclc,EP35,51, NH42,44,46,49,WI,Dc41,44,St [1890?-1963?],NY19,22,26,32,46,Yenser6
Cosmopolitan	Denver	CO		pre 1993	Urban Spectrum
Denver Blade	Denver	CO	w	1961-1977	Ay1969,1970,Pr,Lc83,Oehco,Oclc,WI, EP62-71,St[1961-1970],SPD67,70
Denver Challenge	Denver	CO	w	1946-1948	St
Denver Chronicle	Denver	CO	w	1968-1972	EBA,St[1968-1970],Lb
Denver Dispatch	Denver	CO	w	1957	Oclc,St
Denver Exponent	Denver	CO	w	1892-1895	St
Denver Inquirer	Denver	CO	w	1952-1954	St
Denver Star	Denver	CO	w	1882-1974	Ba,Ay1914,1967,Gr,Go,Oclc,WI,EP37, 49,67,NH42,44,46,49,NY19,22,26,32,46, Dc41,44,SPD67,70,74,Yenser3
Denver Sun	Denver	CO	w	1884-1889	St
Denver Weekly News	Denver	CO	w	1971-1994+	Ga88,90,EBA,BRG,Lb,EP75,93,EH,St, WPN94,SPD79
Drum	Denver	CO	w	1971-1976	EH,St,EP73,75,76
Five Pointer	Denver	CO	w	1943-1946	Ba,NH46,Dc44
Franklin's Paper the Statesmen	Denver	CO	w	1889-1912	Ay1912,Oclc
Independent	Denver	CO	w	1902-1913	Ba,Ay1912,St,Mather
New American Weekly	Denver	CO		1923	St
Observer	Denver	CO	w	1975-1976	EP75,76

TITLE	CITY	ST.	FREQ.	DATES	SOURCES
Statesman	Denver	CO	w	1882-1966	Ba,Ay1894,1921,Cam,Oclc,Eur94,St, Lt1907,Lc83,Fleming
Statesman Exponent	Denver	CO	w	1889-1896	Ba,Ay1896
Urban Spectrum	Denver	CO	m	1987-1993+	Oclc,Urban Spectrum
Woodmen Banner	Denver	CO	w	1925	NY26,Dc44[American Woodmen Bulletin]
Harambee	Fort Carson	CO	bw	1971-1972	Oclc
Megaphone	La Junta	CO	w	1913-1915	Ba,Ay1915
Colorado Eagle	Pueblo	CO	w	1910-1914	Ba,Oehco,NY12
Colorado Times	Pueblo	CO	w	1904-1912	Ba,Ay1912,Oehco,NY12[Times], Lt1907[Times]
Colorado Times Eagle	Pueblo	CO	w	1904-1914	Ay1914
Religious World	Pueblo	CO		1906-1908	Ba
Rising Sun	Pueblo	CO	w	1911-1946	Ba,Ay1921,Br,Go,NY19,22,26,Boris1
Times	Pueblo	CO	w	1894-1896	Ba,Ay1896,Oehco
Tribune	Pueblo	CO	w	1898-1901	Ba,Oehco
Tribune-Press	Pueblo	CO	w	1895-1904	Ba,Oehco
Western Ideal	Pueblo	CO	w	1911-1923	Ba,Cam,Go
Western Ideal	Pueblo	CO	w	1919-1960	Ay1925,1960,EP35,51,NH42,44,46,49,St, NY32,46,Dc41,44,Go
Leader	Trinidad	CO	w	1912-1915	Ba,Oehco,NY12
Beacon	Bridgeport	CT	w	193u-1942	Oclc
Harambee	Bridgeport	CT	m	1968-1975	Oclc[1969-1969],EBA,EH,EP71,72,75,Lb
Harambee Union	Bridgeport	CT	m	1968-1976	Oclc[b1970],EP76
Connecticut World	Danbury	CT		1945-1947	Ba
National Beverage Leader	Farmington	CT	m	1960-1975	Ay1975
Bridgeport Inquirer	Hartford	CT	w	1977-1994+	EP80,93,BRG,SPD87,94
Catholic Transcript	Hartford	CT		1898-1989	EP89,Ay1912[b1876 nlb]
Connecticut Banner	Hartford	CT	w	1892-1896	Ba,Ay1894,1896
Connecticut Chronicle	Hartford	CT	w	1948	Oclc,Ba[New Haven]
Freeman's Chronicle	Hartford	CT		1873-1878	Ba,Br
Hartford Advocate	Hartford	CT	w	1918-1938	Ba,Br,EP37,38
Hartford Chronicle	Hartford	CT	w	1940-1947	Oclc
Hartford Inquirer	Hartford	CT	w	1975-1994+	Ga90-94,Baid90,Oclc,EP77,93,BRG,Na83
Hartford Star	Hartford	CT	w	1969-1974	Oclc,EBA,EP71-74,Lb
Hartford Voice	Hartford	CT	w	1974-1975	Oclc
Herald	Hartford	CT	w	1919-1932	Ba,NY19,22
New England Bulletin	Hartford	CT	w	1949	Oclc
New England Searchlight	Hartford	CT		pre 1937	Yenser4 [Rogers, William Quincy]
New Haven Inquirer	Hartford	CT	w	1976-1994+	Oclc,BRG,EP79,93,SPD87,94
North End Agent's	Hartford	CT	w	1975-1992+	Oclc,BRG
Pilot	Hartford	CT	w	1935	EP35
Springfield Inquirer	Hartford	CT	w	1979-1993+	EP80,91,93,BRG
Waterbury Inquirer	Hartford	CT	w	1975-1993+	EP79,80,91,93,BRG
Botswana Review	Ivoryton	CT		1990-1991+	Ga90,91

TITLE	CITY	ST.	FREQ.	DATES	SOURCES
Black Coalition Weekly	New Haven	CT	w	1971-1972	Lc77,WI
Crow	New Haven	CT	bw	1968-1970	WI,EBA,EP71,Lb
Inner-City News	New Haven	CT	w	1990-1994+	Ga94,API94
New Haven Star	New Haven	CT	w	1971-1978	EH,EP72-74,78,Rw,Bp
Plaindealer	New Haven	CT	w	1913-1915	Ba,Ay1915
Zion Trumpet	New Haven	CT	w	1912	NY12
Journal of the National Medical Association	Norwalk	CT		1987-1993+	Ga87,93
Space Waye	Norwalk	CT		1972-1974	SPD72,74
Zion Trumpet	Norwich	CT	w	1919	NY19
Black Health	Ridgefield	CT	q	1988-1994+	Ga91,94
Black Voice	Waterbury	CT		1971	Unct
Enterprise	Dover	DE	w	1914-1917	Ba,Ay1916
Hornet	Dover	DE	ir	1944-1960	Ay1960
People's Beacon	Dover	DE	ir	1945	Oclc
State College Lantern	Dover	DE	bm	1920-1954	Ay1945,1954,NH42,46,NY46,Dc41,44
Delaware Observer	New Castle	DE	m	1968	Oclc
Advance	Wilmington	DE	w	1899-1901	Ba,Br,Oclc
Advocate	Wilmington	DE	w	1920-1925	Ba,Ay1925,NY22,26,Yenser3
Afro-American Citizen	Wilmington	DE	w	1895-1909	Ba,Ay1905,1909
Arrow	Wilmington	DE	m	1958-1959	Oclc
Defender	Wilmington	DE	w	1965-1992+	Ay1975,Ga90,92,Pr,Oclc[1965-?],EP67,80, SPD70,74,79[1962]
Delaware Advocate	Wilmington	DE	w	1908-1912	Ba,Ay1909,1911,1912,NY12
Delaware Conference Standard	Wilmington	DE		1886-1888	Ba
Delaware Defender	Wilmington	DE	w	1962-1965	Oclc,EBA,BRG[1992],EH[1972],EP71,76, SPD67
Delaware Reporter	Wilmington	DE	w	1940	Oclc
Delaware Spectator	Wilmington	DE	w	1972-1976	Oclc
Delaware Star	Wilmington	DE	m	1976-1978	Oclc
Delaware Twilight	Wilmington	DE	w	1886-1896	Ba,Ay1891,1894,1896,Br
Delaware Valley Defender	Wilmington	DE	w	1967-1992+	Oclc,Ga90[Defender],91
Delaware Valley Star	Wilmington	DE	w,bw	1978-1984	Oclc,EP80,81,NA83
Front Page	Wilmington	DE	w	1944-1946	Ba,Oclc
Herald Times	Wilmington	DE	w	1941-1942	Ba,Oclc
New Era	Wilmington	DE		1899-1900	Ba,Br
Our National Progress	Wilmington	DE		1870-1875	Ba,Penn
People's Pulse	Wilmington	DE	m	1968-1970	Oclc
People's Witness	Wilmington	DE	w	1886-1888	Ba,R1888
Spectator	Wilmington	DE	w	1975-1976	EP75,76
Wilmington Beacon	Wilmington	DE	w	1979-1992+	Ga92,Lb (see also CA)
Wilmington Journal	Wilmington	DE	w	1949	NH49 (see also CA or NC)
Alley Mission Herald	Washington	DC		1890-1892	Mather [Waldron, John Milton]
American	Washington	DC	w	1884-1886	Ay1884,1886

TITLE	CITY	ST.	FREQ.	DATES	SOURCES
American	Washington	DC		1918-1926	Ba
American Visions	Washington	DC	6xy	1986-1994+	Ga88,90,91,94
Argus	Washington	DC	w	1879-1884	Ba,Penn,Cam,DANB,Mather,Boris1
Bee	Washington	DC	w	1882-1884	Ay1884,Sch,Lc91
Bee and Leader	Washington	DC		1886-1892	Ba
Black Box	Washington	DC		1972	WI
Black News Digest	Washington	DC	w	1970-1994+	Ga91,94,Oclc
Building Blocks	Washington	DC		1988	Ga88
Bulletin	Washington	DC		1887-1889	Ba
Bulletin of Medico Chirurigal Society	Washington	DC		1941-1950	Fleming [Cobb, William Montague]
Capital Times	Washington	DC	w	1948-1953	Ay1950,1953,Fleming
Central Methodist	Washington	DC		1887-1892	Ba
Christian Sun	Washington	DC		1896-1900	Ba,Yenser4
Colored American	Washington	DC	w	1893-1904	Ba,R1898,1900,Gr,NWU,Go,Cam,Br,WI, Mather
Columbia Sentinel	Washington	DC	w	1896-1897	Ba,Oclc
Columbian	Washington	DC	m	1973-1976	EP75,76,Bp
Commercial College Outlook	Washington	DC		1919-1922	NY19,22
Commoner	Washington	DC		1875-1879	Ba,Br,DANB657
Conference Journal	Washington	DC	w	1886-1888	Ba,Penn
Daily Sun	Washington	DC	d	1968-1969	Rw
Dawn Magazine	Washington	DC	m	1973-1987	SPD87
Exodus	Washington	DC		1880-1902	Ba
Financial Independence Money Management	Washington	DC	bm	1987	Ga87
Flash	Washington	DC	sm	1937-1944	Ay1940,1944,EP38-40,BJ[e1939]
Focus	Washington	DC		1972-1979	WI
For the People	Washington	DC		1975-1979	WI
Freedmen's Headlight	Washington	DC		1902-1904	Ba
Freeing the Spirit	Washington	DC	q	1971-1983	Ay1983,WI
Freelance	Washington	DC		1883-1884	Ba,Cam
Globe	Washington	DC		1893-1897	Ba
Golden Page	Washington	DC	bm	1976-1987	WI,SPD87
Grass Roots News	Washington	DC	w	1971-1978	WI,EP75-78,Unct
Grit	Washington	DC	w	1883-1884	Ba,Penn,Cam,Lc91,Mather,DANB
Happy News	Washington	DC	m	1938	DANB433
Hilltop	Washington	DC	w	1924-1977	Oclc,NH42,NY46,DC41,Bp,Boris1
Horizon: A Journal of the Color Line	Washington	DC	q	1907-1910	BJ
Howard University Journal	Washington	DC	w	1913-1922	NY19,22,Boris1
Howard University Record	Washington	DC	q	1912-1924	NY19,22,Boris1
Idea	Washington	DC		1969	WI
Impact	Washington	DC	v/q	1971-1987	Sch,WI,SPD87
Industrial Enterprise	Washington	DC		1905-1907	Ba
Journal of Afro-American Issues	Washington	DC	q	1972-1977	BJ

TITLE	CITY	ST.	FREQ.	DATES	SOURCES
Journal of Negro Education	Washington	DC	q	1932-1994+	Ay1940,1983,Ga87,94,EH,EP48,51,BJ, SPD67,70,74,79
Journal of Negro History	Washington	DC	q	1916-1979	Ay1921,1975,EP46,51,BJ,SPD79,Yenser4 (see Atlanta)
Leader	Washington	DC	w	1889-1902	Ba,Cam,Lc91,WI
Liberia	Washington	DC		1892-1909	WI
Lincoln Review	Washington	DC	q	1979-1994+	Ga88,90,91,94
Metro Chronicle	Washington	DC		1990-1994+	Ga90,94,Baid90
Missionary Seer	Washington	DC	m	1920-1944	Yenser6 [Medford, Hampton Thomas]
Morgue	Washington	DC		1925	Boris2 [Petioni, Charles Augustin]
National Afro-American	Washington	DC		1890-1891	Ba
National Christian Congress Record	Washington	DC	w	1909-1912	Ba,Ay1912
National Chronicle	Washington	DC		1992+	BRG
National Crusader	Washington	DC	w	1970-1973	EBA,EP71,Bp,Lb
National Era	Washington	DC	w/d	1847-1860	Lc91,NWU,Br
National Forum	Washington	DC		1910-1911	Ba,Cam
National Industrial Enterprise	Washington	DC		1906-1910	Ba
National Leader	Washington	DC	w	1888-1902	Ba,Cam,Penn,Lc91,WI
National Negro Health News	Washington	DC	q	1944-1950	EP48,50,Dc44
National Notes	Washington	DC	m	1966-1974	SPD67,70,74
National Savings Bank	Washington	DC		1868	Lc91,NWU
National Union	Washington	DC	w	1907-1916	Ba,Ay1912,1915,NY12,Mather
Negro History Bulletin	Washington	DC	q/m	1937-1994+	Ay1945,1975,Ga90,94,WI,EP46,48,51,EH, BJ,SPD67,87,94,Fleming
Negro Music Journal	Washington	DC	m	1902-1903	BJ
Negro Sporting Life	Washington	DC		1944-1946	Ba
Negro Sporting News	Washington	DC	bw	1944-1946	Ba,NY46
New Citizen	Washington	DC		1870s	Rw
New Directions	Washington	DC	q	1973-1994+	SPD87,94
New Era	Washington	DC	w	1870-1870	Ba,Lc91,Sch,Rw
New National Era	Washington	DC	w	1869-1873	Ba,Br,Lc91,Sch,WI,Rw,DANB184 [1870-1874]
New National Era and Citizen	Washington	DC	w	1873-1875	Ba,Lc91,Sch
New Observer	Washington	DC	w	1957-1994+	Ga87,94,Lc91,EP73,93,EH,Baid90,Na83, API94
News Dimensions	Washington	DC	w	1992-1993+	EP93
Nite Life	Washington	DC	w	1939-1951	Ba,EP39,40,51,NY46
Observer	Washington	DC	w	1958-1975	Pr,EP67,75,Bp,SPD87[b1959]
Odd Fellows Journal	Washington	DC		1910-1937	Ba,NY12,19,22,26,32,DANB454,559, Mather
Oracle	Washington	DC	q	1940-1945	Ay1940,1945,Dc44
People's Advocate	Washington	DC	w	1876-1890	Ba,Ay1880,1890,Lc91,WI[e1884?],Penn, Go,Br,Cam,Mather,Boris1,DANB141,236
Pilot	Washington	DC	w	1890-1895	Ba,Ay1891,1892,Boris2
Plaindealer	Washington	DC		1879-1881	Ba,Rw

TITLE	CITY	ST.	FREQ.	DATES	SOURCES
Pulse	Washington	DC	m	1942-1953	Ay1950,1953,EP45,49,BJ[1943-1945]
Pyramid	Washington	DC	q	1942-1960	Ay1960
Quarterly Review	Washington	DC	q	1912	NY12
Record	Washington	DC	w	1899-1912	Ba,Ay1905,NY12,Lt1907
Remark	Washington	DC		1895-1897	Ba
Sentinel	Washington	DC	w	1922-1944	Ba,Ay1935,1940,EP35,NY22,26,32,Br, Yenser6
Sentry	Washington	DC	sm	1942-1946	Ba,NH46,NY46,Dc44
SISTERS	Washington	DC	q	1988-1994+	Ga90,91,92,94
Struggle; Voice of the Black Student Worker	Washington	DC		1971	WI
Stylus Magazine	Washington	DC	ir	1916-1941	BJ
Sunday Item	Washington	DC	w	1880-1883	Ba,Ay1882,Br,Penn,DANB76,Mather
Sunday School News Review	Washington	DC	q	1909-1911	Mather [Pair, James David]
Theatrical Newspicture Magazine	Washington	DC		1946-1948	Fleming [Sewall, Joseph Benson]
Third World	Washington	DC	bw	1969-1976	EP75,76,Bp
Times News	Washington	DC		pre 1972	Lb
Varsity	Washington	DC	sm	1940-1942	NH42,Dc41
Washington Afro American	Washington	DC	2xw	1932-1994+	Ba,Ay1940,1950,Ga87,94,Baid90,Lc91, Oclc,EP38,91,NH42,44,46,49,NY46,Dc41, 44,WPN94,API94
Washington Afro American and Tribune	Washington	DC	2xw	1932-1993	Ga90,91,Lc91,Oclc,WI,EP75,93
Washington American	Washington	DC		1909-1915	Ba,Br,Cam,Lc91,NY12
Washington Bee	Washington	DC	w	1884-1922	Ba,Ay1886,1921,R1898,WI,NY19,22,Br, Go,Lb,Boris2,Bl
Washington Capital Spotlight	Washington	DC	w	1953-1994+	Ga88,94,Bp,Lb,Baid90,BRG,EBA,EP67,93
Washington Daily American	Washington	DC	d	1920-1926	NY26,Yenser3
Washington Daily Citizen	Washington	DC	d	1922	Yenser3 [Petioni, Charles Augustin]
Washington Eagle	Washington	DC	m/w	1912-1961	Ba,Ay1921,1961,EP38,40,NH42,46,NY19, 22,26,32,46,Dc41,44,Go,Yenser3,4
Washington Gaily News	Washington	DC	w	1925-1963	Ba,Ay1963,Sch[b1931?],NH46,EP51, NY46,Dc44
Washington Government	Washington	DC		1883-1884	Cam
Washington Informer	Washington	DC	w	1964-1994+	Ga88,94,Lb,Lc91,EP67,93,WPN94
Washington North Star	Washington	DC	w	1981	Lc91
Washington Sun	Washington	DC	w	1967-1993+	EP90-93
Washington Sun	Washington	DC	w	1914-1915	Ba,Gr,Lc91,Cam,Mather,Boris2
Washington Tribune	Washington	DC	w	1920-1972	Ba,Ay1935,1945,Lc91,Sch,Br,EP38,46, NH42,44,46,EH,NY22,26,46,Dc41,44, Fleming,DANB487
Washington View	Washington	DC	6xy	1989-1994+	Ga91,92,94
Women United	Washington	DC	q	1950-1951	EP50,51
Worker	Washington	DC		1915-1993	NY19,22,Br[Work pre 1946],ABSCHSL, Mather
World	Washington	DC	w	1928-1932	Ba,NY32

TITLE	CITY	ST.	FREQ.	DATES	SOURCES
YSB	Washington	DC	10xy	1993+	Ga94
Zion Methodist	Washington	DC		1924-1928	Yenser4 [Medford, Hampton Thomas]
Kukusu Vitabu	Washington	DC	q	1971-1979	SPD79
Voice of Florida Freedmen	Apalachicola	FL	w	1910-1912	Ba,Ay1911,1912
Arcadia Courier	Arcadia	FL	w	1944	NH44
South Florida Baptist	Arcadia	FL		1900-1903	Ba
Lakeside Shield	Belle Glade	FL	w	1978-1981	Ay1980,1981
Broward Times	Coconut Creek	FL	w	1991+	EP91
Daytona Industrial Advocate	Daytona	FL		1922	NY22
Bulletin Advertiser	Daytona Beach	FL		pre 1979	Lb
Daytona Times	Daytona Beach	FL	w	1978-1994+	Ay1981,Ga87,94,Lb,API90,94,Baid90,92, EP79,93,BRG,WPN94,SPD87
Informer	Daytona Beach	FL		1944-1947	Ba
Voice of the Wildcats	Daytona Beach	FL	q	1974-1994+	Ay1981,Ga87,94,Baid90,92,SPD94
Industrial Herald	De Land	FL	w	1904-1907	Ba,Ay1906
Gold Star News	Deerfield Beach	FL	w	1982	EP82
Summit News	Eaton	FL	w	1960-1976	EP74-76
Cooperator	Eatonville	FL	m	1912-1922	NY12,19,22
Herald	Eatonville	FL	w	1889-1891	Ba,Ay1890,1891
Speaker	Eatonville	FL		1889-1890	Ba
Weekly Observer	Fern Park	FL	w	1972-1976	EP74-76
Watchman	Fernandina	FL		1902-1905	Ba
Fessenden Academy Herald	Fessenden	FL		1919-1922	NY19,22
Florida Spur	Fort Lauderdale	FL	w	1949-1966	Pr,NH49,Lb,SPD67
Gazette	Fort Lauderdale	FL	w	1980-1983	EP80,81,NA83
Spur	Fort Lauderdale	FL	w	1962-1971	EP62,71
Tricity News	Fort Lauderdale	FL	w	1969-1973	EBA,EP71,Bp,Lb
Westside Gazette	Fort Lauderdale	FL	w/sw	1971-1994+	Ga87,94,API90,94,Baid90,92,EP73,93, BRG,EH,WPN94,SPD87,94
Community Voice	Fort Myers	FL	w	1988-1994+	EP91,92,93,BRG,API94
Ebony Star	Fort Myers	FL	w	1971-1974	EP74,Lb
Fort Myers Star News	Fort Myers	FL	w	1971-1976	EH,EP72,73,75,76,Bp
Florida Courier	Fort Pierce	FL	w	1994	API94
Fort Pierce Chronicle	Fort Pierce	FL	w	1957-1994+	Ga90,94,Oclc,EP64,92,BRG,EBA,EH, Baid92,WPN94,SPD67,70,74
Burning Spear	Gainesville	FL	m	1968-1976	Ay1976
Eagle Herald	Gainesville	FL		1900-1902	Ba
Florida Sentinel	Gainesville	FL	w	1887-1895	Ba,Ay1889,1894,Penn,Eur94,Mather [1886-1894]
Messenger	Gainesville	FL		1903-1905	Ba
New Light	Gainesville	FL	w	1903-1906	Ba,Ay1905,1906
Seven Star Defender	Gainesville	FL	w	1903-1906	Ba,Ay1906
Watchman	Gainesville	FL	w	1909-1911	Ba,Ay1911
Havanna Herald	Havanna	FL	w	1992-1994+	BRG,Ga94[b1947 nlb]

TITLE	CITY	ST.	FREQ.	DATES	SOURCES
Weid: the Sensibility Review	Homestead	FL	q	1965-1974	SPD74
Advocate	Jacksonville	FL	w	1891-1938	Ba,Ay1896,Br
Advocate	Jacksonville	FL	w	1966-1994+	Pr,EP67,80,BRG,API94,Lb
American	Jacksonville	FL	d	1895-1896	Ba,Ay1896,DANB354
Bulletin	Jacksonville	FL		1936-1938	Ba
Chronicle	Jacksonville	FL		1988-1993+	EP91,92,93
Courier	Jacksonville	FL	w	1894	Eur94
Courier	Jacksonville	FL	m	1919-1922	NY19,22
Daily Promotor	Jacksonville	FL	w	1912	Mather[Ballou, John Henry]
Defender	Jacksonville	FL	w	1893-1894	Ba,Ay1894,Mather
Florida Alliance	Jacksonville	FL	w	1906-1914	Ba,Ay1908,1909,1911-1913[b1887]
Florida Baptist	Jacksonville	FL	w	1908-1912	Ba,Ay1909,NY12,Boris2
Florida Baptist Weekly	Jacksonville	FL	w	1887-1888	Ba,Ay1888
Florida Daily Times-Union	Jacksonville	FL		1905-1915	Mather [Jenkins, Isaac William]
Florida Evangelist	Jacksonville	FL	w	1896-1903	Ba,Oclc,WI,ABSCHSL,Cam,Mather
Florida Labor Templar	Jacksonville	FL	w	1901-1922	Ba,Ay1908,1909,1911-1914
Florida Press	Jacksonville	FL	w	1944	EP44
Florida Search Light	Jacksonville	FL		1900-1902	Ba
Florida Sentinel	Jacksonville	FL	w	1913-1938	Ay1914,1938,Lc91,NY22,26,32,Cam,Go,Yenser4,Mather[1912]
Florida Standard	Jacksonville	FL	w	1904-1912	Ba,Ay1908,1911,NY12,Lt1907,Mather
Florida Star	Jacksonville	FL	w	1950-1994+	Ay1969,1975,Ga92,API90,94,Bp,Pr,EP62-65
Florida Star News	Jacksonville	FL	w	1966-1994+	EP67,75[1951],80,WPN94[b1968],SPD67,70,74,87
Florida Star Times	Jacksonville	FL	w	1991-1994+	GA91,94,Baid92
Florida Tattler	Jacksonville	FL	w	1934-1966	Ba,Ay1950,1966,EP38,51,Br,NH42,44,46,49,NY46,Dc41,44,SPD67,Fleming
Florida Tribune	Jacksonville	FL		1933-1935	Ba
Florida Workman	Jacksonville	FL	w	1883-1884	Ay1884
Fraternal Ledger	Jacksonville	FL	w	1905-1906	Ba,Ay1905,1906
Free Press	Jacksonville	FL	w	1986-1994+	Oclc,BRG,EP92[1987],93,API94
Jacksonville Advocate Free Press	Jacksonville	FL	w	1978-1991	Oclc,EP91
Labor Templar	Jacksonville	FL	w	1901-1926	Ba,Go,NY19,22,26,Lt1907
Masonic Forum	Jacksonville	FL	w	1903-1919	Ba,Ay1905,1912,NY12,19
Messenger	Jacksonville	FL		1919-1923	Ba
Negro Educational Review	Jacksonville	FL	q	1950-1994+	Ay1960,Ga90,91,Oclc,BJ,SPD87,94
North Florida Star News	Jacksonville	FL	w	1951-1993+	EP91,92,93
Northeast Florida Advocate	Jacksonville	FL	w	1994+	API94
People's Journal	Jacksonville	FL	w	1883-1894	Ba,Ay1884,1886-1888,1891,Eur94
Progressive News	Jacksonville	FL	w	1939-1953	Ba,Ay1950,1953,EP42,51,NH44,49
Royal Lion's Tongue	Jacksonville	FL	w	1909-1914	Ba,Ay1911-1914
Southern Courier	Jacksonville	FL	w	1891-1894	Ba,Ay1894
Southern Leader	Jacksonville	FL	w	1881-1888	Ba,Ay1887,1888

TITLE	CITY	ST.	FREQ.	DATES	SOURCES
Southern Review	Jacksonville	FL	w	1890-1891	Ba,Ay1890
Standard	Jacksonville	FL	w	1915-1923	Ba,Ay1921,Mather
Standard Sentinel	Jacksonville	FL		1918-1919	Ba,NY19
Sunday School Lesson	Jacksonville	FL	w	1900-1922	Ba,Ay1905,1918,NY19,22,Lt1907,Mather
Telegram	Jacksonville	FL		1947	Ba
Together	Jacksonville	FL		1967-1968	ABSCHSL
Togetherness	Jacksonville	FL		1968-1973	ABSCHSL
Watchman	Jacksonville	FL	w	1902-1906	Ba,Ay1906
World	Jacksonville	FL		1932-1940	Ba
Sunday Morning Band Journal	Lake City	FL	w	1903-1922	Ba,Ay1905,1912,NY12,19,22
Weekly Bulletin	Lakeland	FL	w	1970-1973	EBA,EP71,Bp,Lb
Leesburg Herald	Leesburg	FL		1936	Fleming [Wilson, L. Alex]
Outlook	Leesburg	FL	w	1908-1915	Ba,Ay1911,Mather
Star of Bethlehem	Leesburg	FL	w	1910-1911	Ba,Ay1911
Florida Baptist	Live Oak	FL		1909-1910	Ba
Florida Memorial College Herald	Live Oak	FL	m	1922	NY22
Florida Tribune	Marianna	FL	w	1896-1912	Ba,Ay1905,1909,NY12,Lt1907 [Tribune]
Western Florida Bugle	Marianna	FL	w	1913-1927	Ba,Ay1906,1909,NY12,19,22,26,Go,Boris1
Black Miami Weekly	Miami	FL	w	1990-1992+	Ga90,91,Baid90,92
Bronze Confessions	Miami	FL	m	1945-1953	Ay1950,1953
Call	Miami	FL	w	1942-1953	Ay1950,1953
Courier	Miami	FL	w	1953-1969	Ay1953,1969,1970[Pittsburgh]
Florida Courier	Miami	FL	w	1971-1980	Ay1971,EP72-80,Bp,Lb[Florida Courier News]
Florida East Coast News	Miami	FL	w	1904-1911	Ba,Ay1906,1911
Florida Flash	Miami	FL	w	1966-1970	SPD67,70
Florida Sentinel Bulletin	Miami	FL	2xw	1945-1964	Ay1964
Florida Star	Miami	FL	w	1965	EP65
Florida Star News	Miami	FL	w	1967-1970	EP67,69,70
Florida Times	Miami	FL	w	1945-1951	EP45,46,48-51
Industrial Reporter	Miami	FL	w	1902-1905	Ba,Ay1905
Liberty News	Miami	FL	w	1961-1980	WI,EP74-80,Lb,Lc83
Miami Leader	Miami	FL	w	1940-1944	NH42,44,Dc41
Miami Star	Miami	FL	w	1974	EP74
Miami Times	Miami	FL	w	1923-1994+	Ba,Ay1945,1970,Ga87,94,Br,Lc91,WI,NH42,44,46,EP35,93,NY32,46,Dc41,44,API94,WPN94,SPD67,70,74,79,87,94,Fleming
Negro Educational Review	Miami	FL	q	1974-1979	SPD74,79
Progressive News	Miami	FL	w	1945-1946	EP45,46
South Florida Weekly	Miami	FL	w	1983-1990	EP90
Tribune	Miami	FL		1945	Ba
Tropical Dispatch	Miami	FL	w	1929-1970	Ba,Ay1950,NH42,44,46,49,EP48,51 [Tampa],NY46,Dc41,44

TITLE	CITY	ST.	FREQ.	DATES	SOURCES
Whip	Miami	FL	w	1943-1949	Ba,Br,NH44,46,EP44,49,NY46,Dc44
Colored Signal	Milton	FL	w	1925-1926	NY26,Boris1
Times-Herald	New Smyrna Beach	FL		1994+	API94
Beacon Light	Ocala	FL	w	1930-1932	Ba,NY32
Florida Advertiser	Ocala	FL	w	1903-1909	Ba,Ay1905,1906,1908,Lt1907
Florida Ledger	Ocala	FL	w	1887-1892	Ba,Ay1889-1891
Florida News Carrier	Ocala	FL	w	1903-1906	Ba,Ay1905,1906
Forum	Ocala	FL	w	1896-1912	Ba,Ay1911,1912
Hustler	Ocala	FL	sm	1905-1906	Ba,Ay1906
Ocala News	Ocala	FL		1912	NY12
Florida Christian Recorder	Orlando	FL	w	1897-1922	Ba,Ay1906,1912,NY12,19,22,Lt1907
Florida Sun	Orlando	FL	w	1940-1943	EP40,41,43
Florida Sun Mirror	Orlando	FL	w	1932-1987	Ba,EP72-80,NH42,44,Dc41,Lb,SPD67,79,87
Florida Sun Review	Orlando	FL	w	1931-1994+	Ga87,94,Baid90,BRG,EH[1932],WPN94[b1933]
Orlando Times	Orlando	FL	w	1945-1994+	Ba,Ga90,94,Lb,Baid90,EP79,92[b1975],93,SPD87,94
Sun	Orlando	FL	w	1936-1939	Ba,EP36-39
Sun Mirror	Orlando	FL	w	1932-1973	EBA,EH,EP71,Bp
Sun Review	Orlando	FL	w	1932-1994+	EP80,BRG,EP78[1932],81,SPD94
Advocate	Palatka	FL	w	1912-1927	Ba,Ay1917,1925[b1915],Go,Br,NY19,22,26,Boris2
Afro-American	Palatka	FL		1915-1927	Ba,Ay1921,Br,Go
Florida Enterprise & Advertiser	Palatka	FL	w	1902-1906	Ba,Ay1905,1906
Gem City Bulletin	Palatka	FL		1913-1922	Ba
Florida News Herald	Palm Beach	FL		1902-1903	Ba
Record	Palm Beach	FL	w	1940	EP40
World	Panama City	FL		1936-1938	Ba,EP37,38
Brotherhood	Pensacola	FL	w	1905-1915	Ba,Ay1906,1912,NY12
Church School Herald	Pensacola	FL		1928-1937	Yenser4 [Brown, Aaron]
Colored Citizen	Pensacola	FL	w	1912-1958	Ba,Ay1920,1958,NH42,44,46,49,EP35,46,NY19,22,26,32,46,Dc41,44,Go,Boris1
Courier	Pensacola	FL	w	1935-1971	Ba,Ay1950,1971,NH44,49,EP39,51
Exponent	Pensacola	FL	w	1899-1905	Ba,Ay1905
Exposure	Pensacola	FL	w	1972-1973	EH,EP73
Florida Sentinel	Pensacola	FL	w	1895-1913	Ba,Ay1905,1912,Lc91,Oclc,WI[e1912],NY12,Lt1907,Mather
Junion Press	Pensacola	FL		1945-1946	Ba,EP45,46
New American Press	Pensacola	FL	w	1979-1994+	EP91-93,BRG,API94
Pensacola Citizen	Pensacola	FL	w	1959-1973	Ay1958,1959,1965,Bp
Pensacola News Weekly	Pensacola	FL	sm	1986-1990	EP90
Pensacola Times	Pensacola	FL	w	1968-1976	EP71-73,75,76,EBA,Lb,Bp
Pensacola Voice	Pensacola	FL	w	1966-1994+	Ga90,94,EP80,93[b1970],BRG,API94,Baid90,SPD94

TITLE	CITY	ST.	FREQ.	DATES	SOURCES
Negro Weekly	Pinellas	FL		1945	Ba
Broward Times	Pompano Beach	FL	w	1990-1994+	EP92,93,WPN94,API94
Germ of Truth	Ponce de Leon	FL	w	1910-1914	Ba,Ay1911,1912,1913
Golden Rule	Quincy	FL	w	1906-1909	Ba,Ay1909,Lt1907
News	Quincy	FL		1901-1903	Ba
Gold Coast Star News	Riviera Beach	FL	w	1971-1980	EP80,79,Lb
Palm Beach Gazette	Riviera Beach	FL	w	1992+	BRG
Post	Saint Augustine	FL	w	1935-1940	EP35-40
Burning Spear	Saint Petersburg	FL		1970-1974	Unct
Public Informer	Saint Petersburg	FL	w	1928-1940	Ba,Ay1935,1939[1928],EP35-40
Weekly Challenger	Saint Petersburg	FL	w	1965-1994+	Ga88,94,Bp,Baid90,EP69,92[b1967],93, SPD87,94
Weekly Chronicle	Saint Petersburg	FL	w	1973-1977	EP74-77
World	Saint Petersburg	FL	w	1936-1944	Ba,NH42,44,EP36,43,44,DC41
Searchlight	San Mateo	FL		1901-1905	Ba
Weekly Bulletin	Sarasota	FL	w	1959-1994+	Ba,Ga90,94,Lb,Pr,Rw,EP67,92,BRG,EH, WPN94,SPD67,74
Capital City Post	Tallahassee	FL	w	1940-1944	Ba,NH42,EP43,Dc41
Capital Outlook	Tallahassee	FL	bw	1964-1994+	Ga90,94,Baid90,92,EP77,93,BRG,NA83, WPN94[b1975],API94
College Arms	Tallahassee	FL	m	1912-1922	NY12,19,22
Famuan	Tallahassee	FL	w	1919-1994+	Ga90,94,Bp,Baid92,NY46[Famcean]
Front Peoples` Revolutionary News Service	Tallahassee	FL		1971	Unct
Metropolitan	Tallahassee	FL	w	1905-1912	Ba,Ay1906,1912,Go[e1922],Br[b1915], NY12,19
News and Free Press	Tallahassee	FL	w	1975-1976	EP75,76
Primitive Herald	Tallahassee	FL		1892-1893	Ba
Record-Dispatch	Tallahassee	FL	w	1945-1949	Ba,EP48,49
Bulletin	Tampa	FL	w	1914-1958	Ba,Ay1917,1958,Go,Br,NH42,44,46,49, EP35,51,NY19,22,26,32,46,Dc41,44, Brooks,Boris2
Courier	Tampa	FL	w	1951	EP51
Dollar Stretcher	Tampa	FL		1990-1992+	Baid90,BRG,API94[Florida Dollar Stretcher]
East Coast Watchman	Tampa	FL	w	1892-1906	Ba,Ay1906
Florida Intelligencer	Tampa	FL	w	1901-1910	Ba,Ay1905,1909,Lt1907,Mather
Florida Reporter	Tampa	FL	w	1911-1916	Ba,Ay1911-1916
Florida Sentinel	Tampa	FL	w	1945-1958	Ba,Ay1958,NH49,EP48-51
Florida Sentinel Bulletin	Tampa	FL	w/sw	1959-1994+	Ay1969,1980,Ga87,94,API90,94,EP62,93, WPN94,SPD67,79,87
News Reporter	Tampa	FL	w	1966-1992+	Ay1970,1981,Ga91,92,Pr,Lb,Bp,EP75,80, SPD67,79,87
People's News	Tampa	FL	w	1939	EP39
Tampa Sentinel Bulletin	Tampa	FL	w	1945-1992+	EP62,92,NA83
This Is It	Tampa	FL		1945-1947	Ba

TITLE	CITY	ST.	FREQ.	DATES	SOURCES
World	Tampa	FL	w	1932-1936	Ba,Ay1935,EP35,36
Florida Advertiser	Titusville	FL		1936-1938	Ba
Signs of the Times	Wellborn	FL	sm	1901-1905	Ba,Ay1905
Advocate	West Palm Beach	FL		1923-1926	Ba,NY26
Florida News	West Palm Beach	FL	w	1936-1940	Ba,EP36-40
Florida Photo News and Image	West Palm Beach	FL	w	1955-1994+	EP69,93,WPN94 (see Photo News)
Palm Beach Gazette	West Palm Beach	FL	w	1989-1994+	WPN94
Photo News	West Palm Beach	FL	w	1955-1994+	Ay1956,1977,EP63,80,SPD67,70,74,79,87, 94,BRG,API94,EH,EBA,Lb
Tribune	West Palm Beach	FL		1936-1938	Ba
Southern Republican	White Springs	FL	w	1891-1891	Ay1891
Advocate	Winter Park	FL	w	1889-1907	Ba,Ay1894,1896,Lt1907,Eur94
Albany Macon Times	Albany	GA	w	1960-1992+	Baid90,Lb,EP80,90
Albany Times	Albany	GA	w	1960-1988	Ay1981,Ga87,88,Oclc,EP71[1964],79,Lb, SPD67
Enterprise	Albany	GA	w	1937-1954	Ba,Ay1950,1954,NH42,46,49,EP38,51, NY46,Dc41,44
Southwest Georgian	Albany	GA	w	1938-1993+	Ba,Pr,NH44,EP39,93,EH,EBA,BRG,Lb, Bp,SPD67,87
Supreme Circle News	Albany	GA	w	1908-1932	Ba,Go,NY22,26,32,Boris1
Supreme Circle News and Vox Populi	Albany	GA	w	1912-1930	Ay1912[b1903]
Vox Populi	Albany	GA	w	1903-1911	Ba,Ay1905,1911,Lt1907
Chronicle	Americus	GA	w	1907-1922	Ba,Ay1911-1917,NY12,19,22,Go
Chronometer	Americus	GA		1898-1900	Ba,Br
Georgia Investigator	Americus	GA		1899-1902	Ba,Br
People's Messenger	Americus	GA		1894-1896	Ba
Tribune	Americus	GA	w	1891-1894	Ba,Ay1894
Athens Blade	Athens	GA	w	1879-1880	Ba,Br,Cam,Oclc,DANB497
Athens Clipper	Athens	GA	w	1886-1922	Ba,Ay1891,1896,Go,Br,Oclc,Eur94,NY12, 19
Athens Voice	Athens	GA	w	1975	Oclc
Knox Herald	Athens	GA	m	1919-1922	NY19,22
Progressive Era	Athens	GA	sm	1899-1920	Ba,Ay1908,1920,NY12
Republic	Athens	GA		1920-1922	Ba,NY22
Advancement Newsletter	Atlanta	GA		1977-1979	WI
Afra-American Notes for You	Atlanta	GA		1967	WI
African American Family History Assn. Newsletter	Atlanta	GA	q	1987	SPD87
Alumni Update	Atlanta	GA		1980-1989	ABSCHSL
American Citizen	Atlanta	GA	w	1907-1915	Ba,NY12,Bl
Appeal	Atlanta	GA		1899-1901	Ba
Appeal and Southern Age	Atlanta	GA		1896-1899	Ba[1890],Bl
Atheneum	Atlanta	GA	m	1912-1922	NY12,19,22,Lt1907
Atlanta Age	Atlanta	GA	w	1898-1908	Ba,Ay1905,1908,Oclc,Br,WI,Lc83, DANB497,Boris2,Bl

TITLE	CITY	ST.	FREQ.	DATES	SOURCES
Atlanta Constitution	Atlanta	GA		pre 1950	DANB,Fleming
Atlanta Daily World	Atlanta	GA	d	1928-1994+	Ba,Ay1935,1975,Oclc,Gr,NH42,44,46,49, EP35,93,Baid92,EBA,EH,BRG,NY32,46, 52,Dc41,44,Lb,API90,94,Bl,Yenser4, SPD67,70,74
Atlanta Independent	Atlanta	GA	w	1903-1942	Ba,Ay1905-1920,Go,Br,Cam,Brooks,WI, NH42,Lc91,NY12,19,22,26,32,Dc41, Yenser6[1944],Bl
Atlanta Tribune	Atlanta	GA	w	1986-1994+	Ga90,91,92,94,API94,Baid90,92
Atlanta University Bulletin	Atlanta	GA	q	1912-1958	Ay1950,1958,EP51,NY12,19,22
Atlanta Voice	Atlanta	GA	w	1966-1994+	Ba,Ga90,94,EP90,93,API94,Bl
AUC Digest	Atlanta	GA	w	1973-1994+	Ga87,94
A.M.E. Church Review	Atlanta	GA	q	1884-1978	Ay1978,BJ32
Baptist Banner	Atlanta	GA	w	1890-1897	Ba,Ay1896,Bl
Baptist Review	Atlanta	GA	m	1887-1888	Ay1888
Benevolent Design	Atlanta	GA		1899-1903	Ba,Bl
Black and White Magazine	Atlanta	GA	m	1951	EP51
Black Employment and Education Magazine	Atlanta	GA		1993+	Ga94
Blade	Atlanta	GA	w	1879-1882	Ay1882
Campus Mirror	Atlanta	GA	m	1940-1944	NH42,Dc41,44
Church and School Phalanx	Atlanta	GA		1913-1915	Ba,Bl
Church and Society World	Atlanta	GA	m	1902-1903	Bl,Boris1
Clark Atlanta University Magazine	Atlanta	GA		1990-1992	ABSCHSL
Clark University Mentor	Atlanta	GA	m	1922-1940	NY22,EP39,40
Clark University Register	Atlanta	GA	m	1912-1919	NY12,19
College Language Association Journal	Atlanta	GA	q	1957-1982+	BJ
Colored Morticians Bulletin	Atlanta	GA	m	1944-1953	Ay1950,1953,Dc44
Congregationalist Worker	Atlanta	GA		pre 1920	DANB506
Courier	Atlanta	GA	w	1910-1971	Ay1966,1969-1971
Crimson and Gray	Atlanta	GA		pre 1950	DANB,Fleming
Crusader	Atlanta	GA	w/bw	1963-1967	Oclc,WI
Defiance	Atlanta	GA	w	1881-1890	Ba,Ay1882,1886-1889,Oclc,WI,Gr,Cam
Drum Major	Atlanta	GA	m	1971-1987	WI,SPD79,87
Echo	Atlanta	GA		1934-1937	Ba,Bl
Educator	Atlanta	GA		1896-1898	Ba,Bl
Elevator	Atlanta	GA	bw	1881-1889	Ay1888,1889
Evangel	Atlanta	GA		1974-1982	ABSCHSL
Face the Nation	Atlanta	GA		1972-1976	EH,EP73-76,Lb
First World: An International Journal of Black Thought	Atlanta	GA	bm	1977-1987	BJ,SPD87
Foundation	Atlanta	GA	q	1911-1972	Ay1950,1975,EH,EP51,NY12,19,22,Dc44
Georgia Baptist	Atlanta	GA	sm	1880-1953	ba,Ay1950,1953,NH42,46,NY32,46, Bl[1938],Dc41,44,Yenser6
Georgia Broadaxe	Atlanta	GA	w	1910-1914	Ba,Ay1913,1914,Bl,NY12

TITLE	CITY	ST.	FREQ.	DATES	SOURCES
Georgia Congregationist	Atlanta	GA		pre 1920	DANB506
Georgia Guide	Atlanta	GA		1947-1949	Ba,Bl
Georgia News Weekly	Atlanta	GA	w	1992+	BRG
Georgia Sentinel Bulletin	Atlanta	GA		1992-1994+	BRG,API94
Georgia Speaker	Atlanta	GA	w	1895-1897	Ba,Ay1896,Br,Bl
Gospel Trumpet	Atlanta	GA	m	1898	R1898
Herald of United Churches	Atlanta	GA		1887-1889	Ba,Bl
Informer	Atlanta	GA	w	1966-1974	SPD67,70,74
Inquirer	Atlanta	GA	w	1960-1994+	Ay1970,1980,Ga90,94,Baid92,BRG,Oclc, EBA,EH,EP62,93,SPD67,Rw,Bl
Journal of Negro History	Atlanta	GA	q	1916-1994+	Ay1986[1951 DC],Ga87,94,BJ[82 DC]
Justice	Atlanta	GA	w	1904-1908	Ba,Ay1906,1908,Bl
Maroon Tiger	Atlanta	GA	bm/m	1898-1973	Ay1945,1971,NH46,EP46,51,NY46,Dc44, Bp,Rw
Morehouse Alumnus	Atlanta	GA	q	1928-1973	Ay1973
Morehouse College Bulletin	Atlanta	GA	q	1912-1994+	SPD91,94
Mortician Journal	Atlanta	GA	m	1950-1951	EP50,51[See Colored Morticians Bulletin]
New South	Atlanta	GA	m/bm/q	1946-1973	WI,BJ
News	Atlanta	GA	w	1889-1935	Ba,Ay1890,Bl,DANB497
Opinion	Atlanta	GA	d	1895-1898	Ba,Bl
Panther	Atlanta	GA	m	1936-1994+	SPD91,94
People-Going Places-Doing Things	Atlanta	GA	w	1966-1978	EP75-78
People's Advocate	Atlanta	GA	w	1891-1896	Ba,Ay1894,1896,Br,JNH,Bl
People's Crusader	Atlanta	GA	w	1979-1994+	BRG,EP80,90,WPN94[b1971],Lb,SPD87, 94
Phalanx	Atlanta	GA	w	1917-1920	Ba,Ay1918-1920,Bl
Phlyon	Atlanta	GA	q	1940-1994+	EP50,51,BJ,Dc44,SPD94
Post	Atlanta	GA	w	1913-1931	Ba,Ay1915,1925,NY19,22,26,32,Go, SPD87,94,Bl,Boris1
Postal Alliance	Atlanta	GA	m	1914-1922	Ba,Ay1921S,Bl[1921-1922]
Quarterly Bulletin	Atlanta	GA	m	1912-1922	NY12,19,22
Reporter	Atlanta	GA	w	1895-1897	Ba,Ay1896,Br,Bl
Republican	Atlanta	GA	w	1879-1890	Ba,Ay1880,1882,Bl
Republican Leader	Atlanta	GA		1900-1903	Ba,Bl
Sage: A Scholarly Journal on Black Women	Atlanta	GA	2xy	1984-1993+	Ga94,SPD87,94
SCLC Newsletter	Atlanta	GA	m	1962-1970	SPD67,70
Scroll	Atlanta	GA	m	1907-1919	NY19,Lt1907
Scroll and African Methodist Review	Atlanta	GA	m	1912	NY12,Fleming
Sentinel	Atlanta	GA		1885-1887	Ba,Bl
Social Gleaner	Atlanta	GA		1896-1900	Ba,Bl
Soul Force	Atlanta	GA	m	1968-1994+	WI,SPD74,79,87,94
South Today	Atlanta	GA		1969-1973	WI,BJ[e1973]
Southern Age	Atlanta	GA		1891-1901	Ba,Go,Br,Bl,DANB429
Southern Appeal	Atlanta	GA	w	1889-1892	Ba,Ay1890,1891,Eur94,Bl,Penn

TITLE	CITY	ST.	FREQ.	DATES	SOURCES
Southern Changes	Atlanta	GA	bm	1978-1987	SPD87
Southern Christian Recorder	Atlanta	GA	w	1883-1905	Ba,Ay1905,Bl[b1886],R1900,DANB [b1889]
Southern Frontier	Atlanta	GA	m	1940-1954	WI,BJ
Southern Life	Atlanta	GA		1912	NY12
Southern Recorder	Atlanta	GA	w	1886-1888	Ba,Ay1887,1888,Penn
Southern Struggle	Atlanta	GA	m	1942-1978	EP78
Southern Voices	Atlanta	GA	bm	1974	BJ
Southern World	Atlanta	GA		1936	EP36
Spelman Messenger	Atlanta	GA	q/m	1885-1966	Ay1945,1966,NY12,19,22,Lt1907, ABSCHSL
Student Voice	Atlanta	GA		1960-1965	WI
Theological Institute	Atlanta	GA	m	1909-1912	Ba,Ay1911,1912,Blackwell,NY12
Times	Atlanta	GA	w	1890-1894	Ba,Ay1891,Oclc,Eur94,Bl[1893]
Tribune	Atlanta	GA		1899-1900	Ba,Bl
Truth	Atlanta	GA	sm/w	1897-1923	Ba,Ay1911,1912-1920,1921,NY19,22, Lt1907,Bl
United World	Atlanta	GA		1906-1909	Ba[1908],Bl
Upscale	Atlanta	GA	bm	1989-1994+	Ga90,94,Oclc
Voice of Missions	Atlanta	GA	m	1893-1900	Ba,R1898,1900,Cam,Lc91,Oclc,WI,Bl, NY12,DANB[b1892]
Voice of the Negro	Atlanta	GA	m	1904-1907	Ay1905,1906,Oclc,Cam,WI,ABSCHSL, BJ[e1906]Mather,Bl
Voice of the People	Atlanta	GA	sm	1901-1909	Ba,Ay1905,1908,1909,Cam,Bl
Woman's Missionary Recorder	Atlanta	GA		1908-1915	Mather [Turner, Laura Lemon]
Augusta Black Focus	Augusta	GA	w	1981-1994+	EP91,92,BRG[Focus],API94,WPN94
Augusta Mirror	Augusta	GA		pre 1979	Lb
Augusta News	Augusta	GA	w	1919-1922	Ba,Go,NY19,22
Augusta News Review	Augusta	GA	w	1966-1985	Ay1975,1978,Pr,Lb,Bp,Oclc[1971-1985?], EH,EP72-79
Augusta Union	Augusta	GA	w	1889-1904	Ba,Ay1896,Lc91,Br,Oclc,WI,NWU
Augusta Voice	Augusta	GA	w	1970-1976	Oclc,EH,EP73,75,76,Lb
Colored American	Augusta	GA	w	1865-1894	Ba,Gr,Penn,Lc91,Oclc,WI
Eastern Index	Augusta	GA		1930-1935	Ba
Echo	Augusta	GA	w	1914-1946	Ba,Ay1925,1937,NH42,44,46,EP38,46, NY46,Dc41,44
Free Lance	Augusta	GA		1902-1903	Ba
Free Press	Augusta	GA	w	1970-1972	EBA,EP71,Lb
Georgia Baptist	Augusta	GA	w	1880-1949	Ba,Ay1884,1920,R1898,1900,NY12,19,22, Penn,ABSCHSL,Eur94,BJ8,Boris1
Georgia Republican	Augusta	GA		1886-1890	Ba,Penn
Journal	Augusta	GA	w	1936	EP36
Loyal Georgian	Augusta	GA	w/d	1866-1868	Ba,Br,Penn,Lc91,Oclc,WI
Methodist Herald	Augusta	GA		1922	NY22
Methodist Union	Augusta	GA	w	1881-1895	Ba,Ay1891,1894,Eur94

TITLE	CITY	ST.	FREQ.	DATES	SOURCES
Metro County Courier	Augusta	GA	w	1983-1994+	Ga87,94,API90,94,Baid90,92,Oclc, EP90-93,BRG,WPN94
Minority Bus. Soc. and Cult. Dir.	Augusta	GA		1991-1994+	Ga91,94
Regulator	Augusta	GA		1920-1922	Ba,NY22
Sentinel	Augusta	GA	w	1884-1897	Ba,Ay1887,1896,Br,Eur94,Mather, DANB674
Weekly Loyal Georgian	Augusta	GA	w	1884-1887	WI
Weekly Review	Augusta	GA	w	1947-1969	Ay1955,1970,Oclc,Sch,SPD67,NH49, EP48,70,JNH
Advocate	Bainbridge	GA		1901-1904	Ba
Age	Barnesville	GA		1906	Mather [Cobb, Helen Maude Brown]
Globe	Barnesville	GA		1898-1901	Ba
Washington Park Era	Barnesville	GA		1914-1915	Mather [Cobb, Andrew Jackson]
Woman's Missionary Age	Barnesville	GA		1904	Mather [Cobb, Helen Maude Brown]
Messenger	Blakely	GA		1898-1900	Ba
Advocate	Brunswick	GA	w	1907-1926	Ba,Ay1909,1920,NY12,19,22,26,Go, Boris1
American Recorder	Brunswick	GA	w	pre 1928	Boris2 [Sampson, David Solomon]
Appeal	Brunswick	GA		1913-1915	Ba
Gleanor	Brunswick	GA	w	1894-1897	Ba,Ay1896
Herald	Brunswick	GA	w	1896-1909	Ba,Ay1905,1906,1908,1909
Sentinel	Brunswick	GA	w	1939-1940	EP39,40
Union	Brunswick	GA	w	1903-1909	Ba,Ay1905,1906,1908,1909,Lt1907
Worth	Brunswick	GA	m	1919-1922	NY19,22
Advocate	Buena Vista	GA	w	1904-1909	Ba,Ay1909[1908]
Headlight	Camilla	GA	w	1910-1914	Ba,Ay1911,1912,1913,1914
Watchman	Cedartown	GA		1895-1898	Ba
Pointer	Chauncey	GA		1901-1902	Ba
New Century	Clarkesville	GA		1901-1902	Ba
Metro News Weekly	College Park	GA	w	1990-1993+	EP91,92,93
Advocate	Columbus	GA	w	1893-1895	Ba,Ay1894
Advocate	Columbus	GA	w	1939-1941	EP39-41
Columbus Chronicle	Columbus	GA	w	1895-1900	Ba,Lc91,Oclc,WI,Gr
Columbus Messenger	Columbus	GA	w	1883-1890	Ba,Ay1888-1890,Go,Penn
Columbus Times	Columbus	GA	w	1958-1994+	Ay1980,Ga87,94,Oclc[b1970],EP72,93, Baid92[b1970],BRG,EH,Rw,WPN94, API94,SPD87
News	Columbus	GA	w	1966-1970	Ay1971,EP64,71,Pr,Lb,SPD67
Rap	Columbus	GA	ir	1970-1971	Lc83
Rifle	Columbus	GA	w	1890-1893	Ba,Ay1890,1891
Southeastern News	Columbus	GA	w	1966-1994+	EP90,92,93
Southern Christian Recorder	Columbus	GA	w	1883-1916	Ba,Ay1905,1916,NY12
Southern Guide	Columbus	GA	w	1916-1917	Ba,Ay1917
Times	Columbus	GA		1901-1932	Ba,NY26,32,Boris1
Watchman	Columbus	GA		1901-1903	Ba

TITLE	CITY	ST.	FREQ.	DATES	SOURCES
Weekly News	Columbus	GA	w	1930-1932	Ba,NY32
World	Columbus	GA	w	1932-1951	Ba,Ay1950,NH44,EP42,45,46,48,49,51, NY32,Bl
Elevator Exchange	Cordele	GA	w	1903-1906	Ba,Ay1905,1906
Lady	Cordele	GA	w	1908-1911	Ba,Ay1909
Southeastern News	Cordele	GA	w	1979-1994+	Ga91,94,Oclc,Baid92,BRG,EP77,91 [Southeast News b1966],WPN94[b1965]
Southern Planet	Cordele	GA		1903-1904	Ba
Tribune	Cordele	GA		1898-1900	Ba
Advocate	Covington	GA	w	1903-1912	Ba,Ay1905,1906,1908,1909,1911,1912
Ethiopian Phalanx	Covington	GA	w	1909-1914	Ba,Ay1911,1912,1913,1914
Guide Post	Covington	GA		1904-1907	Ba
Weekly Journal of Progress	Cuthbert	GA	w	1878	DANB674
Weekly Sentinel	Cuthbert	GA	w	1878	DANB674
Spectator	Darien	GA		1895-1905	Ba
Independent	Dawson	GA	w	1903	DANB159 (see Atlanta)
Advance	Decatur	GA		1910-1911	Ba (see AL)
Champion	Decatur	GA	w	1993-1994+	EP93,API94
DeKalb Weekly	Decatur	GA	w	1980	EP80
Freedman's Enterprise	Douglas	GA	sm	1905-1906	Ba
Enterprise	Dublin	GA	w	1904-1907	Ba,Ay1906,Lt1907
Record	Dublin	GA	w	1924-1931	Ba,Ay1925
Workers' Herald	Dublin	GA	w	1916-1918	Ba,Ay1917,1918
Negro Exponent	Eastman	GA		1895-1898	Ba
Blade	Eatonton	GA		1894-1896	Ba,Br
Middle Georgia Index	Eatonton	GA	w	1902-1907	Ba,Ay1905,1906,Lt1907
Southern Outlook	Eatonton	GA		1902-1904	Ba
Advance	Fitzgerald	GA	w	1902-1908	Ba,Ay1905,1906,Lt1907
Southern Sentinel	Fitzgerald	GA	w	1907	Lt1907
Critic	Forsyth	GA		1900-1901	Ba
Progressive Journal	Forsyth	GA		1905-1907	Ba
Fort Valley Herald	Fort Valley	GA	w	1986-1994+	Ga90,94,Baid90,92,EP89-93,BRG
Fort Valley Messenger	Fort Valley	GA		pre 1938	DANB336
News	Fort Valley	GA	sm	1904-1906	Ba,Ay1906
Uplift	Fort Valley	GA	m	1909-1919	Ba,NY19,22
Messenger	Gainesville	GA	w	1903-1905	Ay1905
Ebenezer Bugle	Greensboro	GA	m	1917-1920	Ay1920
Enterprise	Greenville	GA		1897-1900	Ba
National Republican	Greenville	GA		1898-1900	Ba,Br
Communicator	Griffin	GA		1913-1915	Ba
Echo	Griffin	GA	w	1888-1922	Ay1890,1917,NY12,22,Eur94
Negro Journal	Griffin	GA	w/q	1906-1913	Ba,Ay1908,1909,1911,1912,1913
Progress	Hagan	GA	w	1908-1909	Ba,Ay1909
Independent	Hawkinsville	GA		1900-1901	Ba

TITLE	CITY	ST.	FREQ.	DATES	SOURCES
Liberty County Herald	Hinesville	GA	w	1975-1976	EP75,76
Star in East	Hope	GA	m	1894	Eur94
South Georgia Advocate	Jesup	GA		1902-1903	Ba
Advocate	La Grange	GA	w	1904-1905	Ba,Ay1905
Emancipator	La Grange	GA		1901-1902	Ba
Georgia Republican	La Grange	GA		1900-1901	Ba
Guide	La Grange	GA	w	1907	Lt1907
Pastoral Echo	La Grange	GA	w	1897-1899	Ba,JNH
People's Christian Visitor	La Grange	GA	m	1908-1912	Ba,Ay1912
Trumpet	La Grange	GA		1895-1899	Ba
Baptist Standard	Macon	GA	w	1910-1927	Ba,Ay1920,1921,1925[1919],NY19,22
Baptist Truth	Macon	GA	w	1901-1922	Ba,Ay1905,1912,NY12,22,Lt1907
Broadcast	Macon	GA	w	1940	EP40
Central City Times	Macon	GA	w	1890-1892	Ba,Ay1890,1891
Critic	Macon	GA		1900-1903	Ba
Dispatch	Macon	GA	w	1906-1914	Ba,Ay1908,1909,1911-1914,NY12
Exponent	Macon	GA	w	1903-1905	Ba,Ay1905
Georgia Broadaxe	Macon	GA	w	1910-1914	Ba,Ay1912
Journal	Macon	GA		1893-1896	Ba
Macon Community Enterprise	Macon	GA	m	197u-1983	Oclc
Macon Courier	Macon	GA	w	1974-1994+	Ga87,88,Oclc,EP77,93,BRG,WPN94,SPD87
Macon Reporter	Macon	GA	w	1964	Oclc
Macon Sentinel	Macon	GA	w	1899-1900	Ba,Gr,Lc91,Br,WI,Oclc
Macon Times	Macon	GA	w	1966-1982	Ay1981,EH,EP72-80,Oclc,Lb
Macon Weekly	Macon	GA	w	pre 1979	Lb
Messenger	Macon	GA		1896-1899	Ba
Metro Times News	Macon	GA	w	1989-1993+	BRG,EP91,92,93
People's Choice	Macon	GA	w	1886-1893	Ba,Ay1887,1889,R1888
Sentinel	Macon	GA	w	1884-1897	Ay1887
Southern Advocate	Macon	GA	w	1892-1895	Ba,Ay1894
Southern Standard	Macon	GA	w	1910-1927	Ba,Ay1913-1920
Sunday School Worker	Macon	GA	bm/m	1911-1950	Ba,Ay1940,1950,NH42,EP38,51,NY46,Dc41
Telegraph	Macon	GA	d	pre 1944	Yenser6,Fleming [Flanagan, Thomas Jefferson]
World	Macon	GA	w	1943-1951	Ba,NH49,EP51
Gleanor	Madison	GA		1898-1901	Ba,Br
Guide Post	Madison	GA	sm	1904-1906	Ba,Ay1906
Exchange	Marietta	GA		1898-1900	Ba
Young People's Recorder	Marietta	GA		1908-1909	Ba
Colored Farmer's Alliance Gazette	Marshallville	GA	w	1889-1891	Ba,Ay1890
Times	Milledgeville	GA		1913-1915	Ba
Vidette	Milledgeville	GA	sm	1905-1906	Ba,Ay1906

TITLE	CITY	ST.	FREQ.	DATES	SOURCES
Advance	Millwood	GA		1902-1903	Ba,Ay1912[b1903 nlb]
Headlight	Monroe	GA		1897-1900	Ba
South Georgia Enterprise	Ocilla	GA	w	1915-1917	Ba,Ay1917
Georgia Post	Roberta	GA	w	1992-1944+	BRG,Ga94[b1922 nlb]
People's Journal	Rome	GA		1890-1895	Ba,Ay1890,1891,Eur94
Rome Enterprise	Rome	GA	w/bw	1903-1954	Ba,Ay1912,1954,NH42,44,46,EP38,49, NY12,19,22,26,32,46,Go,Dc41,44,Lt1907, Boris1
Woman's World	Rome	GA		1894	Jcw
Mouth-Piece	Sandersville	GA		1895-1899	Ba
Advocate	Savannah	GA		1896-1908	Ba
Baptist Truth	Savannah	GA	w	1898-1914	Ba,Ay1914,ABSCHSL
Chatham County Republican	Savannah	GA	w	1903-1910	Ba,Ay1905,1906,1908,1909
Colored Tribune	Savannah	GA	w	1875-1876	Oclc
Crusader	Savannah	GA		1963-1969	WI
Gazette	Savannah	GA		1897-1903	Ba
Georgia Times	Savannah	GA	bm	1962-1963	Sch
Globe	Savannah	GA		1951	EP51
Herald	Savannah	GA	w	1945-1994+	Ba,Ay1969,1980,Ga87,94,Baid90,92,Oclc, NH49,EP49,93,BRG,EH,EBA,WPN94, SPD67,70,74
Independent	Savannah	GA	w	1899-1915	Ba,Ay1905,1915,NY12
Journal	Savannah	GA	m	1912-1926	NY12,19,22,26
Labor Union Recorder	Savannah	GA		1891-1896	Ba
National Republican	Savannah	GA	w	1904-1909	Ba,Ay1906,1909,Lt1907[Republican]
Palmetto Farm	Savannah	GA		1912-1920	Boris2 [Hubert, Benjamin F.]
Phoenix	Savannah	GA		1885-1886	Ba
Pointer	Savannah	GA		1901-1903	Ba
Savannah Banner	Savannah	GA	w	1963-1963	Oclc
Savannah Journal	Savannah	GA	w	1918-1944	Ba,Ay1921,1943,EP35,44,NY19,22,26,32, Go,Br,Yenser6,Boris1
Savannah Tribune	Savannah	GA	w	1875-1878	Ba,Oclc,Cam
Savannah Tribune	Savannah	GA	w	1885-1994+	Ba,Ay1888,1950,Ga90,94,Cam,Oclc,WI, NH42,44,46,49,Baid92,BRG,EP38,93, NY12,19,26,32,46,Dc41,44,Go,Br,WPN94, Bl,Mather
Savannah Weekly Echo	Savannah	GA	w	1878-1884	Ba,Ay1882,1884,Gr,Lc91,Br,Oclc,jcw
Sentinel	Savannah	GA	w	1884-1887	Ay1887
Sentinel	Savannah	GA	w	1962	Ba,Oclc
Southern Gazette	Savannah	GA	w	1897-1916	Ba,Ay1905,1906
Southern News	Savannah	GA	w	1890-1909	Ba,Ay1905,1906,1908,1909,Br
Spy	Savannah	GA	w	1900-1905	Ba,Ay1905
Tan Confessions	Savannah	GA	m	1950-1951	EP51,Fleming[Atlanta]
Tiger's Roar	Savannah	GA	bm	1951	EP51
Union News	Sparta	GA	w	1905-1906	Ba,Ay1906

TITLE	CITY	ST.	FREQ.	DATES	SOURCES
Advocate	Statesboro	GA		1894-1896	Ba
Guide	Statesboro	GA	w	1910-1911	Ba,Ay1911
Negro Progress	Stillmore	GA		1897-1899	Ba
Emancipator	Swainsboro	GA		1902-1904	Ba
Mouth-Piece	Tennille	GA		1895-1898	Ba
News	Thomasville	GA	w	1967-1979	EP71,72,75,76,77,SPD70,74,79
News and Tallahassee Free Press	Thomasville	GA	w	1967-1978	EP78
People's News	Thomasville	GA	w	1907-1913	Ba,Ay1909,1911,1912,1913,NY12
Progress News	Thomasville	GA	w	1967-1967	Oclc
Thomasville Progressive News	Thomasville	GA	w	1967-1972	Oclc,WI,EBA,Chicago PL
Thomasville-Tallahassee News	Thomasville	GA		1967-1973	EH,Lb,Bp
People's Guide	Tifton	GA		1901-1903	Ba
Afro-American Mouthpiece	Valdosta	GA		1899-1901	Ba,Br
Blade	Valdosta	GA	w	1904-1907	Ba,Ay1906,Lt1907
Elevator	Valdosta	GA	w	1902-1906	Ba,Ay1905,1906
Exchange	Valdosta	GA		1902-1903	Ba
News	Valdosta	GA	w	1977	EP77
Plaindealer	Valdosta	GA		1898-1901	Ba,Br
Republican	Valdosta	GA		1897-1899	Ba
Telegram	Valdosta	GA	w	1966-1967	Pr,EP67,SPD67
Banner	Vidalia	GA	w	1937-1940	EP37-40
Enterprise	Warrenton	GA	w	1906-1909	Ba,Ay1908
Missionary Presbyterian	Washington	GA		1902-1910	Ba
Explainer	Waycross	GA	w	1901-1908	Ba,Ay1906,1908
Gazette and Land Bulletin	Waycross	GA	w	1896-1900	Ba,Lc91,Cam,Oclc,WI
Georgia Insight	Waycross	GA		1980	EP80
Georgia Mail	Waycross	GA		1893-1896	Ba
News	Waycross	GA	w	1906-1915	Ba,Ay1915,1908,1911-1914,NY12
South Georgia Baptist	Waycross	GA		1896-1900	Ba
Tribune	Waycross	GA	w	1914-1917	Ba,Ay1915-1917
Chronicle	Waynesboro	GA	w	1920-1922	Ba,Ay1921
Voice of the Union	Waynesboro	GA	w	1902-1905	Ba,Ay1905,1906,1908,1909
Trailer	West Point	GA		1911-1915	Ba[1913-1915],NY12,Mather
Jackson Sun	Winder	GA		1901-1903	Ba
Woodville Times	Woodville	GA		pre 1905	BJ7
National Reflector	Zebulon	GA		1898-1903	Ba
Oahu Papers	Honolulu	HI		1950	Fleming [Davis, Frank Marshall]
Afro-Hawaii News	Pearl City	HI	m	1987-1991+	Oclc
Mahogany	Pearl City	HI	m	1989-1991+	Oclc
Argus	Abingdon	IL	w	1992-1994+	BRG,Ga94[b1952 nlb]
Advance Citizen	Alton	IL	w	1892-1932	Ba,Ay1905,1915,1921
Consciousness	Aurora	IL		1975-1976	EP75,76
American Pilot	Bloomington	IL		1896-1899	Ba,Mather

TITLE	CITY	ST.	FREQ.	DATES	SOURCES
Cooperative News	Bloomington	IL	w	1933-1939	Ba,Ay1935,1938,EP35-39
Voice of the Black Community	Bloomington	IL	sm	1972-1975	Oclc
American	Cairo	IL		1905-1909	Ba
Baptist Truth	Cairo	IL	w	1895-1924	Ba,Ay1912,NY12,19,22,Lt1907
Cairo Gazette	Cairo	IL	w	1882-1889	Ba,Ay1888,Mather[1881-1883],Go,Br
Evangelistic Herald	Cairo	IL		1919-1940	Ba
Illinois Messenger	Cairo	IL		1915-1931	Ba
International Evangelistic Herald	Cairo	IL	m	1921-1940	Ba,Ay1935,1940
Sentinel	Cairo	IL		1892-1895	Ba
Three States	Cairo	IL		1887-1888	Ba
East Central Illinois Voice	Champaign	IL	w	1989	Oclc
Illinois Times	Champaign	IL	bw	1939-1974	Ba,Ay1969,1971,Oclc,NH44,46,EP44,70, Dc44,Br,Lb,SPD67,70,74
Plain Truth: Serving the North End	Champaign	IL		1967-1969	WI
Abbott's Monthly	Chicago	IL	m	1929-1933	BJ,Yenser4
Abbott's Weekly and Illustrated News	Chicago	IL	w	1933-1934	Oclc,Sch
Advance	Chicago	IL		1897-1898	Ba,JH
African Agenda	Chicago	IL		1972-1974	WI
Afro-American Manifesto	Chicago	IL		1972-1974	SPD72,74
All About Us	Chicago	IL		1896-1899	Ba,Br
American Eagle	Chicago	IL		1921-1925	Ba
American Life	Chicago	IL		1926-1928	BJ34
Appeal	Chicago	IL	w	1885-1926	Ba,Ay1905,1921,Go,Br,Cam,Eur94,R1898, 1900
Austin Voice	Chicago	IL	bw	1985-1992+	Oclc
Baptist Observer	Chicago	IL	bw	pre 1901	DANB167
Beacon Light	Chicago	IL		1909	Ba
Bee-Free Speech	Chicago	IL		1888-1895	Ba
Bilalian News	Chicago	IL	w	1961-1981	Ay1981,Oclc,WI[1953?-?],EP78-80,Lb
Black Books Bulletin & Words Work	Chicago	IL	q	1971-1993+	Ga94,SPD79
Black Economy, U. S. A.	Chicago	IL	m	1973-1976	WI,EP75,76
Black Expressions	Chicago	IL	q	1974	SPD74
Black Heritage	Chicago	IL		1961	WI
Black Journalism Review	Chicago	IL	q	1976-1978	Ay1978
Black Liberator	Chicago	IL	w	1968-1976	WI,EP75,76,Bp
Black Rapp	Chicago	IL		1970	Oclc
Black Stars	Chicago	IL	m	1950-1981	Ay1981,EH,SPD79[b1971]
Black Truth Newspaper	Chicago	IL	w	1968-1976	WI,EP75,76,Bp
Black World	Chicago	IL	m	1970-1979	Ay1975,WI[b1942],BJ[b1970](see Negro Digest),SPD72,74,79[DC]
Black Writer	Chicago	IL	q	1974-1994+	Ay1980,Ga88,94
Black X-Press	Chicago	IL	w	1973-1974	Oclc,NWU
Broad Ax	Chicago	IL	w	1899-1935	Ba,Ay1905,1921,Lc91,Oclc,WI,NY12,19, 22,26,32,Gr,Br,Mather

TITLE	CITY	ST.	FREQ.	DATES	SOURCES
Bronzeman	Chicago	IL	m	1929-1933	BJ
Bulletin	Chicago	IL	w	1958-1976	Ay1969,1975,EP70-72,76
Call	Chicago	IL	w/m	1972-1977	EP75,77
Catholic Interracialist	Chicago	IL	m	1941-1954	Ay1954
Catholic Truth	Chicago	IL		pre 1915	Mather [Valle, Lincoln Charles]
Champion Magazine	Chicago	IL	m	1916-1917	BJ,Boris1,DANB351
Chatham Southeast Citizen	Chicago	IL	w	1965-1994+	Ga90,94,Baid90,92,Oclc,EP73,80,BRG
Chicago Advocate	Chicago	IL	w	1925	NY26,Boris1
Chicago Bee	Chicago	IL	w	1909-1949	Ba,Ay1940,1945,Gr,Oclc,NH42,44,46,49, EP38,46,NY26,32,46,Dc41,44,Yenser6
Chicago Citizen	Chicago	IL	w	1965-1994+	Ga90,94,EBA,EH,Baid92,EP71,93
Chicago Crusader	Chicago	IL	w	1940-1994+	Ay1980,Ga90,94,Oclc,Sch,EP91,92,Lb, Baid92,BRG,WI,API90,94,WPN94
Chicago Daily Defender	Chicago	IL	d	1956-1994+	Ay1969,1975,Ga87,88,Oclc,Lc91,EP62,93, BRG,Dc41,44
Chicago Defender	Chicago	IL	w	1905-1987	Ba,Ay1921,1981,Ga87,88,Lc91,Oclc,Gr, WI,NH42,44,46,49,EP35,76,NY12,19,22, 26,32,46,Lb,Yenser3
Chicago Eagle	Chicago	IL	w	1889-1930	Ba,Cam,IL,WI,Gr
Chicago Gazette	Chicago	IL	w	1950-1978	Ay1969,Lb,Bp,EH,EP72-78
Chicago Globe	Chicago	IL		1949-1950	Fleming [Smith, Alfred Edgar]
Chicago Journal	Chicago	IL	w	1976-1981	Ay1980,1981
Chicago Leader	Chicago	IL		1905-1906	Mather [Sweeney, William Allison]
Chicago Leader	Chicago	IL		1896-1897	Yenser6 [Newby, Lawrence Arthur]
Chicago Metro News	Chicago	IL	w	1965-1994+	Ay1975,1980,Ga87,94,Oclc[b1972],WI, Baid92,EP73,92,EH[1972],SPD87,94, BRG
Chicago New Crusader	Chicago	IL	w	1940-1994+	Ay1969,1980,Ga87,API90,Lb,Oclc,EBA, EH,EP63,92,WI,SPD67,79
Chicago Shoreland News	Chicago	IL	w	1974-1994+	Ga91,94,Oclc,BRG,Baid92,WPN94
Chicago Standard News	Chicago	IL	w	1984-1992+	Baid92
Chicago Sun Times	Chicago	IL		1992+	BRG
Chicago Sunday Bee	Chicago	IL	w	1932-1949	EP48,49,Fleming
Chicago Weekend	Chicago	IL	w	1974-1994+	Ga90,94,Oclc,BRG,Baid92,EP78, 79[b1965],WPN94[b1977]
Chicago Whip	Chicago	IL	w	1918-1944	Ba,Ay1935,Br,Oclc,NY22,26,32,Yenser6
Chicago World	Chicago	IL	w	1900-1902	Ba,Oclc,WI,NWU
Christian Educator	Chicago	IL	q	1935	Ay1935
Christian Gibraltar	Chicago	IL		1910-1922	Ba,NY22
Chronicle	Chicago	IL	m	1918-1921	Ay1921
Church Organ	Chicago	IL		1893-1898	Ba,Br
Circuit	Chicago	IL	m	1945-1947	Ay1947
Clipper	Chicago	IL	w	1885-1898	Ba,Br,Eur94
Colored Embalmer	Chicago	IL	m	1939-1940	EP39,40

TITLE	CITY	ST.	FREQ.	DATES	SOURCES
Conservator	Chicago	IL	w	1878-1914	Ba,Ay1888,1905,R1888,Oclc,WI,Eur94,NY12,Br,Go,Cam,Penn,Lt1907,Mather,DANB
Courier	Chicago	IL		1932-1932	Ba
Courier	Chicago	IL	w	1958-1977	Ba,Ay1966,1977,Bp,Lb,Oclc,EP62,76,EBA,EH,Bl,SPD67,70,74
Daily Bulletin	Chicago	IL	d	1921-1921	Ba
Dollars and Sense Magazine	Chicago	IL		1990-1994+	Ga90,94
Dynamite	Chicago	IL	m/w	1936-1939	Ba,Sch
Ebony	Chicago	IL	m	1945-1994+	Ay1950,1975,Ga87,94,EP48,51,BJ,SPD67,70,74,79,Fleming
Ebony, Jr.	Chicago	IL	m/bm	1973-1982+	BJ,SPD79
Economist Publication	Chicago	IL	w	1975-1976	EP75,76
EM: Ebony Man	Chicago	IL	w	1990-1994+	Ga90,94
Engelwood Newspaper & Bulletin	Chicago	IL	w	1973	Bp
Enterprise	Chicago	IL	w	1918-1931	Ba,NY22,26
Favorite Magazine	Chicago	IL	m	1912-1921	Ay1921S
Fellowship Herald	Chicago	IL		1908-1916	Ba
Final Call	Chicago	IL		1991-1994+	Ga91,94,BRG
Fraternal Advocate	Chicago	IL	m	1915-1921	Ay1921S,Boris1,DANB351
Free Lance	Chicago	IL		1895-1926	Ba,Br
Free Speech	Chicago	IL		1888-1898	Ba,Br
Freedmen's Bulletin	Chicago	IL		1865-1866	WI
Freedom's Call	Chicago	IL		1954	WI
Freedom's Journal	Chicago	IL	w	1975-1976	EP75,76
Grapevine	Chicago	IL		1970	WI
Half Century Magazine	Chicago	IL	m	1916-1924	BJ,Yenser3
Hero	Chicago	IL		1889-1891	Ba
Home Circuit	Chicago	IL	m	1950	Ay1950
Hyde Park Citizen	Chicago	IL	w	1987-1994+	Ga91,94,Oclc,BRG,Baid92
Idea	Chicago	IL		1901-1922	Ba,Go,NY19
Illinois Chronicle	Chicago	IL	w	1900-1921	Ba,Oclc[b1909],NY12
Illinois Idea	Chicago	IL	w	1903-1926	Ba,Ay1912,1921,Oclc,NY12,22,26,Mather[e1927]
Illinois Political News	Chicago	IL	w	1939	Oclc
Independent Bulletin	Chicago	IL	w	1958-1994+	Ay1977,Ga90,94,Baid90,92,Bp,Oclc[b1972],EP73,93,EBA,EH,BRG,API94,WPN94[b1963]
Ivy Leaf	Chicago	IL		1920-1994+	Ga87,94,WI
Jet	Chicago	IL	w	1951-1994+	Ay1969,1981,Ga87,94,EH,BJ,SPD67,70,74,79
Lawndale Drum	Chicago	IL	bw	1972-1978	Oclc,WI,EP75-78
Living Blues: A Journal of Black American Blues Tradition	Chicago	IL	w	1970-1982+	BJ
Messenger	Chicago	IL	w	1942-1946	Ba,NH46,Dc44
Metropolitan News	Chicago	IL	w	1930-1939	Ba,Oclc,EP38,39

TITLE	CITY	ST.	FREQ.	DATES	SOURCES
Metropolitan Post	Chicago	IL	w	1940	Ay1940
Mirror	Chicago	IL		1937-1937	Ba
Mirror	Chicago	IL	w	1940-1946	Ba,NH42,44,46,Dc41,44
Mississippi Enterprise	Chicago	IL	w	1933-1992+	Ga91,92,Baid92
Modern Farmer	Chicago	IL	w	1930-1932	Ba,NY32
Muhammad Speaks	Chicago	IL	w	1961-1977	Ay1975,1977,NWU,EP71-76,SPD70,74
Muhammad's Mosque No. 2	Chicago	IL	bw	1962-1979	SPD70,74,79
Muslim Journal	Chicago	IL	w	1961-1994+	Ay1986,Ga87,94,EP90-93,BRG,Baid92
National Aspect	Chicago	IL		1910-1912	Ba
National Negro Insurance Assn. Pilot	Chicago	IL	m	1951	EP51
Negro Digest	Chicago	IL	m	1936-1970	Ay1952,WI,EP48,51,BJ[1942-1951, 1961-1970],Fleming
Negro Heritage	Chicago	IL	bw/m	1961-1967	SPD67,BJ (see Reston VA)
Negro Spearhead	Chicago	IL	w	1968	Oclc
Negro Story	Chicago	IL	bm	1944-1946	BJ
Negro Traveler	Chicago	IL	m	1942-1944	Ay1969,EH,EP50,51,Ga87
New Expression	Chicago	IL	m	1987-1988	Ga87,88
New Negro Traveler and Conventioneer	Chicago	IL	m	1944-1987	Ay1969,1975,Ga87,EH,EP50,51,BJ,SPD79
New Opportunities for Negroes in Medicine	Chicago	IL	ir	1946-1974	SPD67,70,74
New Research Travel and Conventioneer	Chicago	IL	m	1988-1994+	Ga88,94
New Traveler	Chicago	IL	bm	1942-1987	SPD87 [see Negro Traveler]
News Clarion	Chicago	IL	w	1964-1967	Oclc
News Digest	Chicago	IL		1949-1950	Fleming [Goodrich, James Russell]
News-Ledger	Chicago	IL		1938-1939	Ba
Nightmoves	Chicago	IL	2xm	1980-1991+	Ga90,91,Baid90
Northwestern Christian Recorder	Chicago	IL		pre 1915	Mather [Bowling, Alonzo Jesse]
Observer	Chicago	IL	w	1964-1992+	Ay1980,Ga87,90,Baid90,92,Oclc,BRG, EP75,77,SPD87
Opportunity	Chicago	IL		1923-1937	Yenser4 [Johnson, Charles Spurgeon]
Owl	Chicago	IL	w	1962-1963	Oclc,Rw
People's Advocate	Chicago	IL		1900-1922	Ba,Go,NY19,22
People's Voice	Chicago	IL		1942-1944	Oclc,Fleming
Pilot	Chicago	IL		1951-1976	WI
Plain Dealer	Chicago	IL		1888-1922	Ba,NY22,Yenser6
Post	Chicago	IL	d	1952-1953	Ay1953
Reflector	Chicago	IL	w	1895-1900	Ba,Oclc,JH
Republican	Chicago	IL	w	1888-1889	Ba,Ay1888
Review	Chicago	IL		1929-1932	Ba,JH
Revolution	Chicago	IL	w	1975-1976	EP75,76
Royal Messenger	Chicago	IL	w	1922-1932	Ba,NY22,32
Savoyager	Chicago	IL		1932-1932	Ba
Searchlight	Chicago	IL	w	1910-1932	Ba,NY19,22,26,32,Go,Boris1

TITLE	CITY	ST.	FREQ.	DATES	SOURCES
Second Ward News	Chicago	IL	w	1935-1936	Oclc
Sentinel	Chicago	IL	w	1977-1980	EP79,80,Lb
Sophisticates Black Hairstyles and Care Guide	Chicago	IL		1990-1994+	Ga90,94
South End Citizen	Chicago	IL	w	1966-1994+	Ga90,94,Oclc,Baid92,BRG,EP73,79, WPN94[b1954]
South End Review	Chicago	IL	w	1972-1976	EP75,76
South Shore Scene	Chicago	IL	w	1959-1994+	Ay1986,Ga87,94,BRG,Baid92,WPN94 [b1985]
South Side Bulletin	Chicago	IL		1958-1972	WI
South Suburban Citizen	Chicago	IL	w	1967-1994+	Ga92,94[b1983],Oclc,BRG,Baid90,92
Southeast Independent Bulletin	Chicago	IL	w	1972-1978	Oclc,EP77,78
Southeast Sun	Chicago	IL	w	1973-1977	EP73,75-77
Southwest Citizen	Chicago	IL	w	1973-1977	EP73,75-77
Spokesman	Chicago	IL		1932-1932	Ba
Star	Chicago	IL		1910-1922	Ba,NY22
Star (interracial)	Chicago	IL		1946-1948	Ba,Fleming
Supreme Liberty Guardian	Chicago	IL	m	1940-1942	NH42,Dc41
Tan	Chicago	IL	m	1969-1970	Ay1969,1970
Tri City Journal	Chicago	IL	w	1981-1994+	Ga90,94,Baid90,92[1978],BRG,EP90,93, API94
Tuesday	Chicago	IL	m	1963-1979	SPD67,79
Voice	Chicago	IL	w	1940-1942	Oclc
Voice of the First Congressional District	Chicago	IL		1938	Oclc
Voice of the Negro	Chicago	IL	m	1906-1908	Oclc,BJ[1906-1907 Voice],Lc83,Bl,Mather
Voice of the Second Ward	Chicago	IL		1938	Oclc
West Side Torch	Chicago	IL	w,bw	1965-1971	Oclc,WI
West Side Torch Lawndale Edition	Chicago	IL	w,bw	1968-1968	Oclc,WI
Western Appeal	Chicago	IL		1885-1926	Ba,Penn
Western Herald	Chicago	IL		1884	DANB167
Western Opinion	Chicago	IL	w	1906-1909	Ba,Lt1907
Women's National Magazine	Chicago	IL	m	1939-1946	Ay1940,1946,EP39,40
Woodlawn Booster	Chicago	IL	w	1932-1972	Ay1972,Oclc,EH
Woodlawn Observer	Chicago	IL	w	1967-1973	Oclc,EH,EP72,73,Bp,Lb
World	Chicago	IL	w	1918-1953	Ba,Ay1940,1953,Oclc,NH42,44,46,49,Sch, EP38,51,NY32,46
World Muslim News	Chicago	IL	w	1961-1987	SPD87
World News Examiner	Chicago	IL	w	1982	Oclc
Chicago Standard News	Chicago Hts.	IL	w	1984-1994+	Ga87,94,Oclc,WPN94
South Suburban Standard	Chicago Hts.	IL	w	1979-1994+	Ga87,94,Oclc,BRG,Baid92,WPN94
Tri City Journal	Chicago Hts.	IL	w	1980-1983	EP80,NA [see Chicago]
Black Vanguard	Danville	IL		1968	WI
Illinois Times	Danville	IL	w	1940-1944	EP40,41,42,44
International	Danville	IL		1901-1902	Ba,Mather

TITLE	CITY	ST.	FREQ.	DATES	SOURCES
Inter-State Echo	Danville	IL	w	1909-1926	Ba,Ay1915,NY12,19,22,26,Go,Boris1
Decatur Spot-light	Decatur	IL	w/bw	1970-1975	Oclc
Spotlight	Decatur	IL		1969-1970	Oclc
Voice of the Black Community	Decatur	IL	w	1968-1992+	Ga87,94,Baid90,92,Oclc,EP77,93[b1965], NA,BRG,WI,WPN94,API94,SPD87
Weekly News	Decatur	IL	w	1975-1976	EP75,76
Beacon	East St. Louis	IL	w	1966-1967	SPD67
Bi-State Defender	East St. Louis	IL		pre 1979	Lb
Defender	East St. Louis	IL		pre 1979	Lb
Eagle	East St. Louis	IL	w	1908-1914	Ba,Ay1912
East St. Louis Crusader	East St. Louis	IL	w	1941-1992+	Ba,Ay1950,1953,Ga91,92,Oclc,NH46,49, br,Bp,EBA,EH,EP67,80,Baid92,Dc44, SPD67,70,74,79
East St. Louis Monitor	East St. Louis	IL	w	1962-1994+	Ay1969,Ga88,94,SPD67,70,79,Oclc [b1963],EBA,BRG,EH,NA,Baid92,EP67, 93
Empire Weekly News	East St. Louis	IL	w	1966-1974	SPD67,70,74,Lb[Empire Star Bulletin]
Executive Editor	East St. Louis	IL	w	1963-1987	SPD87
Forum	East St. Louis	IL		1904-1929	Ba
Home Guard	East St. Louis	IL		pre 1915	Mather [Borden, Edwin Howard]
Illinois Crusader	East St. Louis	IL		1944	Ba
Missouri Illinois Advance Citizen	East St. Louis	IL	w	1892-1932	Ba,Ay1905,1921,NY26,Boris1
Sentinel	East St. Louis	IL	w	1904-1909	Ba,Lt1907
Southern Illinois Press	East St. Louis	IL	w	1920-1927	Ba,NY22,26,Boris1
Tidings	East St. Louis	IL		1912-1914	Mather [Borden, Edwin Howard]
Baptist Progress	Elgin	IL		1983-1992+	ABSCHSL
Evanston Weekly	Evanston	IL	w	1915-1931	Ba,NY22,Cam
Guide	Evanston	IL		1929-1932	Ba
New Sense	Evanston	IL	q/sa	1974-1987	SPD79,87
Newsette	Evanston	IL		1941	Ba
North Shore Examiner	Evanston	IL	bw	1968-1987	EP72,81,NA83,EH,Lb,SPD87
Central Illinois Advance Citizen	Galesburg	IL		1892-1932	Ba,Ay1915[b1913],1921
Market Journal VII	Grayslake	IL	w	1992-1994+	BRG,Ga94[b1974 nlb] (see Harvey)
Chicago Journal	Harvey	IL	w	1974	EP74
Chicago South Suburban News	Harvey	IL	w	1964-1973	Ay1969,1973,WI,EBA,Lb,Bp
Harvey Chicago Express-American	Harvey	IL	w	1977	EP77
Heights Journal	Harvey	IL	w	1974	EP74
Helper	Harvey	IL		1912	NY12
Joliet Journal	Harvey	IL	w	1974	EP74
Journal	Harvey	IL	w	1970	EP70
Markham Journal	Harvey	IL	w	1974	EP74
Robbins Journal	Harvey	IL	w	1974	EP74
Joliet Voice	Joliet	IL	w	1950-1970	Ay1964,EP67,70,Lb,SPD67[Negro Voice], 70,74
Negro Voice	Joliet	IL	w	1966-1967	SPD67

TITLE	CITY	ST.	FREQ.	DATES	SOURCES
Progressive Era	Kankakee	IL	w	1924-1944	Ba,Ay1935,1942,Oclc,NH42,44,EP35-41, Dc41
Black Rap	Lake Forest	IL	m	1967-1974	WI,SPD74,79
Afro-American Advocate	Litchfield	IL		1892-1893	Ba
Chicago Westside Journal	Markham	IL	w	1992-1994+	BRG,WPN94[b1973],API94
Gentlemen of Color	Matteson	IL	m	1978-1987	SPD87
Suburban Echo Reporter	Maywood	IL	w	1964-1973	EP71,72,73,Bp
Baptist Trumpet	Metropolis City	IL		1896-1900	Ba
Baptist Truth	Metropolis City	IL		1896-1900	Ba
Gazette	Metropolis City	IL	w	1898-1938	Ba,Ay1912,1935,Oclc,Go,Br,EP38,39
Egyptian Sun	Mound City	IL		1920-1922	Ba
Weekly Star	Mound City	IL	w	1908-1926	Ba,Ay1912,Go,NY12,19,22,26,Boris1
Messenger	Mount Morris	IL		1922	NY22
Black Rapper	Peoria	IL	ir	1968	Oclc,WI
Bronze Citizen	Peoria	IL	m	1950	Ay1950
Bronze Informer	Peoria	IL		1946	Ba
Central Illinois Advance Citizen	Peoria	IL		1892-1932	Ba,Ay1915[b1913],1921
Informer	Peoria	IL	w	1936-1938	Ba,EP36
Advance	Quincy	IL	w	1907	Lt1907
Illinois Informer	Quincy	IL	w	1919-1926	Oclc,NY26,Boris1
Illinois Progress	Quincy	IL		1892-1894	Ba
Progress	Quincy	IL		1892-1900	Ba
Herald	Robbins	IL	w	1917-1949	Ba,Ay1945,1950,NH49,EP46,49,NY46
Views and Voices of Chicago and Suburbs	Robbins	IL	w	1951	EP51
Rock Island News Times	Rock Island	IL	m	1971-1978	EP72,75,76,77,78,Bp,Lb
Tri-City Oracle	Rock Island	IL		1898-1900	Ba
Crusader	Rockford	IL	w	1950-1973	Ay1966,1973,Oclc,WI,Bp,SPD67,70,74
Rockford Chronicle	Rockford	IL	w	1981-1983	NA83,EP81
Tuesday at Home	Round Lake Village		m	1975	Ay1975
Tuesday Magazine	Round Lake Village		m	1975	Ay1975
Chicago Heights Journal	South Holland	IL	bw	1965-1978	Ay1975,1978,EP74,76[1970]
Chicago Journal	South Holland	IL	bw	1965-1978	Ay1975,1978,EP74,76[1970]
Joliet Lockport Journal	South Holland	IL	bw	1965-1978	Ay1975,1978,EP74,76[1970]
Lucky Dollar Shopping News	South Holland	IL		1978	EP78
Markham Journal	South Holland	IL	bw	1968-1978	Ay1975,1978,EP74,76[1970]
Robbins Journal	South Holland	IL	bw	1964-1978	Ay1975,1978,EP74,76[1970]
Suburban Journal	South Holland	IL	bw	1964-1978	Ay1975,1978,EP74,76[1970]
Sunday Pictorial Journal	South Holland	IL	w	1971-1978	Ay1978
Argus	Springfield	IL		1912-1915	Ba,NY12
Central Illinois Advance Citizen	Springfield	IL	w	1892-1932	Ba,Ay1912,1921,NY12,19[Advance Citizen],22,32,Go
Eye	Springfield	IL		1890-1893	Ba

TITLE	CITY	ST.	FREQ.	DATES	SOURCES
Forum	Springfield	IL	w	1904-1929	Ba,Ay1912,1921,IL,Oclc[e1927],Cam,Go, NY12,19,22,26,Yenser3
Illinois Chronicle	Springfield	IL	bw,w	1912-1977	Ba,Ay1950,1977,Bp,Lb,EP48,49,Oclc [1917-1950?],NH42,46,49,NY46,Dc41,44
Illinois Conservator	Springfield	IL	w/bw	1902-1958	Ba,Ay1930,1958,Oclc[b1904?],NH42,46, EP37,51,NY19,22,26,46,Dc41,44,Br,Go, Yenser6
Illinois Record	Springfield	IL	w	1897-1907	Ba,Cam,Lc91,Oclc,WI,JQ,Yenser4
Illinois State Informer	Springfield	IL	w	1933-1939	Oclc,EP38,39
Illinois State Messenger	Springfield	IL	w	1897-1900	Ba,IL
Leader	Springfield	IL	w	1902-1918	Ba,Ay1912,1915,NY12
Messenger	Springfield	IL	w	1888-1889	Ba,Ay1888,Oclc
National Standard Enterprise	Springfield	IL		1896-1903	Ba
Negro Democrat	Springfield	IL	sm	1934-1938	Ba,Oclc,EP38
Spirit of Black Springfield	Springfield	IL	m	1968	Oclc
Springfield's Voice of the Black Community	Springfield	IL	bw	1972-1980	Oclc
State Capital	Springfield	IL	w	1886-1915	Ba,Ay1889,1905,R1888,IL,Oclc, WI[e1910],Eur94,NY12,Gr,Penn
Drums	Urbana	IL		1967	WI
Shining Star	Anderson	IN	w	1922	Oclc
Triangle	Angola	IN	w	1946-1982	Ay1980,1982
Army and Navy Musician	Elkhart	IN		pre 1950	Fleming[Adams, Alton Augustus]
Spirit Publications	Elkhart	IN	w	1975-1976	Oclc
American Standard	Evansville	IN		1948-1949	EP48,49
Argus	Evansville	IN	w	1938-1946	Ba,Sch,NH42,44,46,EP41,43,Dc41,44
Chronicle	Evansville	IN		1879-1883	Ba,Penn,jcw,DANB39
Clarion	Evansville	IN	w	1914-1916	Ba,Ay1915
Consolidated News	Evansville	IN	w	1943-1956	Ba,Ay1950,1956,Oclc,EP49,51
Guide	Evansville	IN		1908-1909	Ba
Negro Press	Evansville	IN		1911-1914	Ba
Transcript	Evansville	IN		1906-1907	Ba
Watch Tower	Evansville	IN		pre 1889	Penn (see MD)
Coffee Break	Fort Wayne	IN	w	1966-1968	Oclc
Frost Illustrated	Fort Wayne	IN	w	1968-1994+	Ga87,94,Oclc,BRG,Baid92,EP75,92, SPD87
Weekly Carrier	Fort Wayne	IN	w	1940-1951	Ba,EP40,50,51
Commonwealth	Gary	IN	w	1925-1932	Ba,NY26,32
Crusader	Gary	IN	w	1959-1994+	Ay1969,1982,Oclc,WI,EP64,93[1961], EBA,API94,SPD67,70,74
Dispatch	Gary	IN		1919-1926	Ba,Go,NY22,26
Gary American	Gary	IN	bw/w	1925-1994+	Ba,Ay1935,1980,Ga87,94,Oclc[b1928], NH44,46,49,Gr,EP48,79,NY32,46,Dc44, SPD67,70,WPN94[b1927]
Gary Chronicle	Gary	IN	w	1966-1974	SPD67,70,74,Lb
Gary Colored American	Gary	IN	w	1927-1928	Oclc,Yenser3[North American]

TITLE	CITY	ST.	FREQ.	DATES	SOURCES
Gary Info	Gary	IN	w	1961-1994+	Ay1986,Ga87,94,Oclc,Baid92,EP67,93, BRG,EBA,EH,Bp,SPD87
Lake County Journal	Gary	IN		1921-1925	Ba
Lake County Observer	Gary	IN	w	1946-1951	Ba,Ay1950,1951,NH49,EP48,51,Br
National Defender	Gary	IN		1905-1922	Cam
National Defender and Sun	Gary	IN		1905-1931	Ba,Go,NY19,22
New Crusader	Gary	IN	w	1961-1994+	Ga90,94,API90,BRG,Baid92,EH,EP72,90, Bp
Sun	Gary	IN		1905-1931	Ba,NY26,32,Cam,Boris1
Afro-American Journal	Indianapolis	IN	m/bm/q	1973-1979	WI,BJ16,SPD79
Archon	Indianapolis	IN		1920-1975	WI
Argus	Indianapolis	IN	w	1887-1891	Ba,R1888
Courier	Indianapolis	IN		1893-1900	Ba,Br,Yenser6[1892]
Daily Standard	Indianapolis	IN	d	1921-1924	Ba,Go
Flaming Sword	Indianapolis	IN	m	pre 1927	Boris1 [Boone, Theodore Sylvester]
Freeman	Indianapolis	IN	w/m	1884-1927	Ba,Ay1888,1921,Gr,Penn,Oclc[1888],WI, NY12,19,22,26,Lt1907,Mather,R1888, 1900
Hoosier Herald	Indianapolis	IN	w	1949-1958	Ay1958,Oclc
Indiana Herald	Indianapolis	IN	w	1953-1994+	Oclc,WI,EP62,93,BRG,EBA,EH[b1955], API94,SPD70,74,79
Indiana Herald-Times	Indianapolis	IN	w	1957-1960	Oclc
Indianapolis Herald	Indianapolis	IN	w	1959-1979	EP80,Lb,SPD67
Indianapolis Herald-Times	Indianapolis	IN	w	1957-1957	Oclc
Indianapolis Ledger	Indianapolis	IN	w	1910-1926	Ba,Ay1915,1921[1913],NY19,22,26,Go, Yenser3
Indianapolis Recorder	Indianapolis	IN	w	1895-1994+	Ba,Ay1905,1975,R1900,Ga87,94,Oclc [b1897],Gr,NH42,44,46,49,EP35,92, Baid92,EBA,EH,NY12,19,22,26,32,46, Dc41,44,Lt1907,API90,94,Mather,SPD67, 70,74
Indianapolis Spokesman	Indianapolis	IN	w	1925-1927	NY26,Boris1
Indianapolis World	Indianapolis	IN	w	1883-1932	Ba,Ay1888,1921,Br,Penn,Oclc,WI,R1888, NY12,19,22,26,32,Mather
Leader	Indianapolis	IN	w	1879-1890	Ba,Ay1888,Penn,Mather
Methodist Voice	Indianapolis	IN		1891-1896	Ba
Mid-Western Post	Indianapolis	IN		1943-1946	Ba,Br
National Domestic Magazine	Indianapolis	IN		1896-1898	Mather [Howard, John Dalphin]
Plaindealer	Indianapolis	IN		1912-1926	Ba,NY12,19,22,26
Review	Indianapolis	IN	m	1919-1925	Ba,Ay1921,NY19,22,26,Boris1[1927]
Searchlight	Indianapolis	IN		1919-1924	Ba
Sunset Community Leader	Indianapolis	IN	w	1941	Ba,Br,EP41
World Telegram	Indianapolis	IN	w	1940	EP40
Times	Jasper	IN	w	1876-1889	Ay1889
Noonday Sun	Jeffersonville	IN		1894-1897	Ba
Colored Visitor	Logansport	IN	sm	1879-1879	Ba,Oclc,Lc91,Sch,WI

TITLE	CITY	ST.	FREQ.	DATES	SOURCES
Muncie Times	Muncie	IN	bm	1991-1994+	WPN94
Weekly Review	New Albany	IN	w	1881	Oclc,Lc91,NWU
Blade	Richmond	IN	w	1918-1932	Ba,Oclc[e1922],NY22,26,32,Boris1
Freedmen's Record	Richmond	IN		1865-1866	WI
Indiana Register	Richmond	IN		1909-1915	Ba,NY12
Script	Richmond	IN		1945-1947	Ba
Observer	South Bend	IN		1913-1915	Ba
Reformer	South Bend	IN	w	1967-1978	EBA,EH,EP71-78,Lb
African American Review	Terre Haute	IN	4xy	1993-1994+	Ga94
Afro-American Journal	Terre Haute	IN	2xw	1891-1896	Ba,Eur94
Black American Literature Forum	Terre Haute	IN	4xy	1976-1992	Ga87,92,WI,SPD87,BJ44 (see African American Review)
Citizen	Terre Haute	IN		1919-1926	Ba,Go,NY19,22,26
Eagle	Terre Haute	IN		1901-1903	Ba
Negro American Literature Forum	Terre Haute	IN	4xy	1967-1976	BJ44 (see African American Review)
Right Way	Terre Haute	IN		1896-1898	Ba
Terre Haute Express	Terre Haute	IN		pre 1889	Penn
Times	Terre Haute	IN		1909-1911	Ba
Buxton Advocate	Buxton	IA		1912	NY12
Buxton Gazette	Buxton	IA		1909-1922	Ba,Go,NY19
Eagle	Buxton	IA	w	1903-1905	Ba,Ay1905,WI (see Oskaloosa)
Iowa Colored Workman	Buxton	IA		1907-1910	Ba
Tri-City Advocate	Davenport	IA	w	1907	Lt1907
Tri-City Observer	Davenport	IA		1940	EP40
Afro-Citizen	Des Moines	IA	w	1976-1978	EP77,78
Black Revolutionary	Des Moines	IA		1971	Unct
Challenger	Des Moines	IA	w	pre 1993	Communicator
Communicator	Des Moines	IA	w	1985-1993+	His. Soc. IA
Des Moines Register and Leader	Des Moines	IA		1908-1915	Mather [Hall, Elbert Rufus]
Iowa Baptist Standard	Des Moines	IA	w	1897-1899	Oclc,Cam,Lc91,WI,NWU
Iowa Bystander	Des Moines	IA	w	1934-1950	Ay1935,1975[West Des Moines], SPD67,70,74
Iowa Colored Women	Des Moines	IA		1907-1910	Ba
Iowa Observer	Des Moines	IA	w	1936-1954	Ba,Ay1950,1954,NH42,44,46,49,EP40,49, NY46,Dc41,44,Br
Iowa State Bystander	Des Moines	IA	w	1894-1933	Ay1905,NY12,19,22,26,32,46,Dc41,44, Lt1907,Boris1,Go
New Iowa Bystander	Des Moines	IA	w	1894-1994+	Ga87,94,Baid90,92,Lb,Oclc,WI,NH42,44, 46,49,EP35,80,EBA,SPD87,94
Rising Sun	Des Moines	IA		1883-1885	Ba,Br
Weekly Avalanche	Des Moines	IA	w	1891-1896	Ba,Br,Oclc,WI,Eur94,Cam
Eyes	Iowa City	IA	m	1947-1952	Ay1950,1952
Baptist Herald	Keokuk	IA		pre 1901	DANB167
Buxton Eagle	Oskaloosa	IA		1904-1906	Ba (see also Buxton)
Iowa District News	Oskaloosa	IA		1890-1892	Ba

TITLE	CITY	ST.	FREQ.	DATES	SOURCES
Negro Solicitor	Oskaloosa	IA		1893-1900	Ba
Afro-American Advance	Sioux City	IA	w	1908-1912	Ba,Ay1912
Enterprise	Sioux City	IA	w	1935-1940	EP35,37-40
Searchlight	Sioux City	IA		1899-1902	Ba
Weekly Review	Sioux City	IA	w	1928-1930	Ba,Br
Daily Evening Journal	Washington	IA		1895-1911	Yenser4 [Black, Narris Lehigh]
Observer	Waterloo	IA	w	1941	EP41
Post	Waterloo	IA	w	1952	Treadwell
Special Delivery	Waterloo	IA	w	1987	Treadwell
Waterloo Defender	Waterloo	IA	bw	1963-1977	EH,EP75-77,Lb
Waterloo Star	Waterloo	IA	w	1956	Treadwell
Atchison Blade	Atchison	KS	w	1892-1898	Ba,Ay1894,Gr,Lc91,Oclc,WI,Moten, Ks[1892-1894]
Southern Argus	Baxter Springs	KS	w	1891-1891	Ba,NWU,Lc91,Oclc,WI,Ks
Advocate	Coffeyville	KS	w	1894	Eur94
Afro-American Advocate	Coffeyville	KS	w	1891-1893	Ba,Lc91,Oclc,Gr,WI,Moten,Ks
American	Coffeyville	KS	w	1890-1899	Ba,Gr,Lc91,Oclc,WI[1898-1899],Moten, Ks[1898-1889]
Coffeyville Globe	Coffeyville	KS	w	1918-1925	Ba,Ay1921,1925,NY19,22,Go
Kansas Blackman	Coffeyville	KS		1894-1896	Ba,Cam,Moten
Vindicator	Coffeyville	KS		1906	Mather [Clem, Charles Douglas]
Colored Citizen 1st	Fort Scott	KS	w	1876-1878	Ba,Penn,Oclc[1878-1880],WI [1878-1879],Moten,Cam
Fair Play	Fort Scott	KS	w	1889-1900	Ba,Ks[1898-1898]
Radical	Fort Scott	KS		1876-1879	Ba,Penn
Southern Argus	Fort Scott	KS	w	1891-1893	Ba,NWU,Lc91,Oclc,WI
American Freeman	Girard	KS	w	1929-1951	Ks,Lc83
Blade	Hutchinson	KS	w	1947-1952	Ay1950,1952
Hutchinson Blade	Hutchinson	KS	w	1914-1923	Ba,Ay1916-1921,Ks[1918-1922],Cam,Go
People's Elevator	Independence	KS	w	1892-1943	Ba,Br,Cam,Ks[1926-1930]
American Citizen	Kansas City	KS	w	1887-1912	Ba,Ay1890,1909,Lc91,Oclc,WI[e1909, Moten,Ks[1899-1893],Eur94,NY12, Lt1907,Boris2
Black Progress Shopper News	Kansas City	KS	w	1968-1973	EBA,EH[MO],EP71-73[MO],Bp,Lb
Christian Spiritual Voice	Kansas City	KS	m	1940-1942	NH42,Dc41
Community Challenger	Kansas City	KS	w	1974-1987	Ay1979,EP77,78,SPD87[b1975]
Daily American Citizen	Kansas City	KS	d	1898-1900	Ba,Oclc,WI[1887-1909],Moten, Ks[1893-1900]
Daily Citizen	Kansas City	KS	d	1898-1900	Cam,Lc91
Daily Plaindealer	Kansas City	KS	d	1907-1907	Ba,Cam
Golden Eaglet	Kansas City	KS	w	1940-1944	NH42,44,Dc41
Independent	Kansas City	KS	w	1914-1927	Ba,Ks[1916-1926]
Kansas City Advocate	Kansas City	KS	w	1914-1932	Ba,Ay1921,1925,Lc77,Cam,Br,Moten,Ks, NY22,26,32,Boris1
Kansas City and Topeka Plaindealer	Kansas City	KS	w	1932-1933	Ay1945,Ks

TITLE	CITY	ST.	FREQ.	DATES	SOURCES
Kansas City Globe	Kansas City	KS	w	1972-1980	EP74-80 (see also MO)
Kansas City Independent	Kansas City	KS		1891	Br
Kansas City Independent Negro	Kansas City	KS	w	1915-1916	Lc77,Oclc
Kansas City News	Kansas City	KS		pre 1927	Boris1 [Green, Dorsey]
Kansas City Voice	Kansas City	KS	w	1979-1994+	Ga,92,94,EP79,80,Baid92,Lb
Kansas Daily State Ledger	Kansas City	KS		1893-1893	Ba
Kansas Elevator	Kansas City	KS	w	1916-1920	Ba,Ay1917-1920,br,Moten
Kansas Record	Kansas City	KS	w	1902-1905	Ba,Ay1905
Kansas State Globe	Kansas City	KS	w	1983-1993+	EP90-93
Liberator	Kansas City	KS		1900-1901	Ba
Missouri State Post	Kansas City	KS	w	1986-1990	Oclc
People's Elevator	Kansas City	KS	w	1892-1950	Ba,Ay1940,1950,NH42,44,49,Ks,NY46, Dc41,Br
Plaindealer	Kansas City	KS	w	1931-1970	Ba,Ay1961,Brooks,Lc83[e1960],br, Oclc[e1958?],NH42,44,46,49,Ks [1933-1958],EP35,51,NY46,Dc41,44
Southern Argus	Kansas City	KS		1891-1893	Ba
Western Christian Recorder	Kansas City	KS	w	1920-1932	NY26,32,Boris2
Western Christian Recorder	Kansas City	KS	w	1892-1900	Ba,Cam,Lc91,Oclc,WI,Moten, Ks[1898-1899]
Wyandotte Echo	Kansas City	KS	w	1925-1984	Ba,Ay1938[b1928],1951,NH49,EP36,40, Ks,NY32,46,Br
Colored Radical	Lawrence	KS	w	1876-1876	Moten
Ethnicity and Disease	Lawrence	KS	q	1991-1993+	Ga94
Harambee	Lawrence	KS		1984	Oclc
Historic Times	Lawrence	KS	w	1891-1891	Ba,Lc91,Oclc,WI,Ks,Moten
Kansas Herald and Freeman	Lawrence	KS		1914-1927	Cam
Kansas Herald of Freedom	Lawrence	KS		1855-1859	Lc91
Vindicator	Lawrence	KS	w	1878-1880	Ba,Moten
Advocate	Leavenworth	KS	w	1888-1891	Ba,Ay1891,1890,Lc91,Oclc
Colored Radical	Leavenworth	KS	w	1876-1876	Ba,Moten,Ks
Democratic Standard	Leavenworth	KS	w	1870-1888	Ay1888,Penn[Standard]
Leavenworth Advocate	Leavenworth	KS	w	1889-1891	Ba,Gr,Penn,Lc91,Oclc,WI,Moten,Mather
Leavenworth Herald	Leavenworth	KS	w	1894-1899	Ba,Lc91,Oclc,WI,Moten,Ks[e1898], Ay1896
Nicodemus Cyclone	Nicodemus	KS	w	1887-1889	Ba,Lc91,Oclc,WI,Ks[e1888],NWU
Nicodemus Enterprise	Nicodemus	KS	w	1887-1887	Ba,Oclc,WI,Ks,Cam
Western Cyclone	Nicodemus	KS	w	1886-1887	Ba,Ay1887,NWU,Lc91,Oclc,WI,Ks
Benevolent Banner	North Topeka	KS	w	1887-1887	Ba,Lc91,Oclc,WI,Ks,Moten
Miami Republican	Paola	KS	w	1866-1992+	Ga87,92,Baid90,92,Ay1887,1921,Ks [1871-date]
Western Spirit	Paola	KS	w	1871-1992+	Ga87,92,Baid90,92,Ay1887,1925,Ks [1871-date]
Baptist Globe	Parsons	KS		1895-1897	Ba
Parsons Evening Herald	Parsons	KS	w	1902-1904	Lc77

TITLE	CITY	ST.	FREQ.	DATES	SOURCES
Weekly Blade	Parsons	KS	w	1892-1904	Ba,Ay1894,Lc91,Oclc[e1901],WI[e1901], Ks[e1900],Boris1[1894-1898]
Freeman's Lance	Peru	KS	w	1891-1892	Ay1891,Lc77,Oclc
Sedan Lance	Peru	KS	w	1892-1909	Ks
Afro-American Review	Pittsburg	KS	w	1915-1916	Ba,Ks,Cam
Eclipse	Pittsburg	KS		1974	Oclc
Pittsburg Plain Dealer	Pittsburg	KS	w	1899-1900	Lc91,Oclc,WI,Moten,NWU
Uplift	Pittsburg	KS	w	1914-1914	Ba,Ks,Cam
UNIQUE	Prairie Village	KS	m	1971-1976	Ay1976
Afro-American	Salina	KS		1915-1916	Ba
Salina Enterprise	Salina	KS	w	1908-1912	Ba,Ay1909,NY12,Cam
Afro-American Baptist	Topeka	KS		1892-1894	Ba,Cam,Moten
American Citizen	Topeka	KS	w	1888-1909	Ba,Ay1889,Gr,Penn,Lc91,Oclc,WI[e1907], Moten,Ks[e1907],DANB410
Baptist Headlight	Topeka	KS	w/sm	1893-1894	Ba,Oclc,Lc91,WI,Moten,Ks
Capital Plaindealer	Topeka	KS	w	1937-1940	EP37-40
Chronicle	Topeka	KS	w	1939	EP39
Colored Citizen (1st)	Topeka	KS		1878-1880	Ba,Oclc,Moten,Ks[e1879],Gr,Lc91
Colored Citizen (2nd)	Topeka	KS		1897-1900	Ba,Oclc,WI,Moten,Ks,Gr,Lc91
Colored Patriot	Topeka	KS	w	1882-1882	Ba,Lc91,Oclc,WI,Gr
Colored Woman's Magazine	Topeka	KS	m	1916-1920	Ay1916-1920
Ebony Times	Topeka	KS	w	1972-1978	Oclc,Ks,EP75-78,Lb
Evening Call	Topeka	KS	d	1893-1893	Ba,Lc91,Oclc[1891-1893?],Ks,WI
Helper	Topeka	KS	m	1912-1919	NY12,19
Herald of Kansas	Topeka	KS	w	1880-1880	Oclc,Lc91,WI,Ks,NWU
Kansas American	Topeka	KS	w	1933-1960	Ba,Ay1940,1960,Oclc,NH42,44, Ks[1936-1956],EP38-40,Dc41
Kansas Baptist Herald	Topeka	KS		1911-1913	Ba,Cam,Moten
Kansas Blackman	Topeka	KS	w	1894-1896	Ba,Oclc,WI,Lc91
Kansas Daily State Ledger	Topeka	KS	d	1893	Gr
Kansas Herald	Topeka	KS	w	1880-1880	Ba,Lc91,Oclc,Ks,Moten
Kansas Sentinel	Topeka	KS	w	1960-1961	Ay1961,Ks[1960-1960]
Kansas State Ledger	Topeka	KS	w	1892-1894	Ba,Ay1896[b1894],1906,1908,1909,Gr,Ks, Oclc,Lc91,WI
Kansas State Tribune	Topeka	KS	w	1881-1881	Moten
Kansas Tradesman	Topeka	KS		1922	NY22
Kansas Watchman	Topeka	KS	w	1903-1912	Ba,Ay1906,1908,1909,NY12,Gr,Ks
Little Weekly	Topeka	KS	w	1936-1944	Ba,NH42,44,EP38,Dc41
Messenger	Topeka	KS	w	1969-1970	Ks,Lb
National Watchman	Topeka	KS	w	1914-1915	Ba,Moten,Ks,Cam
Paul Jones Magazine	Topeka	KS		1912	NY12
People's Friend	Topeka	KS	w	1894-1898	Ba,Lc91,WI,Ks[b1896]
Plaindealer	Topeka	KS	w	1899-1900	Ks
State Ledger	Topeka	KS	w	1894-1912	Ba,Ay1905,Lc91,Oclc,Ks,NY12,Gr

TITLE	CITY	ST.	FREQ.	DATES	SOURCES
Third Baptist Church Herald	Topeka	KS		1911-1913	Ba,Cam,Moten[e1911]
Times Observer	Topeka	KS	w	1888-1892	Ba,Oclc,Gr,Lc91
Times-Observer	Topeka	KS	w	1891-1892	Oclc,WI,Ks,Moten
Topeka Call	Topeka	KS	w	1890-1898	Ba,Ay1894,1896,Moten,Eur94,Br,Lc91,Gr, Oclc
Topeka Plaindealer	Topeka	KS	w	1900-1945	Ba,Ay1905,1945,Oclc,Sch,WI,Ks,NY12, 19,22,26,32,Lt1907,Yenser6
Topeka Tribune	Topeka	KS	w	1883-1883	Moten
Tribune	Topeka	KS	w	1880-1881	Ba,Oclc,Moten,Gr
Weekly Call	Topeka	KS	w	1893-1899	Ba,Lc91,Oclc,WI,Ks[1893-1898]
Western Index	Topeka	KS	w	1908-1921	Ba,Ay1914,1916-1921,NY12,Moten, Mather
Western Recorder	Topeka	KS	w	1882-1885	Moten,DANB627[Douglas Co.]
Western Trumpet	Topeka	KS		1908	Mather [Hamlett, James Arthur]
Broad Ax	Wichita	KS		pre 1970	Ba
Colored Citizen	Wichita	KS		1902-1904	Ba,Br,Cam
Enlightener	Wichita	KS	w	1962-1970	EP62,64,65,67,69,70,Lb
Factorian	Wichita	KS	w	1913-1914	Ba,Moten,Cam
Heart of the City	Wichita	KS	w	1993+	Ga94
Kansas Black Journal	Wichita	KS	w	1984	EP84
Kansas Globe	Wichita	KS	w	1887-1889	Ba,Ay1888,Cam
Kansas Headlight	Wichita	KS	w	1894-1895	Ba,Oclc,Ks,Lc91
Kansas Journal	Wichita	KS	w	1940-1944	NH42,44,EP43,Dc41
Kansas Weekly Journal	Wichita	KS	w	1970-1987	Ay1981,SPD87 [see Wichita Times]
National Baptist World	Wichita	KS	w	1894-1894	Ba,Lc91,Oclc,WI,Moten,Ks
National Reflector 1st	Wichita	KS	w	1894-1900	Ba,Cam,lc,Br,WI[1895-1897],Ks [1895-1897]
National Reflector 2nd	Wichita	KS	w	1912-1913	Ba,Cam,Moten
Negro Star	Wichita	KS	w	1908-1954	Ba,Ay1921,1953,Oclc,Lc77,NH42,46, ABSCHSL,Moten[b1920],EP37,49,Ks [1920-1953],NY19,22,26,32,46,Dc41,44, Boris1
News Hawk	Wichita	KS	w	1965-1979	Oclc,EBA,EP71,75,76,Lb
People's Elevator	Wichita	KS	w	1892-1943	Ba,Ks[1924-1926],AY1925[1892]
People's Friend	Wichita	KS	w	1891-1894	Ba,Cam,Lc91,Oclc,WI,Ks
Plaindealer	Wichita	KS	w	1945-1950	Ay1945,1950
Post Observer	Wichita	KS	w	1908-1955	Ay1955,Ks[1953-1954]
Times	Wichita	KS	w	1912-1958	Ay1958,Ay1955
Wichita Globe	Wichita	KS		1887-1889	Ba,Cam
Wichita Protest	Wichita	KS	w	1918-1931	Ba,Ay1921,1925,NY26,Br,Boris1
Wichita Searchlight	Wichita	KS	w	1899-1914	Ba,Ay1905,1914,Oclc,WI,Moten,NY12, Lt1907,Cam
Wichita Times	Wichita	KS	w	1970-1978	EBA,EH,EP71-78,Lb,Bp
Wichita Tribune	Wichita	KS	w	1896-1900	Ba,Lc91,Oclc[1898-1899],WI,Ks [1898-1899],Gr
Colored Teacher		KY		pre 1915	Mather [Foreman, Edgar Seward]

TITLE	CITY	ST.	FREQ.	DATES	SOURCES
Right House		KY		1908	Br
Independent	Ashland	KY		pre 1946	Ba,Br,Ay1912[b1896 nlb?]
Mouthpiece	Bandana	KY		1901-1903	Ba
Citizen	Berea	KY		1922	NY22
Eagle Eye	Bowling Green	KY	w	1903-1904	Ba,Oclc
Liberty	Bowling Green	KY	w	1910-1912	Ba,Ay1911,1912
Watchman	Bowling Green	KY		1888-1892	Ba,Penn
Informer	Cadiz	KY	w	1904-1937	Ba,Ay1909,1935,NY12,19,22,26,32,Boris1
Southern News	Cave Spring	KY		1903-1904	Ba
Suspension Press	Covington	KY	w	1982-1994+	Ga90,94,Oclc,Baid92
Torch Light	Danville	KY	w	1902-1932	Ba,Ay1908,1925,NY12,19,22,26,Go, Lt1907
Tribune	Danville	KY	w	1878-1892	Ba,Ay1887-1889,Penn
Defender	Eminence	KY		1900-1902	Ba
Blue Grass Bugle	Frankfort	KY	w	1898-1915	Ba,Ay1905,1915,Oclc,NY12,Lt1907, Boris1
Kentucky Institute Review	Frankfort	KY	m	1912-1922	NY12,19,22
Kentucky Masonic Herald	Frankfort	KY		1919-1922	NY19,22
Kentucky Thorobred	Frankfort	KY	m	1946-1951	EP51,NY46
Sunday School Union Watch	Fulton	KY		1885-1891	Ba,Ay1889,1890
Kentucky Missionary Visitor	Henderson?	KY		pre 1915	Mather [Kennedy, Paul Horace]
Globe Journal	Hopkinsville	KY	w	1936-1943	Ba,NH42,44,EP36,43,Dc41,44
Glove Democrat	Hopkinsville	KY		1940-1942	Ba
Hopkinsville Times	Hopkinsville	KY		1922-1926	NY22,26
Indicator	Hopkinsville	KY	w	1893-1898	Ba,Ay1894,1896,Eur94,Br
Kentucky News	Hopkinsville	KY	w	1912-1930	Ba,Go
Major	Hopkinsville	KY	w	1897-1904	Ba,R1898,Br
New Age	Hopkinsville	KY	w	1919-1925	Ba,Ay1925,NY19,22,26,Go,Boris1 [e1927]
Saturday News	Hopkinsville	KY	w	1919-1922	NY19,22
Freeman	Lebanon	KY	sm	1909-1912	Ba,Ay1911,1912
Callaloo: A Black South Journal of Arts and Letters	Lexington	KY	3xy	1977-1982+	BJ
Herald	Lexington	KY	w	1886-1888	Ba,Ay1887
Inter-State County News	Lexington	KY	w	1935-1940	EP35-40
Kentucky Soldier	Lexington	KY	w	1889-1892	Ba,Ay1890,1891
Lexington Democrat	Lexington	KY	w	1900	DANB39
Lexington Standard	Lexington	KY	w	1892-1912	Ba,Ay1894,1912,Lc91,Oclc,WI,Lt1907, R1900,Gr,DANB558,Mather
Lexington Times	Lexington	KY	w	1922-1926	NY22,26
News	Lexington	KY	w	1912-1926	Ba,Ay1913,1921,Go,NY12,19,22,26, Mather
Record	Lexington	KY	w	1938	EP38
Visitor	Lexington	KY		1880-1890	Ba
African Mission Herald	Louisville	KY		1897-1905	Ba (see Richmond VA)

TITLE	CITY	ST.	FREQ.	DATES	SOURCES
American Baptist	Louisville	KY	w	1879-1988	Ba,Ay1886,1980,Ga87,88,ABSCHSL, NH42,46,R1888,1898,1900,EH,Eur94, NY12,EP49,72[1880],76,NY19,22,26,32, 46,Penn,Dc41,44,Lt1907,Lb,Boris1
Black Committee for Self-Defense	Louisville	KY		1971	WI
Black Rag	Louisville	KY		1969	WI
Blade	Louisville	KY		pre 1970	Ba
Bulletin	Louisville	KY	w	1879-1885	Ba,Ay1884,Penn,Br,Lc91,Oclc,WI, DANB[e1886]
Champion	Louisville	KY	w	1890-1893	Ba,Ay1891,DANB558
Christian Banner	Louisville	KY		1890-1895	Ba,Penn
Citizen	Louisville	KY		1908-1910	Ba
Columbian	Louisville	KY	w	1899-1917	Ba,Ay1908,1909,1911-1917,NY12
Columbian Herald	Louisville	KY	w	1913-1927	Ba,Go,NY19,22,26,Boris1
Courant	Louisville	KY		1883-1886	Ba
Crescent Magazine	Louisville	KY		1916-1928	Boris2 [Banks, Edward Palmer]
Deep South Patriot	Louisville	KY		1966	WI
Defender	Louisville	KY		1912-1915	Ba,NY12
Fall City News	Louisville	KY	w	1912-1947	Ba,NH42,44,46,Dc41
Independent News	Louisville	KY	w	1936	EP36
Informer	Louisville	KY		1887-1902	Ba
Ivy Leaf	Louisville	KY	q	1940	Ay1940
Jefferson Reporter	Louisville	KY	w	1953-1954	Ay1954
Kentucky Home Finder	Louisville	KY		1913-1922	Ba,NY19,22
Kentucky Home Reporter	Louisville	KY		1922	Go
Kentucky Methodist	Louisville	KY		1872	Penn
Kentucky Reporter	Louisville	KY	w	1913-1953	Ba,Ay1913,1953,NH42,46,EP38,49,NY12, 19,22,26,32,Dc41,44,Go,Br,Boris1
Kentucky Standard	Louisville	KY	w	1898-1912	Ba,Ay1905,1912,DANB559
K.N.E.A. Bulletin	Louisville	KY	bm	1922-1953	Ay1953
K.N.E.A. Journal	Louisville	KY	bm/q	1939-1951	Ay1950,EP39,51
K.T.A. Journal	Louisville	KY	4xy	1922-1956	Ay1956
Louisville Defender	Louisville	KY	w	1933-1994+	Ba,Ay1940,1975,Lc91,Ga87,94,Oclc,WI, NH42,44,46,49,EP35,93,Baid92,EBA, BRG,EH,NY46,Dc41,44,API94,Bl, Fleming
Louisville Herald Tribune	Louisville	KY	w	1938	EP38
Louisville Leader	Louisville	KY	w	1917-1953	Ba,Ay1921S,1953,Br,NH42,44,46,49, EP38,51,Sch,NY22,26,32,46,Dc41,44, Yenser6
Louisville News	Louisville	KY	w	1912-1947	Ba,Ay1913,1925,Cam,NH44,46,49,EP38, 50,NY19,22,26,32,46,Dc44,Go,Mather, Yenser6
Mission Herald	Louisville	KY		1897-1912	Ba[1905],NY12
Moderator	Louisville	KY	w	1912	NY12
New South	Louisville	KY	w	1894-1897	Ba,Ay1896,Br

TITLE	CITY	ST.	FREQ.	DATES	SOURCES
Ohio Falls Express	Louisville	KY	w	1878-1904	Ba,Ay1886,1896,Lc91,Oclc,WI,Eur94,Gr, Penn,R1888
Opinion	Louisville	KY	w	1891-1895	Ba,Ay1894
Our Women and Children	Louisville	KY	m	1888-1890	Ay1889,1890
Planet	Louisville	KY		1872-1875	Ba,Penn
Southern Newsletter	Louisville	KY		1956-1960	WI
Southern Patriot	Louisville	KY	m	1942-1977	EP75,76,77
Standard	Louisville	KY		1922	NY22
Reporter	Mt. Sterling	KY	w	1904-1915	Ba,Ay1908,1909,1911
Defender	New Castle	KY		1900-1901	Ba
New Liberty Parchment	New Liberty	KY		1989	ABSCHSL
Clarion	Owensboro	KY	w	1894	Eur94
Enterprise	Owensboro	KY	w	1922-1925	Ba,Ay1925
Freedman's Clarion	Owensboro	KY		1892-1895	Ba
Kentucky Progress	Owensboro	KY	w	1888-1891	Ay1891
Kentucky Reporter	Owensboro	KY	w	1900-1912	Ba,Ay1905,1906,1912
Ohio Valley Clarion	Owensboro	KY	w	1892-1898	Ba,Ay1894,1896
Rising Sun	Owensboro	KY		1934-1935	Ba
Sunday Unionist	Owensboro	KY	w	1892-1898	Ba,Ay1896,Br
Western Kentucky Progress	Owensboro	KY	w	1888-1890	Ay1890
Baptist Herald	Paducah	KY		1873-1875	Ba,Penn,AAE3
Harrison Street Light House	Paducah	KY	w	1908-1912	Ay1912
Light House	Paducah	KY	w	1908-1937	Ba,Ay1912,1937,NY26,Boris1
Struggler	Paducah	KY	w	1938-1939	EP38,39
Blue Grass Chronicle	Paris	KY	w	1890-1895	Ba,Ay1894
Baptist Voice	Princeton	KY	w	1905-1920	Ba,Ay1907,1911-1913,1915,1916,1918
Sentinel	Richmond	KY	w	1908-1912	Ba,Ay1911,1912,NY12
Zion Western Advocate	Russellville	KY	w	1888-1891	Ba,Ay1891
Lincoln Institute Worker	Simpsonville	KY	q	1919-1922	NY19,22
Mouthpiece	Wickliffe	KY		1901-1902	Ba
Gate City Journal	Winchester	KY		1893-1896	Ba
National Chronicle	Winchester	KY	w	1891-1915	Ay1891,Mather
Advance	Alexandria	LA		pre 1927	Boris1 [Young, Isaac William]
Advance Messenger	Alexandria	LA	w	1909-1938	Ba,Ay1912-1916,Go,NY12,19,22,26,32, Mather
Alexandria Community Leader	Alexandria	LA	w	1978-1997	EP78,79,SPD87
Alexandria News Weekly	Alexandria	LA	w	1975-1994+	Ay1980,Ga87,94,Oclc,Baid92,BRG,EP84, 93[1959],API90,94,SPD87
Louisiana Baptist	Alexandria	LA	w/sm	1898-1916	Ba,Ay1905,1916,Oclc,NY12
News Leader	Alexandria	LA	w	1962-1975	Oclc[1963-1975],EBA,EH,EP64,77,Bp
Observer	Alexandria	LA	w	1942-1949	Ba,NH44,EP42,49
Progressive Age	Alexandria	LA		1897-1901	Ba,Br
Weekly Leader	Alexandria	LA	w	1890	Penn
Lifer	Angola	LA		1973-1976	EP75,76

TITLE	CITY	ST.	FREQ.	DATES	SOURCES
Banner	Baton Rouge	LA	w	1904-1915	Ba,Ay1908,1913,Lt1907,Cam
Baton Rouge Community Leader	Baton Rouge	LA	w	1977-1992+	Ga88,92,API90,Bp,Lb,EP78,90, Oclc[1977-1982?],Baid92,SPD87
Baton Rouge Herald	Baton Rouge	LA	w	1960-1961	Oclc
Baton Rouge News Leader	Baton Rouge	LA	w	1952-1979	Oclc,EBA,EH,EP62,77,SPD67,79,87
Baton Rouge Post	Baton Rouge	LA	w	1983	Oclc
Baton Rouge Post	Baton Rouge	LA	w	1937-1938	Oclc,EP38
Baton Rouge Weekly Press	Baton Rouge	LA	w	1982-1994+	Oclc,API90,94
Capital City Weekly	Baton Rouge	LA	w	1946-1946	Ba,Oclc
Christian Standard	Baton Rouge	LA		1902-1904	Ba
Digest	Baton Rouge	LA	w/bm	1930-1978	Ay1969,1970,1975,1978
Eagle Dispatch	Baton Rouge	LA	w	1930-1932	Ba,NY32
Industrial Letter	Baton Rouge	LA		1900-1902	Ba
Observer	Baton Rouge	LA	w	1899-1900	Ba,Lc91,WI,Gr
Southern University Digest	Baton Rouge	LA	2xm	1946	NY46
Current	Bayou Goula	LA	w	1902-1907	Ba,Ay1906,Lt1907
Watchman	Benton	LA	w/d	1898-1914	Ba,Ay1912,1913,1914
Hurricane	Bossier City	LA	w	1966-1972	Pr,EP67,71[1960],EBA,SPD67,70,74
Davis' Educational Review	Campti	LA	m	1910-1912	Ay1912
Enterprise	Clinton	LA		1901-1907	Ba
Afro-American Citizen	Delhi	LA		1904-1911	Ba
American Citizen	Delhi	LA	w	1904-1912	Ba,Ay1908,1909,1911,NY12
Madison Vindicator	Delta	LA		1878-1882	Ba,Penn
Business Herald	Donaldsonville	LA		1898-1904	Ba,Mather
Fraternal Union	Donaldsonville	LA	w	1906-1909	Ay1908,1909
La Fourche Monitor	Donaldsonville	LA	w	1938	EP38
Monitor	Donaldsonville	LA	w	1940-1942	Ba,NH42,Dc41
Gramblinite	Grambling	LA	w	1936-1973	Bp
Colored American Appeal	Gretna	LA	w	1906-1910	Ba,Ay1908,1909
Southern Racer	Hammond	LA	w	1910-1912	Ba,Ay1912
Terre Bonne Messenger	Houma	LA	w	1895-1897	Ba,Ay1896
Acadian Community Leader	Lafayette	LA	w	1979-1987	EP79,SPD87
Blaze	Lafayette	LA		pre 1979	Lb
Creole Magazine	Lafayette	LA		pre 1979	Lb
Lafayette News Leader	Lafayette	LA	w	1970-1976	Oclc,WI,EBA,EH,EP71-76,Bp
Broad Ax	Lake Charles	LA		1898-1900	Ba
Index	Lake Charles	LA		1897-1899	Ba
Lake Charles Community Leader	Lake Charles	LA	w	1978-1979	EP78,79
Lake Charles News Leader	Lake Charles	LA	w	1965-1973	Oclc,EP69-77,EBA,EH,WI[1968],Bp
New Light Baptist Paper	Lake Charles	LA	w	1911-1912	Ba,Ay1912
Searchlight	Lake Charles	LA		1898-1900	Ba,Br
Wave	Mandeville	LA		1876-1883	Ba,JQ1947
Colored Reformer	Minden	LA	w	1906-1908	Ba,Ay1908
Black Free Press	Monroe	LA	w	1973-1974	Oclc

TITLE	CITY	ST.	FREQ.	DATES	SOURCES
Broadcast	Monroe	LA	w	1932-1936	Ba,EP35,Sch,BJ286
Free Press	Monroe	LA	w/sw	1973-1993+	Oclc,EP69,93[b1969]
Monroe Community Leader	Monroe	LA	w	1979-1987	EP79,SPD87
Monroe Dispatch	Monroe	LA	w	1975-1994+	Oclc,BRG,EP75,93,WPN94
Negro in Louisiana	Monroe	LA	w	pre 1936	BJ286
News Leader	Monroe	LA	w	1962-1976	Oclc,WI,EBA,EH,EP64,76,Bp,SPD70,74
Rapping Black	Monroe	LA	w	1969-1973	Oclc
Southern Broadcast	Monroe	LA	w	1932-1938	Ba,Sch,EP36-39
Twin City Journal	Monroe	LA	w	1940	EP40
Twin City Tribune	Monroe	LA	w	1941-1944	EP41,44
Press	Morgan City	LA		1905-1915	Ba,NY12
African Methodist	New Orleans	LA	w	1898-1906	Ba,Ay1905
Black Collegian	New Orleans	LA	4xy	1970-1994+	Ay1975,1980,Ga87,94,WI,BJ53[b1969]
Black Data Weekly	New Orleans	LA	w	1977-1978	EP77,78
Black PAC Epitaph	New Orleans	LA		197u-1972	Oclc
Black Republican	New Orleans	LA	w	1865-1865	Oclc,NWU,Lc91,WI
Broadcast	New Orleans	LA		1934-1936	Ba
Bulletin	New Orleans	LA		1920-1925	Ba,NY22,26
Business Journal	New Orleans	LA		1912-1915	Ba,NY12
Carrollton Advocate	New Orleans	LA	ir	1970-1970	Oclc,WI
Central Christian Advocate	New Orleans	LA	sm	1940-1960	Ay1950,1960,EP50,51
Christian Herald	New Orleans	LA	w	1888-1896	Ba,Ay1889-1891,1894,Eur94
Claverite	New Orleans	LA		1952-1979	WI
Courier	New Orleans	LA	w	1910-1971	Ay1971
Crusader	New Orleans	LA	w	1889-1898	Oclc,WI
Crusader	New Orleans	LA	d	1887-1896	Ba,Ay1890,Penn,Cam,Lc91,Oclc[b1891]
Daily Spokesman	New Orleans	LA	d	1914	Oclc
Express	New Orleans	LA		1902-1905	Ba
Ferret	New Orleans	LA	w	1891-1903	Ba,Eur94
Ferret and Journal of the Lodge	New Orleans	LA	w	1891-1903	Ba,Ay1894
Free Lance	New Orleans	LA	w	1891-1894	Ba,Eur94
Free Speech	New Orleans	LA		1893	Ba
Herald	New Orleans	LA	bw	1925-1936	Ba,Oclc
Informer and Sentinel	New Orleans	LA	w	1939-1951	Ba,Ay1950,NH46,49,EP45,51,NY46,Dc44
Inside New Orleans	New Orleans	LA	w	1963-1974	Oclc,SPD67,70,74[b1963]
Journal of the Lodge	New Orleans	LA	w	1887-1903	Ba,Ay1896,1891,Penn
Journal of the National Technical Assoc.	New Orleans	LA	w	1988-1994+	Ga88,94
La Tribune de la Nouvelle Orleans	New Orleans	LA	d	1864-1870	Br,DANB601[1864-1868,1869]
Le Dimanche	New Orleans	LA	w	1861-1862	Lc91,Sch,NWU
Louisiana Crusader	New Orleans	LA	w	1903-1907	Ba,Ay1906
Louisiana Daily	New Orleans	LA	d	1870-1888	Br
Louisiana Record	New Orleans	LA	w	1905-1910	Ba,Ay1908,1909
Louisiana Republican	New Orleans	LA	w	1881-1886	Ba,Ay1882,Br,Oclc

TITLE	CITY	ST.	FREQ.	DATES	SOURCES
Louisiana Standard	New Orleans	LA	w	1883-1890	Ba,Ay1884,1887,1889
Louisiana Weekly	New Orleans	LA	w	1925-1994+	Ba,Ay1940,1975,Ga87,94,Oclc,WI,NH42, 44,46,49,EP35,92,Baid92,BRG,EH,EBA, NY32,46,Dc41,44,SPD67,WPN94,API94, Fleming
Louisianian	New Orleans	LA	w/sw	1870-1882	Ba,Ay1880[b1872],1882,Cam,Lc91,Oclc, WI,Go,DANB16,493[e1881],Penn
Messenger	New Orleans	LA	w	1912	NY12
Missionary Messenger	New Orleans	LA	w	1919-1922	NY19,22
Monitor	New Orleans	LA		1893-1896	Ba
National Forecast	New Orleans	LA		1892-1893	Ba
National Negro Voice	New Orleans	LA	w	1924-1938	Ba,Ay1925,NY26,32,Boris1
National Times	New Orleans	LA	w	1938-1946	Ba,NH42,44,46,EP38,Dc41,44
Negro Advocate	New Orleans	LA	m	1917-1926	Ba,Ay1921,NY22,26
Negro Gazette	New Orleans	LA		1872-1874	Ba,Br
Negro South	New Orleans	LA	m	1937-1950	Ay1950,EP46,48,BJ[1946-1947]
New Orleans Daily Creole	New Orleans	LA	d	1856-1857	Lc91,WI
New Orleans Data News Weekly	New Orleans	LA	w	1966-1994+	Ga90,94,Lb,Oclc,EP80,90[b1964], 91[b1920],93,BRG,Baid92,WPN94
New Orleans Tribune	New Orleans	LA	w	1985-1987	EP87
News-Enterprise	New Orleans	LA		1913-1914	Ba
Nkombo	New Orleans	LA	q	1968-1974	WI,SPD74
NSBE Journal	New Orleans	LA		1988-1990	Ga88,90
Observer	New Orleans	LA	w	1878-1882	Ba,Ay1880,Penn
Olio	New Orleans	LA	m/bm	1912-1922	NY12,19,22
Pelican	New Orleans	LA	w	1886-1889	Ay1889
People's Journal	New Orleans	LA		1877-1881	Ba,Penn
Plain Truth of New Orleans	New Orleans	LA	bm,m	1969-1970	Oclc,WI
Republican	New Orleans	LA	w	1893-1896	Ay1896
Republican Courier	New Orleans	LA	w	1899-1900	Ba,Lc91,Oclc,WI,NWU
Republican Liberator	New Orleans	LA	w	1912	NY12
Rescue	New Orleans	LA	w	1893-1896	Ba,Ay1894,Br
Royal Banner	New Orleans	LA		1910-1914	Ba
Saturday Crusader	New Orleans	LA	w	1889-1896	Ba,Ay1896
Semi-Weekly Louisianian	New Orleans	LA	sw	1871-1872	Oclc
SENGA	New Orleans	LA	q	1989-1993+	Ga94
Sentinel	New Orleans	LA	w	1940-1946	Ba,Br,Sch,NH42,44,EP43,44,Dc41
Sepia Socialite	New Orleans	LA	w	1936-1946	Ba,Ay1946,Oclc[1937-1945],Br,NH44,46, EP38,45,Sch,NY46,Dc44,BJ[b1937]
Southern Age	New Orleans	LA	w	1903-1915	Ba,Ay1911[1904],NY12,Mather
Southern Patriot	New Orleans	LA		1942	WI
Southern Republican	New Orleans	LA	w	1898-1907	Ba,Ay1905,1906,NWU,Lc91,WI
Southwestern Christian Advocate	New Orleans	LA	w	1866-1944	Ba,Ay1887,1939[Christian Advocate], NY12,19,22,26,32,Lt1907,Penn,Mather
Spectator	New Orleans	LA	w	1982-1983	Oclc

TITLE	CITY	ST.	FREQ.	DATES	SOURCES
Spokesman	New Orleans	LA	w	1910-1919	Ba,Ay1915,1916,1919,Mather
Standard Pelican	New Orleans	LA	w	1886-1893	Ba,Ay1891,1890,Cam
Sun	New Orleans	LA	w	1950	Ay1950
Tabernacle Journal of U. O.	New Orleans	LA		1919-1922	NY19,22
Tribune	New Orleans	LA		1892-1900	Ba
Tribune de la Nouvelle Orleans	New Orleans	LA	d,w,tw	1864-1870	Ba,Lc91,Oclc,WI (see La Tribune), DANB534,Lc77
Union a.k.a. L'Union	New Orleans	LA	tw,sw	1862-1869	Ba,NWU,Lc91,Oclc,WI,Bl,DANB534 [1862-1864]
Vindicator	New Orleans	LA		1890-1900	Ba,Br
Weekly Louisianian	New Orleans	LA	w	1870-1882	Oclc,WI,NWU
Weekly Pelican	New Orleans	LA	w	1886-1893	Ba,Ay1888,Lc91,Oclc,WI,Penn
Wide Awake	New Orleans	LA	w	1893-1898	Ba,Ay1896
Xavier Herald	New Orleans	LA	m	1943-1951	NH46,EP50,51,NY46,Dc44
Pledge	Norwood	LA		1901-1903	Ba
Baptist Advocate	Opelousas	LA	w	1905-1922	Ba,Ay1906,1911,NY12,19,22,Lt1907
Drum	Ponchatoula	LA	w	1987-1994+	Oclc,API94
Colored Globe	Ruston	LA	w	1904-1905	Ba,Ay1905
New Era	Ruston	LA	w	1904-1908	Ba,Ay1906,1908
Southern Voice	Saint Joseph	LA	w	1907	Lt1907
Progress	Saint Landry	LA		pre 1970	Ba
Echo	Saint Martinville	LA	w	1872-1878	Ba,Lc91,Oclc,WI,NWU
Weekly Messenger	Saint Martinville	LA	w	1912	NY12
Baton Rouge Scotland Press	Scotlandville	LA	w	1975-1979	Oclc
Afro-American	Shreveport	LA	w	1930-1932	Ba,Oclc[192?-1932?],NY32
Christian Messenger	Shreveport	LA	w	1903-1906	Ba,Ay1905,1906
Councilor	Shreveport	LA		1963	WI
Enterprise	Shreveport	LA		1897-1922	Ba
Lantern	Shreveport	LA		1992	ABSCHSL
Louisiana Post Dispatch	Shreveport	LA	w	1935	EP35
Louisiana Searchlight	Shreveport	LA	w	1905-1915	Ba,Ay1906,1913,NY12,Lt1907
Louisiana Standard	Shreveport	LA		1905-1915	Ba
Messenger	Shreveport	LA	w	1901-1905	Ba,Ay1905
New Era	Shreveport	LA	w	1919-1924	Ba,Ay1921
News-Enterprise	Shreveport	LA	w	1897-1926	Ba,Ay1905,1919,NY12,19,22,26,Lt1907, Go
Record	Shreveport	LA		1896-1901	Ba,Br
Royal Banner	Shreveport	LA	w	1911-1921	Ba,Ay1913,1914,1916-1918,1920,1921
Shreveport Ebony Times	Shreveport	LA	w	1972-1983	NA83,EP77,78[1972]
Shreveport Sun	Shreveport	LA	w	1920-1994+	Ba,Ay1925,1980,Ga87,94,Oclc,NH,42,44, 46,49,EP35,93,Baid92,EBA,BRG,EH, NY22,26,32,46,Dc41,44,API90,94, WPN94,Boris1,SPD67,70,74
Shreveport Sun and Business News	Shreveport	LA	w	1964-1966	Oclc

TITLE	CITY	ST.	FREQ.	DATES	SOURCES
Shreveport Community Ebony Tribune	Shreveport	LA	w	1994+	SPD94
Southern Star	Shreveport	LA		1904-1906	Ba,Ay1906
Watchman	Shreveport	LA	d/w	1896-1927	Ba,Ay1905,1911[1883],NY12,19,22,26, Go,Lt1907,Boris1
World	Shreveport	LA	w	1940-1946	Ba,NH42,44,46,EP41,45,NY46,Dc41,44
Echo	Slidell	LA	w	1907-1909	Ba,Ay1909
Negro Voice	Tallulah	LA	w	1908-1912	Ba,Ay1911,NY12
LaFourche Monitor	Thibodaux	LA	w	1904-1939	Ba,Ay1909,1939,NY12,19,22
Tabernacle Herald	Thibodaux	LA	w	1910-1924	Ba,Ay1919-1921
Concordia Eagle	Vidalia	LA	w	1873-1890	Ba,Ay1880,1882,1884,Gr,Lc91,Oclc,WI
MABP Newsletter	Westbrook	ME		1973-1976	EP75,76
Negro Appeal	Annapolis	MD	w	1899-1900	Ba,Lc91,WI,Gr
Afro-American	Baltimore	MD	w	1892-1994+	Ba,Ay1896,1983,Ga87,94,Oclc,EP35,93, Baid92,EBA,EH,NY19,22,26,32,46,Dc41, 44,NH42,44,46,49,API94,WPN94, Yenser3,SPD67,70,74,9
Afro-American Ledger	Baltimore	MD	w	1899-1925	Ba,Ay1905,1917,NY12,Oclc,Rw,Brooks, Mather
Alternative Press Index	Baltimore	MD	4xy	1969-1994+	Ga90,94
American Citizen	Baltimore	MD		1879-1897	Ba,Ay1880,Gr,Lc91,WI,Yenser6
Annapolis Times	Baltimore	MD	w	1994+	API94
Baltimore Spokesman	Baltimore	MD		1893-1895	Boris1 [Hawkins, William Ashbie]
Baltimore Times	Baltimore	MD		1909-1928	Ba[1912-1915],NY12,Mather
Baltimore Times	Baltimore	MD	w	1986-1994+	EP91,92,93,BRG,API94
Baptist Messenger	Baltimore	MD	m	1883-1912	Ba,Ay1884,1912
Callaloo	Baltimore	MD	q	1978-1994+	Ga90,94,Baid92
Church Advocate	Baltimore	MD		1892-1922	Ba[e1898],NY12,22,Mather
Colored Catholic	Baltimore	MD	w/m	1909-1914	Ba,Ay1911-1914,NY12
Colored Harvest	Baltimore	MD	m	1888-1955	Ay1950,1955,EP48-51
Colored Man	Baltimore	MD		1913-1915	Ba
Commonwealth	Baltimore	MD		1886-1887	Ba,Penn,Mather[1884],DANB[1884]
Commonwealth	Baltimore	MD	w	1914-1921	Ba,Ay1921,Lc91,Oclc,WI,NWU,NY19
Companion	Baltimore	MD	w	1907	Lt1907
Crusader	Baltimore	MD	w	1886-1926	Ba,Ay1896,1914,NY12,19,22,26,Br,Go, Lt1907,Mather[1915-1944]
Dawn	Baltimore	MD	m	1887-1908	Ba,Ay1905,1906,1908
Every Wednesday	Baltimore	MD	w	1984-1994+	Ga90,94,Baid92
Examiner	Baltimore	MD		1892-1908	Ba,Ay1894
Golden Enterprise	Baltimore	MD		1879-1882	Ba,Penn
Guide	Baltimore	MD		1903-1907	Ba
Herald	Baltimore	MD	w	1917-1921	Ba,Ay1921
Herald and Commonwealth	Baltimore	MD	w	1917-1937	Ba,Ay1925,1937,NY22,26,32,Go,Br, Boris1
Industrial News Dispatch	Baltimore	MD		1922-1924	Ba

TITLE	CITY	ST.	FREQ.	DATES	SOURCES
Ivy	Baltimore	MD		1887-1890	Ba
Joy	Baltimore	MD		1887-1893	Ba
Lancet	Baltimore	MD	w	1901-1915	Ba,Ay1906,1912,Oclc,NY12,Boris1
Ledger	Baltimore	MD	w	1898-1899	Oclc,DANB58
Lyceum Observer	Baltimore	MD		1863	Oclc,DANB223
Maryland Director	Baltimore	MD		1882-1884	Ba
Maryland Home	Baltimore	MD	m	pre 1940	DANB58
Maryland Voice	Baltimore	MD		1920-1922	Ba,NY22
Morgan State College Bulletin	Baltimore	MD	m	1922-1950	EP50,NY22
Moses Bulletin	Baltimore	MD		1919	NY19
National Education Outlook Among Negroes	Baltimore	MD	m/bm	1937-1940	BJ
Negro Appeal	Baltimore	MD	w	1899-1900	Ba,Oclc
New Era	Baltimore	MD		1899-1909	Ba,Ay1906,1908,1909
Night Club News	Baltimore	MD	w	1938	EP38
Public Ledger	Baltimore	MD	d	1887-1891	Ba,Penn,Br
Race Standard	Baltimore	MD	w	1894-1898	Ba,Br,NWU,Lc91,Oclc,WI
Shore Times	Baltimore	MD		1994+	API94
Spokesman	Baltimore	MD	m	1946-1973	EP51,NY46,Bp
Star	Baltimore	MD	w	1887-1889	Ba,Ay1888,1887
Sunday School Helper	Baltimore	MD		1892	Penn,Rw,DANB463[1890-1896]
Times-Union	Baltimore	MD	w	1898-1912	Ba,Ay1906,1912,Lt1907
Tribune	Baltimore	MD		1910-1915	Mather [Chisum, Melvin Jack]
True Communicator	Baltimore	MD		1865-1866	Ba,Go,Penn
Urban Profile Magazine	Baltimore	MD	m	1988-1993+	Ga94
U.S. Black Engineer	Baltimore	MD	5xy	1980-1994+	Ga90,94,SPD94
Vindicator	Baltimore	MD		1880-1883	Ba,Ay1884,Penn
Record	Cumberland	MD		1900-1903	Ba
Signal	Cumberland	MD		1897-1900	Ba,Br
Delaware Conference Advocate	Easton	MD	m	1902-1906	Ba,Ay1905,1906
Dawn	Elkton	MD	m	1887-1904	Ba,Ay1896,1891,1894
Baptist Watchtower	Evansville	MD		1888-1892	Ba (see Evansville IN)
Afro-American Educator	Frederick	MD		1894-1896	Ba
Educator	Frederick	MD		1894-1897	Ba,Ay1896
Hornet	Frederick	MD	w	1902-1915	Ba,Ay1905,1906,1908,1909,NY12
Central Methodist	Frederick	MD		1886-1889	Ba,Penn
Methodist Banner	Frederick	MD		1889-1892	Ba (see Harpers Ferry, WV)
Message Magazine	Hagerstown	MD	6xy	1898-1994+	Ga90,94
Crusader	Hyattsville	MD	w	1978-1982	Ay1980,1982
Evangel	Laurel	MD		1972-1982	ABSCHSL
Tri-State News	Salisbury	MD		1912	NY12
Penal Colony	Amhurst	MA		1971	WI
Fort Devens Dispatch	Ayer	MA	w	1948-1964	Ay1964
Advance	Boston	MA	w	1896-1907	Ba,Ay1905,1906,Oclc,WI,Lc91

TITLE	CITY	ST.	FREQ.	DATES	SOURCES
Advocate	Boston	MA	w	1885-1890	Ba,Ay1886-1889,Penn,R1888
Alexander's Magazine	Boston	MA	m	1905-1909	BJ
Bay State Banner	Boston	MA	w	1965-1994+	Ay1969,1975,Ga87,94,Oclc,WI,EP70, 79[Roxbury],90[Dorchester],93,Baid92, EH,BRG,EBA,API94
Bayonet	Boston	MA		pre 1927	Boris1 [Gordon, Eugene]
Black Church	Boston	MA	q	1972-1974	BJ53
Boston Chronicle	Boston	MA	w	1915-1966	Ba,Ay1925,1966,Oclc,NH42,44,46,49, EP38,51,NY19,22,26,32,46,Dc41,44,Gr, Go,Br,Boris1,SPD67
Boston Colored Citizen	Boston	MA		1906	Mather [Alexander, Charles]
Boston Courant	Boston	MA	w	1890-1903	Ba,Ay1890,1894,Gr,Go,Br,Lc91,Oclc,WI, Eur94,DANB229[1897]
Boston News	Boston	MA		1976	EP76,Lb
Boston Sun	Boston	MA	w	1962-1970	EP64,SPD67,70,Lb
Challenge	Boston	MA	m/ir	1934-1937	BJ
Citizen	Boston	MA		1895-1906	Ba,Mather[1915]
City News	Boston	MA	w	1965-1974	Pr,EP65,70,SPD67,70,74
Colored American Magazine	Boston	MA	m	1900-1912	Ay1906,1909,1912,BJ[e1909],Mather
Congregationalist	Boston	MA		1897-1898	Ba
Cooperator	Boston	MA		1879-1883	Ba,Penn
Freedmen's Record	Boston	MA		1865-1874	WI
Graphic	Boston	MA	w	1962-1967	EP62,SPD67
Guardian	Boston	MA	w	1901-1959	Ba,Ay1905,1960,Oclc,WI,Go,Rw,NH44, 46,49,EP35,51,NY12,19,22,26,32,46,Dc41, 44,Yenser4
Hub	Boston	MA	w	1879-1885	Ba,Mather,DANB662
Hub and Advocate	Boston	MA		1885-1890	Ba
Jacob's Band Monthly	Boston	MA	m	pre 1950	Fleming [Adams, Alton Augustus]
Leader	Boston	MA	m	1875-1881	Ba,Ay1880,Penn
Mixer and Server	Boston	MA	m	1905-1907	Boris1 [Anderson, Forrest B.]
New Boston Citizen	Boston	MA	w	1966-1970	Pr,EP67,69,70,Lb
New Challenge	Boston	MA	m/ir	1937-1937	BJ
New England Torchlight	Boston	MA		1890-1902	Ba,Mather
New Era	Boston	MA		1916-1917	DANB3265
Observer	Boston	MA		1881-1883,79	Ba,Penn
Opinion	Boston	MA		1923-1925	Ba
Orator	Boston	MA	w	1966-1974	Bp,SPD67,70,74
Pine and Palm	Boston	MA		1845-1865	Ba
Poetic Journal	Boston	MA		1912-1914	Mather,Boris1 [Braithwaite and Oxley]
Reliance	Boston	MA	w	1911-1915	Ba,Boris2
Republican	Boston	MA		1888-1893	Ba
Review	Boston	MA	m	1894-1896	Ay1896,Mather[b1893]
Saturday Evening Quill	Boston	MA	a	1928-1930	BJ
Struggle	Boston	MA	m	1972-1974	WI,EP75,76

TITLE	CITY	ST.	FREQ.	DATES	SOURCES
Times	Boston	MA	w	1943-1970	Ba,Ay1950,1961,Pr,NH49,EP45,67,NY46, SPD67,70
Woman's Era	Boston	MA	m	1894-1900	DANB536,Boris2
Advance	Cambridge	MA		1887-1888	Ba,Boris1,R1888[listed in Cambridge, Maryland]
Advocate	Cambridge	MA	w	1905-1926	Ba,Ay1919,1921,1925,NY12,Mather
Baptist Messenger	Cambridge	MA	w	1902-1909	Ba,Ay1905,1906,1909
Harvard Journal of Afro-American Affairs	Cambridge	MA	sa	1963-1979	BJ,SPD67,70,74,79[Journal of Negro Affairs]
Mirror	Cambridge	MA	w	1906-1910	Ba,Ay1909,Br
Reconstruction	Cambridge	MA	q	1990-1994+	SPD94
Black American Baptist Churchmen News Letter	Roxbury	MA		1971-1973	ABSCHSL
Boston Greater News	Roxbury	MA	w	1983-1992+	Ga88,92,Baid90,92,BRG,EP90[Boston],92
City News	Roxbury	MA	w	1964-1965	Pr,EP64,65
Roxbury Community News	Roxbury	MA	w	1992+	BRG,Lb
Black Women's Log	Springfield	MA		1974	Unct
Bottom Line	Springfield	MA		1993	EP93
Salt	Springfield	MA	w	1971	Oclc
Springfield Star	Springfield	MA	w	1970-1978	EBA,EP71-73,78,Bp
Sun	Springfield	MA	w	1966-1967	Pr,EP67,SPD67
Michigan Representative		MI		1896-1900	Ba
Michigan Age	Ann Arbor	MI		1919-1922	Ba,NY19,Go
Citizen	Benton Harbor	MI	w	1978-1993+	Ga91,92,EP80,93,Baid92
American Catholic Tribune	Detroit	MI	w	1884-1900	Ba,Ay1896
Black Conscience	Detroit	MI	6xy	1972-1979	SPD72,74,79
Black Position	Detroit	MI		1971	WI
Blade Express	Detroit	MI	w	1940-1944	NH42,44,EP44,Dc41
Communist	Detroit	MI		1974-1975	WI
Community Reporter	Detroit	MI	bw	1969-1973	Bp
Correspondence	Detroit	MI		1959-1963	WI
Courier	Detroit	MI	w	1953-1971	Ay1953,1971,EP62,70,Pr,Lb,SPD67,70
Detroit Advocate	Detroit	MI		1901-1903	DANB575
Detroit Contender	Detroit	MI	w	1920-1922	Ba,Gr,Br,NY22
Detroit Independent	Detroit	MI	w	1922-1944	NY26,32,Yenser6,Boris2
Detroit Informer	Detroit	MI	w	1897-1917	Ba,Ay1908,1917,Gr,Br,Lc91,Oclc, WI[e1916],NY12,Lt1907
Detroit Journal	Detroit	MI	m	1992-1993+	Ga94
Detroit Leader	Detroit	MI	w	1909-1923	Ba,Ay1913,1921,NY12,19,22,Go,Mather
Diurnal	Detroit	MI		1945-1946	Ba
DRUM/FREE	Detroit	MI		1972	SPD72
DRUM/FREE	Detroit	MI		1972-1979	SPD72,74,79
Fifth Estate	Detroit	MI		1945-1946	Ba
For My People	Detroit	MI	m	1972-1981	Ay1981,SPD79
Foresight	Detroit	MI		1969-1970	Unct

TITLE	CITY	ST.	FREQ.	DATES	SOURCES
Ghetto Speaks Esvid	Detroit	MI	w	1973-1976	EP75,76,Bp
Goodwill Ambassador	Detroit	MI	sw	1938	EP38
Guardian	Detroit	MI	w	1936-1938	Ba,EP38
Hamtramck-North Detroit Echo	Detroit	MI	w	1940-1942	NH42,Dc41
Headlines and Pictures	Detroit	MI	m	1944-1946	BJ
Illustrated News	Detroit	MI		1960	WI
Inner City Voice	Detroit	MI		1967-1979	WI,Unct,SPD74,79
Journal	Detroit	MI	w	1946-1949	Ba,Ay1949,NH49
Metro	Detroit	MI	w	1973	Bp
Michigan Chronicle	Detroit	MI	w	1936-1994+	Ba,Ay1940,1975,Ga87,94,Lc91,Oclc, NH42,44,46,49,Baid92,BRG,EBA,EH, EP40,93,NY46,Dc41,44,SPD67,79,API94, Fleming
Michigan Independent	Detroit	MI		1922-1938	Ba,Br
Michigan Independent	Detroit	MI		1935-1946	EP37,38,Br
Michigan Scene	Detroit	MI	w	1966-1967	Pr,Lb,EP67,SPD67
Michigan World	Detroit	MI	w	1936-1938	Ba,EP35,36
Militant	Detroit	MI	w	1928-1977	EP75-77
Mission	Detroit	MI	m	1982	ABSCHSL
NAACP Reporter	Detroit	MI	w	1973	Bp
National Baptist Women	Detroit	MI		1989-1992	ABSCHSL
National Independent	Detroit	MI	w	1891-1903	Ba,R1898,Br
National People	Detroit	MI		1886-1887	Mather [Sweeney, William Allison]
New Detroit Now	Detroit	MI		1994+	SPD94
News World	Detroit	MI	w	1935-1939	EP35,39
News & View	Detroit	MI	w	1975-1976	EP75,76
Northwest News	Detroit	MI		1922-1938	Ba,Br
Our Neighbor	Detroit	MI	m	1907	Lt1907
Owl	Detroit	MI	w	1928-1932	Ba,NY32,Boris2
People's News	Detroit	MI	w	1930-1938	Ba,NY32
Plaindealer	Detroit	MI	w	1883-1895	Ba,Ay1886,1894,Penn,Lc91,Oclc,WI, R1888,Eur94,Sch,Mather[1881-1895], DANB487[e1893]
Postal Alliance	Detroit	MI	m	1917-1967	Ay1950,1967,EP51
Pyramid	Detroit	MI	q	1943-1988	Ay1960,1975,Ga87,88,EH[1942]
Reformer	Detroit	MI		1895-1910	Ba [Mather 1911-1915]
River Rouge and Ecorse Esquire	Detroit	MI	w	1947	Ay1947
Rockert	Detroit	MI	w	1953	Oclc
Saint Mathews Lyceum Gazette	Detroit	MI		1879-1884	Ba
Set	Detroit	MI	m	1969-1970	Ay1969,1970
Sound Off	Detroit	MI	w	1971-1976	EP75,76,Bp
Telegram	Detroit	MI	w	1930-1950	Ba,Ay1950,NH49,NY32
Transition	Detroit	MI	w	1972-1976	EP75,76,Bp

TITLE	CITY	ST.	FREQ.	DATES	SOURCES
Tribune	Detroit	MI	w	1920-1970	Ba,Ay1940,1967,Lc91,PR,NH42,44,46,49, EP36,70,NY46,Dc41,44,Lb,Go,Br,SPD67, 70,74,Brooks,Fleming
Tribune Independent	Detroit	MI	w	1935	Ba,Ay1935
Twin City Observer	Detroit	MI	w	1951	EP51
Venture	Detroit	MI		1880-1881	Ba,Penn,DANB487[1879-1883]
West Side Echo	Detroit	MI	w	1947	Ay1947
World Echo	Detroit	MI	w	1938-1949	Ba,Ay1949,NH42,44,EP40,42,Dc41
Grapevine Journal	East Lansing	MI	13xy	1971-1973	Bp
Ecorse Telegram	Ecorse	MI	w	1945-1994+	Ay1980,Ga87,94,Baid92,EBA,EH,BRG, EP71,93,WPN94,API94,SPD87
Brownsville News	Flint	MI	w	1939-1944	EP39,40,42,44,Dc41
Enterprise	Flint	MI	w	1920-1923	Ba,Ay1921S
Flint-Bronzville News	Flint	MI	w	1940-1944	NH42,44
Gazette	Flint	MI	w	1977-1978	EP77,78
Spokesman	Flint	MI	w	1971-1980	EP74-80,Lb
Wolverine State Baptist Herald	Flint	MI	w	1928-1931	ABSCHSL
Echo	Grand Rapids	MI	w	1939	EP39
Grand Rapids Times	Grand Rapids	MI	w	1957-1994+	Ga88,94,Baid92,BRG,EP72,93,WPN94, API94,SPD87
Michigan State News	Grand Rapids	MI		1911-1926	Ba,Br,GRPL,NY26
Detroit World Echo	Hamtramck	MI	w	1943-1949	NH46,49,NY46,Dc44
Echo	Hamtramck	MI	w	1939-1946	EP39,40,NY46
Hamtramck-North Detroit Echo	Hamtramck	MI	m	1942-1946	NH46,EP42,Dc44
North Detroit Echo	Hamtramck	MI	w	1944-1946	EP44,NY46
Drum	Highland Park	MI		1970	Unct
Michigan Citizen	Highland Park	MI	w	1978-1994+	Ga88,94,EP87[1985],93,Baid92,BRG, WPN94
Voice	Inkster	MI	w	1940-1950	Ba,Ay1950,NH49,EP48,49
Blazer and Shopping Express	Jackson	MI	w	1963-1986	Ay1986,EP84
Blazer News	Jackson	MI	w	1963-1994+	Ga87,94,BRG,EP90,93,API94
Echo	Jackson	MI	w	1939	EP39
Jackson Blazer	Jackson	MI	w	1962-1992+	Ga92,Rw,EBA,EH,Baid92[1963],EP72-80, SPD70,74,79
News	Jackson	MI	w	1982-1986	Ay1986
Community Courier	Kalamazoo	MI	w	1972-1976	EP75,76,Bp
Echo	Kalamazoo	MI	w	1939	EP39
Focus News	Kalamazoo	MI	sm	1965-1982	Ay1982,EP76-78
Ledger	Kalamazoo	MI	w	1967-1973	EBA,EP71,72,Bp,Lb
Eye Opener	Lansing	MI	w	1930-1932	Ba,NY32
Lansing Echo	Lansing	MI	w	1940-1949	Ba,NH42,44,46,49,EP44,NY46,Dc41,44
Lansing State Echo	Lansing	MI	w	1939-1944	NH42,44,EP39,40,Dc41
Michigan Sentinel	Lathrup Village	MI	m	1991-1993+	Ga94
Macomb County Echo	Mt. Clemens	MI	w	1940-1944	NH42,EP40,44,Dc41
Macomb County News	Mt. Clemens	MI	w	1939	EP39

TITLE	CITY	ST.	FREQ.	DATES	SOURCES
Challenger	Pontiac	MI		1943-1946	Ba,EP48,49
Commentator	Pontiac	MI	w	1947-1949	Ba,EP48,49
Pontiac Agitator	Pontiac	MI	w	1949	NH49
Pontiac Echo	Pontiac	MI	w	1940-1944	NH42,44,EP40,44,Dc41
Valley Star	Saginaw	MI	w	1970-1975	EP73,75,76,Lb
Conveyor	Ypsilanti	MI		pre 1979	Lb
Washtenaw Sun	Ypsilanti	MI	w	1944-1949	Ba,EP48,49
World	Duluth	MN	w	1895-1897	Oclc
Afro-American Advance	Minneapolis	MN	w	1899-1906	Ba,Ay1905,1906,NWU
Afro-American Independent	Minneapolis	MN		1888-1890	Ba
Banner	Minneapolis	MN	w	1962-1963	Oclc
Minneapolis Messenger	Minneapolis	MN	w	1920-1926	Oclc,NY22,26,Boris1
Minneapolis Observer	Minneapolis	MN	w	1890-1891	Ba,NWU,Lc91,Oclc
Minneapolis Spokesman	Minneapolis	MN	w	1934-1994+	Ba,Ay1940,1986,Ga87,94,Oclc,Lc91, NH42,44,46,49,EP35,93,Baid92,BRG, EBA,EH,NY46,Dc41,44,WI,API90,94, WPN94,SPD67,70,74,87,94,Fleming
Minnesota Daily	Minneapolis	MN	d	1920s	Rw
Minnesota Messenger	Minneapolis	MN	w	1921-1925	Ba,Ay1925,Oclc[1922-1924]
National Advocate	Minneapolis	MN	w	1916-1926	Ba,Ay1921,Oclc,NY19,22,26,Go,Boris1
Northwest Monitor	Minneapolis	MN	w	1930-1932	Ba,Oclc[1903-1931],NY32
Northwestern Vine	Minneapolis	MN	w	1902-1905	Ba,Ay1905
Protest	Minneapolis	MN	w	1892-1892	Oclc
Sphinx It's Journal	Minneapolis	MN		pre 1944	Yenser6 [Canon, Raymond W.]
Timely Digest Magazine	Minneapolis	MN		1931-1932	Fleming [Newman, Cecil E.]
Twin Cities Courier	Minneapolis	MN	w	1966-1992+	Ay1969,1986,Ga87,91,Oclc,WI,EP67,86, Baid92,EBA,EH,Lb,SPD87
Twin City American	Minneapolis	MN		1899-1906	Ba,Gr,Lc91
Twin City Herald	Minneapolis	MN	w	1927-1944	Ba[1930],EP35-44,NY32,Yenser6
Twin City Observer	Minneapolis	MN	w	1943-1977	Ba,Ay1950,1977,Oclc[e1976?],EP67,77, EBA,EH,Lb,Lc91,SPD67,70,74
Twin City Star	Minneapolis	MN	w	1910-1920	Ba,Ay1912,1920,NY12
Twin-City Leader	Minneapolis	MN	w	1940-1944	Oclc,NH42,44,Dc41
Afro-Independent	Saint Paul	MN		1888-1890	Ba,Lc91
Appeal	Saint Paul	MN	w	1889-1929	Ba,Ay1905,1921,Oclc,NY12,19,22,Lt1907, NWU,DANB4
Broad Axe	Saint Paul	MN		1890-1903	Ba,Lc91
Daily Guide	Saint Paul	MN	d	1912-1914	Ba,NY12
Globe News	Saint Paul	MN	w	1939	Oclc
Grand Selby Digest	Saint Paul	MN	m	1971	Oclc
Insight News	Saint Paul	MN	w	1974-1993+	Oclc,BRG,EP91,93
Iroquois	Saint Paul	MN	w	1903-1905	Ba,Ay1905
Negro Star	Saint Paul	MN		1892-1900	Ba
Negro World	Saint Paul	MN		1891-1900	Ba,Lc91,WI
Northwest Monitor	Saint Paul	MN		1930-1932	Ba (see Minneapolis)

TITLE	CITY	ST.	FREQ.	DATES	SOURCES
Northwestern Bulletin	Saint Paul	MN		1922-1924	Lc77,Boris1[1927]
Northwestern Bulletin Appeal	Saint Paul	MN	w	1922-1929	Ba,Ay1925,NY26,Lc77
Saint Paul Echo	Saint Paul	MN	w	1925-1932	ba[1930-1932],NY32,Oclc,Sch
Saint Paul Recorder	Saint Paul	MN	w	1934-1994+	Ba,Ay1945,1975,Oclc,Ga91,94,NH42,44, 49,EP35,93,BRG,EBA,EH,NY46,Dc41, API90,94,WPN94,Fleming
Saint Paul Sun	Saint Paul	MN	w	1941-1977	Ay1969,1977,Oclc[1941-1976],WI,EP67, 77,Pr,Lb,SPD67,74
Twin City Guardian	Saint Paul	MN	w	1895-1923	Oclc,Ay1912 (nlb)
Western Appeal	Saint Paul	MN	w	1885-1888	Ba,Ay1886-1888,Oclc,Lc77,Penn,DANB4
Aberdeen Advance	Aberdeen	MS		1891-1892	Th
Autocrat	Aberdeen	MS		1890-1900	Th,Ba
Practical Pointer	Aberdeen	MS		1902	Th
Practical Pride	Aberdeen	MS		1902-1903	Th,Ba
Blade	Amory	MS		1902-1903	Ba
Benton County Freedom Train	Ashland	MS		1963-1966	Oclc,WI
Devine Word Messenger	Bay Saint Louis	MS	q	1966-1974	Th
In a Word	Bay Saint Louis	MS	m	1983-1994+	Ga91,94
Saint Augustine's Messenger	Bay Saint Louis	MS	m	1923-1966	Th,Ay1950,1959,EP49-51
Times	Benoit	MS		1898-1900	Th,Ba
Avalanche	Beulah	MS	w	1901-1918	Th,Ba,Ay1905,1916,NY12,Lt1907
Baptist Headlight	Biloxi	MS	w	1912-1922	Th,NY12,19,22
Gazette	Biloxi	MS		1899-1900	Th,Ba
Elevator	Booneville	MS		1897-1902	Th,Ba
Backing Up the Farm	Brandon	MS		1911-1915	Mather [Jones, Lawrence Clifton]
Free State	Brandon	MS	w	1898-1905	Th,Ba,Ay1905,Lc91,Oclc,WI
Pine Torch	Brandon	MS	q	1910-1981	Th,NY19,22,Mather
Soldiers of Faith	Brandon	MS		1945	Th
Successful Negro Farmer	Brandon	MS		1911-1915	Mather [Jones, Lawrence Clifton]
Brookhaven Leader	Brookhaven	MS		1940	Th
People's Relief	Brookhaven	MS	w	1909-1910	Th,Ba,Ay1909[b1906]
Canton Citizen	Canton	MS		1869	Th
Colored Messenger	Canton	MS		1938	Th
Mississippi Baptist	Canton	MS	w	1899-1914	Th,Ba,Ay1905,1914,NY12,Lt1907
Baptist Headlight	Carriere	MS	w	1906-1909	Th,Ba,Ay1909
Central Mississippi Signal	Cary	MS		1912-1915	Th,Ba,NY12
Weekly Negro World	Cary	MS	w	1895-1915	Th,Ba,Ay1905,1909,1911,1915,NY12
Charleston Star	Charleston	MS	w	1909-1912	Th,Ba,Ay1911,1912,NY12
Avalanche	Clarksdale	MS	w	1901-1919	Th,Ba,Ay1917-1919
Coahoma Opportunities Inc. Newsletter	Clarksdale	MS	m	1967-1985	Th
Delta Messenger	Clarksdale	MS	w	1936-1939	Th,Ba,Ay1939
Educator	Clarksdale	MS	w	1911-1915	Th,Ba,Ay1912,1915,NY12
Journal	Clarksdale	MS	w	1899-1907	Th,Ba,Ay1905,1906

TITLE	CITY	ST.	FREQ.	DATES	SOURCES
National Defender	Clarksdale	MS		1918-1922	Th,Ba,NY19,Go
Trestle Boards	Clarksdale	MS		1946-1985	Th
Colored Messenger	Coffeeville	MS	w	1939-1946	Th,Ba,NH42,46,Dc41,44
Journal	Coffeeville	MS	w	1910-1911	Th,Ba,Ay1911
Star	Columbia	MS	w	1908-1919	Ay1911,NY12,19
Brotherhood	Columbus	MS	bm	1976	Th
Morning Star	Columbus	MS	sm	1903-1926	Th,Ba,Ay1905,1916,NY12,19,22,26, Lt1907,Go
New Light	Columbus	MS	sm	1886-1923	Th,Ba,Ay1887,1906,Eur94,R1888,Penn
Star	Columbus	MS		1903-1922	Th,Ba,Go
Colored Visitor	Crystal Springs	MS	sm	1898	Th
Woodmen Sentinel	Crystal Springs	MS	m	1915-1919	Th,Ba,Ay1916,1917,1818
Advance	Durant	MS		1898-1900	Th,Ba
Advocate	Durant	MS	w	1899	Th
Benevolent Banner	Edwards	MS	m	1900-1910	Th,Ba,Lt1907
Calanthian Journal	Edwards	MS	w	1904-1915	Th,Ba,Ay1906,1915,NY12
Christian Informer	Edwards	MS	w	1907-1922	Th,Ba,Ay1911-1915,NY12,19,22
Gospel Plea	Edwards	MS	w	1912-1922	Th,NY12,19,22
New Light	Edwards	MS	w/sm	1886-1923	Th,Ba,Ay1911,1916,NY12,Lt1907,Penn
Baptist Trumpet	Enterprise	MS	w	1896-1902	Th
Eastern Banner	Enterprise	MS	w	1900-1907	Th,Ba,Ay1905,1906,Lt1907
National Standard Enterprise	Fayette	MS		1896-1899	Th,Ba
SLRA Newsletter	Forest	MS		1976-1985	Th
Gospel Messenger	Fort Adams	MS		1902-1903	Th,Ba
Baptist Journal	Greenville	MS	w	1880-1889	Th,Ba
Baptist Preachers' Union	Greenville	MS	sm	1895-1907	Th,Ba,Ay1902,1906
Baptist Signal	Greenville	MS	m	1880-1889	Th,Ba,Ay1888,Penn
Baptist Women's Union	Greenville	MS	sm/w	1908-1922	Th,Ba,Ay1909,1912,NY12,19,22
Bee	Greenville	MS		1880	Th
Blade	Greenville	MS	w	1900-1912	Th,Ba,Ay1911,NY12
Bulletin	Greenville	MS	w	1900-1912	Th,Ba
Delta Farmer's Digest	Greenville	MS	w	1948	Oclc
Delta Leader	Greenville	MS	w	1938-1969	Th,Ba,Ay1940,1969,Oclc,NH42,44,46,49, EP41,51,NY46,Dc41,44,Fleming
Delta Lighthouse	Greenville	MS	w	1896-1930	Th,Ba,Ay1905,1921,Oclc,NY12,19, Lt1907,Go
Delta Ministry Report	Greenville	MS		1967	WI
Delta News	Greenville	MS		1894-1895	Th,Ba
Golden Rule	Greenville	MS	w	1887-1905	Th
Greenville Gazette [Owl]	Greenville	MS	w	1920s	Th
Greenville Leader	Greenville	MS	w	1930-1985	Th,Ba,Oclc[e1939],EP35-40
Headlight	Greenville	MS	w	1891-1895	Th,Ba,Ay1891
Herald	Greenville	MS		1961	Th
Herald	Greenville	MS	w	1886-1889	Th,Ba,Ay1887,1888

TITLE	CITY	ST.	FREQ.	DATES	SOURCES
Mississippi Freelance	Greenville	MS	m	1969-1970	Oclc
Mississippi Memo Digest	Greenville	MS	w	1968-1979	Oclc
Mississippi News	Greenville	MS		1974-1976	Th
Mississippiana	Greenville	MS		1942-1947	Th,Oclc
Natchez Weekly Herald	Greenville	MS		1922	Go (See Natchez)
Negro Leader	Greenville	MS	m	1962-1976	Th,EBA,EH,EP67,76,Lb
New	Greenville	MS		1964	Th
Pathfinder	Greenville	MS	w	1899-1906	Th,Ba,Ay1905,1906
Southern Forum	Greenville	MS	w	1901-1912	Th,Ba,Ay1906,1912,NY12,Lt1907
Southern Leader	Greenville	MS	w	1940-1944	Th,NH42,44,EP43,44,Dc41
Taborian Leader	Greenville	MS	w	1904-1922	Th,Ba,Ay1906,1913,NY12,19,22
Voice of Shimp	Greenville	MS		1975-1985	Th
Zion Harp	Greenville	MS	sm	1895-1922	Th,Ba,Ay1905,1917,Oclc,NY12,19,22, R1898,1900,Lt1907
Beacon Light	Greenwood	MS		1909-1910	Th,Ba
Center Light	Greenwood	MS		1950s	Th
Colored Veteran	Greenwood	MS		1927-1928	Th
Golden Rule	Greenwood	MS	w	1887-1894	Th,Ba,Ay1888,1894
Negro Star	Greenwood	MS	w	1908-1919	Th,Ba,Ay1909,1919,NY12,Mather
Progressive Torchlight	Greenwood	MS		1918-1919	Th,Ba,NY19,Go
Sun	Greenwood	MS		1896-1898	Th,Ba
News	Grenada	MS	w	1886-1889	Th,Ba,Ay1888,1889
Gulfport World	Gulfport	MS	w	1960	Th
Informer	Gulfport	MS		1918-1922	Th,Ba,NY19,Go
Vanguard	Gunnison	MS		1902-1903	Th,Ba
Beacon Light	Hattiesburg	MS		1909-1915	Ba,NY12
Galaxy	Hattiesburg	MS		1970s	Th (late 1970s)
Herald	Hattiesburg	MS	w	1898-1905	Th,Ba
Hub City Community News	Hattiesburg	MS	w	1983-1987	Th,Oclc
Times	Hattiesburg	MS	w	1898-1922	Th,Ba,Ay1906,1909,NY12,19,22,Go, Mather
Union Messenger	Hattiesburg	MS	bm	1934	Oclc
New Era	Hernando	MS	w	1888-1922	Th,Ba,Ay1911,1916,NY12,19,22
Saturday Times	Hollandale	MS	w	1904-1915	Th,Ba,Ay1906,1912,NY12,Lt1907
Marshall Herald	Holly Springs	MS	w	1903-1909	Th,Ba,Ay1906,1909,Lt1907[Herald]
Mississippi Industrial College News	Holly Springs	MS		1983	Th
Mississippi Old Fellows	Holly Springs	MS	w	1907-1918	Th,Ba,Ay1909,1917,NY12,19
Rust College Sentinel	Holly Springs	MS	m	1946-1985	Th
Rust Enterprise	Holly Springs	MS	q	1919-1922	NY19,22
Rustorian	Holly Springs	MS	m	1935-1985	Th
Southern Advocate	Holly Springs	MS		1900-1902	Th,Ba
Southern Progress	Holly Springs	MS		1913-1915	Th,Ba
Woodmen Sentinel	Holly Springs	MS	m	1901-1915	Th,Ba,Ay1911,1914,NY12
Mileston Minute	Holmes Co.	MS		1964	Th,WI

TITLE	CITY	ST.	FREQ.	DATES	SOURCES
Negro Reminder	Houston	MS	w	1910-1911	Th,Ba,Ay1911
People's Elevator	Independence	MS	w	1933-1935	Th,Ba
New Era	Indianola	MS	sm	1905-1926	Th,Ba,Ay1909,1918,NY12,19,22,26,Go, Mather
Review	Itta Bena	MS		1980-1985	Th
Valley Voice	Itta Bena	MS		1980-1985	Th
BAMS Keynotes	Jackson	MS	m	1972-1985	Th
Baptist Messenger	Jackson	MS	w/m	1887-1890	Th,Ba,Ay1889,1890,ABSCHSL[1883], Penn
Baptist Record	Jackson	MS	w	1878-1922	Th,Ay1915,1921,NY12,19,22,Lt1907
Baptist Reporter	Jackson	MS	w	1900-1922	Th,Ba,Ay1906,1916,NY12,19,22,Mather
Baptist Signal	Jackson	MS		pre 1890	Th
Baptist Teacher	Jackson	MS		1880	Th
Blue and White Flash	Jackson	MS	w	1940-1985	Th
Calanthian Journal	Jackson	MS	bm	1916-1917	Ba,Ay1916
Child Development Group of Mississippi Newsletter	Jackson	MS	bm	1967-1985	Th
Christian Informer	Jackson	MS	bm	1907-1916	Ba,Ay1916
Close UP Magazine	Jackson	MS	q	1967-1973	Th
Colored Citizen	Jackson	MS		pre 1891	Ba,Penn
Colored Citizen's Monthly	Jackson	MS	m	1868-1870	Th
Colored Journal	Jackson	MS	w	1890-1894	Th,Ba,Ay1890,1891,1894
Colored Journal of Mississippi	Jackson	MS	w	1922-1938	Th,Ba,Ay1925,EP35-38,NY26,32
Delta Leader	Jackson	MS		1939-1943	Th,Ba
Douglas Report	Jackson	MS		1983-1985	Th
Drummer	Jackson	MS		1971-1972	Th,Oclc,Unct,WI
Eagle Eye	Jackson	MS	w	1944-1950s	Th
Enterprise	Jackson	MS	w	1939-1940	EP39,40 (see Mississippi Enterprise)
Farish Street Baptist Church Newsletter	Jackson	MS		1976-1985	Th
Field Hand	Jackson	MS		pre 1947	Th
Forty Acres and a Mule	Jackson	MS	m	1978-1981	Th
Free Press	Jackson	MS	w	1964-1965	EP64,65
Headlight	Jackson	MS		1891-1900	Th
Herald	Jackson	MS		1920s	Th
Highlighter	Jackson	MS	m	1974-1976	Th
Jackson Advocate	Jackson	MS	w	1937-1994+	Th,Ba,Ay1950,1976,Ga88,94,Rw,Lc83, Baid90,92,Oclc,WI,NH42,44,46,49,EP41, 93,EBA,EH,NY46,Dc41,44, WPN94[b1938],SPD67,70,74,79,87
Jackson College Journal	Jackson	MS	sm	1912-1922	NY12,19,22
Jackson Mississippian	Jackson	MS		1854-1860	NWU
Jackson State University Researcher	Jackson	MS	q	1980-1985	Th
Jackson State University Review	Jackson	MS	q	1968-1980	Th
Jackson Tiger	Jackson	MS		1938	Th

TITLE	CITY	ST.	FREQ.	DATES	SOURCES
Jackson Tribune	Jackson	MS		1883-1891	Th,Ba[1888-1891],Penn
Jacob's Watchman	Jackson	MS	sm	1902-1910	Th,Lt1907
Lancet	Jackson	MS		1901-1905	Th,Ba
Leader	Jackson	MS	w	1901-1905	Th,Ba,Ay1905
Light	Jackson	MS	w	1892-1910	Th,Ba,Ay1894
Messenger	Jackson	MS	w	1881-1894	Th,Ba,Oclc,Penn
Metropolitan Observer	Jackson	MS	w	1976	Th
Mississippi Educational Journal	Jackson	MS	m/y	1924-1976	Th
Mississippi Enterprise	Jackson	MS	w	1938-1992+	Th,Ba,Ay1950,1971,Ga87,90,Oclc,NH42, 44,46,49,EP41,78,NY46,Dc41,44,Lb, Baid90
Mississippi Free Press	Jackson	MS	w	1961-1979	Th,Oclc,WI,EP67,70,Lb,SPD67,70,74,79
Mississippi Independent Beauticians Assoc. Newsletter	Jackson	MS		1941-1985	Th
Mississippi Mirror	Jackson	MS	ir	1978-1985	Th
Mississippi Weekly	Jackson	MS	w	1936-1940	Th,Ba,EP36-40
Monitor	Jackson	MS	m	1982-1985	Th
MTA Newsletter	Jackson	MS	m	1924-1976	Th
MTA Newsletter-NOW	Jackson	MS	bw	1970-1977	Th
National Association of Landowners of Mississippi, Inc.	Jackson	MS	m	1976-1985	Th
New African	Jackson	MS	m	1971-1985	Th
New South	Jackson	MS	w	1893-1895	Th,Ba,Ay1894
Outlook Magazine	Jackson	MS	m	1974-1985	Th
People's Adviser	Jackson	MS	w	1882-1915	Th,Ba,Ay1884
People's Defender	Jackson	MS	w	1889-1915	Ba,Ay1890,1909,NY12,Lt1907,Br,Eur94
People's Journal	Jackson	MS		1870-1881	Th,Ba,Penn
People's Light	Jackson	MS		pre 1885	Penn
People's Relief	Jackson	MS	w	1906-1915	Th,Ba,Ay1911,1913,1914,NY12
Reconciler	Jackson	MS	m	1977-1985	Th
Reflector	Jackson	MS	w	1916-1919	Th,Ba,Ay1917-1919
Southern Register	Jackson	MS	w	1922-1934	Th,Ba,Ay1925,EP35-38,NY26,32
SPAR Southern Popular Athletic Review	Jackson	MS	w/bw	1977-1985	Th
Street Talk	Jackson	MS	m	1978-1985	Th
Truth [Holiness]	Jackson	MS	w	1907-1922	Th,NY12,19,22,Lt1907
Weekly Communicator	Jackson	MS	w	1975-1985	Th
Weekly Recorder	Jackson	MS	w	1939-1949	Th,Ba,NH42,44,46,EP39,48,Dc41,44
Central Mississippi Signal	Kosciusko	MS	m	1906-1922	Th,Ba,Ay1909,NY12,19,22,Go
Preacher and Teacher	Kosciusko	MS	sm	1893-1904	Th,Ba
Preacher Safeguard	Kosciusko	MS		1894-1905	Mather [Buchanan, Charles Andrew]
Star	Lambert	MS	sm	1913-1916	Th,Ba,Ay1914,1916
News Journal	Laurel	MS	w	1902-1912	Th,Ba,Ay1905,1906,1909,NY12
Progress	Laurel	MS	w	1910-1915	Th,Ba,Ay1911-1915
Voice of the People	Laurel	MS	w	1926	Th,Oclc

TITLE	CITY	ST.	FREQ.	DATES	SOURCES
Baptist Sentinel	Lexington	MS	w	1906-1922	Th,Ba,Ay1909,NY12,19,22
New Light	Lexington	MS	w	1886-1923	Th,Ba,Ay1921
Sentinel-Signal	Lexington	MS	w	1906-1920	Th,Ba,Ay1911-1920
Alcorn A & M College Bulletin	Lorman	MS	q	1871-1944	Th
Alcorn Herald	Lorman	MS	m	1930-1985	Th
Alcorn Report	Lorman	MS	m	1981-1985	Th
Alumnus Magazine	Lorman	MS		1952-1985	Th
Record	Lucedale	MS	w	1907	Lt1907
Observer	Macon	MS		1898-1899	Th
Negro Herald	Magnolia	MS	sm	1904-1907	Th,Ba,Ay1906
News Messenger	Marks	MS	sm	1908-1910	Th,Ba,Ay1909
Mayersville Spectator	Mayersville	MS	w	1877-1911	Th,Ay1911,1912
Voice of the Black Youth	Mayersville	MS		1968	Th
Ardis Times	McComb	MS	w	1909-1911	Th,Ba[b1910 Slocumb MS],Ay1911 (see Slocumb AL)
District Gazette	McComb	MS	w	1926-1931	Th,Ba
Freedom's Journal	McComb	MS	w	1964	Th
Pike County Tribune	McComb	MS	w	1901-1903	Th,Ba
Hunter's Horn	McLeod	MS	m	1919-1922	NY19,22
Simpson Co. Welfare Rights Organization Newsletter	Mendenhall	MS		1970-1985	Th
Appeal	Meridian	MS	w	1898-1912	Th,Ba,Ay1905,1906,1909,NY12
Blade	Meridian	MS	w	1900-1916	Th,Ba,Ay1913-1916
Fair Play	Meridian	MS	w	1889-1895	Th,Ba,Ay1889,1894,Penn,Mather
Harris Newsletter	Meridian	MS		1956-1970	Th
Headlight	Meridian	MS	w	1907-1912	Th,Ba,Ay1909,NY12
Meridian Morning Sun	Meridian	MS		1958-1961	Th
Mississippi Memo Digest	Meridian	MS	w	1961-1994+	Th,Oclc,Ga87,94,EP72[1966],93,EH,Baid90,92,WPN94,SPD87
Mississippi Monitor	Meridian	MS	w	1903-1922	Th,Ba,Ay1911-1913,NY19,Go
Star	Meridian	MS	w	1896-1898	Th,Ba
Teacher and Preacher	Meridian	MS		1905-1912	Th,Ba
Weekly Echo	Meridian	MS	w/sm	1923-1960	Th,Ba,Oclc,NH42,46,EP48,51,Dc41,44
Journal	Moss Point	MS		1902-1911	Th,Ba
Pas Point Journal	Moss Point	MS	w	1976-1985	Th
People's Pilot	Moss Point	MS	w	1908-1911	Th,Ba,Ay1911
Advance	Mound Bayou	MS		1919-1926	Th,Ba,NY19,22,26,Go
Advance Dispatch	Mound Bayou	MS	w	1914-1933	Th,Ba,Ay1921,1925,Br
Baptist Echo	Mound Bayou	MS	m	1909	Th
Baptist Women's Union	Mound Bayou	MS	sm	1906-1922	Th,Ba,Ay1912,1914,1915,NY12,19,22
Defender	Mound Bayou	MS	w	1890s	Th
Delta Progress	Mound Bayou	MS	w	1899-1902	Th
Demonstrator	Mound Bayou	MS	w	1900-1919	Th,Ba,Ay1905,1919,NY12,Lt1907
Light	Mound Bayou	MS	m	1976	Th

TITLE	CITY	ST.	FREQ.	DATES	SOURCES
Mound Bayou News Digest	Mound Bayou	MS	w	1944-1966	Th,Oclc,Pr,NH44,49,EP51
Mound Bayou Sentinel	Mound Bayou	MS	sm	1952-1954	Th,Oclc
National News Digest	Mound Bayou	MS	w	1919-1927	Th,Ba,Ay1921,1925,NY19,22,26,Go, Boris1
News-Dispatch	Mound Bayou	MS	w	1914-1919	Ba,Ay1917-1919
Southern Advocate	Mound Bayou	MS	w	1933-1941	Th,Oclc,NH42,EP38-40,Dc41
Taborian Bulletin	Mound Bayou	MS		1947-1963	Th
Taborian Star	Mound Bayou	MS	q/m	1923-1959	Th,Ba,Ay1950,1959
Vindicator	Mound Bayou	MS	w	1890s	Th
Voice	Mound Bayou	MS	w	1968-1971	Th,Oclc
Weekly	Mound Bayou	MS	w	1966-1970	Th,EP67,69,70
Weekly Recorder	Mound Bayou	MS	w	1942-1944	Th,NH42
Baptist Signal	Natchez	MS	m	1881-1890	Th,Ba,Ay1887,1889,1890,Penn
Baptist Signal Messenger	Natchez	MS	w	1891-1894	Th,Ba,Ay1891,1894,Penn,Eur94
Bluff City Post	Natchez	MS	bm	1978-1985	Th,Oclc
Brotherhood	Natchez	MS	m	1887-1900	Th,Ba,Ay1889,1896,R1888,Eur94,Br
City Bulletin	Natchez	MS	m	1958-1963	Th
Guide	Natchez	MS	w	1904-1907	Th,Ba,Ay1906,Lt1907
Herald	Natchez	MS	w	1901-1920	Th,Ba,Ay1906,1915,NY12,19,Mather
Mississippi World	Natchez	MS	w	1935	EP35
Natchez News Leader	Natchez	MS	w	1971-1976	Th,Oclc,WI,EH,EP72,76,Lb,Bp
Natchez Weekly Reporter	Natchez	MS	w	1890-1938	Th,Ba,Ay1890,1935,Eur94,NY12,19,22, Br[1909],Go,Mather
Republican	Natchez	MS	w	1889-1891	Th,Ay1890,1891
Community Citizen	New Albany	MS	w/sm	1947-1977	Th,Ay1950,1973,Oclc,EP51
Conservative Echo	Okolona	MS		1898-1900	Th,Ba
Mississippi Letter	Okolona	MS		1902-1965	Th,NY19,22,Yenser4
Race Pride	Okolona	MS		1902-1903	Th,Ba
South Central Athletic Conference Bulletin	Okolona	MS		1924-1949	Th
Enterprise	Oxford	MS	w	1897-1902	Th,Ba,Yenser3
Soul Force!	Oxford	MS	m	1970-1985	Th,Oclc
Spectator	Oxford	MS		1971-1974?	Th
Workmen of the World	Oxford	MS	sm	1913-1917	Th,Ba,Ay1917
Baptist Advocate	Port Gibson	MS	m	1896-1898	Th,Ba
Claiborne	Port Gibson	MS		1980-1981	Th
Lever	Port Gibson	MS	w	1910-1915	Th,Ba,Ay1914,1915
Searchlight	Port Gibson	MS	sm	1903-1907	Th,Ba
Golden Rule	Quitman	MS		1901-1902	Th
Taborian Herald	Renova	MS	w	1909-1913	Ba,Ay1911,1912,1913
Mississippi Brotherhood	Robinsonville	MS	w	1899-1901	Th,Ba
Citizen	Rosedale	MS		1902-1903	Th,Ba
Negro Star	Rosedale	MS	w	1898-1900	Th,Ba
Negro Star	Rosedale	MS	w	1919-1925	Ay1925

TITLE	CITY	ST.	FREQ.	DATES	SOURCES
Star	Rosedale-Floreyville	MS		1870s	Th
Cotton Farmer	Scott	MS	w	1917-1928	Th,Ba,Ay1925[1919],NY19,22,26,Go, Boris1
Gulf Coast Vigilante	Scranton	MS	w	1891-1895	Th,Ba,Ay1894
Colored People's Messenger	Senatobia	MS	w	1915-1919	Th,Ba,Ay1917-1919
Mississippi Baptist Herald	Senatobia	MS	w	1888-1909	Th,Ba,Ay1889,1909,Oclc,Eur94
Christian Plea	Shaw	MS	sm	1902-1906	Th,Ba,Ay1905,1906
Delta Progress	Shelby	MS		1899-1902	Ba
American	Signal	MS	sm	1907-1913	Th,Ba,Ay1911,1912
Real	Smith Co.	MS		1937	Th
Afro-American Newsletter	Starksville	MS		1971-1972	Th
New Light	Stratton	MS	w	1923-1939	Th,Ba,Ay1925,1935,1939
Republican Times	Summit	MS	w	1896-1898	Th,Ba
Rising Sun	Toomsuba	MS	w/sm	1909-1921	Th,Ba,Ay1911,1921,Mather
Furrows	Tougaloo	MS		1972-1974	SPD72,74
Harambee	Tougaloo	MS	m	1969-1985	Th
Mississippi Newsletter	Tougaloo	MS		1966-1970	Th
Tougaloo Enterprise	Tougaloo	MS		1884-1889	Th
Tougaloo News	Tougaloo	MS		1890-1985	Th,NY19,22
Tougaloo Quarterly	Tougaloo	MS	q	1889	Th
Colored Promoter	Tunica	MS		1898	Th
Progressive Together	Tupelo	MS	m	1947	Th
Southern Afro-American	Tupelo	MS	w	1909-1911	Th,Ba,Ay1911
Tutwiler Whirlwind	Tutwiler/Clarksdale	MS	w	1978-1980	Th
Living Blues	University	MS	6xy	1970-1994+	Ga90,94,WI[Chicago]
Black People Speak	Utica	MS	m	1954-1973	Th
Bull Dog Growl	Utica	MS		pre 1954	Th
Maroon and Gold Flash	Utica	MS	m	1974-1985	Th
Southern Notes	Utica	MS		1927-1962	Th[b1903?]
Utica News	Utica	MS	sm	1907-1932	Th,NY19,22
Colored Alliance Advocate	Vaiden	MS	w	1888-1889	Th
Advance-Dispatch	Vicksburg	MS	w/sm	1914-1946	Th,Ba,Ay1935,1937,NH42,46,EP43,44, Dc41,44,Boris1
Advocate Journal	Vicksburg	MS	w	1904-1920	Th,Ba,Ay1912-1920,NY12
African Methodist Advocate	Vicksburg	MS	w	1895-1900	Th,Ba
American	Vicksburg	MS	w	1941-1942	EP41,42
Anchor	Vicksburg	MS		1922	Go
Baptist Herald	Vicksburg	MS	w	1898-1903	Th,Ba
Black Man	Vicksburg	MS	m	1918-1937	Ba,Ay1921,1925,1935,1937
Citizens' Appeal	Vicksburg	MS	w	1964-1974	Th,Pr,Lb,WI,EP57,70,SPD67,70,74
Colored Citizen	Vicksburg	MS		1867-1870	Th,Go
Delta Beacon	Vicksburg	MS	w	1889-1892	Ba,Ay1891
Evening Post	Vicksburg	MS	d	1884-1885	Penn,Oclc?
Golden Eagle	Vicksburg	MS	w	1910-1914	Th,Ba,Ay1911,1912,1914

TITLE	CITY	ST.	FREQ.	DATES	SOURCES
Golden Rule	Vicksburg	MS	w	1898-1907	Th,Ba,Ay1906,1909,WI,Oclc
Light	Vicksburg	MS	m,w	1891-1926	Th,Ba,Ay1896,1920,Oclc,WI,NY12,19,22, 26,Lt1907,Go,Br,Lc91,Boris1
Mississippi Republican	Vicksburg	MS		1877-1883	Th,Ba,Penn
Mississippi Tribune	Vicksburg	MS	w	1935	EP35
National Star	Vicksburg	MS	w	1900-1922	Th,Ay1905,1911,NY12,19,Go
New Light	Vicksburg	MS		1908-1915	Th
Vicksburg Tribune	Vicksburg	MS	w	1940-1946	Th,Ba,NH44,46,EP44,45,Dc44
Mid South Informer	Walls	MS	w	1965	Th
Blade	West Point	MS	m	1896-1899	Th,Ba
Conservative	West Point	MS		1902-1903	Th,Ba
Eagle	West Point	MS	m	1980-1985	Th
Growl	West Point	MS	m	1960-1980	Th
Preacher's Safeguard	West Point	MS	w	1893-1905	Th,Ba,Ay1905,Mather
Reflections	West Point	MS	m	1970?-1985	Th
Advocate	Winona	MS	sm	1898-1904	Th,Ba
Wilkinson County Appeal	Woodville	MS	w	1902-1907	Th,Ba,Ay1905,1906
Afro-American Courier	Yazoo City	MS	bm	1930-1935	Oclc
Century Voice	Yazoo City	MS	m	1941-1956	Th,Ba,Ay1955,Oclc,EP51
Church Journal		MO		1891-1915	Mather [McDonald, J. Frank]
Central Missouri Star	California	MO	w	1900-1902	Ba,MO
Anchor	Caruthersville	MO	w	1911-1923	Ba,Ay1921,Oclc,NY19,22
Charleston Spokesman	Charleston	MO	w	1934	Oclc
Professional World	Columbia	MO	w	1901-1921	Ba,Ay1905,1921,MO,Oclc,NY12,Lt1907
Hannibal Register	Hannibal	MO	w	1926-1944	NH42,44,EP35,43,Dc41,Br
Home Protective Record	Hannibal	MO	w	1908-1919	Ba,Ay1919,Oclc
Missouri State Register	Hannibal	MO	w	1919-1942	Ba,Ay1921,MO,NY19,22,Go,Br
People's Elevator	Independence	MO		1935	Ay1935
Campus Magazine	Jefferson City	MO	m	1949-1951	EP49-51
Lincoln Clarion	Jefferson City	MO	w/sm	1932-1954	Ay1945,1954,NH42,46,EP45,51,NY46, Dc41,44
Lincoln University Journalism Newsletter	Jefferson City	MO		1946	NY46
Midwest Journal	Jefferson City	MO	q	1948-1956	BJ
Missouri Baptist Together	Jefferson City	MO		1987	ABSCHSL
Reporters News	Jefferson City	MO		pre 1927	Boris1 [Spencer, James Oscar]
Weekly Herald	Jefferson City	MO	w	1913-1916	Ba,Ay1914-1916,MO,Gr,Mather
Western Messenger	Jefferson City	MO	w	1899-1922	Ba,Ay1909,1915,MO,NY12,19,22,Gr,Go, Br
Afro-American Leader	Joplin	MO	w	1915-1918	Ba,Ay1918
Joplin Uplift	Joplin	MO	w	1926-1928	Oclc
Joplin-Springfield Uplift	Joplin	MO	w	1926-1935	Oclc,EP35
Reminder	Joplin	MO	w	1916-1917	Ba,Ay1917
Advocate	Kansas City	MO		1914-1927	Ba

TITLE	CITY	ST.	FREQ.	DATES	SOURCES
Baptist Record	Kansas City	MO	w	1921-1926	Ba,Ay1925,NY26
Career Focus	Kansas City	MO	6xy	1988-1994+	Ga90,94
Christian Advocate	Kansas City	MO		pre 1946	Ba,Br
Colored Messenger	Kansas City	MO	w	1900-1902	Ba,MO
Dispatch	Kansas City	MO	w	1886-1892	Ba,Ay1887-1890,R1888
Free Press	Kansas City	MO		1880-1889	Ba,Penn
Future State	Kansas City	MO	w	1892-1896	Ba,Ay1896,Moten,MO
Gate City Press	Kansas City	MO	w	1880-1889	Ba,Ay1888,MO,Penn
Independent	Kansas City	MO	w	1914-1927	Ba
Kansas City American	Kansas City	MO	w	1927-1940	Ba,Oclc[e1936],NY32,Br,Yenser4
Kansas City Call	Kansas City	MO	w	1919-1994+	Ba,Ay1921,1975,MO,Oclc,Ga87,94,NH42, 44,46,49,EP36,93,NY22,26,32,46,Dc41,44, lc,API90,94,WPN94,Fleming
Kansas City Globe	Kansas City	MO	w	1972-1994+	Ga90,94,Lb,Baid92,EP75,93,WPN94 (see also KS)
Kansas City Observer	Kansas City	MO	w	1896-1902	Ba,Lc91,Oclc,WI,Gr
Kansas-Missouri Enterprise	Kansas City	MO	w	1881-1886	Ba,Ay1884[Enterprise],MO
Liberator	Kansas City	MO	w	1901-1911	Ba,Ay1905,1911,MO,Oclc,Lt1907,Gr
Missouri Messenger	Kansas City	MO	w	1894-1900	Ba,Lc91,MO,Oclc
Missouri State Post	Kansas City	MO	w	1990-1990	Oclc
National Mirror	Kansas City	MO	w	1885-1922	Ba,Ay1912,1918,NY12,19,Go,MO
National Notes	Kansas City	MO		1920-1930	NYPL,NUC,Sch
New Dawn	Kansas City	MO	m/bm	1949-1953	BJ286
New Day: the People's Magazine	Kansas City	MO		1947-1949	BJ286
New Missouri	Kansas City	MO	w	1894-1898	Ba,Ay1896,MO
NHSA Newsletter	Kansas City	MO	q	1964-1967	SPD67
Record Searchlight	Kansas City	MO	w	1908-1927	Ba,Ay1913,1925[Searchlight],MO
Rising Sun	Kansas City	MO	w	1896-1920	Ba,Ay1905,1915,MO,Oclc[e1918],WI, NY12,Gr
Signal	Kansas City	MO	w	1908-1912	Ba,Ay1909,1911,1912,NY12,MO
Son	Kansas City	MO	w	1908-1917	Ay1911-1914,1916,1917,NY12
Southern Argus	Kansas City	MO	w	1892-1893	Ba,Moten
Sun	Kansas City	MO	w	1908-1925	Ba,Ay1911,1921,Oclc,NY19,22,Gr,Mather
Times-Observer	Kansas City	MO	w	1891-1892	Oclc
UNIQUE	Kansas City	MO	m	1975	Ay1975
Western Argus	Kansas City	MO	w	1891-1893	Ba,MO
Western Christian Recorder	Kansas City	MO	w	1896-1921	Ba,Ay1909,1921,NY12,22,MO,Mather
Western Messenger	Kansas City	MO	w	1919-1922	NY19,22
Western Recorder	Kansas City	MO		1882-1885	Ba,Penn
Western Sentinel	Kansas City	MO		1879-1887	Ba,Penn
World	Kansas City	MO		1885-1888	Ba,Penn
Missouri Messenger	Macon	MO	w	1894-1900	Ba,Lc91,Oclc,WI
Western Christian Recorder	Macon	MO	m	1896-1921	Ba,Ay1905,1908,1911,1912,1916
Western Messenger	Macon	MO	w	1901-1922	Ba,MO,ABSCHSL

TITLE	CITY	ST.	FREQ.	DATES	SOURCES
Brother's Optic	Moberly	MO	w	1888-1895	Ba,Ay1888-1891,1894,MO
Western Optic	Moberly	MO	w	1895-1897	Ba,Ay1896,Br,MO
Critic	Richmond	MO	w	1889-1889	Ay1889 (see also VA)
Appeal	Saint Joseph	MO	w	1913-1921	Ba,Ay1915,1921,MO,NY22
Mirror	Saint Joseph	MO	w	1885-1904	Ba,Ay1888,1896,MO,Br
National Protest	Saint Joseph	MO	w	1897-1929	Ba,Ay1925,MO
Radical	Saint Joseph	MO	w	1887-1922	Ba,Ay1887,1909,NY12,Br,MO
Times-Observer	Saint Joseph	MO	w	1891-1892	Oclc
Advance	Saint Louis	MO	w	1881-1896	Ba,Ay1886,1906,MO,Oclc[1881-1908], Brook92
Afro-American	Saint Louis	MO	w	1906-1910	Ba,Mather
Afro-American News	Saint Louis	MO	w	1873-1893	MO
American Eagle	Saint Louis	MO	w	1894-1908	Ba,Ay1905,1908,MO,Lc91,Oclc,WI,Gr
Call	Saint Louis	MO	w	1935-1942	Ba,Ay1940,1942,NH42,EP36,41,42,Dc41
Central Afro-American	Saint Louis	MO	w	1909-1915	Ba,Ay1911,1912,NY12,MO,Mather
Chronicle	Saint Louis	MO		1929-1932	BJ (St. Elizabeth Chronicle & Interracial Review NY)
Clarion	Saint Louis	MO	w	1914-1926	Ba,Ay1920,NY26,MO,Boris1
Contributor	Saint Louis	MO	w	1883-1886	Ba,Ay1884,br,MO
Daily Christian Index	Saint Louis	MO	d	1914-1914	Mather [Bouey, Forrest Lee]
Evening Whirl	Saint Louis	MO	w	1938-1994+	Ga87,94,Oclc,EH,BRG,Baid92,EP72, 93[1964],Bp,SPD87
Flashes of Negro Life	Saint Louis	MO	m	1944-1950	Ay1950
Freeman's Journal	Saint Louis	MO	w	1877-1882	Ba,Penn,MO
Intelligencer	Saint Louis	MO	w	1902-1903	Craighead
Metro-Sentinel	Saint Louis	MO	w	1971-1992+	Oclc,EH,EP71,79[1968-1979],WI
Missouri Citizen	Saint Louis	MO	w	1880-1890	Ba,MO
Missouri Illinois Advance Citizen	Saint Louis	MO	w	1892-1922	Ba,Ay1921,1925[Advance Citizen 1892-1925],Lt1907
National Tribune	Saint Louis	MO	w	1876-1882	Ba,Penn,MO
Negro World	Saint Louis	MO	w	1875-1890	Ba,Ay1884,MO
Negro: A Journal of Essential Facts about the Negro	Saint Louis	MO	m/bm	1942-1950	Ay1950,BJ[1943-1948]
New Citizen	Saint Louis	MO	w/bw	1966-1970	Pr,EP67,SPD67,70
People's Guide	Saint Louis	MO	w	1968-1993+	EP71,93,Bp,Lb,SPD70,74,79,87
Pine Torch	Saint Louis	MO	w/m	1940-1951	NH42,46,EP50,51,NY46,Dc41,44
Postal Alliance	Saint Louis	MO	m	1914-1940	Ba,Ay1925,1937,EP39,40
Proud	Saint Louis	MO	m/q	1970-1994+	BJ,SPD87,94
Race Problem	Saint Louis	MO		1891-1893	Ba
Recorder	Saint Louis	MO		1943-1948	Ba,Br
Saint Elizabeth Chronicle	Saint Louis	MO		1928-1929	BJ (Chronicle & Interracial Review)
Saint Louis American	Saint Louis	MO	w	1927-1994+	Ba,Ay1935,1975,Oclc,Ga87,94,WI,NH42,44, 46,49,EP38,93,Baid92[1928],EBA,BRG,EH, NY32,46,Dc41,44,API90,94,Gr,Rw

TITLE	CITY	ST.	FREQ.	DATES	SOURCES
Saint Louis Argus	Saint Louis	MO	w	1912-1994+	Ba,Ay1920,1975,Ga90,94,MO,Oclc,NH42, 44,46,49,EP35,93,Baid92,EBA,BRG, NY19,22,26,32,46,Dc41,44,Bp,API90,94, WPN94,Fleming
Saint Louis Chronicle	Saint Louis	MO		pre 1979	Lb
Saint Louis Crusader	Saint Louis	MO	w	1963-1994+	Ga90,94,Pr,Lb,EP67,80,BRG,Baid92,EBA, EH,Bp,WPN94[b1961],SPD67
Saint Louis Defender	Saint Louis	MO	w	1966-1967	Pr,EP67,Lb
Saint Louis Globe-Democrat	Saint Louis	MO		pre 1950	Fleming [Walton, Lester Aglar]
Saint Louis Independent News	Saint Louis	MO		1919-1922	Ba,NY19,22,Go
Saint Louis Independent-Clarion	Saint Louis	MO	w	1914-1922	Ba,Ay1921,NY19,Br,Go
Saint Louis Mirror	Saint Louis	MO	w	1955-1973	EP67,75,EBA,Rw,Lb,Bp
Saint Louis Monitor	Saint Louis	MO		pre 1901	DANB167
Saint Louis New Crusader	Saint Louis	MO	w	1966-1974	EP67,69,70,SPD67,74
Saint Louis Palladium	Saint Louis	MO	w	1884-1912	Ba,Ay1905,1912,MO,Oclc,WI,NY12, Lt1907,Lc77,Br
Saint Louis Post Dispatch	Saint Louis	MO		pre 1950	Fleming [Walton, Lester Aglar]
Saint Louis Sentinel	Saint Louis	MO	w	1968-1994+	Ga90,94,Lb,Oclc,EP69,93,BRG,Baid92, EBA,EH,API90,94,Rw,lc,Bp
Saint Louis Star Sayings	Saint Louis	MO		1902-1906	Fleming [Walton, Lester Aglar]
Saint Louis Star-Times	Saint Louis	MO		pre 1950	Fleming [Walton, Lester Aglar]
Saint Louis Tribune	Saint Louis	MO		1877-1880	Ba,Penn
Show Down	Saint Louis	MO	m	1939	EP39
Standard	Saint Louis	MO		1923-1925	Ba
Tri-State Tribune	Saint Louis	MO	w	1936-1938	Ba,EP39
United World	Saint Louis	MO	w	1930-1938	Ba,NY32
Vanguard	Saint Louis	MO	w	1881-1911	Ba,Ay1894,1909,1911,MO
Welcome Friend	Saint Louis	MO		1870-1880	Ba,Penn
Western Christian Recorder	Saint Louis	MO	sm	1909-1952	Ay1952,EP49
Western Messenger	Saint Louis	MO		1901-1922	Ba
Whirl-examiner	Saint Louis	MO	w	1994+	WPN94[b1938]
World	Saint Louis	MO		1936-1938	Ba
Review	Sedalia	MO		1903-1924	Ba
Searchlight	Sedalia	MO	w	1908-1924	Ba,Ay1914-1921,NY19,22
Sedalia Weekly Conservator	Sedalia	MO	w	1903-1909	Ba,Ay1906,1909,Gr,Oclc,Lc83,Lt1907
Times	Sedalia	MO	w	1893-1905	Ba,Ay1896,Gr,MO,Lc91,Oclc,WI
Southeast Missouri World	Sikeston	MO	w	1939	Oclc
Southern Sun	Sikeston	MO	sm	1954-1954	Oclc
Afro-American	Springfield	MO		1896-1898	Ba
American Negro	Springfield	MO	w	1890-1891	Ba,MO,Oclc,WI,Lc77
Headlight	Springfield	MO		1888-1889	MO
Headlight	Springfield	MO		1898-1900	Ba
Tribune	Springfield	MO	w	1888-1890	Ba,MO
Tribune	Springfield	MO	w	1884-1888	Ba,Ay1887,MO
New Age	Butte	MT	w	1902-1904	Ba,aba,Mont.HS

TITLE	CITY	ST.	FREQ.	DATES	SOURCES
Colored Citizen	Helena	MT	w	1894-1894	Aba,Mont.HS
Reporter	Helena	MT		1899-1901	Ba
Montana Plaindealer	Helena	MT	w/ir	1906-1912	Ba,Ay1908,1911,Mont.HS[e1911],aba
Everybody	Missoula	MT	m	1959-1987	SPD87 (see Omaha)
Mode	Farnam	NE	m	1961-1962	Ay1962
Lincoln Leader	Lincoln	NE		1899-1907	Mather [Kemp, William Paul]
Voice	Lincoln	NE	w	1946-1953	Ay1950,1953,EP51
Weekly Review	Lincoln	NE	w	1933-1934	Ba
Afro-American Sentinel	Omaha	NE	w	1892-1911	Ba,Ay1894,Gr,Br,Lc91,WI, Oclc[1893-1899]
Chronicle	Omaha	NE		1936-1938	Ba
Enterprise	Omaha	NE	w	1892-1915	Ba,Ay1905,1915,Oclc,WI[1893-1914], NY12,Lc77,Fleming
Everybody	Omaha	NE	m	1959-1981	Ay1970,1981,WI[e1977],EH,Bp[Kansas City]
Everyone	Omaha	NE	m	1959-1974	Ay1969,SPD70,74
New Era	Omaha	NE	w	1920-1926	Ba,Gr
Omaha Guide	Omaha	NE	w	1927-1962	Ba,Ay1935,1962,NH42,44,46,49,EP35,46, NY32,46,Dc41,44,Gr
Omaha Monitor	Omaha	NE	w	1915-1932	Ba,Ay1916,1921,NY19,22,26,32,Gr,Go, Boris1
Omaha Star	Omaha	NE	w	1938-1992+	Ba,Ay1950,1956,Oclc,NH44,49,EP45,90, EH,EBA,BRG,NY46,Baid90,Bp,SPD67,70
Progress	Omaha	NE	w	1889-1905	Ba,Ay1890,1896,NY12,Br,Lc91,Oclc
Progressive Age	Omaha	NE		1913-1915	Ba
Tan Pride	Omaha	NE	m	1968-1981	Ay1970,1981,SPD72,74,79
Las Vegas Sentinel Voice	Las Vegas	NV	w	1963-1994+	Ga88,94,Lb,WI,BRG,EBA,Chic.PL, EP90-93[1980]
Voice	Las Vegas	NV	w	1963-1977	EP67,77,EH,SPD70,74
Reno Observer	Reno	NV	w	1975-1983	NA,EP75,76
A.M.E. Sunday School Teachers' Quarterly		NJ		pre 1915	Mather [Hood, Solomon Porter]
New Jersey Weekly News		NJ	w	1994+	SPD94
Central Jersey Post	Asbury Park	NJ	w	1961-1974	Pr,NJ,EP62,67,SPD67,70,74
Monmouth Vindicator	Asbury Park	NJ	w	1893-1894	Ba,NJ
New Jersey Trumpet	Asbury Park	NJ	w	1895	NJ
Apex News	Atlantic City	NJ	m,bm,q	1928-1949	NJ,EP39,40
Atlantic Advocate	Atlantic City	NJ	w	1912-1926	Ba,Go,NJ,NY12,19,22,26, Mather[1915-1927],Yenser3
Atlantic City Crusader	Atlantic City	NJ	w	1966-1973	EBA,EP71,Lb,Bp
Atlantic City Eagle	Atlantic City	NJ	w	1936-1946	Ba,NJ,EP36-40
Atlantic City Review	Atlantic City	NJ		1914-1915	Boris1 [Billups, Pope Barrow]
Beacon	Atlantic City	NJ	w	1908-1911	NJ
Messenger	Atlantic City	NJ	w	1908-1915	Ba,Ay1912,1915,NJ
National Public Record	Atlantic City	NJ	w	1900-1908	Ba,NJ
Public Record	Atlantic City	NJ	w	1896-1898	R1898,NJ

TITLE	CITY	ST.	FREQ.	DATES	SOURCES
Seaside News	Atlantic City	NJ	w	1900-1903	Ba,NJ
State Register	Atlantic City	NJ	w	1904-1906	Ba,NJ
Telegram	Atlantic City	NJ	w	1935	EP35
Topics	Atlantic City	NJ	w	1908-1913	Ba,Ay1912,NJ
W. Frank Patterson's Weekly	Belmar	NJ	w	1892-1901	Ba,NJ
County Sword	Beverly	NJ	w	1924	NJ
Ironsides Echo	Bordentown	NJ	m	1940-1942	NH42,Dc41
Ironsides Letter	Bordentown	NJ	m	1919-1922	NY19,22
Black Observer	Camden	NJ	w	1969-1970	NJ,Gl
Camden Daily Courier	Camden	NJ	d	1897-1900	Yenser3 [Davenport William Henry]
Camden Jersey Beat	Camden	NJ	w	1955-1976	NJ,EBA,EP71-76,Bp
Camden News	Camden	NJ	w	1915	NJ
Camden Union Recorder	Camden	NJ	w	1920	NJ
Musical Enterprise	Camden	NJ		pre 1950	Fleming [Adams, Alton Augustus], Ay1912[b1888 nlb]
New Jersey Spokesman	Camden	NJ	w	1930-1932	Ba,NJ,NY32
Tribune	Camden	NJ	w	1920-1922	Ba,NJ,NY22
Union Recorder	Camden	NJ	w	1918	NJ
Union Recorder & Messenger	Camden	NJ	w	1918	NJ
Afro-American	East Orange	NJ	w	1940-1992+	Ga91,92,Baid92
Essex Forum	East Orange	NJ	w,bw,m	1972-1975	Ay1975[Newark],Oclc,EP75,Bp
Grafrica News	East Orange	NJ	w	1975-1987	Ay1979,1982,EP78,80,Lb,SPD87[1975]
Innovator	East Orange	NJ	w	1973-1978	EP77,78
Jersey Voice	East Orange	NJ	w	1977-1978	EP77,78
New Jersey Forum	East Orange	NJ	sw	1975-1978	Ay1975,1978
New Jersey Voice	East Orange	NJ	w	1973-1987	EP75-76,Bp,SPD87
Appeal	Jersey City	NJ	w	1902-1912	Ba,Ay1905,NY12,NJ
Courier	Jersey City	NJ	w	1905-1906	Ba,NJ
Globe	Jersey City	NJ	w	1910-1913	Ba,Ay1912,NJ
New Day	Jersey City	NJ	w	1932-1973	Bp
New Day Inter-Denominational Inter-Racial Newspapers	Jersey City	NJ	w	1975-1976	EP75,76
New Jersey Trumpet	Jersey City	NJ	w	1887-1889	NJ
Coast Appeal	Long Branch	NJ		1898-1900	Ba
Echo	Long Branch	NJ	w	1904-1910	Ba,NJ,Oclc,Mather
American Monitor	Montclair	NJ	w	1912-1915	Ba,Ay1915,NJ
Eastern Observer	Montclair	NJ	w	1914-1926	Ba,Go,NJ,NY19,22,26,Boris2[1912]
Monitor	Montclair	NJ	w	1909-1912	Ba,Ay1912,NJ,NY12
New Jersey Observer	Montclair	NJ	w	1918-1919	NJ
New Jersey Times	Montclair	NJ		pre 1970	Ba
North Jersey News	Montclair	NJ		pre 1946	Ba,Br,NJ
Weekly Inquirer	Montclair	NJ	w	1936-1938	Ba,Br,NJ,EP38
Black Voice/Carta Boricua	New Brunswick	NJ	w	1969-1994+	Ay1986,Ga87,94,NJ,Baid92
Review of Black Political Economics	New Brunswick	NJ	q	1970-1994+	Ga90,94,SPD94

TITLE	CITY	ST.	FREQ.	DATES	SOURCES
American Star	Newark	NJ	w	1888-1898	Ba,Ay1888
Black New Ark	Newark	NJ		1972-1973	Bp
Black Voice	Newark	NJ		1971-1975	WI,Unct
City News	Newark	NJ	w	1992-1994+	BRG,API94
Community Alert	Newark	NJ	w	1980	EP80
Forum	Newark	NJ	bw	1974-1978	Oclc,EP75-78,Ay1975[Essex Forum]
Greater News/ New Jersey	Newark	NJ		1981-1992+	BRG,EP81
Herald Advance	Newark	NJ	w	1966	NJ
Hi Rise	Newark	NJ		1974-1976	EP75,76
Information	Newark	NJ	w	1972-1973	EP76,Bp
Jersey Mail	Newark	NJ	w	1930	NJ
New Day	Newark	NJ	w	1936-1938	Ba,NJ
New Jersey Afro-American	Newark	NJ	w	1941-1992+	Ba,Ay1941,1977,Ga88,91,NJ,Oclc,WI, NH44,46,49,EP45,80,Baid92,BRG,EBA, Bp,NY46,Dc41,44,SPD67,70,74,79,87
New Jersey Guardian	Newark	NJ	w	1934-1944	Ba,Ay1940,NJ,Oclc,NH42,EP38-42,Dc41, 44
New Jersey Herald	Newark	NJ	w	1940	Ay1940
New Jersey Herald Guardian	Newark	NJ		1934-1942	Ba,Br
New Jersey Herald News	Newark	NJ	w	1938-1970	Ba,Ay1945,1967,Br,Pr,NJ,EP39,67, Oclc[1938-1966],NH42,44,46,49,Dc41,44, SPD67
New Jersey Informer	Newark	NJ	w	1919-1923	Ba,Go,NJ,NY19
New Jersey Observer	Newark	NJ	w	1914-1927	Ba,NJ,NY22,26
New Jersey Record	Newark	NJ	w	1934-1951	Ba,Ay1945,1951,Br,NJ,NH46,49,50,51, Dc44
New Jersey Review	Newark	NJ	m	1866-1866	NJ
New Jersey Trumpet	Newark	NJ	w	1889-1900	Ba,Br,Penn,NJ
Newark Age	Newark	NJ	w	@1893	NJ
Newark Herald	Newark	NJ	w	1927-1939	Ba,Ay1935,1939,Oclc,EP36-39,NY32,NJ
Nite Lite Publication	Newark	NJ	w	1958-1976	NJ,EP71-76,Bp
Telegram	Newark	NJ	w	1944-1949	Ba,NJ,NH49,NY46
Unity and Struggle	Newark	NJ	m	1972-1975	EP75,76
World Telegram	Newark	NJ	w	1949-1950	EP49,50
North Jersey News	Newfoundland	NJ	w	1936	NJ
Bronze Thrills	North Bergen	NJ	m	1951-1981	Ay1981 (see Fort Worth)
Harambee	Orange	NJ		1990-1991+	Oclc
Triple Star Z	Orange	NJ	w	1972-1973	Bp
Union	Orange	NJ	w	1898-1920	Ba,Ay1905,1912,1915,NJ
Women's Missionary Recorder	Orange	NJ	w	1935-1938	Ba,NJ
Industrial Watchman	Paterson	NJ	bw/w	1899-1936	Ba,Ay1912,1935,NJ,Lt1907
New Jersey Herald	Paterson	NJ	m	1902-1905	NJ
North Jersey Independent	Paterson	NJ	w	1951	EP51
Model Cities Voice	Perth Amboy	NJ	w	1973	Bp
Herald	Plainfield	NJ	w	1904-1907	Ba,Ay1905,Lt1907,NJ

TITLE	CITY	ST.	FREQ.	DATES	SOURCES
Voice	Plainfield	NJ	w	1968-1974	NJ,Bp,Lb,Oclc,EP71-74
Trumpet	Princeton	NJ	W	1888-1897	NJ
Echo	Red Bank	NJ	w	1910-1943	Ba,Ay1912,1943,Gr,NJ,EP35,40,NY12,19, 22,26,32,Boris1
Mail and Express	Red Bank	NJ	w	1903-1907	Ay1905,NJ
Our Mail and Express	Red Bank	NJ	w	1900-1903	NJ
Word UP!	River Edge	NJ	m	1987-1993+	Ga94
A. P. Smith's Paper	Saddle Brook	NJ	w	1881-1891	NJ
Landscape	Saddle Brook	NJ	w	1887-1901	NJ
New Jersey Twilight	Salem	NJ	w	1900-1902	NJ
Connection	Teaneck	NJ	bw	1982-1994+	Oclc,EP87[1986],90-93
North Jersey Connection	Teaneck	NJ	bw	1983-1992+	Oclc,BRG
Right On!	Teaneck	NJ	m	1971-1990	Ga88,90
Journal of the National Medical Assoc.	Thorofare	NJ	m	1909-1994+	Ga90,94 (see CT)
Action News	Trenton	NJ	w	1976-1978	EP77,78
Black Journal	Trenton	NJ	w	1973	Bp
Black Weekly	Trenton	NJ	w	1973	Bp
Expositor	Trenton	NJ	w	1880-1880	NJ
Model Cities Action	Trenton	NJ	w/m	1968-1976	EP75,76,Bp
New Jersey Afro-American	Trenton	NJ	w	1940-1943	Ba,Ay1943
New World	Trenton	NJ	m	1946-1947	NJ
New World News	Trenton	NJ	m	1947-1947	NJ
Observer	Trenton	NJ	w	1960-1960	NJ
Rank & File	Trenton	NJ	w/m	1972-1976	EP75,76,Bp
Sentinel	Trenton	NJ	w	1880-1882	Ba,NJ,Lc91,Oclc,WI,NWU
Thoughts on Blackness	Trenton	NJ		1979	SPD79
Trenton Sun	Trenton	NJ		1951	NJ
Trenton Tribune	Trenton	NJ	w	1961	NJ
United Progress News	Trenton	NJ	w	1966-1966	NJ
African News	Vineland	NJ	m	1889-1891	Lc77
Corporate Headquarters	Westfield	NJ		1990-1991+	Ga90,91
Tri County News	Willingboro	NJ	w	1981-1982	EP81,82
South Jersey Defencer	Woodbury	NJ	w	1907	Lt1907
Cornish-Russwurm Chronicle	Albuquerque	NM	m/ir	1989-1991	Alb. PL
Cornish-Russwurm Chronicle	Albuquerque	NM	m/ir	1993+	Alb. PL
New Age	Albuquerque	NM	w	1911-1915	Ba,NM,NY12
Southwest Review	Albuquerque	NM	w	1922-1932	Ba,NM,NY32
Western Star	Albuquerque	NM		1940-1941	Ba
Harambee	Las Cruces	NM		1972-1973	Oclc
Western Voice	Las Cruces	NM		1938-1940	Ba
Albany Liberator	Albany	NY		1967-1968	WI
Capital	Albany	NY		1894-1896	Ba,Br
Dialogue	Albany	NY		1990	ABSCHSL

TITLE	CITY	ST.	FREQ.	DATES	SOURCES
Elevator	Albany	NY		1841-1843	Ba,Rw,Penn,NY12[1842]
Enterprise	Albany	NY		pre 1946	Ba,Br
Genius of Freedom	Albany	NY		1845-1847	Ba,Penn
Legacy	Albany	NY		1989	ABSCHSL
Liberator	Albany	NY		1968-1971	WI
Northern Star and Freeman's Advocate	Albany	NY		1842-1843	Ba,Lc91,Lc83,WI,NWU
People's Weekly	Albany	NY	w	1966-1974	Pr,EP67,SPD67,70,74
Together; We Shall Overcome	Albany	NY		1990-1991	ABSCHSL
Urban Star Bulletin	Albany	NY		pre 1979	Lb
Bulletin	Auburn	NY		pre 1915	Mather [Brooks, Edward Ulysses Anderson]
Western Echo	Bath/Utica	NY		1877	Penn
Afro American Times	Brooklyn	NY	w	1990-1994+	Ga90,94,BRG,Baid92
Afro-America	Brooklyn	NY	6xy	1966-1974	WI (see Brooklyn),SPD72,74
Ansaru Allah Publications	Brooklyn	NY	w	1973-1975	EP75,76,Bp
Bayano Publications	Brooklyn	NY		1973-1977	EP75-77
Big Red News	Brooklyn	NY	w	1975-1993+	Ay1986,Ga87,90,EP90-93,BRG,Baid92, API90
Black News a Black Nationalist Publication	Brooklyn	NY	w	1969-1979	WI,SPD74,79
Blackbird Fly	Brooklyn	NY		1974	SPD74
Brooklyn Monitor	Brooklyn	NY		1885-1890	Penn
City Sun	Brooklyn	NY	w	1984-1994+	Ga87,94,Baid92,EP90-93,BRG,WPN94, SPD87
Harmony Magazine	Brooklyn	NY	q	1982-1993+	Ga94
Home News	Brooklyn	NY		pre 1930	Yenser3 [Allen, Cleveland G.]
Long Island Tribune	Brooklyn	NY	w	1941-1943	Ba,NY46
Metropolitan Courier	Brooklyn	NY	w	1965-1973	Ay1973
National Baptist	Brooklyn	NY		1889-1915	Penn,Mather
National Monitor	Brooklyn	NY	w	1870-1902	Ba,Eur94,DANB167
Network Journal	Brooklyn	NY	w	1993-1994+	API94
New Entertainer	Brooklyn	NY	w	1975-1976	EP75,76
New York Beacon	Brooklyn	NY	w	1976-1994+	Ga94,API94
New York Daily Challenge	Brooklyn	NY	d/sw	1972-1994+	Ga94,Lb,Lc83,Bp,EP73,93[and Afro Times],BRG,EH,SPD87
New York Echo	Brooklyn	NY	w	1974-1976	Lc83,EP75,76
New York Eye	Brooklyn	NY	w	1908-1917	Ba,Ay1912,1915,Boris1
New York Recorder	Brooklyn	NY	w	1953-1994+	Ay1956,1980,Ga92,94,Sch[1935], EBA[1958],Bp,EH,BRG,Baid92,WI,EP67, 82,SPD67,70,74,79
Sentinel	Brooklyn	NY		1889-1892	Ba
Standard Union	Brooklyn	NY	d	pre 1927	Ay1912[nlb],Boris1
Sunbeam	Brooklyn	NY		1865-1867	Ba,BJ50
Third World Edition	Brooklyn	NY	w	1975-1976	EP75,76

TITLE	CITY	ST.	FREQ.	DATES	SOURCES
Tribune	Brooklyn	NY	w	1945-1946	Ba,NY46
Western Sunrise	Brooklyn	NY		1975-1976	EP75,76
Sisterhood Newsletter	Brooklyn	NY	q	1987-1994+	SPD87,94
Advocate	Buffalo	NY	w	1923-1935	Ba,Ay1935,Br,NY26
Afro-Americans in New York Life & History	Buffalo	NY	2xy	1977-1994 +	Ga91,94,WI,Baid90,SPD87
American	Buffalo	NY	w	1895-1931	Ba,NY22,26,32,Boris1
Black Academy Review	Buffalo	NY	q	1970-1979	BJ44,SPD79
Black American	Buffalo	NY	d	1920-1926	Buff.& Erie HS
Black News	Buffalo	NY	w	1970	WI,Unct
Broadcaster	Buffalo	NY		1939-1947	Ba,Br,EP39,41
Buffalo Spokesman	Buffalo	NY	w	1940-1946	Ba,Br,NH42,44,46,NY46,Dc41,44
Buffalo Star	Buffalo	NY	w	1932-1950	Ba,Ay1950,Br,NH42,44,46,49,EP36,48, NY46,Dc41,44
Challenger	Buffalo	NY	w	1962-1994+	Ay1969,Ga88,94,BRG,Baid92,EH,Bp, EP72,93,EBA,API94,WPN94
Conch	Buffalo	NY	sa	1969-1987	SPD87
Criterion	Buffalo	NY	w	1925-1994+	Ba,Ay1959,1973,Ga90,94,Lc83,NH42,44, 46,49,BRG,EP38,93,NY46,Dc41,44, API94,WPN94,Bp,SPD67,70
Empire Star	Buffalo	NY	w	1951-1971	Ay1951,1971,WI,EP67,70,Rw,Lb,SPD67, 70
Empire State Bulletin	Buffalo	NY	w	1962-1970	EP62,67,69,70,Lb
Fine Print News	Buffalo	NY	w	1970-1994+	Ga91,94,Baid92,BRG,EH,EP51,73,80, WPN94
Gazetteer and Guide	Buffalo	NY	m	1912	Ay1912,NY12,Mather
National Advocate	Buffalo	NY		1894	Rw
Outlet	Buffalo	NY		pre 1946	Ba
People's Weekly	Buffalo	NY	w	1966-1974	Pr,EP67,SPD67,70,74
Progressive Herald	Buffalo	NY	w	1930-1932	Ba,NY32
Pyramid	Buffalo	NY	q	1942-1956	Ay1950,1956
Spectator	Buffalo	NY		1894-1901	Ba
Black Perspective in Music	Cambria Heights	NY		1973-1982	BJ
East Elmhurst News	Corona	NY	w	1967-1969	EP67,69,Lb,SPD67,70
East Elmhurst News & Queens Voice	Corona	NY	w	1963-1970	EP63,64,70
Education: A Journal of Reputation	Corona	NY		1935-1936	BJ
New York Voice-Harlem USA	Flushing	NY	w	1958-1994+	Ga91,94,Lc83,BRG,Baid92,EP90,93, WPN94
Obsidian	Fredonia	NY		1975-1994+	WI,SPD94
Westchester County Press	Hastings on Hudson	NY	w	1910-1980	Ay1968,EP62,80,Bp,EBA,EH, Fleming[Mt.Vernon],SPD67
Long Island Observer	Hempstead	NY	w	1977	EP77
Long Island Rapper	Hempstead	NY		1959-1975	EP75,76[1973]
N.Y.L.I. Courier	Hempstead	NY	w	1980	EP80
Hempstead Beacon	Hicksville	NY	w	1992-1994+	BRG,Ga94[Hempstead nlb b 1950]
Uniondale Beacon	Hicksville	NY	w	1992-1994+	BRG,Ga94[Uniondale nlb b 1951]

TITLE	CITY	ST.	FREQ.	DATES	SOURCES
Black Odyssey	Jamaica	NY	m	1979-1982+	BJ70
Brooklyn & Long Island Informer	Jamaica	NY	w	1920-1926	Ba,Ay1921,NY22,26
Chocolate Singles	Jamaica	NY	bm	1987-1994+	Ga91,94,SPD87
Empire State Gazette	Jamaica	NY	w	1930-1932	Ba,NY32
Informer	Jamaica	NY		pre 1970	Ba
Jamaica Gleaner	Jamaica	NY		1946	Ba,Br
Long Island Call	Jamaica	NY	w	1952-1953	Ay1953
New York Voice	Jamaica	NY	w	1958-1974	SPD74
Queen's Voice	Jamaica	NY	w	1957-1971	Ay1969,1970,Pr,Lc83,Bp,EP67,69, Ch.P.L.[1967-1978],SPD70
Shopping and Entertainment Guide	Jamaica	NY	w/sm	1989-1993+	Ga94
Voice	Jamaica	NY		1972-1979	EH,EBA,EP71[1958],72-79
Responsibility	Massapequa	NY	3xy	1966-1994+	SPD67,70,74,87,94
Color Line	Mount Vernon	NY	m/bm	1946-1947	WI,BJ
Westchester Observer	Mount Vernon	NY	w	1947-1992+	Ga91,92,Baid92,EP67,77,EBA,EH,Bp, SPD67
A.M.E. Zion Quarterly Review	New Rochelle	NY	q	pre 1927	Boris1 [Carrington, W. O.]
League [Journal]	New Rochelle	NY		1908-1914	Ba
African Opinion	New York City	NY	bm	1950-1954	Ay1954
African Progress	New York City	NY	m	1971-1975	Ay1975,SPD74
African: Journal of African Affairs	New York City	NY	m	1945-1948	BJ16
Afro-American Beacon Light	New York City	NY	m	1898	R1898
Afro-American Page	New York City	NY	w	1909-1915	Mather [Dodson, Nathaniel Barnett]
Age	New York City	NY	w	1974-1976	EP76
Al Fann Theatrical Ensemble	New York City	NY	m	1973	Bp
Amalgamated Publishers, Inc. Newsletter	New York City	NY	q	1991-1994+	API94
American and West Indian News	New York City	NY	w	1928-1933	Yenser3 [Grey, Edgar Mussington]
American Baptist	New York City	NY		1885-1890	Ba
American Freedman	New York City	NY		1866-1869	WI
American Recorder	New York City	NY	w	pre 1928	Yenser6 [Sampson, David Solomon]
Amistad	New York City	NY	2xy	1970-1971	BJ35
Amsterdam News	New York City	NY	w	1909-1919	Ba,Ay1912,Lc83,WI,Sch,NY19,22,26,Bp, Mather
Anglo-African	New York City	NY	w	1863-1865	Lc83,Sch
Antillean Caribbean Echo	New York City	NY	w	1969-1973	Lc83,Bp
Babylon	New York City	NY		1971-1972	Unct
Baptist	New York City	NY	m	1987	ABSCHSL
Baptist Herald	New York City	NY	w	1912-1922	NY12,19,22
Beauticians Journal and Guide	New York City	NY	m	1946-1952	Ay1952
Black America	New York City	NY		1965	WI
Black American	New York City	NY	w	1960-1994+	Ga90,94,Lc83,Baid92,BRG,EP75,92, SPD87
Black Bulletin	New York City	NY		1972-1974	SPD72,74
Black Creation	New York City	NY	q	1970-1975	WI,BJ59

TITLE	CITY	ST.	FREQ.	DATES	SOURCES
Black Enterprise	New York City	NY	m	1970-1994+	Ay1975,Ga87,94,WI,BJ64
Black Health	New York City	NY		1990+	Ga90
Black Informer	New York City	NY		1972	WI
Black is Beautiful	New York City	NY		1974	SPD74
Black Liberation Journal	New York City	NY		1977	WI
Black Marker	New York City	NY		1945	Ba
Black Mask	New York City	NY		1966-1970	Unct,Gl
Black Press	New York City	NY	bm	1972-1973	Bp
Black Republican & Officer Holders Journal	New York City	NY	w	1865-1867	Ba,Lc91,Lc83,WI
Black Review	New York City	NY	ir	1971-1987	WI,BJ,SPD79,87
Black Sports	New York City	NY	m	1970-1982	Ay1975,BJ
Black Stars	New York City	NY	m	1950-1980	Ay1975,1980
Black Theatre	New York City	NY	m	1968-1974	BJ,SPD74
Black Tress	New York City	NY	bm	1978-1982	Ay1980,1982
Black Worker	New York City	NY	m	1929-1968	Ba,Lc83,WI
Brownies' Book	New York City	NY	m	1920-1921	Ay1921S,WI,BJ
Bulletin	New York City	NY	m	1947-1950	Fleming [Adams, Alger Leroy]
Business World	New York City	NY		1921-1922	DANB,Yenser3 [Petioni, Charles Augustin]
Calvin News	New York City	NY		1935-1939	Yenser6 [Calvin, Floyd Joseph]
Campus Magazine	New York City	NY	m	1951-1963	Ay1963,EP51
Carib News	New York City	NY	w	1982-1992+	Ga87,90,BRG,Baid92
Caribbean Express	New York City	NY	m	1973	Bp
Cateret Gazetteer & Guide	New York City	NY	q	1940	Ay1940
Chronicle	New York City	NY		1888-1890	Ba,DANB76[1897]
Citizen	New York City	NY		1919-1921	Ba
Class Magazine	New York City	NY	m	1979-1994+	Ga90,94,SPD87
College Weekly	New York City	NY	w	1951-1963	Ay1963
Colored American	New York City	NY	w	1837-1842	Ba,Lc91,Lc83,NY12,Bir.PL[1840-1841]
Colored American Magazine	New York City	NY	m	1900-1907	Lt1907,Mather,DANB277[b1900]
Colored Citizen	New York City	NY		1912-1915	Ba,NY12
Colored Man's Journal	New York City	NY		1848-1861	Ba,Gr,Br,NY12,Penn
Commoner	New York City	NY	w	1919-1922	Ba,Ay1921,NY19,Go
Contact	New York City	NY	m/q	1970-1975	Ay1970,1975
Contender	New York City	NY		1926-1930	Ba
Courier	New York City	NY	w	1962-1972	EBA,EP62,72,Lb,SPD67
Crescent	New York City	NY		1935-1950	Fleming [Reddick, Lawrence Dunbar]
Crisis	New York City	NY	m/bm	1909-1994+	Ay1915,1980,Ga94,WI,EP39,51,EH, NY12,BJ,SPD72,74,79[b1968]
Crusader	New York City	NY	m	1918-1923	Ba,Ay1921,BJ[e1921]
Daily Citizen	New York City	NY	d	1933-1944	Ba[1933-1934],Yenser6
Daily Informer	New York City	NY	d	1927-1929	Ba
Daily World	New York City	NY	w	1970-1979	Lc83,Bp,SPD74

TITLE	CITY	ST.	FREQ.	DATES	SOURCES
Defender	New York City	NY		1909-1910	Ba
Defender	New York City	NY		1930-1931	Yenser3 [Grey, Edgar Mussington]
Despite Everything	New York City	NY		1968	Unct
Dispatch	New York City	NY	w	1920-1925	Ba,Ay1921S,Boris1
Dominant Metronome	New York City	NY		pre 1950	Fleming [Adams, Alton Augustus]
Educating in Faith	New York City	NY	m	1907-1981	Ay1975,1986,WI,Ay1983[DC],SPD87
Education	New York City	NY		1935-1936	WI
Emerge	New York City	NY	10xy	1989-1994+	Ga90,94
Encore American & Worldwide News	New York City	NY	q/bm/m	1972-1982	Ay1975,1980,1981,WI,BJ
Enterprise	New York City	NY	w	1883-1890	Ba,Ay1888
Equal Justice	New York City	NY		1970-1971	WI
Equality	New York City	NY		1944-1945	WI
Essence	New York City	NY	m	1970-1994+	Ay1975,1982,Ga87,94,WI,SPD70,74,79,87
Ethiopian World	New York City	NY		1917-1934	Ba
Evangelist	New York City	NY		1846-1847	Ba
Evening Gazette	New York City	NY		1913-1915	Ba
Expansions	New York City	NY	q	1971-1976	EP75,76
Fight Back	New York City	NY	m	1974-1987	SPD79,87
Fire!!: Devoted to Younger Negro Artists	New York City	NY		1926-1926	BJ,DANB590,Boris1
For You	New York City	NY	bm	1948-1949	EP48,49
Freedom	New York City	NY		1950-1955	WI
Freedom North	New York City	NY		1964-1966	WI
Freedom's Journal	New York City	NY	w	1827-1829	Ba,WI,NY12,Lb,BJ
Freedomways	New York City	NY	q	1961-1988	Ga87,88,BJ,SPD67,70,74,79,87
Freeman	New York City	NY	w	1884-1887	Ba,Penn,Lc91,Sch,DANB236
Gibson Report	New York City	NY	m	1966-1979	SPD67,74,79
Gladiator	New York City	NY		1990-1991	Ga90,91
Globe	New York City	NY		1879-1884	Ba,Penn,Go,Lc91,Mather, DANB236[b1881]
Golden Legacy	New York City	NY	5xy	1966-1979	SPD79
Harlem Digest	New York City	NY		1950-1951	EP50,51
Harlem Heights Daily Citizen	New York City	NY	w	1933-1934	Sch,Yenser4
Harlem Liberator	New York City	NY		1933-1934	Ba
Harlem News	New York City	NY		1967-1971	WI
Harlem Quarterly	New York City	NY	q	1949-1950	BJ
Harlem Star	New York City	NY		1933	Yenser3 [Grey, Edgar Mussington]
Herald Tribune	New York City	NY		1931	Fleming [Walton, Lester Aglar]
Home Journal News	New York City	NY	w	1933-1938	Sch,EP38,Yenser3[1931-1933 Harlem Home Journal]
Hotel Messenger	New York City	NY		1917-1917	BJ
Howard Medical News	New York City	NY	3xy	1924-1940	EP49,40,Boris2
Imani	New York City	NY		1971-1987	SPD74,79,87,Unct
Independent	New York City	NY		1879-1882	Ba,BJ23[1906]

TITLE	CITY	ST.	FREQ.	DATES	SOURCES
Inside Out	New York City	NY	bw	1973	Bp
Interracial News Service	New York City	NY		1920-1965	WI
Interracial Review	New York City	NY	m/ir	1917-1971	Ay1945,1964,EP46,49,BJ[1933-1971]
Interstate Tattler	New York City	NY	w	1921-1939	Ba,Ay1935,1939,Sch[1925],NY32,Yenser4
Ivy Leaf	New York City	NY		1928-1944	Yenser3 [Berlack, Thelma E.]
Journal of the National Medical Assoc.	New York City	NY	bm	1939-1951	Ay1940,1975,EP39,40,46,50,51
Liberation	New York City	NY		1965-1970	WI
Liberator	New York City	NY	m	1961-1974	WI,BJ,SPD67[1965],70,[b1961],74
Liberator	New York City	NY	w	1929-1935	Ba,Sch,NY32,Lc77,DANB160
Listener News	New York City	NY	w	1938-1941	Ba,Sch,Br,EP40,41
Long Island Star	New York City	NY	w	1953	Sch
Looking Glass	New York City	NY		1925	DANB590
Manhattan Tribune	New York City	NY	w	1968-1973	WI,EBA,EH,EP70-73,Bp,Lb
Masonic Quarterly	New York City	NY	q	pre 1924	DANB76
Masses	New York City	NY		1912	Boris1 [Harrison, Hubert Henry]
Messenger	New York City	NY	m	1917-1928	Ay1921,WI,BJ,Boris[1906-1944], DANB476
Militant	New York City	NY	w	1928-1994+	BRG,Bp,Ga94[nlb]
Mirror of Liberty	New York City	NY		1838-1841	DANB537
Missionary Seer	New York City	NY		1901-1977	WI
Modern Business	New York City	NY	m	1946	EP46
Music Dial Magazine	New York City	NY	m	1945-1946	EP45,46
Nation	New York City	NY		1976	EP76
National Black Monitor	New York City	NY	m	1975-1994+	BRG,SPD87,94
National Eye	New York City	NY		1890-1891	Ba
National Freedman	New York City	NY		1865-1866	WI
National Leader	New York City	NY		1884-1886	Ba
National News	New York City	NY	w	1932-1932	Sch,Fleming
National Principia	New York City	NY	w	1858-1866	Sch,WI
National Review	New York City	NY	w	pre 1928	Boris2 [Simmons, Roscoe]
National Scene	New York City	NY	m	1965-1991+	Ay1969,1980,EH,Ga91,SPD70,74,79
Negro Book Club Newsletter	New York City	NY	bm	1966-1974	SPD67,70,74
Negro Champion	New York City	NY		1925-1929	Lc77
Negro Churchman	New York City	NY	m/ir	1923-1931	Rw,BJ
Negro Liberator	New York City	NY	w	1932-1935	Ba,Sch
Negro Peace Echo	New York City	NY		pre 1933	Rw
Negro Press Digest	New York City	NY	m	1961-1970	SPD67,70
Negro Times	New York City	NY	d	1920-1922	Ba,Rw,Boris1,DANB76
Negro Worker	New York City	NY	w	1912-1935	Ba,Ay1921S,Bir.PL[1931-1937],Lc77
Negro World	New York City	NY	w	1912-1935	Ba,Ay1921S,Lc77,NY19,22,26,32,Bir.PL, Boris1,DANB76,221,470
New Africa	New York City	NY	m	pre 1950	Fleming [Hunton, William Alphaeus]
New African	New York City	NY		1990-1991	Ga90,91

TITLE	CITY	ST.	FREQ.	DATES	SOURCES
New Day	New York City	NY	w	1936-1943	Ba,Ay1940,BJ[b1937]
New Negro	New York City	NY		1918-1919	DANB490[b1916],Boris2
New Sign	New York City	NY	w	1940-1951	NH42,EP50,51,Dc41
New York Age	New York City	NY	w	1887-1970	Ba,Ay1888,1960,Penn,Lb,R1888,1898, 1900,WI,NH42,44,46,49,EP38,51,NY12, 19,22,26,32,46,Dc41,44,Lc83,Lt1907, Yenser6
New York Age Defender	New York City	NY	w	1953-1957	Lc77,Lc91,Sch
New York Amsterdam News	New York City	NY	w	1919-1994+	Ay1915,1950,Ga90,94,Br,Lc91,Lc83, NH42,44,46,49,EP35,93,Baid92,BRG,EH, NY12,22,26,32,46,Dc41,44,API94
New York Citizen Call	New York City	NY	w	1960-1967	Sch
New York Courier	New York City	NY	w	1962-1972	EBA,Lb,SPD74[b1971]
New York Dispatch	New York City	NY	w	1909-1926	Ay1915,1921,NY22,26
New York Freeman	New York City	NY	w	1884-1887	Ba,Sch,Penn,Lc91,WI
New York News	New York City	NY	w	1913-1935	Ba,Ay1915,1935,NY19,22,26,32,Go,Br, Yenser6[e1944],BJ
New York Observer	New York City	NY	w	1987-1994+	WPN94
New York State Contender	New York City	NY	w	1929	Sch
New York Tribune	New York City	NY		1868	Penn
New York Voice	New York City	NY	w	1971-1980	Lc83,EP80
On Guard	New York City	NY		1961	WI
On the Ball Magazine	New York City	NY	w	1973	Bp
Opportunity: Journal of Negro Life	New York City	NY	m/q	1923-1948	Ay1935,1945,EP39,49,BJ,Fleming, DANB348
Our Colored Missions	New York City	NY	m	1907-1973	Ay1970,1973,EH
Our World	New York City	NY	m	1946-1955	Ay1955,1990,EP48-51,BJ
Pearson's Magazine	New York City	NY		1919-1921	Boris1 [Kelley, William Melvin]
People's Journal	New York City	NY		1870	Penn,Go
People's Press	New York City	NY		1843-1844	Ba,Go,Penn,NY12
People's Voice	New York City	NY	w	1942-1951	Ba,Ay1951,NH44,46,EP43,48,NY46,Dc44, Rw,Br,BJ
People's Weekly	New York City	NY	w	1966-1967	SPD67
Pilot	New York City	NY		1913-1915	Ba
Pine and Palm	New York City	NY		1845-1865	Ba,Penn
Prince Hall Sentinel	New York City	NY	m	1951	EP51
Probe	New York City	NY	m	1972-1974	SDP72,74
Progressive American	New York City	NY	w	1871-1887	Ba,Ay1886,Penn,Go,Rw, Mather[1902-1905],DANB39
Progressive Labor	New York City	NY	w	1973	Bp
Race Relations and Industry	New York City	NY	m	1966-1974	SPD67,70,74
Race: Devoted to Social, Political,and Economic Equality	New York City	NY	q	1935-1936	BJ
Ram's Horn	New York City	NY	w	1847-1848	Ba,Penn,Go,Lc91,WI,NY12
Re Up	New York City	NY	w	1950	Sch
Record Beat	New York City	NY		1966-1967	SPD67

TITLE	CITY	ST.	FREQ.	DATES	SOURCES
Reporter	New York City	NY		1902-1903	Ba
Republican	New York City	NY		1896-1903	Ba,Br
Review of Black Political History	New York City	NY		1970-1982	BJ
Right On!	New York City	NY	m	1971-1994+	Ga91,94,WI,SPD94
Rights and Reviews	New York City	NY	bm	1965-1974	SPD67,70,74
Rights of All	New York City	NY		1828-1829	Ba,Penn,Go,Lc91,WI,NY12
Rumor	New York City	NY	w	1880-1880	Ba,Penn,DANB236
Say	New York City	NY	bw	1954-1974	Ay1969,1974,EH,SPD67,70,74
Sentinel	New York City	NY		1892-1895	Ba
Small's Illustrated Monthly	New York City	NY	m	1905	Mather [Small, Thomas Frederick]
Small's Negro Trade Journal	New York City	NY		1906-1912	NY12,Mather
Spirit of the Times	New York City	NY		1836-1842	Ba
Spoken Word	New York City	NY	sw	1936	BJ
Spokesman	New York City	NY		1924-1927	BJ,Boris1,Yenser4
Store	New York City	NY		1921-1923	Ba
Tattler	New York City	NY		1930-1932	Ba
Times of Freedom	New York City	NY		1845-1847	Ba
Together: Baptist Educational Center Newsletter	New York City	NY		1957-1963	ABSCHSL
Transition Press	New York City	NY	w	1969	Rw
Triple Jeopardy	New York City	NY	bm	1970-1975	EP75,76
Union Times	New York City	NY	w	1892-1895	Ba,Eur94
Uptown	New York City	NY		1987-1994+	SPD87,94
Urban League News	New York City	NY	m	1970-1974	SPD74
Vanguard	New York City	NY	m	1943-1949	Ay1949
Voice	New York City	NY		1916-1919	Ba,Boris1,Yenser3
Voice	New York City	NY	w	1970-1971	Lc83,Bp
Voice of Ethiopia	New York City	NY		1938-1941	Ba,Br,Lc91
Voice of Missions	New York City	NY	6xy/bm	1892-1994+	Ba,Ay1912,1975,Ga87,94,EP48,51,NY19,22,26,SPD94
Weekly Advocate	New York City	NY	w	1837-1842	Ba,Penn,Lc91,NY12
Weekly Anglo-African	New York City	NY	w/m	1859-1862	Ba,Br,Penn,Go,Lc91,Lc83,WI,Sch,NY12,BJ39
Welfarer	New York City	NY	m	1946-1950	Fleming [Aldridge, Madeline Aray]
World	New York City	NY		1922-1931	Fleming [Walton, Lester Aglar]
World Herald	New York City	NY	w	1936	BJ
World Peace Echo	New York City	NY		1917-1934	Ba,Lc83
World Telegram	New York City	NY		1933	Yenser3 [Grey, Edgar Mussington]
World To-Morrow	New York City	NY		1926	Boris1 [Thurman, Wallace]
Zion Standard & Weekly Review	New York City	NY		1865-1869	Ba,Penn
Hudson Valley Black Press	Newburgh	NY	w	1983-1994+	Ga90,94,Baid92,BRG,API94
Salaam	Nyack?	NY		1969	WI
Mid Hudson Herald	Poughkeepsie	NY	bw	1977-1994+	EP77,78,80,81,Lb,SPD87,94
About Time	Rochester	NY	m	1972-1994+	Ga90,94,WI,BJ[b1973],SPD87

TITLE	CITY	ST.	FREQ.	DATES	SOURCES
American Negro	Rochester	NY	w	1962-1967	Pr,EP62,63,64,67,SPD67
Communicade	Rochester	NY	w	1972-1994+	Ay1980,Ga87,94,EP73-80,Baid92,BRG, EH,Lb,SPD87
Douglass's Monthly	Rochester	NY	m	1860-1863	WI[1858-1863],Rw,NWU,BJ
Frederick Douglass' Paper	Rochester	NY		1851-1860	Ba,Lc91,WI,Penn,NWU
Frederick Douglass Voice	Rochester	NY	bm	196u-1984	Rw,EP84[1934]
Liberty Party Paper?	Rochester	NY		1851	Rw
North Star	Rochester	NY	w	1949	NH49
North Star	Rochester	NY	w	1847-1851	Ba,Penn,Lb,Lc91,NY12,DANB170
People's Weekly	Rochester	NY	w	1966	Pr
Rochester Sentinel	Rochester	NY	w	1910-1912	Ay1912,NY12
Rochester Voice	Rochester	NY	w/bm	1933-196u	Ba,Ay1950,1954,NH42,44,46,EP37,51, Dc41,44,Rw,Br
Star	Rochester	NY	w	1947-1953	Ay1950,1953
Ekklesia	Springfield Gardens	NY		1986-1991	ABSCHSL
Challenger	Syracuse	NY		1970-1971	Rw
Gazette	Syracuse	NY	w	1970-1981	Ay1981,EP76-80,Lb
Gazette News Weekly	Syracuse	NY	w	1971-1975	EP75
Home Town News	Syracuse	NY	w	1967-1968	Rw
Impartial Citizen	Syracuse	NY		1848-1856	Ba,Penn
Impartial Citizen	Syracuse	NY	6xy	1980-1994+	Ay1982,Ga87,94[nlb],SPD87,Baid90,EP81
Liberated Voice	Syracuse	NY		1968	Rw
Palladium	Syracuse	NY		1889-1892	Ba
Progressive Herald	Syracuse	NY	w	1933-1959	Ba,Ay1940,1959,NH42,44,46,49,EP38,51, NY46,Dc41,44,Br,Rw
Clarion	Troy	NY		1846-1846	Ba,NY12,DANB253
National Watchman	Troy	NY		1842-1843	Ba,Penn,NY12,DANB253
Long Island Courier	Uniondale	NY	w	1972-1994+	EP77,SPD87,94
Long Island Courier & Hawk	Uniondale	NY		1978	EP78
Westchester County Press	White Plains	NY	w	1928-1992+	Baid92(see Mt.Vernon,Yonkers, Hasting-on-Hudson)
Progressive Inquirer	White Plains	NY		1906-1908	Ba
Progressive Inquirer	Yonkers	NY	w	1906-1915	Ba,Ay1912,NY12
Standard	Yonkers	NY	w	1907-1911	Ba,Mather,DANB76[b1908]
Standard Journal	Yonkers	NY	w	1912-1915	Ba,Ay1912,NY12
Westchester County Press	Yonkers	NY	w	1910-1994+	Ay1980,Ga87,94[b1928],API90,94,Baid92, EP51[NYC],EP70
Voice	Ashboro	NC	sm	1910-1918	Ba,Ay1914-1918
Advocate	Asheville	NC	w	1894	Eur94
Asheville Advocate	Asheville	NC	w	1987-1993+	Oclc,Asheville Advocate
Asheville Enterprise	Asheville	NC		1918-1944	Ba[1930-1932],NY26,32,Yenser6
Black Post	Asheville	NC	w	1975-1976	Lb,Gp
Church and Southland Advocate	Asheville	NC		1935	Ba
Colored Enterprise	Asheville	NC		1897-1900	Ba
Freeman's Advocate	Asheville	NC	w	1892-1896	Ba,Ay1894,NC[1892-1893]

TITLE	CITY	ST.	FREQ.	DATES	SOURCES
Light Beaver & People's Record Magazine	Asheville	NC	m	1945-1951	EP45,46,48-51
Mountain Gleanor	Asheville	NC		1884-1886	Ba,Penn
Record	Asheville	NC	w	1934-1944	Ba,Ay1940,1941,NH42,44,EP35,44,Dc41, Br
Southern News	Asheville	NC	w/bw	1936-1975	Ba,Ay1945,1955,NH44,46,49,EP37,76,EH, NY46,Dc41,44,Br,Bp,Lb
World	Asheville	NC		1936-1938	Ba
Tribune	Baden	NC		1919-1921	Ba
News	Beaufort	NC		1901-1914	Ba
Joseph K. Brick News	Bricks	NC	m	1919-1922	NY19,22
Minorities and Women in Business	Burlington	NC	6xy	1984-1994+	Ga90,94
Sentinel	Carthage	NC	w	1909-1911	Ba,Ay1911
Advertiser	Charlotte	NC	w	1904-1922	Ba,Ay1906,1919,NY12,19,22,Lt1907,Go
Africo-American Presbyterian	Charlotte	NC	w	1879-1939	Ba,Ay1894,1935,Lc91,Oclc,WI,NY12,19, 22,26,32,NWU,Yenser6
Argue	Charlotte	NC		1919-1922	NY19,22
A.M.E. Zion Quarterly Review	Charlotte	NC	q	1889-1940	EP39,40,Mather
Carolina Post	Charlotte	NC		1922	Ba
Carolina Tribune	Charlotte	NC	w	1926-1945	Ba,Ay1945
Charlotte Post	Charlotte	NC	w	1918-1994+	Ay1935,1969,Ga87,94,Br,Lc91,NH44,49, EP35,93,EH,EBA,BRG,Baid92,NY32,46, API90,94,Bp,SPD67,70,74
Charlottean	Charlotte	NC		1946-1946	Ba
Church School Herald-Journal	Charlotte	NC		1951-1977	WI
Eagle	Charlotte	NC		1946-1951	Ba,EP48-51,Fleming
Enterprise	Charlotte	NC	w	1891-1892	Ba,Ay1892
Gazette	Charlotte	NC	w	1903-1926	Ba,Ay1905,1912,NY12,19,22,26,Go
Messenger	Charlotte	NC	w	1882-1890	Ba,Ay1887,1888,NC[1882-1888],Penn
Metrolinian News	Charlotte	NC	w	1970-1975	EH[1971],EP73-78,Gp,Bp,Lb
National Enquirer	Charlotte	NC		1880-1887	Ba,Penn
Post	Charlotte	NC		1906-1911	Ba
Progressive Messenger	Charlotte	NC		1913-1932	Ba,NY32
Quarterly Review of Higher Education Among Negroes	Charlotte	NC	q	1933-1971	Ay1945,1971,EH,EP49-51,BJ[e1960]
Queen City Gazette	Charlotte	NC	w	1964-1974	Pr,Lb,EP64,70,SPD67,70,74
Safe Guard-Enterprise	Charlotte	NC		1895-1899	Ba
Star of Zion	Charlotte	NC	w	1876-1994+	Ba,Ay1896,1975,Ga87,94,Penn,NH42,46, EP38,80,BRG,Baid92,NC,EH,Bp,NY12, 19,22,26,32,46,Dc41,44,Lt1907,Lb, WPN94,R1898,1900,Mather,SPD87,94
Sunday School Literature	Charlotte	NC		1896-1900	Mather [Blackwell, George Lincoln]
Zion's Harp	Charlotte	NC		1890-1899	Ba
Blue Ridge Eagle	Cherrylane	NC		1906-1909	Ba
Cotton Boll	Concord	NC	w	1897-1898	NC
Independent Pilot	Concord	NC		1878-1884	Ba,Penn

TITLE	CITY	ST.	FREQ.	DATES	SOURCES
Piedmont	Concord	NC		1896-1898	Ba
Piedmont Index	Concord	NC		1896-1898	Ba
Light-House	Dallas	NC	bw	1872-1887	Ba,NC[1884-1886]
Advance	Durham	NC		1901-1902	Ba
Africa News	Durham	NC	w	1973-1987	Sch,SPD79,87
African Expositor	Durham	NC		1870s	Penn
Black Aging	Durham	NC		1975	WI
Bulletin	Durham	NC	q	1919-1922	NY19,22
Campus Echo	Durham	NC	bm	1940-1978	Ay1969,1978
Carolina Times	Durham	NC	w	1919-1994+	Ba[1922],Ay1945,1975,Ga87,94,Lc91,WI, NH42,46,49,EP38,93,Baid92,EBA,EH, BRG,Gp,NY46,Dc41,44,API90,94,Bp, Yenser3,SPD67,70,74,79
Carolina Tribune	Durham	NC	w	1938-1944	Ba,Ay1940,NH44
Champion	Durham	NC	w	1960	Sch
Ex Umbra	Durham	NC		1965-1969	WI
Reformer	Durham	NC	w	1898-1938	Ba,Ay1911,1912,1913,NY12
Sunday Star	Durham	NC		1945	Ba
Eastern Herald	Edenton	NC	w	1895-1900	Ba,NC[1896-1898]
Herald	Edenton	NC		1917-1919	Ba
Christian Star	Elbow	NC	sm	1904-1905	Ba,Ay1905
Christian Eagle	Elizabeth City	NC		1898-1900	Ba
Eastern Herald	Elizabeth City	NC	w	1896-1901	Ba,NC[1869-1900]
Gazette	Elizabeth City	NC		1903-1904	Ba
Industrial Advocate	Elizabeth City	NC		1913-1915	Ba
Our Carolina World	Elizabeth City	NC	w	1907-1911	Ba,Ay1911
Roanoke Tribune	Elizabeth City	NC	w	1905-1922	Ba[1905-1910],Ay1908,1909,NY12,19,22
Signs of the Times	Elizabeth City	NC	sm	1902-1926	Ba,Ay1908,1911,NY12,19,22,26,Go, Mather
Neuse River Times	Enfield	NC	w	1904-1908	Ba,Ay1908
Black Times/Recap	Fayetteville	NC	w	1986-1992+	Ga87,91,Baid90,92,BRG,EP87,90
Buffalo	Fayetteville	NC	m	1980-1982	BJ
Carolinian	Fayetteville	NC		1944-1970	Ba,EP48,49
Challenge	Fayetteville	NC		1992+	BRG
Educator	Fayetteville	NC		1875-1880	Ba,Penn
Enterprise	Fayetteville	NC		1877-1881	Ba,Penn
Home Review	Fayetteville	NC		pre 1915	Mather [Kyles, Linwood W.]
North Carolina Sun	Fayetteville	NC	w	1893-1897	Ba,Ay1896
Sun	Fayetteville	NC	w	1883-1885	NC
What's Happening Now	Fayetteville	NC	w	1973-1976	EP74-76,Gp[1976]
Christian Star	Franklin	NC	sm	1915-1917	Ba,Ay1917[1908]
Fremont Enterprise	Freemont	NC		pre 1927	Boris1 [Skinner, John Henry]
Gaston Times	Gastonia	NC	w	1972-1976	EH,EP73-76,Lb
Carolina Enterprise	Goldsboro	NC	w	1881-1885	Ba,Ay1882,Gp[1881-1882],Br

TITLE	CITY	ST.	FREQ.	DATES	SOURCES
Enterprise	Goldsboro	NC		1881-1884	Ba,Penn
Golden Rule	Goldsboro	NC	w	1887-1890	Ba
Metro Times	Goldsboro	NC	w	1978-1994+	Ga90,91,94[nlb],Baid90,92,BRG,EP84, 93[Goldsboro Times],WPN94
Negro Herald	Goldsboro	NC	w	1925-1926	Ba,Ay1925S
Progress	Goldsboro	NC	w	1890-1891	Ba,Ay1890,NC
Star	Goldsboro	NC	w	1936-1940	Ba,Ay1940
United American Free Will Baptist Advocate	Goldsboro	NC		1990-1992	ABSCHSL
Echo	Graham	NC	m	1910-1915	Ba,Ay1911,1912,1914
A & M College Bulletin	Greensboro	NC	q	1912-1922	NY12,19,22
A & T Register	Greensboro	NC	2xw	1892-1994+	Ay1969,1980,Ga87,94,WI[1928?],NY46, EP51,Bp
African World	Greensboro	NC	w	1971-1976	WI,EP75,76,Bp,NWU
Carolina Citizen	Greensboro	NC	w	1940-1944	NH42,44,EP43,44,Dc41
Carolina Methodist	Greensboro	NC	w	1890-1892	Ba,Ay1891
Carolina Peacemaker	Greensboro	NC	w	1965-1994+	Ay1969,1975,Ga87,94,BRG,Baid92,EBA, EH,Gp[1967],EP71,92[1967],93,WPN94, API94,Bp
Cuttings	Greensboro	NC	w	1937	EP37
Democrat	Greensboro	NC		pre 1946	Ba,Br
Future Outlook	Greensboro	NC	w	1934-1978	Ay1969,1978,EP62,76,EBA,Bp,Lb,SPD67, 70,74
Gate City Argus	Greensboro	NC		1913-1922	Ba,Go,NY19,22
Greensboro Daily News	Greensboro	NC	d	1909-1984	Oclc,Sch
Greensboro News and Record	Greensboro	NC	d	1984	Oclc
Greensboro North Carolina Patriot	Greensboro	NC		pre 1946	Br
Greensboro Record	Greensboro	NC		1983	Oclc
Herald	Greensboro	NC	w	1913-1915	Ba,Ay1914,1915
North Carolina Sun	Greensboro	NC		1893-1898	Ba
People's Sentinel	Greensboro	NC		pre 1915	Mather [Rush, James Buchanan]
Post	Greensboro	NC		1936-1938	Ba
Public Post	Greensboro	NC	w	1981-1991	Ga91 (see Laurinburg)
Register	Greensboro	NC	m	1883-1885	NC
Share	Greensboro	NC		1971-1974	WI
SOBU	Greensboro	NC		1971-1974	SPD74,NWU
Tribune	Greensboro	NC	w	1936-1945	Ba,Ay1945,NH42,44,EP43,44,Dc41
W.C.T.U. Tidings	Greensboro	NC	m	1907	Lt1907
Carolina Citizen	Greenville	NC	w	1943-1944	EP43,44
Progressive Messenger	Greenville	NC	w	1914-1916	Ba,Ay1915
"M" Voice Newspaper	Greenville	NC	m	1897-1993+	Ga94
Messenger and Review	Hamlet	NC		1906-1909	Ba
Southern Watchman	Hamlet	NC	w	1913-1919	Ba,Ay1916-1919
Messenger	Hartford	NC	bm	1908-1911	Ay1911
Christian Star	Henderson	NC	sm	1912-1915	Ba,Ay1913,1914

TITLE	CITY	ST.	FREQ.	DATES	SOURCES
Union Christian Star	Henderson	NC	m	1908-1912	Ba,Ay1909,1911,1912
Mountain News	Hendersonville	NC	w	1939-1950	Ba,Ay1940,1950,NH42,44,49,EP43,NY46,Dc41
Colored American	High Point	NC		1919-1922	Ba,Go,NY19,22
Tribunal Aid	High Point	NC	w	1973-1976	Gp
Advance	Jamestown	NC		1896-1910	Ba
City Paper	Kenly	NC		1926-1927	Boris1 [Skinner, John Henry]
East Carolina News	Kinston	NC	w	1913-1917	Ba,Ay1915,EP40
Free Will Baptist Advocate	Kinston	NC	w	1906-1937	Ba,Ay1908,1935,EP35,40,NY12,19,22
People's Chronicle	Kinston	NC		1948	EP48
Searchlight	Kinston	NC		1898-1900	Ba
Standard	Kinston	NC		1894-1896	Ba
Messenger	Kittrell	NC		1919-1922	NY19,22
Laurinburg Post	Laurinburg	NC	w	1895	Oclc
Public Post	Laurinburg	NC	w	1981-1994+	Ga90,94,Baid92 (see Greensboro)
Scotland Times	Laurinburg	NC		1895-1904	Ba
Colored Industrial	Lincolnton	NC		1899-1903	Ba
Baptist Pilot	Littleton	NC	w/m	1887-1895	Ba,Ay1894,Eur94
True Reformer	Littleton	NC	w	1899-1909	Ba,Ay1905,1909,Lc91,Oclc,WI,NC,Br,DANB679
Blade	Maxton	NC	w	1890-1907	Ba,Ay1905,1906,Lt1907
Crusader Weekly Newsletter	Monroe	NC	w	1960	WI
Freedom	Monroe	NC		1963	WI
Enterprise	Mount Airy	NC		1897-1900	Ba
Afro-American Vindicator	New Bern	NC	w	1888-1892	Ba,Ay1891
Golden Rule	New Bern	NC	w	1887-1890	Ba,Ay1888,Penn
People's Advocate	New Bern	NC	w	1886-1887	Ba,Ay1886,Gr,Penn,Lc91,Oclc,NC
Star of Zion	New Bern	NC		1876-1890	Ba,Penn
World	New Bern	NC	w	1932-1942	Ba,Ay1940,1942,EP35-39
Baptist Pilot	Newton	NC		1887-1893	Ba (see also Winton NC)
Parmele Institute Herald	Parmele	NC	m	1919-1922	NY19,22
Herald	Pee Dee	NC	w	1897-1898	NC
News	Pee Dee	NC		1894-1896	Ba
Eastern Index	Pittsboro	NC	w	1918-1920	Ba,Ay1918,1919
North Carolina Index	Pittsboro	NC	sm/w	1903-1922	Ba,Ay1906,1916,NY12,19,22
Public Post	Raeford	NC	w	1981-1994+	Ay1986,Ga87,91,BRG,API94
African Expositor	Raleigh	NC	q	1880-1890	Ba,Ay1884,1890,ABSCHSL,Penn
Augustinian	Raleigh	NC	m	1919-1922	NY19,22
Banner	Raleigh	NC	w	1881-1884	Ba,Ay1882,Br,Penn
Banner Enterprise	Raleigh	NC	w	1881-1884	Ba,Penn,NC,Ay1884[Winston-Salem]
Baptist Informer	Raleigh	NC	m	1878-1994+	Ay1986,Ga87,88,ABSCHSL,Ga94[nlb]
Baptist Quarterly	Raleigh	NC	q	1896	ABSCHSL
Baptist Sentinel	Raleigh	NC	w	1898-1927	Ba,Ay1912,1915,NY12,19,22
Baptist Standard	Raleigh	NC		1881-1927	Ba,Penn

TITLE	CITY	ST.	FREQ.	DATES	SOURCES
Blade	Raleigh	NC		1891-1901	Ba
Carolina Times	Raleigh	NC	w	1930-1938	Ba,NY32
Carolina Tribune	Raleigh	NC	w	1926-1946	Ba,Ay1935,1946,Br,NH42,44,46,EP35,44,NY32,Dc41,44,Fleming
Carolinian	Raleigh	NC	w	1920-1994+	Ba,Ay1950,1978,Ga87,94,WI[b1941],NH49,Baid92,EP45,93,EBA,BRG,EH[1940],Gp,Bp,Lc91,WPN94,API94,SPD67
Gazette	Raleigh	NC	w	1883-1898	Ba,Ay1896,R1898,Br,NWU,Lc91,Oclc,WI,Eur94,NC[1883-1898?],Mather
Home Mission College Review	Raleigh	NC	w	1927-1930	ABSCHSL
Independent	Raleigh	NC	w	1917-1926	Ba,Go,Sch,NY19
Journal of Industry	Raleigh	NC		1877-1882	Ba,Penn
Kinston Greenville Dispatch	Raleigh	NC	w	1990	EP90
Liberator	Raleigh	NC		1908-1909	Ba
Light House	Raleigh	NC		1884-1886	Ba,Penn
Mountain Gleanor	Raleigh	NC		1884-1886	Ba
North Carolina Gazette	Raleigh	NC	w	1884-1890	Ba,Penn,Oclc,NC[1885-1891]
North Carolina Teachers Record	Raleigh	NC	q	1930-1970	Ay1969,1970
Outlook	Raleigh	NC	w	1887-1889	Ba,R1888,NC[1887-1888]
Progressive Educator	Raleigh	NC		1881-1885	Ba,Penn
Raleigh Greenville Dispatch	Raleigh	NC	w	1940-1994+	WPN94
Searchlight	Raleigh	NC		1910-1915	Mather [Vincent, Andrew Brown]
Shaw Journal	Raleigh	NC	m	1940-1987	NH42,Dc41,ABSCHSL,Bp
State Republican	Raleigh	NC	w	1895-1897	Ba,Ay1896,NC
Union Reformer	Raleigh	NC	w	1902-1937	Ba,Ay1921,1925,1937,NY32
Voice	Reidsville	NC	sm	1910-1921	Ba,Ay1920,1921
Pee Dee Union	Rockingham	NC		1896-1900	Ba
Republic	Rockingham	NC		1898-1900	Ba
Herald	Rocky Mount	NC		1894-1896	Ba
Herald	Rocky Mount	NC	w	1905-1907	Ba,Ay1906
Rocky Mount Dispatch	Rocky Mount	NC	w	1976-1990	EP90[Raleigh],API90
Voice	Rocky Mount	NC	w	1919-1931	Ba,Ay1920,1925[1920],NY22,26,Go,Boris1
News	Roxboro	NC	w	1935-1944	Ba,NH42,44,EP35,38,Dc41
Person County Times	Roxboro	NC	w	1937-1940	EP37-40
Industrial Messenger	Salisbury	NC	bm	1919-1922	NY19,22
Livingstone	Salisbury	NC	m	1889-1927	NC,NY12,19,22,Yenser3
News	Salisbury	NC	w	1936-1938	Ba,EP36-38
Piedmont Advocate	Salisbury	NC	w	1907-1916	Ba,Ay1911-1914,1916,NY12,Yenser6
Piedmont Sun	Salisbury	NC		1988-1992+	EP91,92
Samaritan Journal	Salisbury	NC		1883-1886	Ba,Penn
Star of Zion	Salisbury	NC	w	1876-1888	Ba,Ay1882,1886-1891
Enterprise	Sanford	NC	w	1922-1940	Ba,Ay1938,EP35,40,NY32
Express	Sanford	NC		1886-1939	Ba

TITLE	CITY	ST.	FREQ.	DATES	SOURCES
Index-Herald	Shelby?	NC		1922-1926	Yenser4 [Roberts, John Wesley]
Southern Weekly	Smithfield	NC	w	1907	Lt1907
Do it Loud	Spring Lake	NC		1970	Unct
Iredell County News	Statesville	NC	w	1980-1994+	Ga90,94,Baid92,BRG,EP84,93,WPN94
Piedmont Sun	Statesville	NC	w	1896-1898	Ba,NC
Piedmont Sun	Statesville	NC	w	1988-1993+	EP93
Times	Statesville	NC		1897-1899	Ba
People's Friend	Sunlight	NC	sm	1902-1916	Ba,Ay1905,1912-1916
North Carolina Sentinel	Tarboro	NC		1883-1886	Ba,Penn,DANB156
People's Friend	Thelma	NC		1902-1904	Ba
Voice	Thomasville	NC	sm	1910-1913	Ba,Ay1911,1912,1913
Anson Future	Wadesboro	NC		1896-1898	Ba
Enterprise	Wadesboro	NC	w	1908-1912	Ba,Ay1911,1912
Baptist Sentinel	Warrenton	NC		1945	Ba
Christian Star	Warrenton	NC		1905-1906	Ba
Sun	Warsaw	NC	w	1924-1925	Ba,Ay1925
NC Republican & Civil Rights Advocate	Weldon	NC	w	1884-1884	Ba,Lc91,Oclc,Penn,WI,NWU
Neuse River Herald	Weldon	NC		1899-1905	Ba
Neuse River Times	Weldon	NC		1904-1906	Ba
Africo-American Presbyterian	Wilmington	NC	w	1879-1891	Ba,Ay1880,1891,Penn,R1888
Bulletin	Wilmington	NC	w	1887-1889	Ba,Ay1888
Cape Fear Journal	Wilmington	NC	w	1927-1945	Ba,Ay1940,1945,NH42,44,EP38,49,Gp,NY46,Dc41,Br
Challenger	Wilmington	NC	w	1988-1993+	EP91,92,93
Daily Record	Wilmington	NC	d	1898	Oclc
Golden Rule	Wilmington	NC		1887-1890	Ba
Home News	Wilmington	NC	w	1907-1926	Ba,Ay1909,920,NY12,19,22,26,Go
People's Advocate	Wilmington	NC		1881-1888	Ba,Penn
Record	Wilmington	NC	w	1895-1900	Ba,Oclc,DANB589[pre 1887]
Sentinel	Wilmington	NC	w	1894-1898	Ba,Ay1896,NC
Southern Evangelist	Wilmington	NC		1877-1880	Ba,Penn
Wilmington Journal	Wilmington	NC	w	1945-1994+	Ba,Ay1950,Ga87,94,Br,NH49,EP51,93,Baid92[1927],BRG,EH,EBA,Gp,API90,94
News	Wilson	NC	bw	1880-1886	Ba,Ay1882,Penn
Record	Wilson	NC	w	1938-1940	Ba,Ay1940
Home Journal	Windsor	NC	w	1890-1891	Ay1890,1891
Afro-American Signboard	Winston-Salem	NC		1925-1931	Ba
Black College Sports Review	Winston-Salem	NC		1991-1994+	Ga91,94
Enterprise	Winston-Salem	NC	w	1935	EP35
Informer	Winston-Salem	NC		1990	ABSCHSL
News	Winston-Salem	NC	w	1919-1932	Ba,NY19,22,26,32,Go
News-Dispatch	Winston-Salem	NC	w	1942-1943	EP42,43
Odd Fellows' Times	Winston-Salem	NC		1906-1908	Ba

TITLE	CITY	ST.	FREQ.	DATES	SOURCES
Outlook	Winston-Salem	NC	w	1938	EP38
People's Spokesman	Winston-Salem	NC	w	1945-1949	Ba,Ay1949,Oclc,NH49,EP48,49,NY46
Post	Winston-Salem	NC	w	1936-1943	Ba,EP37-39,41,43
Salem Post	Winston-Salem	NC	w	1940	EP40
Star	Winston-Salem	NC	w	1913-1915	Ba,Ay1913
Telegram	Winston-Salem	NC	w	1944	EP44
Winston Salem Chronicle	Winston-Salem	NC	w	1974-1994+	Ga87,94,WSJ,API90,94,Lc91,Baid92, BRG,EP75,93,WPN94
Baptist Pilot	Winton	NC	sm	1887-1891	Ba[Newton e1893],Ay1889-1891,Penn
Chowan Pilot	Winton	NC	w	1880-1885	Ba,Penn,NC[1884-1892]
Waters Institute Journal	Winton	NC	m	1919-1922	NY19,22
Akron Brown Mirror	Akron	OH		@1946	Gutg
Akron Bulletin	Akron	OH		@1936	Gutg
Akron Informer	Akron	OH		1921-1922	Gutg
Akron Informer	Akron	OH		1946-1960	Gutg
Akron Post	Akron	OH		1931-1941	Yenser3 [Smith, Alvin D.]
Akron Reporter	Akron	OH	w	1969-1994+	Ga90,94,Oclc,Lc83,EP75,93,BRG,Baid92, Bp
Akron Umpire	Akron	OH		1961-1961	Gutg
Akron Vindicator	Akron	OH		@1943-1944	Gutg
Akronite	Akron	OH	w/m	1963-1965	GON,Oclc
Baptist Progress	Akron	OH		1983-1992	ABSCHSL
Black and White Chronicle	Akron	OH	w	1924-1930	OHS
Call and Post	Akron	OH	w	1983-1994+	EP84,WPN94[b1927]
Ohio Informer	Akron	OH	w	1946-1960	Ay1956,1960
Recorder	Akron	OH	w	1936	EP36
Bedford Times Register	Bedford Hts.	OH	w	1992+	BRG,Ga94[b 1888 nlb]
Cleveland Metro	Bedford Hts.	OH	w	1955-1980	EBA,EH,EP71-80,Bp,Lb
Clarion Post News	Canton	OH	w	1970-1971	GON
Educator	Canton	OH	w	1949	NH49
Freedom's Journal	Canton	OH	w	1970-1972	GON
Afro-American	Cincinnati	OH	w	1882-1886	Ba,Br,Penn
American Catholic Tribune	Cincinnati	OH	w	1884-1894	Ba,Ay1887,1888,1894,OHS,Eur94
American Reformer	Cincinnati	OH		1892-1894	Mather [Anderson, William Louis]
Applause!; for Cincinnati's Black Lifestyle	Cincinnati	OH	bm	1990-1992+	Jpd
Black Dispatch	Cincinnati	OH	3xm	1969-1972	EBA,EP71
Brotherhood	Cincinnati	OH	w	1896-1922	Ba,Ay1905,1914,NY12,19,22,OHS
Bulletin	Cincinnati	OH	w	1930-1932	Ba,NY32,Yenser4[1927-1937]
Call and Post	Cincinnati	OH	w	1950-1994+	Ba,Ay1967,1971,Oclc,Jpd,EBA,EH,EP64, 79,API90,94,Lb
Catholic Tribune	Cincinnati	OH	w	1884	Mather [Valle, Lincoln Charles]
Cincinnati Commercial Guide	Cincinnati	OH		1883	Penn,DANB657

TITLE	CITY	ST.	FREQ.	DATES	SOURCES
Cincinnati Herald	Cincinnati	OH	w	1954-1994+	Ay1969,1975,Ga88,94,Oclc,WI,BRG, EH[1956],EBA,Baid92,EP62,93,WPN94, API94,SPD67,70,74,87
Cincinnati Herald of Freedom	Cincinnati	OH		1885	OHS
Cincinnati Leader	Cincinnati	OH	w	1952-1955	Ay1955,OHS
Cincinnati News	Cincinnati	OH	w	1963-1970	OHS,Lb,SPD67,70
Cincinnati News Recorder	Cincinnati	OH		1893	OHS
Cincinnati Pilot	Cincinnati	OH		1911-1912	Mather [Anderson, William Louis]
Colored American	Cincinnati	OH		1863-1869	Ba
Colored Citizen	Cincinnati	OH	w	1863-1869	Ba,Br,Gr,Go,Lc91,GON,Oclc,Jpd,Mather
Colored Patriot	Cincinnati	OH	w	1883-1884	GON,Mink
Declaration	Cincinnati	OH		1876	OHS
Disfranchised American	Cincinnati	OH		@1843	OHS
Forum	Cincinnati	OH		1936-1938	Ba,EP38
Fraternal Monitor	Cincinnati	OH	m	1901-1923	Ba,Ay1915,1919-1921,NY19,22
Genocide; Weekly Newsletter and Information Sheet	Cincinnati	OH	w	1970	WI,Jpd
Independent	Cincinnati	OH	w	1939-1956	Ba,Ay1950,1956,NH44,49,EP40,51
Journal	Cincinnati	OH		1919-1922	Ba,Go,NY19,22
Ohio Republican	Cincinnati	OH	w	1884-1888	Ba,Ay1884,Br,OHS
Plaindealer	Cincinnati	OH	w	1883-1895	Oclc
Pythian Monitor	Cincinnati	OH	m	1901-1923	Ba,Ay1914,NY12
Queen City Bee	Cincinnati	OH	w	1902-1909	Ba,Ay1908
Rostrum	Cincinnati	OH		1897-1902	Mather [Anderson, William Louis]
Union	Cincinnati	OH	w	1907-1954	Ba,Ay1908,1950,Gr,Go,Br,Mink,Lc91, Oclc[e1952],NH42,44,46,49,EP38,51, NY12,19,22,26,32,46,Dc41,44,Yenser6
Voice of the People	Cincinnati	OH		pre 1992	OHS
West End News	Cincinnati	OH		1940	GON
Advocate	Cleveland	OH	w	1914-1925	Ba,Ay1921,Gr,Go,Br,Oclc,Lc91,NY19,22, 26,Mink,DANB
Advocator	Cleveland	OH		1969	Rw,Lb
Aliened American	Cleveland	OH	w	1852-1857	Ba,Lc91,GON,Oclc[1853-1854],Jpd,WI, NY12,Penn,Mink,DANB164
American Negro Woman	Cleveland	OH	m	1974	Jpd
Call	Cleveland	OH	w	1919-1931	Ba,Ay1925[b1920],Gr,Oclc,WI[CC&P], NY26,Mink,Brooks,Boris1,DANB453
Call and Post	Cleveland	OH	w	1932-1994+	Ba,Ay1935,1969,Ga87,94,Lc91,Oclc, WRHS,NH42,44,46,49,EP35,93,BRG, Baid92,EBA,EH,NY32,46,Dc41,44,API94, WPN94,Mink,Fleming
Cleveland Guide	Cleveland	OH	w/sm	1931-1963	Ba,Ay1940,1963,Br,NH42,44,46,49,EP46, 51,NY46,Dc41,44,Fleming
Cleveland Herald	Cleveland	OH	w	1938-1970	Ba,Ay1940,1950,Br,Mink,GON,Oclc,NH, 42,44,46,49,EP46,51,NY46,Dc41,44
Clubdate Magazine	Cleveland	OH	6xy	1979-1994+	Ga87,94,SPD87
Courier	Cleveland	OH	w	1957-1964	Ay1960,EP62-64

TITLE	CITY	ST.	FREQ.	DATES	SOURCES
Eagle	Cleveland	OH	w	1933-1942	Ba,Ay1940,1942,EP35-39
Gazette	Cleveland	OH	w	1883-1945	Ba,Ay1886,1946,Gr,Go,Br,Brooks,Penn, Lc91,Oclc,Jpd,WI,NH42,44,EP38,41, Eur94,NY12,19,22,26,32,46,Dc41,Lt1907, Yenser6
Globe	Cleveland	OH	w	1885-1892	Ba,Ay1888-1891,Penn
Gracious Living	Cleveland	OH	q	1964-1970	Ay1968,SPD67,70
Inner City Voice	Cleveland	OH		1970	Unct
It's Happening	Cleveland	OH		pre 1979	Lb
Journal	Cleveland	OH	w	1903-1913	Ba,Ay1906,1913,NY12,Lt1907,Mink,Oclc, Gr,DANB225
National Guide	Cleveland	OH	m	1929	Yenser3 [Cheeks, Eugene Francis]
New Negro World	Cleveland	OH		1940	Rw49
Odd Fellows' Signal	Cleveland	OH	sm	1883-1892	Ba,Ay1887-1889,1891
Ohio State Pioneer	Cleveland	OH		1926	NY26
People's Exposition	Cleveland	OH		pre 1860	DANB164
Public Enterprise	Cleveland	OH	w	1944	NH44
Queen's Garden	Cleveland	OH	m	1907	Lt1907
Ringwood's Home Magazine	Cleveland	OH	m	1891-1896	Ay1894,1896,DANB136
Southeast Times	Cleveland	OH	w	1979-1992+	Ga91,Lb,BRG,Baid92,EP79,80
Vibration	Cleveland	OH	q	1968-1994+	Jpd,SPD87,94
Vindicator	Cleveland	OH	bw	1970	Oclc
Voice of the League	Cleveland	OH	ir	1937-1941	Oclc,WI,NWU
Voice of the People	Cleveland	OH		pre 1937	Yenser4 [Rogers, William Quincy]
Advocate	Columbus	OH	w	1936-1944	Ba,NH42,44,EP37,44,Dc41
Afro-American	Columbus	OH	w	1901-1907	Ba,Lt1907
American	Columbus	OH	w	1945-1949	Ba,Ay1947,NH49
Challenger	Columbus	OH	w,m	1963-1975	Pr,GON,Oclc,Jpd,WI,EP67,70,Lb
Christian Plea	Columbus	OH	m	1950-1951	EP50,51
Colored World	Columbus	OH	w	1905-1908	Ba,Ay1908,1906,Lt1907
Columbus Call & Post	Columbus	OH	w	1960-1994+	Ay1965,1971,GON,Jpd,EP64,93,BRG,EH, EBA,WI,API90,94,Lb
Columbus Dispatch	Columbus	OH		1905	DANB613,614
Columbus Recorder	Columbus	OH	m/w	1921-1932	Ba,GON,Mink,NY32
Columbus Standard	Columbus	OH		1901	WI
Communicator News	Columbus	OH	w	1991-1994+	Oclc,BRG,API94
Free American	Columbus	OH	w	1887-1888	Ba,Lc91,GON,Oclc,Lc83,Jpd
Independent	Columbus	OH	w	1913-1914	Boris2 [Snelson, Floyd Grant, Jr.]
Informer	Columbus	OH		1914-1915	Ba
Ohio Baptist News	Columbus	OH	m	1926-1933	Ba,Boris1
Ohio Sentinel	Columbus	OH	w	1949-1966	Ba,Ay1964,GON,Oclc,EP51,64,Lb,SPD67
Ohio State Informer	Columbus	OH	w	1945-1946	Ba,NY46
Ohio State Journal	Columbus	OII	w	1905	DANB614[nlb]
Ohio State Monitor	Columbus	OH	w	1918-1925	Ba,Ay1925,NY22,26,Mink,GON, DANB614

TITLE	CITY	ST.	FREQ.	DATES	SOURCES
Ohio State News	Columbus	OH	w	1935-1970	Ba,Ay1940,1953,GON,Oclc[e1952],NH42,44,46,49,EP38,51,NY46,Dc41,44,Mink,Br,Fleming
Ohio State Tribune	Columbus	OH	w	1884-1886	Ba,Ay1886
Ohio Torch	Columbus	OH	sm	1928-1930	Ba,GON
Onyx News	Columbus	OH	w	1971-1982	Ay1982,GON,EP77,78
Our Choking Times	Columbus	OH	ir	1970-1974	GON
Palladium of Liberty	Columbus	OH	w	1839-1844	Ba,Mink,GON,Oclc,DANB345[b1842]
Recorder	Columbus	OH		1921-1932	Ba
Republican Vindicator	Columbus	OH		1897-1901	Ba
Saturday Evening News	Columbus	OH	w	1906-1913	Ba,Ay1909,1911,1912,1913
Standard	Columbus	OH	w	1898-1901	Ba,NWU,Lc91,Lc83,Jpd
Vindicator	Columbus	OH		pre 1970	Ba
Voice	Columbus	OH	w	1883-1942	Ba,Ay1940,1942,EP36,41,GON,NY26,Br
Advocate	Dayton	OH	w	1971-1972	Oclc,EP72,Lb,OHS
Black Press	Dayton	OH	bw	1972-1981	Oclc,Jpd,Lb
Cincinnati and Dayton Forum	Dayton	OH	w	1940-1943	EP43,Dc41
Citizen	Dayton	OH	w	1951	EP51
Confrontation/Change Review	Dayton	OH	q	1976-1994+	Ay1980,Ga87,94
Daily Bulletin	Dayton	OH	d	1941-1947	Ba,Br,GON,Oclc,Lc83,Jpd,NH44
Daily Express	Dayton	OH	d	1946	NY46
Dayton Bulletin	Dayton	OH	w	1944-1948	EP44-46,48
Dayton Cincinnati Forum	Dayton	OH	w	1945	EP45
Dayton Defender	Dayton	OH	bw	1986-1992+	Jpd
Dayton Express	Dayton	OH	w	1960-1970	Pr,GON,Oclc[b1964],Lc83,EP67,71,EBA[b1972],Bp
Dayton Express Urban Weekly	Dayton	OH	w	1970-1971	GON,Oclc,Lc83
Dayton Forum	Dayton	OH	w	1913-1949	Ba,Ay1921S,1949,Mink,Oclc,Jpd,NH42,44,EP35,49,NY19,22,26,32,46,Dc41,Go,Br,Boris1
Dayton Globe	Dayton	OH	w	1941	Oclc
Dayton Standard	Dayton	OH		1906	Oclc
Dayton Tattler	Dayton	OH	w	1890-1891	Oclc,GON
Guide	Dayton	OH	w	1923-1925	Ba,Ay1925
Informer	Dayton	OH	w	1903-1907	Ba,Ay1906
Jetstone News	Dayton	OH	w	1974-1987	Ay1982,Oclc,EP75-80,Lb,SPD87
New Dayton Express	Dayton	OH	w	1971-1971	Oclc,Lc83,EP70,GON
Ohio Daily Express	Dayton	OH	d	1942-1955	Ba,Ay1950,1955,GON,Jpd[1946-1955],NH49,EP48-51,Br
Ohio Eagle	Dayton	OH	w	1964	Oclc
Progress	Dayton	OH	w	1936-1939	Ba,EP38,39
Record	Dayton	OH	w	1910-1915	Ba,Ay1912-1915,NY12
Republican	Dayton	OH	w	1887-1888	Ba,Ay1888
Tribune	Dayton	OH	w	1962	EP62

TITLE	CITY	ST.	FREQ.	DATES	SOURCES
Butler County American	Hamilton	OH	w	1938-1969	Ba,Ay1947,Pr,NH44,46,EP50,69,NY46, Dc44,Lb,SPD67,70[b1939]
Enterprise	Hamilton	OH		1920-1922	Ba,NY22
Fort Hamilton American	Hamilton	OH		1970	EP70
Negro Printer & Publishers	Hamilton	OH		1951	EP51
Spokesman	Ironton	OH		1883-1887	Ba,Penn
Post	Lima	OH	w	1953-1956	Ay1956,Oclc,Jpd
Lincoln Heights Times	Lincoln Heights	OH		pre 1950	Fleming [Smith, Alvin Dean]
Speaker	Lincoln Heights	OH	w	1977-1978	EP77,78
Mansfield Star	Mansfield	OH	ir	1982	Oclc
New Visions	Maple Heights	OH	6xy	1989-1994+	Ga91,94
Girl's Guide	Oberlin	OH	m	1933-1944	Yenser6 [Barnes, Margaret E.]
Nommo	Oberlin	OH	ir	1969-1971	Oclc
Plantation Missionary	Oberlin	OH	bm	1905-1907	Jpd
Queen's Gardens	Oberlin	OH	m	1941-1944	Yenser6 [Barnes, Margaret E.]
Pilot	Portsmouth	OH	w	1924-1926	Ba,Ay1925
Anti-Slavery Bugle	Salem	OH		1851-1861	Lc91
Baptist Beacon	Springfield	OH	m	1886-1887	Ay1887,ba[IL]
Informer	Springfield	OH	w	1925-1933	GON,Lc83,NY26,Yenser3
Ohio Express	Springfield	OH		1943-1943	Ba
Ohio Springfield	Springfield	OH		pre 1946	Br
Ohio State Tribune	Springfield	OH	w	1884-1886	Ba,Ay1884,Br
Springfield Post	Springfield	OH	w	1956-1960	Ay1960
Equator	Steubenville	OH		1884-1924	SI
Bronze Raven	Toledo	OH	w	1945-1976	Ay1956,1976,GON,Oclc[1948-1976], EP67,76,EH,EBA,Pr,Bp,Lb,SPD67
Eagle	Toledo	OH	w	1889-1891	Ba,Ay1890,1891
Independent	Toledo	OH	w	1889-1889	Ba,Ay1889
Observer	Toledo	OH	w	1930-1940	Ba,EP35-40,NY32
Observer	Toledo	OH	w	1971	ONG
Pioneer	Toledo	OH		1920-1922	Ba,NY22
Press	Toledo	OH	w	1936-1945	Ba,NH42,44,EP36,45,Dc41
Progress	Toledo	OH	w	1907-1908	Ba,Ay1908
Script	Toledo	OH	w	1943-1951	Ba,GON,Oclc,Lc83,WI,EP48,49,51
Sentinel	Toledo	OH	w	1930-1932	Ba,NY32
Star	Toledo	OH		1944-1946	Ba
Toledo Journal	Toledo	OH	w	1975-1994+	Ga90,94,Baid90,92,Oclc,Jpd,EP78,93, BRG,WPN94
Toledo Sepia City Press	Toledo	OH	w	1948-1950	GON,Oclc,Lc83,WI
Toledo Voice	Toledo	OH	w	1944	NH44
Tri City News	Toledo	OH	w	1940	EP40
Voice	Toledo	OH	w	1940-1945	EP40-42,44,45
Informer	Urbana	OH	m	1897-1925	Ba,Mink,Oclc,Lc83,GON,Jpd,NY12,19,22
Alumni Journal	Wilberforce	OH	q	1950	Ay1950

TITLE	CITY	ST.	FREQ.	DATES	SOURCES
Gold Torch	Wilberforce	OH	w	1950-1975	Ay1966,1969,1970,1975,Oclc
Interpreter	Wilberforce	OH	3xy	1935-1964	Ay1964
Journal of Human Relations	Wilberforce	OH	q	1952-1973	BJ
Negro College Quarterly	Wilberforce	OH	q	1945-1950	Ay1945,1950,EP48,BJ[1943-1947]
Negro Journal of Religion; an Interdenominational Review	Wilberforce	OH	m	1935-1940	EP39,40,Jpd,BJ[e1939]
Newsletter; The National Afro-American Museum and Cultural Center	Wilberforce	OH	q	1990+	Jpd
Ohio Standard and Observer	Wilberforce	OH	w	1897-1907	Ba,GON,Jpd[1897-1903]
Sodalian	Wilberforce	OH	m	1906-1922	Ay1912,1915,NY12,19,22
Wilberforce Student	Wilberforce	OH	ir	1943-1946	NH46,NY46,Dc44
Wilberforcian	Wilberforce	OH		pre 1927	Boris1 [Braddock, Edna B. Johnson]
Herald of Freedom	Wilmington	OH	w	1851-1855	Penn,Go,Mink,NY12
Ohio Standard	Xenia	OH		1901	NWU
Ohio Standard and Observer	Xenia	OH	w	1897-1907	Ba,Lc91,Oclc,Lc83[1897-1903],WI
Buckeye Review	Youngstown	OH	w	1937-1994+	Ba,Ay1950,1975,Ga87,94,Oclc,Lc83,Jpd,NH42,44,46,49,EP38,93,BRG,EBA,EH,NY46,Dc41,44,Bp,Lb,SPD67
Call and Post	Youngstown	OH	w	1982-1994+	EP84,WPN94
Challenger	Youngstown	OH	w	1934-1940	Ba,EP35-40
Critique	Youngstown	OH	sm	1967-1973	Oclc
Mahoning County Observer	Youngstown	OH	w	1973	EP72[1967],Bp
Mahoning Valley Challenger	Youngstown	OH	w	1967-1976	Ay1969,1976,GON,Oclc,EH,EP73,Jpd[1967-1974],Lb
Recorder	Youngstown	OH		1931-1941	Yenser3 [Smith, Alvin D.]
Torch	Youngstown	OH	w	1930-1932	Ba,NY32
Advocate	Zanesville	OH	w	1909-1914	Ba,Ay1911,1912,1913,1914
Missionary Baptist of OK		OK		1900	NEW
Pythian Monitor		OK		1907	NEW
Ardmore Sun	Ardmore	OK		1907-1911	NEW,Lc83,Br
Baptist Rival	Ardmore	OK	w	1902-1917	Ba,Ay1906,1917,NY12,NEW
Chickasaw Rival	Ardmore	OK	w	1902-1907	Ay1905,Lt1907[Rival],NEW
Indian Territory Sun	Ardmore	OK	bm	1901-1907	Ba,Ay1906,NEW,Br,Lc83[1904-1907],Lt1907
Oklahoma Sun	Ardmore	OK	w	1906	NEW
Sun	Ardmore	OK	w	1908-1912	Ba,Ay1908,NY12,NEW,Lc83
Western World	Ardmore	OK	w	1902-1904	Ba,Lc83
World	Ardmore	OK	w	1907-1908	Mather [Franklin, Buck Colbert]
World Sun	Ardmore	OK		1907	NEW
People's Protector	Atoka	OK		pre 1915	Mather [Guess, Henry Augustus]
Oklahoma Negro News	Bartlesville	OK	w	1937-1940	EP37-40
Voice	Bartlesville	OK		1936-1938	Ba,EP37
Beacon	Boley	OK	w	1907-1909	Ba,NEW,Oclc,WI,NY12
Boley Elevator	Boley	OK	w	1920-1926	Ba,NEW,NY22,26

TITLE	CITY	ST.	FREQ.	DATES	SOURCES
Boley Informer	Boley	OK	w	1910-1912	Ba,Ay1912,Oclc,WI,NEW
Boley News	Boley	OK	w	1918-1938	Ba,Ay1919[b1904],Oclc,WI,EP35,38, NEW
Boley Progress	Boley	OK	w	1905-1926	Ba,Ay1908,1918,NEW,Go,Oclc,WI,NY12, 19,22,26,Mather
Express	Boley	OK		1920-1922	Ba
Greater Boley Area Newsletter	Boley	OK		1975-1976	WI
Marriott's Advertiser	Boley	OK	m	1917-1925	Ba,Ay1925
Star	Boley	OK	w	1913-1914	Ba,Ay1914
Tribune	Boley	OK		1926-1928	Ba
Trumpet	Boley	OK		1926-1927	Ba
Bookertee Searchlight	Bookertee	OK	w	1917-1919	Ba,NEW,Oclc,Lc83,WI
Chandler and Falls Express	Chandler	OK		1904	NEW
Western World	Chandler	OK	w	1902-1904	Ba,Lc83
Clearview Patriarch	Clearview	OK	w	1911-1926	Ba,Ay1912,1918,NY12,19,22,26,NEW,Go, Oclc,Lc83,WI[e1917],Boris1
Clearview Tribune	Clearview	OK	w	1904-1904	NEW,Oclc,Lc83,WI
Informer	Clearview	OK	w	1909-1911	Ba,Ay1911
Lincoln Tribune	Clearview	OK	w	1904-1905	Ba,NEW,Ay1905,Oclc
Oklahoma Star	Enid	OK	w	1903-1905	Ba,Ay1905,NEW
Informer	Eufaula	OK		1902-1903	Ba
Fallis Blade	Fallis	OK	w	1904-1905	Ba,NEW,Oclc,Lc83
Citizen	Fort Gibson	OK	w	1897-1900	NEW
Western Advocate	Fort Gibson	OK		1906	NEW
Garvin Pioneer	Garvin	OK	w	1908-1912	Ba,Ay1911,1912,NEW,Yenser6
Avalanche	Guthrie	OK	w	1901	NEW
Baptist Safeguard	Guthrie	OK	w	1917-1919	Ay1917,1918,1919[b1894]
Constitution	Guthrie	OK	w	1892	NEW
Guthrie Progress	Guthrie	OK	w	1902-1914	NEW,Oclc,Lc83[1902-1905],WI
Health Bulletin	Guthrie	OK	q	1918-1921	Ay1920,1921
Labor Advocate	Guthrie	OK		1902-1903	WI
Little Missionary	Guthrie	OK	m	1905	NEW
Oklahoma Enterprise	Guthrie	OK		1908	NEW
Oklahoma Guide	Guthrie	OK	w	1892-1925	Ba,Ay1894,1921,NEW,Go,Oclc,Lc83, Eur94,NY12,19,22,26,Lt1907,Boris1
Oklahoma Safeguard	Guthrie	OK	w	1894-1916	Ba,Ay1906,1916,NEW,WI,NY12, Oclc[1905-1915],Mather
Oklahoma School News	Guthrie	OK		1910	NEW
People's Elevator	Guthrie	OK	w	1900-1923	Oclc[ks 1922-1924],WI
Taborian Monitor	Guthrie	OK	m	1904-1921	Ba,Ay1911-1921,Lc83
Twice a Week Sun	Guthrie	OK	2xw	1911-1914	NEW,Lc83,WI
Western World	Guthrie	OK	w	1902-1904	Ba,Lc83
Kingfisher Constitution	Kingfisher	OK	w	1894-1899	Ba,NEW,Eur94
Oklahoma Constitution	Kingfisher	OK	w	1891-1894	Ay1894
Western Home	Kingfisher	OK	w	1907-1908	Ba,Ay1908,NEW

TITLE	CITY	ST.	FREQ.	DATES	SOURCES
Western World	Kingfisher	OK	w	1902-1904	Ba,Lc83
Church and State	Langston City	OK	w	1911	Oclc,Lc83,WI
Church Review	Langston City	OK		1902	NEW
Headlight	Langston City	OK		1904	NEW
Langston City Herald	Langston City	OK	w	1891-1902	Ay1894,Gr,NEW,Lc91,Oclc,Lc83,WI, Eur94,DANB208
Living Age	Langston City	OK	m	1904-1909	Ba,Ay1905,Lc83,NEW
Negro School Journal	Langston City	OK	w	1913	NEW
Oklahoma Church and State News	Langston City	OK	w	1911	NEW
Southwestern Journal	Langston City	OK	q	1944-1951	EP50,51,BJ
Western Age	Langston City	OK	w	1904-1909	Ba,Ay1906,1908,NEW,Oclc,Lc83,WI
Community Guide	Lawton	OK	w	1971-1980	EH,EP72-80,Bp,Lb
Voice of the People	McAlester	OK		1900-1905	NEW,Mather
Afro-American	Muldrow	OK		1902-1903	Ba
Mulhall Enterprise	Mulhall	OK		1893-1911	WI,Ay1912[nlb]
Baptist College Searchlight	Muskogee	OK	w	1899-1912	Ba,Ay1905,1906,1908,1911,NEW
Baptist Informer	Muskogee	OK	w	1909-1925	Ba,Ay1911,1925,NEW,NY12,19,22
Blade	Muskogee	OK		1906	NEW
Cimeter	Muskogee	OK	w	1901-1932	Ba,Ay1905,1921,Go,NEW,Lc83,NY12,19, 22,26,32,Oclc[1899-1930?],Lt1907, Mather[1897],Boris1
Daily Searchlight	Muskogee	OK	d	1905-1906	NEW,Oclc,Lc83,WI,Br
Dispensation	Muskogee	OK	w	1905-1906	NEW,Lc83,WI
Enterprise	Muskogee	OK	w	1910-1913	Ba,Ay1911,1912,1913
Herald	Muskogee	OK	w	1932-1968	Ay1968,Pr,Lb,EP67,SPD67
Lantern	Muskogee	OK	w	1902-1943	Ba,Ay1935,1942,NEW,Go,Br,Oclc,Lc83, WI,EP35,38,NY19,22,32
Ministerial Voice	Muskogee	OK	w	1919-1922	NY19,22
Muskogee Comet	Muskogee	OK	w	1904	NEW,Oclc,Lc83
Oklahoma Eagle	Muskogee	OK		1978	EP78 (see Tulsa)
Oklahoma Independent	Muskogee	OK	w	1932-1965	Ba,Ay1945,1965,NH42,44,46,49,EP37,51, NY46,Dc41,44,Br
Our Brother in Black	Muskogee	OK	w	1880-1883	Ba,NEW
Our Brother in Black	Muskogee	OK	w	1890-1891	Ba,Ay1891,NEW
Pioneer	Muskogee	OK	w	1898-1907	Ba,Oclc,NEW,Lc83,WI
Republican	Muskogee	OK	w	1905-1913	Ba,Ay1908,1913,Br,NY12,NEW[Daily Republican 1905,1907-1912]
Saturday Evening Tribune	Muskogee	OK	w	1912-1915	Ba,NEW,Oclc,Lc83[b1912],WI
Searchlight	Muskogee	OK	d	1905-1907	Ba,Ay1906,Lt1907
Southwestern World	Muskogee	OK		1904-1905	NEW
Southwesterner	Muskogee	OK		1905	WI
Star	Muskogee	OK	w	1912-1913	Ba,Ay1913,Br,NEW,Lc83,WI, Mather[b1911]
Sun	Muskogee	OK	w	1893-1895	Ba,Ay1894,NEW
Tattler	Muskogee	OK	w	1915-1917	Ay1917,NEW,Oclc,Lc83,WI

TITLE	CITY	ST.	FREQ.	DATES	SOURCES
Tribune	Muskogee	OK		1926-1928	Ba
Watchman-Lantern	Muskogee	OK	w	1901-1943	Ba,Ay1921,Lc83,NY22,26
Weekly Progress	Muskogee	OK	w	1926-1932	Ba,NEW,Oclc,Lc83,WI,NY32
Western World	Muskogee	OK	w	1903-1905	NEW,Lc83,WI
YMCA Bulletin	Muskogee	OK		1914	NEW
Clarksville Echo	Muskogee Co.	OK		1905	NEW
Oklahoma Trumpet	Newkirk	OK		1925-1928	Ba
Castle News	Okfuskee	OK		1908	NEW,WI[Castle]
Black Chronicle	Oklahoma City	OK	w	1979-1994+	NEW,Ga90,94,BRG,EP80,93,Baid92, API90,94
Black Dispatch	Oklahoma City	OK	w	1909-1981	Ba,Ay1921,1981,Bp,Lb,Gr,Oclc[b1915], Lc83,WI,NH42,44,46,49,EP35,80,NY19, 22,26,32,46,Dc41,44,SPD67,70,74, 79,Fleming,DANB204
Ebony Tribune	Oklahoma City	OK	w	1986-1993+	EP91,92,93,BRG
Gazette	Oklahoma City	OK		pre 1970	Ba
Occidental Lighthouse	Oklahoma City	OK	sm	1899-1907	Ba,Ay1905,1906
Oklahoma Defender	Oklahoma City	OK	w	1936-1942	Ba,NH42,EP36-40,Dc41
Oklahoma Dispatch	Oklahoma City	OK	w	1981-1988	Ay1986,Ga87,88,SPD87
Oklahoma Guide	Oklahoma City	OK	w	1889-1903	Ba,NEW,Gr,Lc91,Oclc[b1897], Lc83[b1898],WI
Oklahoma Traveler	Oklahoma City	OK		1939	EP39
Oklahoma Tribune	Oklahoma City	OK	w	1907-1915	Ba,Ay1912,NEW
Western World	Oklahoma City	OK	w	1902-1905	Ba,Ay1905,NEW,Oclc,Lc83, Mather[b1901]
Okmulgee Observer	Okmulgee	OK	w	1927-1963	Ba,Ay1950,1963,NEW,NH42,44,46,49, EP38,51,Sch,NY46,Dc41,44
Paden Press	Paden	OK	w	1908-1909	Oclc,WI
Paden Times	Paden	OK	w	1904-1908	Oclc,WI
Redbee	Redbird	OK	w	1912-1914	Ba,Ay1913,1914
Rentiesville News	Rentiesville	OK		1913-1926	Ba,Go,NY19,22,26,Mather
Western World	Shawnee	OK		1902-1904	Ba
Informer	Taft	OK		1910-1912	Ba
News	Taft	OK	w	1912-1918	Ba,Ay1916-1918
Taft Enterprise	Taft	OK	w	1910-1915	Ba,Ay1912-1915,Lc83,WI
Western Age	Taft	OK		1904-1910	Ba
Cherokee Advocate	Tahlequah	OK	w	1856-1906	Ay1882,1896,1906,Penn,Oclc
Appeal	Tulsa	OK	w	1941-1955	Ba,Ay1955,NH42,44,46,49,EP49-51, NY46,Dc41,44
Oklahoma Eagle	Tulsa	OK	w/sw	1920-1994+	Ba,Ay1925[b1922],1981,Ga90,94,Oclc, Lc91,Lc83,WI,NH44,46,49,EP39,93, Baid92[b1921],EBA,BRG,NY26,32,46, Dc41,44,API94,Lb,Bp,Boris1,SPD67,70, 74,87
Oklahoma Sun	Tulsa	OK		1920-1924	Ba,Go,NEW,NY22
Tulsa Guide	Tulsa	OK	w	1906-1912	Ba,Ay1908,NY12,Gr,Oclc

TITLE	CITY	ST.	FREQ.	DATES	SOURCES
Tulsa Star	Tulsa	OK	d/w	1912-1921	Ba,Ay1914-1921,Oclc,Lc83,NY19,Gr,Go, NEW,Mather
American	Wagoner	OK		1910-1918	Ba,Ay1912,1913,1914,NY12,NEW
Lantern	Wagoner	OK	w	1908-1913	Ba,Ay1910,1912,1913
Oklahoma Freeman	Watonga	OK		1901-1903	Ba
Oklahoma Hornet	Waukomis?	OK		1899-1908	Ay1905,1921,NEW
Advocate	Portland	OR	w	1903-1937	Ba,Ay1908,1937,Br,Lc83,EP35,40,NY19, 22,26,32,Lt1907,Go,Mather,DANB572
African-American Journal	Portland	OR	w	1989-1992+	EP91,92
Inquirer	Portland	OR		1900-1946	Ba,EP45,46
Negro Times	Portland	OR	w	1909-1924	Ba,Ay1921
New Age	Portland	OR	w	1896-1905	Ba,Ay1905,Lc91,Oclc,Lc83
Northwest Clarion	Portland	OR	w	1944-1967	Ba,NH49,EP50,51,67,SPD67
Northwest Clarion Defender	Portland	OR	w	1944-1973	Pr,EBA,EP71,72[1960],Bp
Observer	Portland	OR		1900-1903	Ba
Portland New Age	Portland	OR	w	1905-1907	Lc91,Oclc,Lc83,WI,NWU
Portland Observer	Portland	OR	w	1970-1994+	Ga90,94,API90,94,EP72,93,Baid92,EH, WPN94
Portland Observer	Portland	OR	w	1939-1951	EP39,51
Portland Skanner	Portland	OR	w	1975-1994+	Ga87,94,Baid90,92,Lc91,EP77,93,WPN94
Times	Portland	OR	d	1911-1912	Lc83
A.M.E. Zion Quarterly Review	Bedford	PA	q	1890-1977	WI
Defender	Bryn Mawr	PA	w	1897-1909	Ba,PA
Crusader	Chester	PA	w	1945-1949	Ba,Ay1948,NH49,PA
Flash News	Chester	PA	w	1943-1945	Ba,NY46
Cheyney Record	Cheyney	PA	m	1913-1955	Ay1940,1955,NH42,46,EP46,48,NY46, Dc41,44
Record	Coatesville?	PA		1925-1927	Boris1 [Anderson, Thomas Jefferson]
Bulletin	Dowingtown	PA	m	1925-1958	Ay1950,1958,NH42,EP49,50,51,Dc41
Afro-American	Frankford	PA		1902-1904	Ba
Advocate Verdict	Harrisburg	PA	w	1881-1926	Ba,Ay1908,1920,PA,NY12,19,22,26,Go, Boris2
Central Pennsylvania Network Chronicle of the African American Community	Harrisburg	PA	m	1989	Oclc
Harrisburg Journal	Harrisburg	PA	m	1976	Oclc
Home Journal	Harrisburg	PA	w	1882-1885	Ba,PA,Lc83
Howard's American Magazine	Harrisburg	PA	m	1897-1904	R1900,Mather,DANB[b1896]
Howard's Negro America Magazine	Harrisburg	PA	m	1880-1891	Ay1889-1891,Mather
Inter-State Journal	Harrisburg	PA		1902-1903	Mather [Nelson, Robert John]
New Era	Harrisburg	PA		1911-1915	Mather [Howard, James H. W.]
Pennsylvania Post	Harrisburg	PA	w	1914-1920	Ba,Ay1920,PA
People's Forum	Harrisburg	PA		1907-1915	Yenser4 [Nelson, Robert John]
Progressive News	Harrisburg	PA	w	1912-1914	Ba,Ay1913
Sentinel Gazette	Harrisburg	PA	w	1895-1899	Ba,PA

TITLE	CITY	ST.	FREQ.	DATES	SOURCES
State Journal	Harrisburg	PA	w	1882-1885	Ba,Ay1882,1884,PA,Lc91,Oclc,WI,Lc83, Mather[1885-1890]
Times	Harrisburg	PA	w	1880-1895	Ba,Ay1894,1890,PA,Eur94
Little Voice	Homestead	PA	bw	1936-1940	EP36,37,38,40
Commonwealth	Mansfield Valley	PA	w	1887-1892	Ba,R1888,Ay1890,1891
Leader	New Hope	PA	w	1963-1993+	Ga94 [main entry nlb]
Afro-American	Philadelphia	PA	w	1938-1979	Ba,Ay1940,1956,Br,Bp,PA,WI,NH44,44, 46,49,EP38,80,EBA,EH,NY46,Dc41,44
Afro-American Press	Philadelphia	PA		1920-1922	Ba,NY22
American	Philadelphia	PA	w	1919-1925	Ba,Ay1921,Go,PA,NY22,26,Boris2
American Herald	Philadelphia	PA	w	1901-1912	Ba,Ay1906,NY12
A.M.E. Church Review	Philadelphia	PA	q	1884-1928	Ay1888,1912,R1900,BJ,Mather,Boris1
Baptist World	Philadelphia	PA	w	1919	NY19
Black Business Digest	Philadelphia	PA	m	1970-1979	Ay1975,1979,Lc83,Lc77,BJ,SPD74,79,
Black Careers	Philadelphia	PA	6xy	1965-1994+	Ay1975,1980,Ga87,94,EH,BJ[b1971], SPD79
Black Opals	Philadelphia	PA	2xy	1927-1928	BJ72
Bronze Woman	Philadelphia	PA	m	1946-1950	Ay1950
Brown American	Philadelphia	PA	q/m	1936-1945	Ay1945,WI,BJ
Caravan	Philadelphia	PA		1975-1976	EP75,76
Christian Banner	Philadelphia	PA	w	1888-1920	Ba,Ay1894,1919,PA,Lc91,Oclc,WI,Lc83, NY12,ABSCHSL,Penn,Mather
Christian Herald	Philadelphia	PA		1848-1852	NY12
Christian Record	Philadelphia	PA	w	1912-1922	NY12,19,22
Christian Recorder	Philadelphia	PA	w	1848-1946	Ba,Ay1888,1925,PA,WI,NH42,46,Eur94, EP39,R1888,1900,NY12,19,22,26,32,46, Dc41,44,Lt1907,Mather,Yenser4,BJ50
Christian Review	Philadelphia	PA	w	1913-1952	Ba,Ay1916,1952,PA,NH42,46,EP36,51, ABSCHSL,NY19,22,32,46,Dc41,44, Yenser4
Church Weekly	Philadelphia	PA	w	1975	EP75,76
Color	Philadelphia	PA	m	1944-1956	Ay1956
Colored World	Philadelphia	PA	w	1915-1916	Ba,Ay1916,PA
Courant	Philadelphia	PA	w	1901-1926	Ba,Ay1908,1920,Go,PA,NY12,19,22,26, Mather
Craftsman	Philadelphia	PA		1919-1922	NY19,22
Decoder	Philadelphia	PA	m,bw	1971-1972	Oclc
Defender	Philadelphia	PA	w	1897-1912	Ay1908,Br,NWU,PA,Lc91,Oclc,WI,Lc83, NY12
Dig This Now	Philadelphia	PA		1969-1971	EP72,Lb,Rw97
Easterner Magazine	Philadelphia	PA	m	1946-1958	Ay1949,EP48,49
Garvey's Voice	Philadelphia	PA		1975-1976	EP75,76
Graphic	Philadelphia	PA		1892-1892	Ba
Herald Mission	Philadelphia	PA		1920-1922	Ba,NY22
Independent-Advocate	Philadelphia	PA	w	1891-1895	Ba,PA
Industrial Statesman	Philadelphia	PA		1960	WI

TITLE	CITY	ST.	FREQ.	DATES	SOURCES
Informer	Philadelphia	PA	q/m	1950-1955	Ay1950,1952,1955,EP50,51
It's What's Happening	Philadelphia	PA		1969	Rw
Journal	Philadelphia	PA	w	1892-1892	Oclc
Kappa Alpha Psi Journal	Philadelphia	PA	q	1927-1951	Ay1940,1950,EP48-51,Fleming
Lincoln University Herald	Philadelphia	PA		1919-1922	NY19,22
Lincolnian	Philadelphia	PA	m	1929-1994+	Ay1950,Ga87,94,Baid90,NH42,46,NY46, Dc41,44
Mac	Philadelphia	PA		1975-1976	EP75,76
Masonic Herald	Philadelphia	PA		1879-1882	Ba,Penn
McGirt's Magazine	Philadelphia	PA	m/q	1903-1912	Ay1912[b1909],NY12,BJ[e1909], DANB416[e1910]
Miss Black America	Philadelphia	PA	bm	1974-1987	SPD74,79,87
Mission Herald	Philadelphia	PA	m	1930-1951	Ba,EP51,NY32[MO]
Missionary Seer	Philadelphia	PA		1898-1910	Ba
Monthly Echo	Philadelphia	PA	m	1882-1890	Ay1890,1891,Penn
National Beverage Leader	Philadelphia	PA	m	1969-1973	Ay1969,1970,Bp,EH
National Leader	Philadelphia	PA		1982-1984	EP84
National Public Record	Philadelphia	PA	w	1900-1909	Ba,Ay1905,1909,R1900
National Reformer	Philadelphia	PA		1837-1840	Ba,DANB643
Negro Statesmen	Philadelphia	PA	m	1936-1945	Oclc
Neighbors	Philadelphia	PA	bm	1971-1974	SPD74
New Day	Philadelphia	PA	w	1936-1962	Sch
New Era	Philadelphia	PA	w	1925-1927	NY26,Boris1
Nite Life	Philadelphia	PA	w	1953-1987	Ay1981,EBA,EH,EP71-78,Bp, SPD87[b1955]
Nite Owl	Philadelphia	PA	w	1958-1992+	BRG,EBA,EH,EP71-78,Bp
Nite Scene	Philadelphia	PA	w	1967-1978	EP71-78,EBA,EH,Bp
Nite Scene Tap and Tavern Guide	Philadelphia	PA		1968-1978	EP78
North City Free Press	Philadelphia	PA	w	1973-1978	Ay1970,EP75-78,Bp
Odd Fellows Journal	Philadelphia	PA	w	1897-1917	Ba,Ay1913,1915,PA,Lc91,Oclc,WI,Lc83, NY12,NWU
Pennsylvania Freedmen's Bulletin	Philadelphia	PA		1865-1868	WI
Pennsylvania Freeman	Philadelphia	PA		1952	Aba
Philadelphia Flame	Philadelphia	PA		1971	Oclc,WI
Philadelphia Independent	Philadelphia	PA	w	1931-1971	Ba,Ay1940,1971,Br,Pr,PA,NH42,44,46,49, EP36,78,NY12,32,Lc83,NY46,Dc41,44, SPD67,70,Yenser4
Philadelphia Metro	Philadelphia	PA	w	1978-1993+	EP91,92,93,API90
Philadelphia New Observer	Philadelphia	PA	w	1975-1994+	Ay1986,Ga87,94,Baid92,BRG,EP77,93, API94,SPD87
Philadelphia Spirit	Philadelphia	PA		1981-1983	EP81,82,83
Philadelphia Sunday Sun	Philadelphia	PA	w	1993+	EP93

TITLE	CITY	ST.	FREQ.	DATES	SOURCES
Philadelphia Tribune	Philadelphia	PA	w	1884-1994+	Ba,Ay1888,1975,Ga87,94,Penn,Gr,Lc91, Oclc,WI,NH42,44,46,49,BRG,Lc83, Baid92,EBA,EP35,92,NY12,19,22,26,32, 46,Dc41,44,API90,94,SPD67,70,74,87,94, Mather
Philly Talk	Philadelphia	PA	m	1971-1973	Rw,Bp,BJ
Picture News Weekly	Philadelphia	PA	w	1936-1946	Ba,NH42,46,EP38,NY46,Dc41,44
Pilot	Philadelphia	PA	w	1907-1915	Ba,Ay1908,NY12,PA
Pilot	Philadelphia	PA	w	1884-1884	Ay1884,PA
Political Digest	Philadelphia	PA	d	1943-1951	NH46,EP51,Dc44
Pride Magazine	Philadelphia	PA	bm	1970-1975	Ay1970,1975,BJ,SPD72,74
Project Magazine	Philadelphia	PA	bm	1969-1971	BJ50
Public Journal	Philadelphia	PA	w	1920-1931	Ba,Ay1925,NY22,32,PA,Go,Yenser4
Responsibility	Philadelphia	PA		1949-1950	Fleming [Whord, Eureka Berneda]
Review	Philadelphia	PA	q	1841-1968	Ay1968
Scoop	Philadelphia	PA	w	1959-1992+	Oclc,EBA,BRG,EH,EP71-78,Bp
Sentinel	Philadelphia	PA		1902-1903	Ba
Sentinel	Philadelphia	PA	w	1884-1892	Ba,Ay1886,1888,1890,1891,PA,Penn
Smithford Press	Philadelphia	PA		1905-1906	Ba
Solid Rock Herald	Philadelphia	PA	w	1901-1922	Ba,PA,NY19,22,Mather
Southwestern Christian Advocate	Philadelphia	PA		18??	Ba,Br
Spokesman	Philadelphia	PA	w	1930-1932	Ba,NY32
Standard Echo	Philadelphia	PA	w	1881-1900	Ba,Ay1894,1891,Br,PA,DANB457
State Journal	Philadelphia	PA	w	1890-1894	Ay1890,1891,1894
Sunday Caret	Philadelphia	PA	w	1908-1913	Ba,Ay1913,PA
Sunday Herald	Philadelphia	PA	w	1896-1897	Ba,Mather
Sunday Journal	Philadelphia	PA		1895-1897	Ba
Suss-Lee Community News	Philadelphia	PA		1977-1978	EP78
Temple University News	Philadelphia	PA	d	1921-1968	PA,Lc83,Rw96
Temple University Weekly	Philadelphia	PA	w	1920-1927	Lc83
United Golfers and Other Sports	Philadelphia	PA		1939-1940	EP39,40
Voice	Philadelphia	PA		1975	EP75,76
Weekly Advocate	Philadelphia	PA	w	1937-1942	Lc83
Weekly Prophet	Philadelphia	PA	w	1913-1918	Oclc
Witness	Philadelphia	PA	w	1918-1920	Ba,Ay1920,PA
Afro-American Presbyterian	Pittsburgh	PA		1887-1890	Ba
Afro-American Spokesman	Pittsburgh	PA	w	1888-1891	Ba,Ay1890,Penn
Afro-Dispatch	Pittsburgh	PA	w	1940	Ba,EP40,Br
American	Pittsburgh	PA	w	1918-1925	Ba,Ay1921,PA,NY22,26,Go,Boris1
Balance Sheet	Pittsburgh	PA	m	1951	EP51
Black Lines	Pittsburgh	PA	q	1970-1974	WI,SPD74
Broad Axe	Pittsburgh	PA	w	1896-1901	Ba,PA
Colored Citizen	Pittsburgh	PA	w	1880-1884	Ba,Penn,PA,jcw
Commoner	Pittsburgh	PA	w	1884-1884	Ay1884

TITLE	CITY	ST.	FREQ.	DATES	SOURCES
Commonwealth	Pittsburgh	PA	w	1887-1889	Ba
Competitor	Pittsburgh	PA	m	1920-1921	WI,BJ
Crier	Pittsburgh	PA	w	1933-1938	Ba,Ay1935,1938,EP35,PA
Criterion	Pittsburgh	PA	w	1935	EP35
Crusader	Pittsburgh	PA	w	1936-1938	Ba,Br,EP36-38
Detroit Courier	Pittsburgh	PA	w	1953-1987	Ay1953,1971,EP80,Pr,Lb,SPD87
Examiner	Pittsburgh	PA	w	1930-1942	Ba,Br,NH42,EP38,40-42,Dc41
Georgia Courier	Pittsburgh	PA	w	1973-1980	EP75,77,80,Bp
Guard	Pittsburgh	PA	w	1926-1929	Ba,PA
Homewood Brushton News	Pittsburgh	PA	w	1935-1994+	PA,EP77,84,Lb,SPD87,94
Independent	Pittsburgh	PA	w	1900-1906	Ba,Ay1906,PA
Industrial Register	Pittsburgh	PA		1920-1922	Ba,NY22
Journal	Pittsburgh	PA	w	1893-1896	Ba,Ay1896,PA
Kodesh Herald	Pittsburgh	PA	bm	1941-1946	Ba,NH46,Dc44
Mystery	Pittsburgh	PA	w	1843-1848	Ba,NY12,DANB170
New Informer	Pittsburgh	PA		1992+	BRG
New Pittsburgh Courier	Pittsburgh	PA	w	1966-1994+	Ay1970,1975,Ga87,94,Lc91,Baid92,Bp, EBA,BRG,EP71,93,WSJ,API90,94, WPN94
News	Pittsburgh	PA	w	1882-1885	Ba,Ay1884,PA
Philadelphia Courier	Pittsburgh	PA	w	1953-1971	Ba,Ay1953,1971,EP62,80
Pittsburgh Courier	Pittsburgh	PA	w	1908-1966	Ay1919,1925[b1910],1953,Go,Bp,WI, Lc91,Oclc,NH42,44,46,49,EP35,78,NY19, 22,26,32,46,Dc41,44,SPD67,70,74, Yenser6,Fleming
Pittsburgh News	Pittsburgh	PA		1975-1976	EP75,76
Pittsburgh Renaissance News	Pittsburgh	PA	w	1967-1994+	BRG,WPN94,API94
Plaindealer	Pittsburgh	PA		1889-1901	Ba
Ploughshare	Pittsburgh	PA		1900-1901	Ba
Progressive Afro-American	Pittsburgh	PA	w	1906-1910	Ba,PA,NY12
Shooting Star Review	Pittsburgh	PA	q	1987-1994+	Ga90,94,SPD94
Smith's Broad Axe	Pittsburgh	PA	w	1885-1892	Ba,R1888,Ay1891,1886
Spiritual Sunbeam	Pittsburgh	PA		1897	Boris1 [Withrow, Chauncey Isaiah]
Telegram	Pittsburgh	PA	w	1943-1944	EP43,44
Triangle Advocate	Pittsburgh	PA	w	1935-1955	Ba,Ay1940,1955,NH42,Dc41
Vanguard	Pittsburgh	PA		pre 1970	Ba
Western Enterprise	Pittsburgh	PA	w	1896-1897	Ba,PA
Pennsylvania Black Observer	Reading	PA	m	1973-1978	Ay1975,1978
Plain Dealer	Rochester	PA	w	1904-1908	Ba,Ay1906,1908,PA
Press	Steelton	PA	w	1890-1916	Ba,Ay1894,1916,PA
Afro-American Signal	Uniontown	PA	w	1904-1905	PA
Courier Digest	Uniontown	PA	w	1936-1946	Ba,NH42,EP38,43
Journal	Uniontown	PA	w	1893-1895	Ba,Ay1894,PA
Journal	Uniontown	PA	w	1926-1927	Ba,PA
News	Uniontown	PA		1908-1917	Ba

TITLE	CITY	ST.	FREQ.	DATES	SOURCES
People's Advocate	Uniontown	PA		1912	NY12
Together Community Witness Newsletter	Valley Forge	PA		1963-1966	ABSCHSL
Black Music Review	West Pittston	PA		1974-1979	SPD74,79
Advocate	Wilkes-Barre	PA	w	1900-1922	Ba,Ay1905,1915,NY19,22,Go,Mather
Voice of the People	Wilkes-Barre	PA		1899-1901	Ba
Newport and Boston Union	Newport	RI		pre 1915	Mather [Small, Thomas Frederick]
Triangle	Newport	RI		1920-1922	Ba,NY22
Pawtucket Evening Times	Pawtucket	RI	d	1900-1904	Boris1 [Minkins, John Carter], Ay1912[b1885]
Advance	Providence	RI	w	1906-1942	Ba,Ay1908,1942,Oclc,go,Br,EP38,NY12, 19,22,26,32,Mather
Chronicle	Providence	RI	w	1924-1958	Ba,Ay1958,Oclc,EP44,51
Citizen	Providence	RI	w	1968	Oclc
Eastern Review	Providence	RI		1878-1883	Ba,Penn
Ebenezer Grapevine	Providence	RI	m	1978-1980	Oclc
Evening Telegram	Providence	RI		1904-1906	Boris2 [Minkins, John Carter]
North Star	Providence	RI	m	1977	Oclc,Lb
Ocean State Grapevine	Providence	RI	sm	1986-1994+	Ga91,94,Oclc,Baid90,92
Providence American	Providence	RI	bw	1986-1993+	Oclc,EP91,92,93
Providence News	Providence	RI	d	1891-1912	Ay1912[nlb],Boris1
Republican Sun	Providence	RI	w	1895-1897	Ba,Ay1896
Rhode Island Examiner	Providence	RI	w	1911-1915	Ay1912[nlb],Boris1
Rhode Island Independent	Providence	RI		1913-1915	Ba
Telegram	Providence	RI		1893-1900	Boris1 [Minkins, John Carter]
Torchlight	Providence	RI	w	1894	Eur94,Mather[New England Torchlight 1890-1900]
Tribune	Providence	RI	d	1915-1944	Yenser6 [Minkins, John Carter]
Watchman	Providence	RI		1901-1903	Ba
Methodist Messenger		SC		1887-1889	Mather [Burroughs, Edward Butler]
Pee Dee Times		SC		1994+	API94 (see Florence)
Journal of Enterprise	Abbeville	SC		1883	SC
Odd Fellows' Journal of SC	Abbeville	SC	m	1910-1914	Ba,Ay1911-1914,NY12
Piedmont Voice	Abbeville	SC	w	1910-1914	Ba,Ay1914
Herald	Aiken	SC		1898-1901	Ba
Journal	Aiken	SC		1940-1942	Ba,SC[1943-1945]
Little Observer	Aiken	SC	sm	1895	SC
Schofield School Bulletin	Aiken	SC	m	1912-1922	NY12,19,22
Allendale Advocate	Allendale	SC		1913-1922	Ba,Go,NY19
Anderson Herald	Anderson	SC	w	1962-1979	Pr,EP67,70,SC,Lb,SPD67,70,74,49
Messenger	Anderson	SC	w	1936-1938	Ba,EP36
Beaufort County News	Beaufort	SC	w	1904-1915	Ba,Ay1906,1912,NY12
New South	Beaufort	SC	w	1889-1898	Ba,Ay1890,1896,SC[1880-1885],Penn, Eur94
Sea Island News	Beaufort	SC	w	1879-1891	Ay1882,1886,1887,1889-1891,Oclc

TITLE	CITY	ST.	FREQ.	DATES	SOURCES
Sea Island News	Beaufort	SC	w	1910-1913	Ba,Ay1911,1912,1913
South Carolina Churchman	Beaufort	SC	w	1904-1909	Ba,Ay1906,1908,1909
Baptist Monitor	Bennettsville	SC	w	1890-1891	Ba,Ay1891,Penn
Pee Dee Educator	Bennettsville	SC	sm	1890-1906	Ba,Ay1890,1906,Oclc,SC[1879-1899]
Afro-American Recorder	Bishopville	SC	w	1907-1909	Ba,Ay1909
Progressive Church Record	Branchville	SC	sm	1913-1915	Ba,Ay1915
Elevator	Brunson	SC	sm	1894	Eur94
Hampton County Elevator	Brunson	SC	sm/w	1891-1895	Ba,SC
New Light	Brunson	SC		1896-1897	Ba
Bee	Camden	SC	w	1907-1911	Ba,Ay1909,1911
Camden Chronicle	Camden	SC	w	1967-1979	EP67,70,Lb,SPD67,70,74,79
Afro-American	Charleston	SC	w	1954-1955	Ay1955
Afro-American Banner	Charleston	SC		1899-1902	Ba
Afro-American Citizen	Charleston	SC	w	1899-1900	Gr,Lc91,Oclc,WI
Baptist Tribune	Charleston	SC	w	1887-1890	Ba,DANB61
Charleston Advocate	Charleston	SC	w	1867-1869	Ba,Lc91,Oclc,WI
Charleston Black Times	Charleston	SC	w	1970-1994+	Ay1983,Ga87[Columbia],94,BRG, EP78[1972],WPN94,API94
Charleston Enquirer	Charleston	SC	w	1895	SC
Charleston Inquirer	Charleston	SC	w	1963-1964	SC
Charleston Journal	Charleston	SC		1866-1911	Ba,Br
Charleston Leader	Charleston	SC		1868-1870	Ba,Go
Charleston Messenger	Charleston	SC	w	1894-1946	Ba,Ay1906,1946,NH42,EP35,41,Go,Br, NY12,SC[1900-1937],NY19,22,26,32,46, Dc41
Chronicle	Charleston	SC	w	1971-1994+	Ay1983,Ga87,94,Oclc,Bp,EP73,93,Baid92, BRG,EH,API94
Church Herald	Charleston	SC		1927-1937	Yenser4 [Baskerville, Erasmus Lafayette]
Coastal Times	Charleston	SC	w	1983-1994+	Ga91,94,Baid92,BRG,EP87,93
Esquire	Charleston	SC		1894-1900	Ba
Free Press	Charleston	SC	w	1868-1870	Ba,Lc91,Oclc,WI
Hamitic Palladium	Charleston	SC		1902-1905	Ba,SC
Lighthouse	Charleston	SC	w	1939-1941	Ba,Oclc,EP43,44
Lighthouse and Informer	Charleston	SC	w	1940-1944	Oclc,NH42,EP41,42,Dc41
Missionary Record	Charleston	SC	w	1868-1879	Ba,Lc91,Oclc,WI[e1874], DANB85[e1872],KSWilliams 1877,SC
Monitor	Charleston	SC	w	1888	SC
New Citizen	Charleston	SC	w	1948-1952	Ay1950,1952,SC
New Era	Charleston	SC	w	1922-1932	Ba,Go,SC[1934-35],NY22,26,Boris1
New Era	Charleston	SC		1880-1884	Ay1882,1884,SC
Observer	Charleston	SC	w	1899	SC
Palmetto Press	Charleston	SC	w	1882-1887	Ba,Ay1884,SC
People's Watchman	Charleston	SC		1880-1881	Ba,Penn
Protective League Journal	Charleston	SC	w	1905-1909	Ba,Ay1909
Recorder	Charleston	SC	w	1883-1887	Ba,Ay1887,SC

TITLE	CITY	ST.	FREQ.	DATES	SOURCES
South Carolina Leader	Charleston	SC	w	1865-1868	Ba,Lc91,Oclc,WI,DANB85
South Carolina Methodist	Charleston	SC		1903-1905	Ba
South Carolina Tribune	Charleston	SC		1887-1891	Ba
Southern Reporter	Charleston	SC	w	1900-1920	Ba,Ay1905,1920,NY12,Mather
Telegram	Charleston	SC	w	1935-1939	Ba,EP35,36
World	Charleston	SC		1876-1882	Ba
Carolina News	Cheraw	SC	w	1909-1914	Ba,Ay1912,1913,1914
Monitor	Cheraw	SC	w	1883	SC
South Carolina Herald	Chester	SC	w/sm	1891-1895	Ba,Ay1894,Eur94,SC
Torchlight	Chester	SC	w	1907	Lt1907
Allen Journal	Columbia	SC		1942	SC
Allen Student	Columbia	SC		1922	NY22
Barnwell Recorder	Columbia	SC		1892	SC
Bee	Columbia	SC	w	1910-1912	Ba,Ay1912
Benedict Newsletter	Columbia	SC		1991	ABSCHSL
Carolina Panorama	Columbia	SC	w	1991-1992+	EP91,92
Christian Soldier	Columbia	SC	w	1899	SC
College Journal	Columbia	SC	m	1919-1922	NY19,22
Columbia Black News	Columbia	SC	w	1970-1994+	Ay1983,92,Ga87,94,Oclc,Baid90,EP77, 93[b1973],BRG,API94,WPN94
Columbia Bowler	Columbia	SC		1962-1963	SC
Columbia Courier	Columbia	SC	w	1986-1987	EP87
Comet	Columbia	SC		1939	SC
Florence Black Sun	Columbia	SC	w	1970-1994+	Ga87,94,Baid92,BRG,EP78,93,WPN94, API94
Greenville Black Star	Columbia	SC	w	1983-1994+	Ay1983,Ga87,94,Baid90,92,BRG,EP78,93, WPN94,API94
Informer	Columbia	SC		1919-1937	Ba,NY19,22,26,Go
Light	Columbia	SC	w	1907-1928	Ba,Ay1909,1925,Oclc[b1916],NY12,19, 22,26,SC,Go,Boris1
Lighthouse	Columbia	SC		1963	Bl
Lighthouse and Informer	Columbia	SC	w	1938-1954	Ba,Ay1950,1955,Oclc,Br,NH44,46,49, EP45,51,SC,NY46,Dc44
Monitor	Columbia	SC	m	1907	Lt1907
Odd Fellows' Journal	Columbia	SC	m	1905-1909	Ba,Ay1906,1908,1909
Orangeburg Black Voice	Columbia	SC	w	1970-1994+	Ay1983,Ga87,94,EP78[1972],93,BRG, Baid92,WPN94,SPD87,94
Palmetto Gleaner	Columbia	SC	w	1890-1892	Ba,Ay1890,1891,SC
Palmetto Leader	Columbia	SC	w	1925-1970	Ba,Ay1935,1960,Br,NH42,44,46,49,EP35, 51,SC,NY32,46,Dc41,44,Yenser6[b1920]
Palmetto Post/Greenville Leader	Columbia	SC	w	1983-1990	EP87,90
Palmetto Times	Columbia	SC	w	1962-1970	Pr,EP64,65,67,SC,SPD67,70
People's Recorder	Columbia	SC	w	1893-1940	Ba,Ay1896,1925,Gr,Lc91,Oclc[e1905?], WI,SC,NY32
Plowman	Columbia	SC		1906-1922	Ba,Go,NY19

TITLE	CITY	ST.	FREQ.	DATES	SOURCES
Pythian World	Columbia	SC		1912	NY12
Record	Columbia	SC		1896-1897	Ba
Recorder Indicator	Columbia	SC	w	1893-1927	Ba,SC,NY26,Boris
Rock Hill Black View	Columbia	SC	w	1970-1994+	Ay1983,Ga87,94,WPN94,API94,Baid92, EP93
Shopping Guide and News	Columbia	SC		pre 1979	Lb
South Carolina Baptist	Columbia	SC		1918-1920	SC
South Carolina Herald	Columbia	SC	w	1907-1919	Ba,Ay1911,1912,NY12,19
South Carolina Methodist	Columbia	SC	w	pre 1962	SC
South Carolina Standard	Columbia	SC		1896-1904	Ba
Southern Indicator	Columbia	SC	w	1898-1935	Ba,Ay1916,1925[b1903],Lc91,WI, Oclc[1913-1924],SC[1913-1924],NY19,22, NWU
Southern Ploughman	Columbia	SC	sm	1906-1916	Ba,Ay1911,1914,NY12,SC[1908-1910]
Southern Sun	Columbia	SC	w	1902-1912	Ba,Ay1905,1909,Oclc,NY12,SC
Standard	Columbia	SC	w	1919-1927	Ba,Ay1921S,1925,Oclc,SC[b1899],NY19, 22,Lt1907
Sumter Black Post	Columbia	SC	w	1970-1994+	Ay1983,Ga87,94,Oclc,Baid92,API94, WPN94
Venture	Columbia	SC	m	1978-1979	Oclc
Watchman	Columbia	SC	w	1903	SC
Farmer's Courier	Darlington	SC	w	1905-1916	Ba,Ay1906,1908,1909,1911-1914,1916
Union	Darlington	SC	m	1935-1953	Ba,NH42,SC,Dc41,ABSCHSL
Century Dawn	Dillon	SC	w	1902-1905	Ba,Ay1905
Baptist Chronicle	Florence	SC	m	1916-1923	Ba,Ay1916-1920
Baptist Herald	Florence	SC	sm	1889-1895	Ba,Ay1890,1891,1894,Eur94,SC
Chronicle	Florence	SC	m	1896-1915	Ba,Ay1906,1912-1915[b1902],Lt1907
Florence Black Times	Florence	SC	w	1983	Ay1983 (see Columbia)
Joint Enterprise	Florence	SC	w	1910-1911	Ba,Ay1911
Key	Florence	SC	w	1980-1983	EP80,81,83
Pee Dee Weekly	Florence	SC	w	1935-1938	Ba,EP35,36
Pee Times	Florence	SC	w	1992+	BRG (See Pee Dee Times)
Chronicle	Gaffney	SC	w	1896-1923	Ba,Ay1921[1915]
District Herald	Gaffney	SC		pre 1928	Boris2 [Miller, Samuel M.]
Negro Journal	Gaffney	SC	w	1915-1920	Ba,Ay1918-1920
Sun	Gaffney	SC	w	1905-1906	Ba,Ay1906
Advocate	Georgetown	SC	w	1902-1905	Ba,Ay1905
People's Advocate	Georgetown	SC		1903-1907	Ba
Planet	Georgetown	SC	w	1873-1875	Ba,Lc91,Oclc,WI
Carolina News and Guide	Greenville	SC	w	1963-1964	SC
Crusader	Greenville	SC		1940-1963	Ba,SC
Enterprise	Greenville	SC	w	1905-1908	Ba,Ay1908
Focus	Greenville	SC	w	1973-1977	EP74-77
Greenville American	Greenville	SC	w	1952	SC
Lancet	Greenville	SC	w	1890-1891	Ba,Ay1891

TITLE	CITY	ST.	FREQ.	DATES	SOURCES
Log	Greenville	SC	w	1940-1943	NH42,EP43,Dc41
Negro Chronicle	Greenville	SC		1916-1922	Ba,Go,NY19
People's Record	Greenville	SC	w	1901-1909	Ba,Ay1906,1909
World	Greenville	SC	w	1932-1940	Ba,Ay1939,1940,EP35-37
Piedmont Voice	Greenwood	SC	w	1910-1914	Ba,Ay1911-1913
Sentinel	Greenwood	SC		1902-1904	Ba
Messenger	Hertford	SC		1908-1911	Ba
Lowcountry Newsletter	John's Island	SC		1968	WI
Carolina Sun	Kingstree	SC	w	1966-1979	EP67,69,70,Bp,Lb,SPD67,70,74,79
Voice	Kingstree	SC	w	1987-1990	EP87,90
Williamsburg Republican	Kingstree	SC	w	1873-1877	Oclc
People's Record	Laurens	SC		1901-1905	Ba
Pee Dee Observer	Marion	SC	w	1981-1984	EP84
Plane	Marion	SC	w	1905-1906	Ba,Ay1906
Southland Herald	Mayesville	SC	m	1905-1916	Ba,Ay1912,1913,1916
Industrial Enterprise	McCormick	SC	sm	1908-1912	Ba,Ay1909
Laing School Visitor	Mount Pleasant	SC		1912-1922	NY12,19,22
People's Advocate	Mount Pleasant	SC	w	1903-1906	Ba,Ay1906
Weekly Observer	Myrtle Beach	SC	w	1974-1977	EP75-77
Stylus	Newberry	SC	m	1907	Ay1912[b1897 nlb],Lt1907
Afro Weekly	Orangeburg	SC	w	1980-1983	EP80,83
Black Future	Orangeburg	SC	q	1987	SPD87
Gospel Banner	Orangeburg	SC		1890-1892	Ba
Orangeburg Herald	Orangeburg	SC	w	1957-1973	EBA,Bp,Lb
Panther	Orangeburg	SC	2xy	1973	Bp
People's Recorder	Orangeburg	SC	w	1893-1922	Ba,Ay1906,1920,Go,NY12,19,22,Lt1907
Plain Speaker	Orangeburg	SC	w	1886-1892	Ba,Ay1889-1891,Mather
Plaindealer	Orangeburg	SC		1888-1892	Ba
State College Review	Orangeburg	SC	m	1919-1922	NY19,22
View South News	Orangeburg	SC	w	1979-1994+	Ga90,94,Baid92,BRG,API94
Vue South	Orangeburg	SC	m	1964-1974	Ay1969,1974,EH,SPD70,74
Record	Pendleton	SC		1906-1907	Ba
True Light	Ridgeland	SC		1897-1899	Ba
Friendship Banner	Rock Hill	SC	w	1903-1922	Ba,Ay1906,1920,NY12,19,22
Messenger	Rock Hill	SC	w	1896-1932	Ba,Ay1905,1921,Gr,Lc91,Oclc,WI,Boris1, NY12,19,22,26,32
Sunday School Headlight	Rock Hill	SC		1906-1908	Mather [Eichelberger, James W., Jr.]
Carolina Freeman	Saint George	SC		1901-1903	Ba
Gospel Banner	Saint Matthews	SC	sm	1890-1891	Ba,Ay1890,1891
News	Society Hill	SC	w	1910-1911	Ba,Ay1911
Advance	Spartanburg	SC	w	1894-1897	Ba,Ay1896
Baptist Advocate	Spartanburg	SC	w	1895-1897	Ba,Ay1896
Link	Spartanburg	SC	w	1902-1906	Ba,Ay1905,1906
Negro Index	Spartanburg	SC	w	1916-1922	Ba,Ay1902,1921

TITLE	CITY	ST.	FREQ.	DATES	SOURCES
Piedmont Indicator	Spartanburg	SC	w	1896-1900	Ba,SC
Southern Indicator	Spartanburg	SC	w	1898-1935	Ba,Ay1911,1913,1920
Southern Reporter	Spartanburg	SC		1900-1903	Ba
Baptist Informer	Sumter	SC	q	1963	SC
Daily Christian Advocate	Sumter	SC		1908	Mather [Jacobs, Charles Cook]
Defender	Sumter	SC	w	1903-1920	Ba,Ay1908,1920,Oclc[1903-1913],NY12, Lt1907
People's Informer	Sumter	SC		1937-1940	EP39,40,ba,SC
Samaritan Herald	Sumter	SC	w	1909-1942	Ba,Ay1920,1925,[b1912],1942,Oclc, NH42,46,49,EP38,43,NY22,Dc41,44
Samaritan Herald and Voice of Job	Sumter	SC	w	1943-1952	Ay1943,1955,Oclc,EP48,49[God],SC, NY46
Samaritan Leader	Sumter	SC	w	1944	NH44
Vindicator	Sumter	SC		1883	SC
Weekly Advocate	Sumter	SC	w	1902	Mather [Jenkins, Isaac William]
Defender	Timmonsville	SC		1911-1931	Ba
Joint Stock News	Timmonsville	SC	sm	1914-1915	Ba
Pee Dee Watchman	Timmonsville	SC	w	1910-1914	Ba,Ay1911,1912,1913,1914
Pee Dee Watchman and Defender	Timmonsville	SC	w	1915-1919	Ba,Ay1915-1919
Watchman and Defender	Timmonsville	SC	w	1920-1931	Ba,Ay1921,1925,NY26,Boris1
Star	Union	SC		1897-1898	Ba
Carolina Tribune	Vaucluse	SC		1891-1894	Ba,Ay1891,1894,Eur94,SC
Messenger of the Day	Wedgefield	SC		1909-1910	Ba
Watchman	Athens	TN	w	1891-1895	Ba,Ay1894,1891,Kfb
Haywood Republican	Brownsville	TN	w	1888-1903	Ba,Ay1889-1891
Tennessee Baptist Standard	Brownsville	TN		1899-1900	Ba
African-American Community Business Newsletter	Chattanooga	TN	m	1992-1993+	AAMC
Aurora	Chattanooga	TN		1946	EP46
Baptist	Chattanooga	TN		1898-1899	Ba
Baptist Recorder	Chattanooga	TN	w	1902-1912	Ba,Ay1905,1906,1912
Blade	Chattanooga	TN	w	1898-1916	Ba,Ay1905,1915,Kfb,NY12
Chattanooga Defender	Chattanooga	TN	w	1916-1944	Ba,Ay1919,1937,EP35,40,Kfb,Go,Br, NY19,22,26,Boris1
Chattanooga Journal	Chattanooga	TN	w	1925-1926	NY26
Chattanooga Observer	Chattanooga	TN	w	1935-1974	Ba,Ay1937,1953,NH44,46,49,Pr,Lb,EP35, 71,Kfb,NY46,Dc44,SPD67,70,74
Citizen	Chattanooga	TN		1944-1949	Ba,EP48,49,Kfb
Colored Citizen	Chattanooga	TN	w	1908-1912	Ba,Ay1909,1910,Kfb,NY12
Defender	Chattanooga	TN	w	1978	EP78
Freeman	Chattanooga	TN		1896-1897	Ba,Kfb
Harambee	Chattanooga	TN		1974	Kfb
Heritage	Chattanooga	TN	w	1977	EP77
Independent Tribune	Chattanooga	TN	w	1886-1886	Ba,Ay1886,Kfb
Industrial Search Light	Chattanooga	TN		1891-1904	Ba,Kfb[1899-1904]

TITLE	CITY	ST.	FREQ.	DATES	SOURCES
Journal	Chattanooga	TN		1973-1974	Kfb
Justice	Chattanooga	TN	w	1887-1889	Ba,Ay1889,NWU,Lc91,Oclc,WI,Kfb,bu
National Democracy	Chattanooga	TN	w	1918-1921	Ba,Ay1921,Kfb
News Weekly	Chattanooga	TN	w	1986-1993+	AAMC,TNSLA
Observer	Chattanooga	TN	w	1887-1895	Ba,Ay1891,1894,1890,Kfb[1890-1895]
Radiance	Chattanooga	TN		1978	Kfb
Southern American	Chattanooga	TN		1884-1887	Ba,Br,Kfb
Sun	Chattanooga	TN		1913-1915	Ba,Kfb
Tribune	Chattanooga	TN	w	1928-1931	Ba,Kfb,NY32
World	Chattanooga	TN		1930	Kfb,Bl
Clarksville Connection	Clarksville	TN	w	1992-1993+	Mont. Co. PL
Negro Index	Clarksville	TN		1901-1903	Ba,Kfb
News Herald	Clarksville	TN	w	1913-1939	Ba,Ay1914-1917,EP38,39,Kfb
Press	Clarksville	TN	w	1991-1992	EP91,92
Sun	Clarksville	TN	w	1950	Kfb
Headlight	Columbia	TN	w	1893-1895	Ba,Ay1894,Kfb
Advocate	Fayetteville	TN	w	1900-1905	Ba,Ay1905,Kfb
Banner of Light	Fayetteville	TN	m	1879-1882	Ay1882
Colored Cumberland Presbyterian	Fayetteville	TN	w/sm	1884-1906	Ba,Ay1891,1906,Eur94
Rising Sun	Fayetteville	TN		1895-1899	Kfb
Major	Gallatin	TN	sm	1905-1914	Ba,Ay1906,1913,Kfb,NY12
Herald of Truth	Henderson	TN	w	1881-1886	Ay1886
Afro-American Journal	Humboldt	TN	w	1904-1909	Ba,Ay1909
Afro-American Sentinel	Jackson	TN		1890-1891	Ay1891,Kfb
Afro-American Standard	Jackson	TN	w	1903-1906	Ba,Ay1905,1906,Kfb
Christian Index	Jackson	TN	w	1867-1966	Ba,Ay1882,1966,Oclc,NH42,46,EP38,51, Eur94,Kfb,NY12,19,22,26,32,46,Dc41,44, Lt1907,Mather,Yenser3
Everready Magazine	Jackson	TN	m	1920	Ay1920
Gazette	Jackson	TN		1910-1912	Ba,Kfb
Headlight	Jackson	TN	w	1899-1900	Ba,NWU,Lc91,Oclc,WI,Kfb
Herald of Truth	Jackson	TN		1881-1886	Ba
Jackson Times	Jackson	TN	bw/w	1936-1944	NH42,EP36,43,44,Dc41
Lane College Reporter	Jackson	TN	m	1912-1922	NY12,19,22
Medical and Surgical Observer	Jackson	TN	m	1892-1895	Ba,Ay1894,Boris1
Metro Forum	Jackson	TN		1992-1994+	BRG,API94
News	Jackson	TN	w	1906-1907	Ba,Kfb,Lt1907
Aurora	Knoxville	TN	m	1886-1953	Ay1940,1953,NH46,NY12,19,22,46,Dc44, Lt1907
Baptist Family Companion	Knoxville	TN	w	1876-1882	Ba,Ay1880,Penn
Daily Monitor	Knoxville	TN	d	1949	NH49
East Tennessee News	Knoxville	TN	w	1906-1949	Ba,Ay1911,1948,NH42,44,49,EP38,49, Kfb,NY12,19,22,26,32,Dc41,Go,Boris1
Enquirer	Knoxville	TN	w	1939-1944	EP43,44,Kfb,NH42,44,Dc41

TITLE	CITY	ST.	FREQ.	DATES	SOURCES
Flashlight Herald	Knoxville	TN	w	1931-1964	Ba,Ay1940,1964,NH42,EP35,64,Kfb, NY46,Dc41
Gleanor	Knoxville	TN	w	1891-1900	Ba,Ay1894,1896,Kfb,Eur94, Mather[e1915]
Herald	Knoxville	TN		1927-1946	Ba,Ay1931-1935,Kfb[1927-1935], Br,NY32
Independent Call	Knoxville	TN		1952-1961	Kfb
Keyana	Knoxville	TN		1974-1974	Kfb
Keyana Spectrum	Knoxville	TN		1974-1975	Kfb
Knoxville Examiner	Knoxville	TN		1878-1885	Ba,Penn,Kfb
Knoxville Times	Knoxville	TN	w	1964-1971	Ay1969,Kfb[1964-1966],EP72,73,Bp
Messenger	Knoxville	TN		1908-1910	Ba,Kfb
Monitor	Knoxville	TN	w	1944-1954	Ba,Ay1950,1954,EP46,51,Kfb
Negro World	Knoxville	TN		1928	WI
Negro World	Knoxville	TN		1887-1895	Ba,Ay1889-1891,R1888,WRHS,Oclc,Go, Br,Kfb,Eur94
New South	Knoxville	TN	w	1887-1895	Ba,Ay1894,Kfb
Public Guide	Knoxville	TN		1935-1938	Ba,EP35-38
Review	Knoxville	TN	w	1904-1910	Ba,Ay1906,1909,1910,Kfb
Spectrum	Knoxville	TN		1975-1975	Kfb
Voice	Knoxville	TN		1949	Kfb
Afro-American	Liberty	TN		1899-1902	Kfb
Blount County Democrat	Maryville	TN	w	1879-1882	Ba,Ay1880,1882,Kfb
Maryville Democrat	Maryville	TN	w	1878-1879	Kfb
Maryville Monitor	Maryville	TN	w	1873-1876	Kfb
Maryville Republican	Maryville	TN	w	1867-1877	Lc91,WI,Kfb
Republican	Maryville	TN	w	1873-1878	Ba,Lc91,Oclc
Afro-American	Memphis	TN		1895	Kfb
Baptist Herald	Memphis	TN	w	1901-1920	Ba,Ay1906,1920[b1907],Lt1907
Bluff City News	Memphis	TN	w	1902-1922	Ba,Ay1906,1920,Kfb,NY12,19,Lt1907,Go
Bulletin	Memphis	TN	m	1919-1922	NY19,22
Christian Index	Memphis	TN	2xm	1968-1994+	Ga90,94,WI[1866-1968]
Colored Citizen	Memphis	TN	w	1900-1921	Ba,Ay1905,1921,Kfb,NY12,Lt1907
Colored Wage Earner	Memphis	TN	sm	1938	EP38
Dixie Journal	Memphis	TN	bw	1936	EP36
Dublin Weekly Bulletin	Memphis	TN	w	1920-1922	Ba,Kfb,NY22
Evening Striker	Memphis	TN		1903-1904	Ba (see Memphis Daily Striker)
Free Speech	Memphis	TN		1889-1893	Ba,Lb,Rw,Mather,DANB
Free Speech and Headlight	Memphis	TN		1888-1890	Ay1890,Kfb
Head and Hand	Memphis	TN	w	1902-1922	NY19,22,Lt1907,Kfb
Headlight	Memphis	TN		1886-1888	Ba,Kfb
Index	Memphis	TN	w	1923-1936	Ba,Ay1931,1932,1935,Br
Industrial World	Memphis	TN		1913-1915	Ba
Living Way	Memphis	TN	w	1883-1892	Ba,Ay1884,1886,1888-1891,Rw

TITLE	CITY	ST.	FREQ.	DATES	SOURCES
Memphis Citizen	Memphis	TN	w	1969-1972	EBA,EP71-73,Lb
Memphis Daily Striker	Memphis	TN	d	1905	Mather [Holloway, Isaac H.] (see Evening Striker)
Memphis Journal	Memphis	TN		1936-1938	Ba,Kfb,Br
Memphis Silver Star News	Memphis	TN	w	1990-1994+	Ga90,94,Baid90,92,BRG,API94
Memphis Star Times	Memphis	TN	w	1954-1957	Ay1956,Kfb
Memphis World	Memphis	TN	w/sw	1931-1974	Ba,Ay1945,1952,Br,NH42,44,46,49,EP35,73,EBA,Kfb[e1972],NY46,Dc41,44,Rw,Lb,SPD67,70,74,Fleming,Bl
Mid-South Express	Memphis	TN	w	1979-1986	EP80-83,86[1980],Kfb
Mid-Weekly Progress	Memphis	TN	w	1905-1912	Ba,Kfb,NY12
Moon Illustrated Weekly	Memphis	TN	w	1905-1906	WI,Kfb,BJ
National Beacon Light	Memphis	TN		1904-1917	Ba,Ay1917
Negro Journal of Industry	Memphis	TN		1946	Ba,Br
Outlook	Memphis	TN	w	1902-1906	Ba,Ay1905,1906,Kfb[1920s]
Planet	Memphis	TN		1879-1882	Ba,Penn,Kfb[1872-1876]
Record	Memphis	TN		1920-1922	Ba,Kfb,NY22
Scimitar	Memphis	TN		1898-1900	Ba,Kfb
Signal	Memphis	TN	w	1901-1916	Ba,Ay1905,1916,Kfb,NY12,Lt1907
Southern Sentiment	Memphis	TN	2xm	1904-1905	Ba,Ay1905
Sphinx Magazine	Memphis	TN	q	1935-1951	Ay1945,1950,EP39,51,Fleming
Sun	Memphis	TN		1913	Kfb
Times	Memphis	TN	w	1918-1937	Ba,Ay1921S,1925,1937,NY19,22,26,Go
Triangle	Memphis	TN	w	1930-1932	Ba,NY32
Tri-State Defender	Memphis	TN	w	1951-1994+	Ay1956,1975,Ga90,94,Lc91,Oclc,EP62,93,EBA,BRG,EH,Kfb,Bp,API90,94,WPN94,SPD67,70,74,79,87,94
Tri-State Tribune	Memphis	TN	w	1930-1932	Ba,Kfb,NY32
U.W.T. News	Memphis	TN	m	1922	NY22
Watchman	Memphis	TN	w	1878-1897	Ba,Ay1884,1886-1889,1894,1896,Br
Western World Reporter	Memphis	TN	w	1919-1925	Ba,Ay1925[1914],NY19,22,26,Go,Boris1
Whole Truth	Memphis	TN	m	1925-1978	Ba,Ay1945,1978,NH42,46,EH,NY46,Dc41,44
Colored Cumberland	Milan	TN	w	1922-1932	Ba,NY22,26,32
Reporter	Morristown	TN	sm	1920-1921	Ba,Ay1921,Kfb
Murfreesboro News	Murfreesboro	TN	w	1952-1987	Ay1969,1971,Kfb[1956-1966],EP73,Lb,SPD67,70,74,79,87
Murfreesboro Times	Murfreesboro	TN		pre 1972	EP72
Union	Murfreesboro	TN	w	1920-1950	Ba,Kfb,NY22,26,32,Fleming
780 Countdown	Nashville	TN	w	1962-1964	Ay1964,Kfb,TNM
Advanced Quarterly	Nashville	TN	q	1885-1935	Ay1917,1935,Boris2 [Birmingham]
Allen Christian Endeavor	Nashville	TN		pre 1915	Mather [Calswell, Julian Carr]
American Negro Mind	Nashville	TN	m	1933-1951	Ay1940,1951
A.M.E. Christian Recorder	Nashville	TN	w	1846-1994+	Ay1969,1983,Ga87,88,WI,BRG,EH,EP72-78,Lb,WPN94[b1848]

TITLE	CITY	ST.	FREQ.	DATES	SOURCES
A.M.E. Church Review	Nashville	TN	q	1883-1972	Ay1920,1925[b1884],1969,1975,EH, NY12,WI
A.M.E. Sunday School Union	Nashville	TN		1908	Mather [Bryant, Ira T.]
Baptist Training Union Leader	Nashville	TN		1958-1964	ABSCHSL
Black Church Development	Nashville	TN		1990-1992	ABSCHSL
Block Bulletin	Nashville	TN		1950	TNM,Kfb
Broadcaster	Nashville	TN	q	1923-1977	Ay1940,1977,EP48,49,EH
Brown Book	Nashville	TN	m	1915-1920	Ay1917,1920
Bulletin	Nashville	TN	m	1950-1951	EP50,51
Capital City Defender	Nashville	TN	bm	1963-1970	Oclc,Kfb,EP73,TNM,Lb,SPD67,70
Catholic Mentor	Nashville	TN	bm	1986-1992+	Ga91,92,Baid92
Central Christian Advocate	Nashville	TN	sm	1961-1968	Ay1961,1968
Christian Plea	Nashville	TN	m	1892-1949	Ba,Ay1949
Citizen	Nashville	TN	w	1893-1905	Ba,Ay1896,1898,1899,1905,Kfb
City Examiner	Nashville	TN	w	1962-1966	Oclc,Kfb,TNM
Clarion	Nashville	TN	w	1902-1950	Ba,Ay1905,1937,NH42,44,EP35,40,Kfb, NY12,19,22,26,32,TNM,Dc41,Fleming
Colored Tennessean	Nashville	TN	w	1865-1866	Ba,Gr,Penn,Go,Br,IL,Lc91,Oclc,WI,Kfb, TNM
Corner Stone	Nashville	TN	m	1881-1892	Ba,Ay1888-1891
Courier	Nashville	TN	w	1993+	AAMC
Defender	Nashville	TN	w	1938-1946	Ba,Oclc,NH42,44,46,EP39,40,TNM,Dc41, 44[susp.]
Ebony Gazette	Nashville	TN	w	1975-1976	Oclc,Kfb,TNM
Educator and Reformer	Nashville	TN		1879-1881	Ba,Penn,DCH
Emigration Herald	Nashville	TN		1879-1879	DCH,Kfb
Enterprise	Nashville	TN		1884-1885	Boris1 [Greene, Robert Royster]
Ethnicity	Nashville	TN		1985-1989	ABSCHSL
Fisk Expositor	Nashville	TN	y	1885	DCH
Fisk Herald	Nashville	TN	m	1883-1948	Ay1884,1915,1969,NY12,19,EP46,49
Fisk News	Nashville	TN	w	1925-1994+	Ay1945,1983,Ga88,94,WI,Bp,Baid92, EP46,51
Fisk University News	Nashville	TN	m	1919-1922	NY19,22
Fraternal Gazette	Nashville	TN		1919-1922	NY19,22
Free Lance	Nashville	TN	w	1885-1887	Ba,Ay1886,1887,Kfb,Penn
Globe and Independent	Nashville	TN	w	1937-1954	Ba,Ay1940,1954,Oclc,NH42,44,46,EP37, 51,NY46,Dc41,44,Lc91
Herald and Pilot	Nashville	TN	w	1873-1880	Ay1880,Kfb,DCH[1879-1885?]
Herald Examiner	Nashville	TN	w	1976-1976	TNM,Kfb
Hope Magazine	Nashville	TN	m	1885-1961	ABSCHSL,EP45
Independent	Nashville	TN	w	1929-1938	Ba,Oclc,Kfb[1929-1938],TNM, Yenser6[1944]
Independent Chronicle	Nashville	TN	w	1966-1970	Pr,EP69,67,70,71,Lb
Intermediate Quarterly	Nashville	TN	q	1885-1925	Ay1917,1920,1925

TITLE	CITY	ST.	FREQ.	DATES	SOURCES
Journal of the National Medical Association	Nashville	TN	q	1909-1919	NY12,DANB533
Kappa Alpha Psi Journal	Nashville	TN	w	1951-1969	Ay1969,1970,1975,EP51
Landmark Baptist	Nashville	TN		1895-1898	Ba
Message Magazine	Nashville	TN	m	1934-1951	Ay1940,1950,EP48-51,WI
Metropolitan	Nashville	TN	w/ir	1979-1993+	TNSLA,Kfb
Mid State Observer	Nashville	TN		1978	TNM,Kfb
Modern Farmer	Nashville	TN	m	1936-1956	Ba,Ay1950,1956,NH42,46,EP39,40,43,50,Dc41,44
Monthly Summary of Events and Trends in Race Relations	Nashville	TN	m	1943-1948	DANB348
Nashville Commentator	Nashville	TN	w/bm	1948-1974	Ay1969,1972,Oclc,EP69,Pr,Kfb,EBA,Lb,EP67,71,SPD67,70,74
Nashville Globe	Nashville	TN	w	1906-1960	Ba,Ay1914,1935,Oclc,Gr,Go,Kfb,EP38,49,TNM,NY12,19,22,26,32,Mather,DANB56
Nashville News-Star	Nashville	TN	w	1960-1961	Oclc,Kfb,TNM
Nashville Pride	Nashville	TN	w	1988-1994+	EP91,92,93,BRG,API94
Nashville Sun	Nashville	TN	w	1950-1951	Oclc,TNM
Nashville Tennessean	Nashville	TN		1924-1944	Yenser6 [McClellan, James Fennimore]
National Baptist Concert Quarterly	Nashville	TN	q	1898-1925	Ay1917,1920,1925
National Baptist Convention Quarterly	Nashville	TN	q	1939-1945	EP39-45
National Baptist Magazine	Nashville	TN		1884-1901	ABSCHSL
National Baptist Metoka and Galeda Magazine	Nashville	TN	q	1912-1925	Ay1917,1920,1925
National Baptist Union Review	Nashville	TN	w/bm	1896-1992+	Ba,Ay1906,1925[b1899],1976,EP38,76,ABSCHSL,NH42,46,NY12,19,22,26,32,Dc41,44,Mather
National Baptist Voice	Nashville	TN	bm/m/w	1916-1991	Ba,Ay1935,1955,ABSCHSL,Go,NH42,EP48,49,NY19,22,26,32,46,Dc41,Boris1,Fleming
National Baptist Young Peoples Quarterly	Nashville	TN	q	1911-1940	Ay1925,EP39,40
National Gospel Digest	Nashville	TN	q	1940	Ay1940
National Negro Magazine	Nashville	TN	m	1917-1920	Ay1917,1920
Negro Educational Review	Nashville	TN	a	1950-1974	SPD67,70,74
Negro School News	Nashville	TN	m	1949-1951	EP49-51
New South Student	Nashville	TN		1964-1969	WI
News	Nashville	TN	w	1914-1918	Ba,Ay1916-1918,Kfb
Palladium	Nashville	TN	m	1883-1909	Ba,Ay1889,1909,Kfb
Pilot	Nashville	TN	w	1878-1882	Ba,Penn,Kfb,DCH[1878-1879]
Primary Quarterly	Nashville	TN	q	1885-1935	Ay1917,1920,1925,1935
Race Relations	Nashville	TN		pre 1992	WI
Recorder	Nashville	TN	w	1951	EP51
Republican	Nashville	TN		1891-1892	Ba
Roger Williams Record	Nashville	TN		1886	ABSCHSL
Senior Quarterly	Nashville	TN	q	1905-1935	Ay1917,1920,1925,1935

TITLE	CITY	ST.	FREQ.	DATES	SOURCES
Southern Christian Recorder	Nashville	TN	w	1886-1967	Ba,Ay1890,1925[b1889],1967,EP49, NY19,22,26,32,46,Boris1
Southern Education Report	Nashville	TN		1965-1969	WI
Southern School News	Nashville	TN		1954-1965	WI
Standard	Nashville	TN		pre 1889	Penn
Sun	Nashville	TN		1950-1951	Kfb
Sunday School Board	Nashville	TN		1923-1944	Yenser6 [Brown, Jacob Tileston]
Sunday School Teacher	Nashville	TN		1921-1944	Yenser6 [Vass, Samuel Nathaniel]
Teacher	Nashville	TN	m	1887-1937	Ay1917,1920,1921,1925,1937,NY12
Tennessean	Nashville	TN	w	1866-1868	Ba,Gr,Penn,Go,Br,IL,Lc91,Oclc,WI,TNM
Tennessee Baptist	Nashville	TN	w	1890-1898	Ba,Ay1896
Tennessee Star	Nashville	TN	w	1886-1891	Ba,Ay1887,1891,Lc91,Oclc,WI,Kfb,Gr,Br
Tribune	Nashville	TN	w	1912-1913	Ba,Ay1913,Kfb
Union Review	Nashville	TN	w	1966-1979	Pr,EP67,71,Lb,SPD67,70,74,79
Uplift	Nashville	TN		1973-1976	Kfb
Western Christian Recorder	Nashville	TN	sm	1950	Ay1950
World	Nashville	TN	w	1932-1938	Ba,Ay1935,1938,Oclc,EP35,38,Kfb,TNM
Young Allenite Monthly	Nashville	TN	m	1912-1922	NY12,19,22,Mather
Yours	Nashville	TN		1949	Kfb
Headlight	Paris	TN	w	1909-1911	Ba,Ay1911[1910],Kfb
Cumberland Flag	Union City	TN	m	1915-1980	Ba,Ay1950,1980,EP49-51
People's Advocate	Washington	TN		pre 1915	Mather [Causler, Charles Warner]
Negro Enterprise	Winchester	TN		1899-1900	Ba,Kfb
Herald	Amarillo	TX		1936-1938	Ba
Austin Mirror	Austin	TX	w	1958-1961	Oclc,Cwg
Austin Sun	Austin	TX	w	1993+	EP93
Capital City Argus	Austin	TX	w	1962-1992+	Oclc[b1971],EP71,80,EBA,BRG,EH, Cwg[1961],Bp,Lb
Capital City Argus and Interracial Review	Austin	TX	w	1969-1971	Oclc
Colored Alliance	Austin	TX	w	1890-1891	Ba,Ay1890
Express	Austin	TX		1912-1915	Ba,Ay1915,NY12
Free Man's Press	Austin	TX	w	1868-1869	Ba,IL,Lc91,Oclc
Freedman's Press	Austin	TX	w	1868-1868	Lc91,Oclc,WI
Gold Dollar	Austin	TX		1876-1876	Ba,Gr
Herald	Austin	TX	w	1890-1931	Ba,Ay1891,1925,Oclc,NY12,19,22,26,Gr, Go,Br,Boris1
Illustrated News	Austin	TX	w	1923-1937	Oclc
Informer	Austin	TX	w	1939-1946	Ba,Ay1940,1946
Interracial Review	Austin	TX	m	1970-1976	EH,EP75,76
Monitor	Austin	TX		1921-1922	Ba
National Union	Austin	TX		1890-1892	Ba
Nokoa Observer	Austin	TX	w	1987-1993+	Oclc,EP91,92,93,BRG
People's Mouthpiece	Austin	TX	w	1920-1928	Ba,Ay1921S,1925,Cwg,NY26

TITLE	CITY	ST.	FREQ.	DATES	SOURCES
Rams' Voice	Austin	TX	q	1948-1973	Bp
Searchlight	Austin	TX	w	1896-1909	Ba,Ay1905,1909,Cwg
Silver Messenger	Austin	TX		1897	Cwg
Sunday School Herald	Austin	TX	w	1891-1893	Ba,Oclc[e1892],Lt1907
Texas Blade	Austin	TX	w	1886-1889	Ba,Ay1888,Cwg,Mather[1895]
Texas Headlight	Austin	TX		1895-1903	Ba,Br,Cwg
Texas Illuminator	Austin	TX		189?	Cwg
Texas Interracial Review	Austin	TX	m	1941-1969	Oclc,Lb
Tilloston Tidings	Austin	TX	m/bm	1912-1922	NY12,19,22
Tribune	Austin	TX	w	1970-1983	Ay1980,1983,Oclc
Villager	Austin	TX	w	1973-1994+	Ga87,94,Baid90,92,Oclc,BRG,EP75,93
Villager and Tribune	Austin	TX	w	1973-1974	EP74
Watchman	Austin	TX	w	1901-1926	Ba,Ay1911,1919,Cwg,Go,NY12,19,22,26, Lt1907
Weekly Bulletin	Austin	TX	w	1900-1922	Oclc,NY12,19,22
Avinger Advance	Avinger	TX	sm	1919-1922	NY19,22
Advertiser	Beaumont	TX		1896-1898	Ba
Echo	Beaumont	TX	w	1893-1897	Ba,Ay1896
Industrial Era	Beaumont	TX	w/bw	1903-1949	Ba,Ay1912,1947,br,NH42,44,46,EP35,49, Cwg,NY12,19,22,26,32,Dc41,44,Lt1907, Go,Boris1
Monitor	Beaumont	TX	w	1920-1926	Ba,Ay1921S,Cwg,NY22,26,Boris1
Progress Reporter	Beaumont	TX	w	1969	Cwg
Recorder	Beaumont	TX	w	1889-1891	Ba,Ay1889,1890,Cwg
Reformer	Bellville	TX		1899-1901	Ba
Register	Brenham	TX		1903-1905	Ba
Watchword	Brenham	TX	w	1913-1917	Ba,Ay1914-1917,Cwg
Baptist Telephone Messenger	Brownwood	TX		1901-1903	Ba
Silhouette	Bryan	TX	bm	1980-1984	Oclc
Torchlight	Bryan	TX	w	1912-1913	Ba,Ay1913,Cwg
Alliance Vindicator	Calvert	TX		1892-1893	Ba
Bugle	Calvert	TX	w	1912-1932	Ba,NY12,19,22,26,32
Calvert Eagle	Calvert	TX		1922	Go
Seven Mansions	Calvert	TX		1885-1888	Ba
Liberator	Cameron	TX	w	1907-1908	Ba,Ay1908,Cwg
Journal	Center	TX	w	1910-1912	Ba,Ay1911,1912
Republican	Colmesneil	TX		1889-1893	Ba,Cwg
Trinity Valley Baptist	Colmesneil	TX		1900-1903	Ba
United States Republican	Colmesneil	TX	w	1889-1893	Ba,Ay1890,1891
Taborian Banner	Conroe	TX	m	1902-1914	Ba,Ay1912,1913
Voice of Missions	Conroe	TX	wm	1909-1911	Ba,Ay1911,Cwg
Informer	Corpus Christi	TX	w	1937-1946	Ba,Ay1940,1946
Baptist Journal	Corsicana	TX	m	1878-1887	Ba
Oil City Afro-American	Corsicana	TX	w	1898-1902	Ba,Lc91,Oclc,WI,Gr

TITLE	CITY	ST.	FREQ.	DATES	SOURCES
Taborian Banner	Corsicana	TX	m	1900-1942	Ba,Ay1935,1942,EP36-40
Baptist Journal	Dallas	TX		pre 1915	Mather [Griggs, Allen Ralph]
Black Tennis Magazine	Dallas	TX	m	1977-1994+	Ga87,94
Brotherhood Eyes	Dallas	TX		1930-1939	Ba,Cwg
Christian Star	Dallas	TX	sm	1881-1888	Ba,Ay1886-1888
Colored Methodist	Dallas	TX	m	1884-1888	Ba,Ay1886,1887
Daily Metropolitan	Dallas	TX	d	1912	NY12
Dallas Appeal	Dallas	TX		pre 1915	Mather [Griggs, Allen Ralph]
Dallas Examiner	Dallas	TX	w	1986-1994+	Ga90,94,Baid90,92,BRG,EP90,93,API93
Dallas Express	Dallas	TX	w	1893-1972	Ba,Ay1894,1975,Bp,Rw,Lc91,Oclc, WI[e1970],NH42,44,46,49,Gr,EP35, 74[e1972],EBA,NY12,19,22,26,46,Dc41, 44,Lt1907,Mather,Yenser3,SPD67,70,74
Dallas Leaflet	Dallas	TX		pre 1915	Mather [Griggs, Allen Ralph]
Dallas Post Tribune	Dallas	TX	w	1946-1994+	Ay1970,1975,Ga87,94,Baid90,92,Rw,Bp, API90,94,Lc91,Oclc,EP63,93,BRG, WPN94
Dallas Weekly	Dallas	TX	w	1953-1994+	Ay1983,Ga87,94,EP74,93,Lb,Baid92 [b1955],WPN94[b1960]
Echo	Dallas	TX	w	1884-1884	Ay1884
Elite News	Dallas	TX	w	1966-1972	EH,EP71,Lb
Enterprise	Dallas	TX	sm	1887-1889	Ba,Ay1888,1889,Cwg
Freedom's Journal	Dallas	TX	w	1978-1983	Ay1981,1982,EP81,83
Gazette	Dallas	TX	w	1930-1938	Ba,Cwg,EP38,39,NY32
Great Circle West	Dallas	TX	w	1971-1976	EP76
Herald of Truth	Dallas	TX		1885-1887	Ba,Penn
In Sepia	Dallas	TX	w	1953-1971	EP71,72,Cwg
Informer	Dallas	TX	w	1939-1945	Ba,Ay1940,1945
Item	Dallas	TX	w	1891-1901	Ba,Oclc,WI,Lc91
Key News	Dallas	TX	w	1960-1987	EP71,80,EBA,EH,Cwg,Lb,Bp,SPD79,87
Link	Dallas	TX	w	198u-1986	Oclc
Mahogany	Dallas	TX	w	1972-1987	SPD87
Metropolitan	Dallas	TX		1906-1910	Ba,Cwg
Mutual Enterprise	Dallas	TX	w	1889-1890	Ay1889,1890,Cwg
National Baptist Bulletin	Dallas	TX	sm	1902-1905	Ba,Ay1905,ABSCHSL
Oak Cliff Eagle	Dallas	TX	w	1977-1978	EP78,Ay1912[b1909 nlb]
Odd Fellows Budget	Dallas	TX		1919-1922	NY19,22
Post Tribune	Dallas	TX	w	1948-1987	Ay1969,Oclc,WI[1959?-1979?],EH,EBA, EP80,SPD67,87
Preacher and Teacher	Dallas	TX		pre 1915	Mather [Griggs, Allen Ralph]
Reporter	Dallas	TX	bw	1900-1912	Ba,Ay1909,1912,NY12
Star Post	Dallas	TX	w	1950-1964	Ay1964,Oclc,Cwg,EP62,64,65
Texas Baptist Star	Dallas	TX	w	1888-1900	Ba,Ay1891,1896
Texas Protest	Dallas	TX		1894-1896	Ba,Ay1895,Cwg
Texas Recorder	Dallas	TX	w	1904-1907	Ba,Ay1905,1906,Cwg

TITLE	CITY	ST.	FREQ.	DATES	SOURCES
Tribune	Dallas	TX		1887-1891	Ba,Ay1890
Western Index	Dallas	TX	sm	1912-1943	Ba,Ay1940,1943,NH42,EP37,40,NY19,22, Dc41,Mather
Western Star of Zion	Dallas	TX		1902-1917	ABSCHSL,Mather
World	Dallas	TX	w	1902-1905	Ba,Ay1905,Cwg
World	Dallas	TX	w	1976	EP76
Colored Farmer	Denison	TX		1920-1922	Ba,NY22
Gate City Bulletin	Denison	TX	sm	1913-1931	Ba,Ay1918,1925,Go,Cwg,NY22,26,32, 19[Gem City],Boris1
Texas Reformer	Denison	TX	w	1890-1894	Ba,Ay1890,1891,Cwg,Eur94,Penn
Southwestern Torch	El Paso	TX	w	1941-1944	EP41,44
Scimitar	Ennis	TX	w	1910-1920	Ba,Ay1912,1914-1920,Cwg
Texas Hornet	Forney	TX		1891-1893	Ba,Cwg
Afro-American	Fort Worth	TX		1902-1903	Ba
Black Dispatch	Fort Worth	TX		1898-1901	Ba,Cwg
Bronze Texan News	Fort Worth	TX	w	1964-1974	Ay1969,1974,Pr,Oclc,Cwg,EBA,EP71,Lb, SPD67
Bronze Thrills	Fort Worth	TX	m	1951-1978	Ay1969,1978,WI[e1969],EH,SPD67,70,74, 79
Church Week	Fort Worth	TX	w	1976	EP76
Como Weekly	Fort Worth	TX	w	1940-1978	Ay1969,1978,Pr,Bp,Lb,EP67,69,EBA,EH, Cwg
Defender	Fort Worth	TX	w	1944-1951	Ba,NH46,EP51,NY46,Dc44
Defender and Baptist Herald	Fort Worth	TX	w	1950	Ay1950
Eagle Eye	Fort Worth	TX	w	1930-1944	Ba,Lc91,NH42,44,EP38-41,Dc41
Fort Worth Como Monitor	Fort Worth	TX	w	1971-1980	EP71[1940],75,76,77,78,80
Fort Worth Mind	Fort Worth	TX	w	1931-1980	Ba,Ay1945,1954,Oclc,NH42,44,46,49, EP35,80,EBA,EH,Cwg,NY46,Dc41,44,Bp, Lb,SPD67,70,74
Hep	Fort Worth	TX	m	1955-1975	Ay1969,1975,SPD67,70,74,79
Hornet	Fort Worth	TX	w	1918-1926	Ba,Ay1921,NY19,22,26,Go
Item	Fort Worth	TX	w	1890-1912	Ba,Ay1891,1911,Cwg,NY12,Eur94,R1898
Jive	Fort Worth	TX	m	1951-1975	Ay1969,1975,SPD67,70,74
La Vida	Fort Worth	TX	w	1958-1994+	Pr,EBA,EH,BRG,Cwg,EP67,77,Lb,Bp, API94
Lake Como News	Fort Worth	TX	w	1940-1959	Ay1950,1959,EP51,Cwg[1943]
Light	Fort Worth	TX	w	1930-1932	Ba,NY32
Masonic Quarterly	Fort Worth	TX	q	1919-1922	NY19,22
Metro Cities News	Fort Worth	TX	w	1965-1981	Ay1975,1980,1981,EP74,80
Negro Achievements	Fort Worth	TX	m	1947-1951	EP51,BJ
Negro Progress	Fort Worth	TX	q	1968-1979	SPD70,74,79
Organizer	Fort Worth	TX	w	1895-1897	Ba,Ay1896
People's Contender	Fort Worth	TX		1930-1932	Ba,Br[1946?],NY32
Sepia	Fort Worth	TX	m	1950-1982	Ay1969,1978,Rw,Bp,BJ[b1952],WI [e1979],EH,SPD67,70,74[b1954],79
Soul Teen	Fort Worth	TX	m	1957-1982	Ay1980,1982

TITLE	CITY	ST.	FREQ.	DATES	SOURCES
Sports News	Fort Worth	TX	m	1945-1946	Ba,NY46
Texas Times	Fort Worth	TX	w	1973-1994+	BRG,Lb[Dallas],API90,94
Times	Fort Worth	TX	w	1980-1987	EP80,NA83,SPD87
Torchlight Appeal	Fort Worth	TX	w	1886-1894	Ba,Ay1890,1891[b1888],Penn,NWU,Lc91, Oclc,WI[e1893]
URE News in Sports	Fort Worth	TX		1945-1946	Ba
Weekly	Fort Worth	TX	w	1966-1987	SPD67,79,87
Western Star	Fort Worth	TX		1924-1944	Yenser6 [Boone, Theodore Sylvester]
White Man and the Negro Magazine	Fort Worth	TX	y	1939	EP39
World	Fort Worth	TX	w	1912-1976	EP74,76,Bp
World's Messenger	Fort Worth	TX	m	1950-1951	EP50,51
Informer	Galena Park	TX	w	1966-1967	SPD67
West Texas Voice	Galena Park	TX	w	1966-1967	Pr,EP67,SPD67
Argus	Galveston	TX		1890-1893	Ba,Cwg
Banner	Galveston	TX	w	1925-1936	Ba,Cwg[1935],Gr,EP35,NY32
City Times	Galveston	TX	w	1898-1931	Ba,Ay1905,1925,Gr,Br,Cwg,NY12,22,26, 32,Lt1907,Boris1
Colored American	Galveston	TX	w	1920-1926	Ba,Ay1925[b1922],Br,Oclc,Cwg,NY22,26, Boris1
Examiner	Galveston	TX		1938-1940	Ba,Oclc
Free Man's Press	Galveston	TX	w	1868-1869	Ba,Gr,IL,Lc91,WI,Cwg,Sch
Freeman's Journal	Galveston	TX	w	1887-1894	Ba,Ay1888-1891,Lc91,Oclc,WI[e1891], Eur94,Cwg,Penn,Gr
Galveston Sentinel	Galveston	TX	w	1932-1940	Ba,EP35-40,Cwg[1935],Gr
Galveston Voice	Galveston	TX	w	1931-1949	Ba,Oclc,NH44,EP35,49,Gr
Informer	Galveston	TX		1939-1946	Ba,Ay1940,1946
New Idea	Galveston	TX	w	1896-1932	Ba,Ay1905,1921,Go,Oclc,Cwg,NY12,19, 22,26,32,Lt1907,Boris1
Spectator	Galveston	TX	w	1873-1887	Ba,Penn,Cwg
Test	Galveston	TX		1890-1892	Ba,Ay1890,1891
Texas Blade	Galveston	TX	w	1886-1889	Ba,Ay1888
Consolidated Colored Alliance	Giddings	TX		1889-1890	Cwg,Ay1890?
Conservative Counselor	Gonzales	TX		1908-1911	Ba,Ay1911
Colored Methodist	Henderson	TX	sm	1884-1890	Ba,Ay1888,1889
Educator	Henderson	TX		1886-1888	Ba,Ay1887
Afro-American	Houston	TX		1897	Cwg
Baptist Headlight	Houston	TX		1891-1893	Ba
Christian Examiner	Houston	TX	w	1943-1946	NH46,Dc44
Citizen	Houston	TX	w	1881-1888	Cwg
Dallas Express	Houston	TX		1948	EP48
Dallas Informer	Houston	TX		1940	Dc41
Examiner	Houston	TX		1937	Cwg
Forward Times [Metro]	Houston	TX	w	1960-1994+	Ay1969,1983,Ga87,94,Oclc,WI,Baid92, EP69,93,Cwg,EBA,BRG,EH,Bp,API94, SPD67,70,74,79,87

TITLE	CITY	ST.	FREQ.	DATES	SOURCES
Free Lance	Houston	TX		1898-1899	Cwg
Globe Advocate	Houston	TX	w	1965-1983	EP71,80,EBA,EH,NA83,Bp,Lb
Guide	Houston	TX		1936-1938	Ba
Guiding Star of Truth	Houston	TX		1922	NY22
Headlight	Houston	TX	m	1894	Eur94
Herald	Houston	TX	w	1947-1992+	Ay1969,1983,Ga87,91,Baid92,NUC, SPD87
Hoo-Doo	Houston	TX		1973	WI
Houston Call	Houston	TX	w	1969-1972	Oclc,EBA,Cwg,EP71,Lb
Houston Defender	Houston	TX	w	1930-1994+	Ba,Ay1940,1950,Ga87,94,Oclc,Gr,NH42, 44,46,EP37,93,Baid92,BRG,EBA, EH[1934],Cwg,NY46,Dc41,44,Yenser4
Houston Freeman	Houston	TX	w	1893-1966	Ay1966,Br,DANB549
Houston Informer	Houston	TX	w	1919-1994+	Ba,Ay1921S,1966,Oclc,Gr,Ga90,94,Br, WI[e1973?],NH42,44,46,49,EP35,93,EBA, BRG,EH,Cwg[1893],NY19,22,26,32,Dc41, API90,94,Fleming
Houston Newspages	Houston	TX	w	198u-1994+	Oclc,BRG,API94
Houston Observer	Houston	TX	w	1916-1932	Ba,Ay1921S,Go,Gr,Cwg,NY19,22,26,32, Boris1
Houston Sentinel	Houston	TX	w	1927-1932	Ba,Cwg[1931],NY32,Br
Houston Sun	Houston	TX	w	1983-1994+	Ga90,94,BRG,Baid92,EP90,93,SPD87
Independence Heights Record	Houston	TX		1902-1926	Ba,Go,NY19,22,26
Independent	Houston	TX	w	1898-1906	Ba,Ay1905,1906,Gr,Lc91,Oclc,WI [e1905],Cwg
Informer & Texas Freeman	Houston	TX	w	1931-1994+	Ay1950,1978,Lc91,Br,Oclc,EP48,69[I&F], 78,NY32,46,API94
Metropolitan	Houston	TX	w	1961	Oclc
Metropolitan Civic News	Houston	TX		1946	Ba
National Alliance	Houston	TX		1889-1893	Ba,Mather
Negro Labor News	Houston	TX	w/fn	1930-1976	Ba,Ay1940,1976,Oclc,Bp,Lb,NH42,46, EP43,49,Cwg[1931],NY46,Dc41,44, DANB143
New Age	Houston	TX	w	1981-1990	EP88-90
New Orleans Informer and Sentinel	Houston	TX		1948	EP48
Old Ironsides' Monthly	Houston	TX	m	1947-1950	Oclc
San Antonio Informer	Houston	TX	w	1948-1949	EP48,49
Southern Guide	Houston	TX		1879-1881	Ba,Penn
Southwestern Banner	Houston	TX		1901-1903	Ba,Cwg
Space City	Houston	TX	w	1975-1976	EP75,76
Sunnyside Digest	Houston	TX	w	1966-1967	SPD67
Tempo	Houston	TX	w	1965-1977	EH,EP74-78,Lb
Texas Citizen	Houston	TX	w	1881-1889	Ba,Ay1888
Texas Courier	Houston	TX		1913-1915	Ba
Texas Examiner	Houston	TX	w	1942-1946	Ba,Br,Oclc,NH46,NY46,Dc44
Texas Freeman	Houston	TX	w	1893-1972	Ba,Ay1896,1925,Go,Gr,EH[b1892],Cwg, NY12,19,22,26,Rw,Boris1

TITLE	CITY	ST.	FREQ.	DATES	SOURCES
Tips News Illustrated	Houston	TX	w	1973-1976	EP74-76
TSU Herald	Houston	TX	w	1947-1973	Oclc,Bp
Van	Houston	TX		1879-1903	Ba,Cwg
Voice of Hope	Houston	TX	w	1966-1978	Oclc,WI[b1968],Cwg[b1967],EBA,EH, EP71,78,Bp,Lb
Western Index	Houston	TX	w	1938	Moten
Western Star	Houston	TX	w	1881-1932	Ba,Ay1905,1925,Oclc,WI[1893-1932], Cwg[1893-1919],NY12,19,22,26,Go, Lt1907,Mather
Witness	Houston	TX	w	1905-1912	Ba,Ay1906,1912,Lt1907
Bugle	Huntsville	TX		1897-1900	Ba
East Texas Messenger	Huntsville	TX	w	1935	EP35
Free Lance	Huntsville	TX		1898-1900	Ba
Messenger	Kendleton	TX	w	1966-1987	EP75,76,Bp,SPD67,79,87
New Test	Lockhart	TX	w	1893-1899	Ba,Ay1896,Cwg[1890]
Flyer	Longview	TX		1901-1902	Ba,Cwg
Great Circle News	Longview	TX	w	1969	EP74-76[1971],Cwg
Informer	Longview	TX	w	1939-1946	Ba,Ay1940,1946
Reporter	Longview	TX		1900-1902	Ba,Cwg
Western Christian Advocate	Longview	TX		1878-1883	Ba
Informer	Lovelady	TX	w	1939-1946	Ba,Ay1940,1946
Lubbock Digest	Lubbock	TX	bw	1977-1983	Oclc,EP80,NA83
Lubbock Southwest Digest	Lubbock	TX	w	1972-1994+	Ga87,94,Baid92[b1977],BRG,EP88,93, WPN94
Manhattan Heights Times	Lubbock	TX	w	1961-1965	Oclc
Manhattan Heights Times and West Texas Times	Lubbock	TX	w	1965	Oclc
West Texas Times	Lubbock	TX	w	1960-1987	Ay1975,1980,Oclc,EP71[1962],80,Bp,Lb, EBA,EH,Cwg[1962],SPD87
Texas Colored Citizen	Luling	TX	w	1907-1908	Ba,Ay1909,Cwg
Manor Appeal	Manor	TX		pre 1915	Mather [Clayton, Joseph Edward]
Voice	Manor	TX	w	1910-1912	Ba,Ay1911,1912,Cwg,NY12
Colored Texan	Marlin	TX		1895-1898	Ba
Republican Appeal	Marlin	TX		1902-1903	Ba,Ay1903,Cwg
Baptist Journal	Marshall	TX		1877-1883	Ba
Campus Lens	Marshall	TX	sm	1940-1946	NH42,46,Dc41,44
Christian Advocate	Marshall	TX	m	1878-1882	Ay1882
Informer	Marshall	TX	w	1939-1946	Ba,Ay1940,1946
People's Union	Marshall	TX	w	1913-1919	Ba,Ay1915-1919
Texas and Louisiana Watchman	Marshall	TX	w	1904-1913	Ba,Ay1905,1906,1909,1911,1912
Tribune	Marshall	TX	w	1935	EP35
Wiley Reporter	Marshall	TX	m/6xy	1904-1973	Ay1950,1953,NY12[w],19,22,46,Bp
Banner	Mexia	TX		1925	Cwg
National Negro Retailers Journal	Mineral Wells	TX	sm	1940-1942	NH42,Dc41
Bugle	Navasota	TX	m	1897-1906	Ba,Ay1905,1906

TITLE	CITY	ST.	FREQ.	DATES	SOURCES
Colored Knights of Liberty Alliance	Navasota	TX		1893-1896	Ba
Texas Messenger	Navasota	TX	w	1895-1898	Ba,Ay1896
Success	Orange	TX	w	1909-1911	Ba,Ay1911,Cwg
Informer	Palestine	TX	w	1939-1947	Ba,Ay1940,1945,1946,1947
Plaindealer	Palestine	TX	w	1894-1915	Ba,Ay1909,1912-1915,Cwg,NY12
Texas Guide	Palestine	TX	w	1910-1915	Ba,Ay1912,1914,1915[b1891]
Helping Hand	Paris	TX	m	1896-1911	Ba,Ay1911[b1897],Lt1907
Living Age	Paris	TX		1891-1893	Ba,Cwg
People's Informer	Paris	TX	w	1882-1883	Ba,Ay1884,Mather[1880-1884]
Flash	Port Arthur	TX	w	1940	EP40
Herald	Port Arthur	TX	w	1930-1932	Ba,NY32
Review	Port Arthur	TX	w	1923-1927	Ba,Ay1925,Cwg,NY26,Boris1
Panther	Prairie View	TX	bw	1946-1973	EP50,51,NY46,Bp
Prairie View Standard	Prairie View	TX	w	1912-1951	NH42,46,EP51,NY12,19,22,Dc41,44, Yenser6
Enterprise	San Angelo	TX	w	1936-1938	Ba,EP38
Alamo Eagle	San Antonio	TX	w	1907	Lt1907
Conservator	San Antonio	TX		1900-1901	Ba,Cwg
Express	San Antonio	TX		1884-1891	Ba
Guard	San Antonio	TX	w	1940-1946	Ba,NH42,46,NY46,Dc41,44
Hephzibah Herald	San Antonio	TX		1920-1924	Ba,Ay1921S,Cwg
Hustler	San Antonio	TX	w	1910-1918	Ba,Ay1912,1919,Cwg,NY12
Informer	San Antonio	TX	w	1939-1949	Ba,Ay1948,NH49,EP45,46,48,49,NY46
Inquirer	San Antonio	TX	w	1906-1942	Ba,Ay1917,1925,Go,Br,EP35,40,Cwg, NY12,19,22,26,32,Lt1907,Boris1, Ay1912[nlb]
National S.N.C.C.	San Antonio	TX		1968-1968	WI
New Generation	San Antonio	TX	w	1972-1976	EH,EP75,76,Lb
People's I Opener	San Antonio	TX	w	1930-1932	Ba,NY32
San Antonio Informer	San Antonio	TX	w	1988-1993+	EP91,92,93
San Antonio Reformer	San Antonio	TX	w	1946	NH46 (see Informer)
San Antonio Register	San Antonio	TX	w	1930-1994+	Ba,Ay1935,1975,Br,NH42,44,46,49,EP35, 93,BRG,EH,EBA[b1933],NY46,Dc41,44, Rw,API90,94,WPN94,SPD67,70,74
Sentinel	San Antonio	TX	w	1920-1932	Ba,NY22,26,32,Boris1
Snap News	San Antonio	TX	w	1947-1993+	EP67,93,EBA,Cwg,Bp
Texas Illuminator	San Antonio	TX		1892	Cwg
Tonguelet	San Antonio	TX		1892-1893	Cwg
Austin County Enterprise	Sealy	TX		1898	Cwg
Texas Christian Recorder	Sealy	TX	w	1909-1913	Ba,Ay1912,1913
Texas News	Seguin	TX		1895-1900	Ba
New American	Seguin	TX	w	1913-1927	Ba,Ay1915-1917,Cwg
Texas Reformer	Sherman	TX	w	1890-1894	Ba,Ay1891,Eur94
Indicator	Sour Lake	TX	w	1919-1923	Ba,Ay1920,1921,Cwg
Western Star	Temple	TX		1924-1933	Yenser3 [Boone, Theodore Sylvester]

TITLE	CITY	ST.	FREQ.	DATES	SOURCES
Afro-American Voice	Texarkana	TX		1892-1944	Yenser6 [Preston, W. A.]
Appreciator	Texarkana	TX		1898-1922	Ba
Courier	Texarkana	TX	w	1975-1983	EP77,78,81,83,NA83
Informer	Texarkana	TX	w	1939-1946	Ba,Ay1940,1945,1946
Inter-State Blade	Texarkana	TX		1897-1900	Ba,Cwg
Texarkana Courier	Texarkana	TX	w	1975-1987	SPD87
Texarkana Sun	Texarkana	TX		1888-1890	Penn
The Colony Leader	The Colony	TX		1992+	BRG
Progressive Age	Timpson	TX		1898-1900	Ba,Ay1900,Cwg[1899]
Union	Timpson	TX	w	1904-1905	Ba,Ay1905,Cwg
Caret	Tyler	TX	w	1971-1976	EP75,76
East Texas Guard	Tyler	TX	w	1906-1908	Ba,Ay1908,Cwg
Informer	Tyler	TX	w	1939-1946	Ba,Ay1940,1945,1946
Texas Steer	Tyler	TX	m	1973	Bp
Tyler Leader	Tyler	TX	w/bw	1962-1973	EH[b1951],EBA[b1969],Cwg[b1956], EP71,75[b1951],76,Bp
Tyler Tribune	Tyler	TX	w	1950	Cwg
Guard	Victoria	TX	w	1912-1925	Ba,Ay1916-1921,Cwg,NY19,22,26,Go
Guide	Victoria	TX	w	1894-1909	Ay1896,1909,1908,Cwg
Southwestern Herald	Victoria	TX		1900-1904	Ba
Texas Guide	Victoria	TX	w	1894-1922	Ba,Ay1905,Go,NY12,19
Baptist Journal	Waco	TX		1880-1884	Ba
Baptist Pilot	Waco	TX	w	1884-1889	Ba,Ay1887,1888
Cen-Tex Reflections	Waco	TX	w	1984	Oclc
Clarion	Waco	TX	w	1921-1936	Ba,Ay1925,1935,Cwg,NY22,26,Br,Boris1
Colored Observer	Waco	TX	w	1915-1921	Ba,Ay1917-1921,Cwg
Conservative Counselor	Waco	TX	w	1909-1922	Ba,Ay1912,1921,Cwg[b1915],NY19,Go
Enterprise	Waco	TX		1898-1900	Ba,Cwg
Helping Hand	Waco	TX	m/bm	1912-1939	Ba,Ay1912,1939,Oclc,NY12,19,22
Paul Quinn Monthly	Waco	TX	m	1886-1900	Ay1890,1891,1894,1896,Penn
Paul Quinn Weekly	Waco	TX	w	1900-1916	Ba,Ay1906,1916,Lc91,Oclc,Lt1907, WI[1886-1903],NWU
Social Gleaner	Waco	TX		1894-1900	Ba
Southern Herald	Waco	TX		1894-1900	Ba,Cwg
Texas Interracial Review	Waco	TX	sm	1940	Oclc
Texas Searchlight	Waco	TX		1893-1895	DANB421,Boris1
Waco Good News	Waco	TX	w	1880	Oclc
Waco Messenger	Waco	TX	w	1927-1994+	Ba,Ay1935,1975,Ga87,91,Br,NH42,44,46, EP35,93,BRG,Cwg[1932],EH,NY46, EBA[1929],Baid92[1929],Dc41,44, WPN94,Lb,SPD67,70,74,Fleming
Elevator	Wharton	TX		1897-1899	Cwg
Pilot	Wharton	TX		1896-1898	Ba
Southern Monitor	Wharton	TX		1887-1890	Ay1890,Cwg
Eagle	Ogden	UT		1946-1947	Ba

TITLE	CITY	ST.	FREQ.	DATES	SOURCES
Broad Ax	Salt Lake City	UT	w	1895-1899	Ba,Lc91,Oclc,WI
Tri-City Oracle	Salt Lake City	UT		1902-1903	Ba
Utah Plain Dealer	Salt Lake City	UT	w	1895-1909	Ba,Ay1906,1908,1909,Boris2
Mountain West Minority Reporter and Sentinel	West Valley City	UT	bm	1990+	Oclc
Clipper	Alexandria	VA	w	1892-1898	Ba,Ay1894
Eaf Vea	Alexandria	VA	w	1890-1891	Ba,Ay1890
Home News	Alexandria	VA	w	1901-1907	Ba,Ay1905,1906
Horizon; A Journal of the Color Line	Alexandria	VA		1907-1910	WI
Industrial Advocate	Alexandria	VA	w	1880-1910	Ba,Ay1905,1906,1908,1909
Leader	Alexandria	VA	w	1880-1895	Ba,Ay1890,1891,1894,Eur94
Leader and Clipper	Alexandria	VA	w	1895-1902	Ba,Ay1896
NSBE Bridge	Alexandria	VA	q	1990-1993+	Ga94
NSBE Magazine	Alexandria	VA		1922-1994+	Go,Ga94[b1985],SPD94
People's Advocate	Alexandria	VA	w	1876-1885	Ba,Penn,Lc91,Oclc,DANB141
Post and National Echo	Alexandria	VA		1884-1885	Ba
SBE Journal	Alexandria	VA		1991	Ga91
Virginia Post	Alexandria	VA		1880-1883	Ba
Midland Express	Boydton	VA	w	1891-1895	Ba,Lc91,Oclc,NWU
Colored Churchman	Bradford City	VA		1898-1900	Ba
Freedmen's Friend	Cambria	VA	q	1912-1922	NY12,22,Mather
Peninsula News	Cape Charles	VA	sm	1902-1906	Ba,Ay1905
Albemarle Tribune	Charlottesville	VA	w	1954-1994+	EP71,93,BRG,EH,NA83,SPD67,Bp,Lb, Ga94[nlb]
Messenger	Charlottesville	VA	w	1909-1932	Ba,Ay1911,1925,NY19,22,26,32,Go, Mather[b1908]
Tribune	Charlottesville	VA	w	1950-1969	Ay1954,EP62,70,SPD67,70,74,87
Virginia Headlight	Charlottesville	VA	w	1908-1922	Ba,Ay1911-1913,NY12,19,Go
Colored Union	Clifton Forge	VA	w	1901-1909	Ba,Ay1905,1906,1908,1909
Bath Times	Covington	VA		1908-1910	Ba (see also Hot Springs, VA)
Virginia Echo	Covington	VA		1920-1923	Ba
Sumner Tribune	Culpepper Courthouse	VA		1886-1892	Ba,Penn
Midland Guide	Cumberland	VA	m	1904-1909	Ba,Ay1906,1908,1909
News and Observer	Danville	VA	w	1974-1983	Ay1980,1981,EP77,82,Lb,NA83
Independent Observer	Enfield	VA	w	1951	EP51
Virginia Statesman	Ettrick	VA	sm	1943-1946	NH46,NY46,Dc44
News	Franklin	VA		1896-1898	Ba
Studies in Black Literature	Fredericksburg	VA	q	1970-1977	BJ[b1976],SPD74
Gum Springs News	Gum Springs	VA		1967-1968	ILNL264
American Problem	Hampton	VA		1905-1915	Ba,Ay1909,1911,NY12,Br
Fisherman's Net	Hampton	VA		1904-1912	Ba,Ay1911,NY12,HU
Hampton Institute Journal of Ethnic Studies	Hampton	VA	a	1976-1982+	BJ
Hampton Roads Metro Weekender	Hampton	VA		1990-1994+	API90,94

TITLE	CITY	ST.	FREQ.	DATES	SOURCES
Hampton Script	Hampton	VA	bw	1925-1993+	Ay1945,1960,NH42,46,EP46,51,NY46, Dc41,44,HU[b1928],Bp
Hampton Student	Hampton	VA	m	1912-1922	NY12,19,22,HU
Journal of Afro-American Studies	Hampton	VA	a	1971-1972	BJ
Southern Workman	Hampton	VA	m	1872-1939	Ay1880,1939,WI,HU,BJ[b1868],NWU
Virginia Teachers Bulletin	Hampton	VA	q	1946	NY46
Virginia Post	Harrisonburg	VA		1880-1883	Ba,Penn[1877-1880]
Black Family	Herndon	VA	6xy	1980-1994+	Ga92,94 (see also Reston)
Black Information Index	Herndon	VA		1970-1972	WI
Virginia Messenger	Hopewell	VA	w	1913-1919	Ay1919
Bath Times	Hot Springs	VA		1908-1910	Ba (see also Covington VA)
Augustinian	Lawrenceville	VA	m	1912	NY12
Colored Churchman	Lawrenceville	VA		1898-1904	Ba
C.I.A.A. Bulletin	Lawrenceville	VA	a	1946	NY46
Saint Paul Bulletin	Lawrenceville	VA	q	1919-1922	NY19,22
Southern Missionary	Lawrenceville	VA	sm	1894-1922	Eur94,NY22
Colored Churchman	Luray	VA	w	1908-1918	Ba,Ay1918,NY19,ba (see also Shenandoah)
Valley Churchman	Luray	VA	w	1930-1938	ABSCHSL
Eastern Clarion	Lynch Station	VA	w/sm	1911-1916	Ba,Ay1913-1915
Baptist Herald	Lynchburg	VA		1909-1910	Ba
Christian Organizer	Lynchburg	VA	w	1899-1919	Ba[e1909],NY12,19,Lt1907,ABSCHSL
Counselor and Herald	Lynchburg	VA	w	1891-1897	Ba
Expected	Lynchburg	VA		1936-1965	ABSCHSL
Industrial Day	Lynchburg	VA		1889	Penn
Interpreter	Lynchburg	VA	w	1903-1907	ba,Ay1905,1906,Lt1907,Br
Laborer	Lynchburg	VA		1886-1888	Ba,Ay1887,Br,Penn
Laboring Man	Lynchburg	VA		1886-1888	Ba,Br
Lynchburg Opportunity	Lynchburg	VA	w	1919	NY19
Southern Forge	Lynchburg	VA		1895-1896	Ba
Virginia Churchman	Lynchburg	VA		1917	ABSCHSL
Virginia News Herald	Lynchburg	VA	w	1925-1932	Ba,NY26,32
Bulletin of National Dental Association	Manassas	VA	q	1948-1951	Ay1950,EP48-51
News and Observer	Martinsville	VA	w	1974-1978	EP78
American Problem	Newport News	VA	m	1905-1914	Ba,Ay1911-1914
Caret	Newport News	VA	w	1885-1896	Ba,R1888,Br
Common Sense	Newport News	VA		1945	Fleming [Ivy, James Waldo]
Evening Recorder	Newport News	VA	w,d	1893-1904	Ba,Gr
Herald	Newport News	VA		1920-1922	Ba,NY22
Journal and Guide	Newport News	VA	w	1940-1944	Ba,Ay1944
Leadway Standard	Newport News	VA		1948	Ba
Light of the Race	Newport News	VA		1905-1922	Ba[1910],NY12,19,22
Newport News Post	Newport News	VA		1946	Ba,Br

TITLE	CITY	ST.	FREQ.	DATES	SOURCES
Newport News Star	Newport News	VA	w	1901-1939	Ba,Ay1912[b1903],1935,Go,Br,EP35,39, NY12,19,22,26,32,Boris1
Advance	Norfolk	VA	w	1893-1895	Ba,Ay1894,Br
Afro-American Churchman	Norfolk	VA		1886-1888	Ba,Ay1888,WI
American Ethiopian	Norfolk	VA	w	1903-1907	Ba,Ay1905,1906,Br
Citizen Advocate	Norfolk	VA	w	1920-1932	Ba,NY22,26,32
Herald	Norfolk	VA	w	1919-1922	NY19,22
Industrial Way	Norfolk	VA		1889	Penn
Journal and Guide	Norfolk	VA	w	1901-1994+	Ba,Ay1909,1975,Ga87,94,Br,Oclc,WI, NH42,44,46,49,EP35,92,NY12,19,22,26, 32,46,Dc41,44,Yenser4
New Century	Norfolk	VA		1908-1915	Ba,NY12,Mather
News and Advertiser	Norfolk	VA	w	1900-1908	Ba,Ay1905,1906,1908
Omega Bulletin Oracle	Norfolk	VA		1951	EP51
Rambler	Norfolk	VA		1894-1898	Ba
Recorder	Norfolk	VA	d	1893-1900	Ba,Ay1896,Br
Republican	Norfolk	VA	w	1882	Mather,Boris1[Tidewater Republican]
Right Way	Norfolk	VA		1885-1885	Ba,Penn
Speaker	Norfolk	VA		1889-1893	Ba
Spectator	Norfolk	VA	w	1887-1892	Ba,Ay1889,1890[b1889],1891
Standard	Norfolk	VA	w	1889-1892	Ba,Ay1890,1891,Br
True Southerner	Norfolk	VA		1865-1867	Penn,Bl
Afro American Churchman	Petersburg	VA		1886	Lc77,DANB58
American Sentinel	Petersburg	VA		1880-1881	Ba,Penn (see also Norfolk VA)
Church Advocate	Petersburg	VA		1894-1937	DANB58,Yenser4
Clarion	Petersburg	VA		1919-1922	NY19,22
Colored Virginian	Petersburg	VA	w	1912-1927	Ba,Go,NY19,22,26,Boris1
Digest and Reporter	Petersburg	VA		pre 1972	EP72,73,74,Lb
Herald	Petersburg	VA	w	1888-1899	Ba,Ay1889-1891,1894,1896,Br
Ivy Leaf	Petersburg	VA	q	1945-1948	Ay1945,EP48
Lancet	Petersburg	VA	w	1882-1937	Ba,Ay1884,R1888,Eur94,Yenser6, DANB58[e1886]
Lancet Recorder	Petersburg	VA		1893-1896	Ba
Masonic Visitor	Petersburg	VA	w	1887-1890	Ba,Ay1888,Penn
National Pilot	Petersburg	VA	w/q	1886-1900	Ba,Ay1890,1891,Lc91,Oclc,WI
Review	Petersburg	VA	w	1922-1931	Ba,Ay1925,NY22,26,Br,Go
Southern Tribune	Petersburg	VA		1883-1884	Ay1884
Southside Virginia Star	Petersburg	VA	w	1989-1993+	EP91-93
Star of Zion	Petersburg	VA	w	1881-1886	Ba,Ay1884
Union Republican	Petersburg	VA		1865-1870	Ba,Bl
Virginia Lancet	Petersburg	VA	w	1882-1894	Ay1886,1894,Penn,R1888
Virginia Statesman	Petersburg	VA	bw	1927-1965	Ay1950,1965,NH42,EP49,51,Dc41
Virginian Messenger	Petersburg	VA	w	1913-1922	Ba,Ay1919,NY22
V.N. & I. I. Gazette	Petersburg	VA	q	1908-1922	NY12,19,22,DANB250

TITLE	CITY	ST.	FREQ.	DATES	SOURCES
Zion Herald-News	Petersburg	VA		1991-1992	ABSCHSL
Industrial Messenger	Pocahontas	VA		1890-1892	Ba
Southwestern Press	Pocahontas	VA		1890-1892	Ba
Press	Port Royal	VA	sm	1893-1898	Ba,Ay1894,1896,Lt1907
American Ethiopian	Portsmouth	VA		1902-1903	Ba
Baptist Companion	Portsmouth	VA		1880-1882	Ba,Penn
Enterprise	Pulaski	VA	w	1908-1916	Ba,Ay1911-1914
People's Light	Pulaski	VA		1893-1895	Ba,Br
Black Family	Reston	VA	bm	1987-1990	Ga90,SPD87[b1979]
Black Heritage	Reston	VA	bm	1977-1982	BJ,SPD79[b1961]
Negro Heritage	Reston	VA	bm	1961-1977	BJ,SPD70
African Mission Herald	Richmond	VA		1897-1905	Ba (see Louisville KY)
African Missions	Richmond	VA		1880-1883	Ba
Afro-American and the Richmond Planet	Richmond	VA	w	1891-1939	Oclc,WI,EP39,40,Bl[1945],Ay1975
Baptist	Richmond	VA	w	1907	Lt1907
Baptist Companion	Richmond	VA		1883-1889	Penn,AAE5
Baptist Headlight	Richmond	VA		1922	NY22
Baptist Herald	Richmond	VA		1951-1973	ABSCHSL
Critic	Richmond	VA		1889-1890	Ba (see MO)
Domestic Worker	Richmond	VA		1946	NY46
Education Bulletin	Richmond	VA	m	1950-1951	EP50,51
Enquirer	Richmond	VA	w	1935	EP35
Fraternal Bulletin	Richmond	VA		1900-1920	Ba
Industrial Day	Richmond	VA		1888-1891	Ba,Br
Industrial Herald	Richmond	VA		1886-1902	Ba
Lott Carey Herald	Richmond	VA		1921-1991	ABSCHSL
Negro Advocate	Richmond	VA		1902-1904	Ba
Negro Criterion	Richmond	VA	w	1905-1909	Ba,Ay1906,1908,1909,Br
News Letter	Richmond	VA	bw	1919	NY19
Panther	Richmond	VA	w/m	1900-1973	Ay1940,NH42,Dc41,Bp
Pilot	Richmond	VA		1888	Penn
Planet	Richmond	VA	w	1883-1945	Ba,Ay1884,1945,R1898,1900,Br,Go,Bp, Oclc,WI,EP35,36,NY12,19,22,26,32, Lt1907,Boris2,Bl
Progress Record	Richmond	VA	q	1946-1951	EP51,NY46
Reformer	Richmond	VA	w	1895-1931	Ba,Ay1905,1925,Br,Lc91,Oclc,WI,NY12, 19,22,Lt1907,Mather
Reporter	Richmond	VA	w/d	1890-1894	Ba,Ay1890,1891,Eur94,Mather[daily 1891-1892]
Richmond Afro American	Richmond	VA	w	1938-1994+	Ba,Ay1940,1970,Ga87,94,Br,Bp,NH44,46, 49,EP48,92,NY46,Dc41,44,API90,94, SPD70,74
Richmond Colored American	Richmond	VA	d	1922-1927	Ba,Go
Richmond Free Press	Richmond	VA	d	1993-1994+	API94

TITLE	CITY	ST.	FREQ.	DATES	SOURCES
Saint Luke Fraternal Bulletin	Richmond	VA	m	1897-1962	Ay1950,1962,EP48-51,NY46
Saint Luke Herald	Richmond	VA	w	1901-1937	Ba,Ay1921S,1935,NY12,19,22,26,32, DANB626[b1902],Yenser4
Southern News	Richmond	VA	w	1892-1895	Ba,Ay1894,Oclc,Lc91,WI,NWU
Spotlight	Richmond	VA		1936-1938	Ba,EP38
Star	Richmond	VA		1878-1889	Ba
True Southerner	Richmond	VA		1865-1868	Ba
Union-Hartshorn Journal	Richmond	VA	m	1919-1922	NY19,22
Vigilant Reporter	Richmond	VA	w	1890-1893	Ba
Virginia Baptist	Richmond	VA	w	1894-1909	Ba,Ay1896,1905,1906,1908,1909
Virginia Mutual Benefit Life Co. Bulletin	Richmond	VA	w	1946-1951	EP51,NY46
Virginia Star	Richmond	VA	w	1877-1888	Ba,Penn,Gr,Lc91,Oclc,WI
Virginia Union Bulletin	Richmond	VA		1946	NY46
Voice	Richmond	VA	w	1918-1926	Ba,Ay1921S,1925,Br,NY22,26
Voice	Richmond	VA	w	1985-1994+	EP91,92,93,BRG,API94
Young Man's Friend	Richmond	VA		1889-1890	Penn,Mather[DC],ba[1875?-1882]
Press	Roanoke	VA	w	1891-1897	Ba,Br
Roanoke Daily Press	Roanoke	VA	d	1891-1894	Eur94,Br
Roanoke Tribune	Roanoke	VA	w	1938-1994+	Ba,Ay1950,1975,Ga87,94,NH49,EP45,93, Baid92,BRG,EH,API90,94,EBA[b1940], Bp,WPN94
Virginia Advocate	Roanoke	VA		1919-1922	Ba,Go,NY19,22
Colored Churchman	Shenandoah	VA	w	1908-1912	Ay1912
Boston Banner	South Boston	VA	w	1893-1899	Ba,Ay1894,1896
Halifax Enterprise	South Boston	VA		1886-1888	Ba,Penn
News and Observer	Southside	VA	w	1974-1978	EP78
Beverly Times	Staunton	VA	w	1935-1940	EP35,36,37,38,40
Critic	Staunton	VA		1884-1888	Penn
Reporter	Staunton	VA	w	1905-1923	Ba,Ay1908,1921,NY12
Southern Tribune	Staunton	VA	w	1891-1897	Ba
Tribune	Staunton	VA	w	1875-1933	Ba,Ay1894,1896[b1891],Br,NY32
Valley Index	Staunton	VA	w	1897-1905	Ba,Ay1905,Br
Virginia Critic	Staunton	VA	w	1884-1889	Ba,Ay1888
Christian Visitor	Suffolk	VA		1891-1893	Ba
Colored Universalist	Suffolk	VA	m	1912-1922	NY12,19,22
Pioneer	Waverly	VA		1894-1896	Ba
Free Baptist Herald	Winchester	VA		1917-1928	ABSCHSL
Free Baptist Quarterly	Winchester	VA		1928-1929	ABSCHSL
Golden Epoch	Winchester	VA		1898-1900	Ba
Rising Sun	Everett	WA		1912	NY12
Western Journal of Black Studies	Pullman	WA	q	1977-1994+	Ga87,94,SPD87,91,BJ
Afro-American Journal	Seattle	WA	w	1967-1971	Oclc,EP71,72,EH,Lb
Cayton's Monthly	Seattle	WA	m	1921-1922	Oclc

TITLE	CITY	ST.	FREQ.	DATES	SOURCES
Cayton's Weekly	Seattle	WA	w	1916-1921	Ba,Oclc,Lc72
Enterprise	Seattle	WA	w	1920-1932	Ay1925,NY22,26,32
Fact News	Seattle	WA	w	1961-1994+	Ga87,94,Bp,Lb,Oclc,WI,EP67,93,BRG, EBA,EH,WPN94
K-ZAM Kazette	Seattle	WA	w	1962	Oclc
Medium	Seattle	WA	w	1970-1994+	Ga87,94,Bp,EBA,BRG,EH,Baid92,EP71, 93,WPN94
Messenger	Seattle	WA	w	1964	Oclc
Metro Home Maker	Seattle	WA	w	1992+	BRG
Northwest Bulletin	Seattle	WA	w	1937-1940	Oclc,EP38
Northwest Enterprise	Seattle	WA	w	1920-1962	Ba,Ay1935,1953,Gr,Br,Oclc,EP37,51, Lc72[1921-1953],NH42,44,46,NY46, Dc41,44
Northwest Herald	Seattle	WA	w	1970-1992+	Ga92,Lb
Northwest Herald	Seattle	WA	w	1935-1946	Ba,Sch,Oclc,NH44
Pacific Dispatch	Seattle	WA	w	1946-1947	Oclc
Pacific Leader	Seattle	WA	w	1952-1956	Oclc
Pacific Northwest Bulletin	Seattle	WA	sm	1944-1948	Ay1945-1948
Progressive Herald	Seattle	WA	m	1933	Oclc
Puget Sound and Inland Empire Observer	Seattle	WA	s	1959	Oclc
Renaissance Courier	Seattle	WA	w	1969	Oclc
Republican	Seattle	WA	w	1893-1915	Ba,Ay1896,1915,Lc91,Oclc,Lc77, WI[b1894],NY12,Lt1907
Searchlight	Seattle	WA	w	1904-1925	Ba,Ay1908,1925,Go,NY12,19,22,26, Mather
Seattle Dispatch	Seattle	WA	w	1947-1949	Oclc,NH49
Seattle Medium	Seattle	WA		1935-1946	Br
Seattle Observer	Seattle	WA	w	1964	Oclc
Seattle Skanner	Seattle	WA	w	1992+	BRG
Soul Town Review	Seattle	WA	w	1992+	BRG
Tacoma True Citizen	Seattle	WA	w	1974-1994+	WPN94
Trumpet	Seattle	WA	m	1967	Oclc
World	Seattle	WA	w	1898-1903	Ba,Lc91,Oclc,Lc77,WI
Citizen	Spokane	WA	w	1908-1915	Ba,Ay1911,1912,Oclc[e1913],NY12
Forum	Spokane	WA	m	1908-1912	Ba,Ay1909,1911,1912
Star	Spokane	WA		1946	Ba
Voice of the West	Spokane	WA		1912-1915	Ba,NY12
Fact News	Tacoma	WA	w	1969-1979	EP73-39,EH,Lb
Facts	Tacoma	WA	w	1970-1980	Oclc,Bp
Forum	Tacoma	WA	w	1903-1920	Ba,Ay1906,1920,NY12,Lc72,Oclc
Kitsap County Dispatch	Tacoma	WA	w/d	1988-1994+	WPN94
Northwest Courier	Tacoma	WA	w	1969-1972	EBA,EP71,73,Lb
Northwest Dispatch	Tacoma	WA	w/d	1981-1994+	Ga87,94,Oclc,EP83,93,BRG,Baid92, WPN94[b1982]

TITLE	CITY	ST.	FREQ.	DATES	SOURCES
Northwest Journal-Reporter	Tacoma	WA	w	1970	Oclc,EP71[Tacoma J-R],Lb
Pacific Northwest Review Bulletin	Tacoma	WA	w	1936-1949	Ba,Ay1949,NY46
Progress Messenger	Tacoma	WA	w	1970-1971	Oclc
Sunday Morning Echo	Tacoma	WA	w	1907-1909	Ay1909,Ba[Sunday School Echo]
Tacoma New Courier	Tacoma	WA	w	1969-1973	Bp
Tacoma True Citizen	Tacoma	WA	w	1975-1994+	Ga90,94,Oclc,EP75,93,Baid90,92
Thurson County Dispatch	Tacoma	WA	w	1989-1994+	BRG,WPN94
Bluefieldian	Bluefield	WV	bw	1921-1983	Ay1940,1983,Bp,NH42,EP46,48,49,NY46, Dc41
West Virginia Clarion	Bluefield	WV	w	1923-1931	Ba,NY26,32
Advocate	Charleston	WV	w,m	1894-1926	Ba,Ay1905,1913,WVU,Go,Lc72,NY12,19, 22,26,Mather
American	Charleston	WV		1920-1926	Ba,NY22,26
Color Magazine	Charleston	WV	m	1943-1954	Ay1950,1954,Br,EP45,51,NY46
Messenger	Charleston	WV		1922-1930	Ba,Br
Mountain Leader	Charleston	WV		1910-1926	Ba,Go,NY12,19,22,26
Observer	Charleston	WV		1919-1926	Ba,Go,NY19,22,26
Star-Journal	Charleston	WV	w	1946-1949	Ba,EP48,49
West Virginia Digest	Charleston	WV	w	1940-1949	Ba,Br,WVU,NH42,44,46,EP43,49,Dc41,44
West Virginia Enterprise	Charleston	WV	w	1885-1888	Ba,Ay1886,WVU,R1888,DANB484,87
West Virginia Weekly	Charleston	WV	w	1935-1938	Ba,WVU,EP35
Clarion	Clarksburg	WV		1912	NY12
Harpers Ferry Messenger	Harpers Ferry	WV		pre 1900	DANB203
Methodist Banner	Harpers Ferry	WV		1887-1890	Penn (see Frederick MD)
Storer Record	Harpers Ferry	WV	m	1912-1922	NY12,19,22
Miner	Hill Top	WV	w	1912-1913	Ba,Ay1912
Baptist Pioneer	Huntington	WV	w	1890-1893	Ba,Ay1890,1891,Penn[Pioneer]
Huntington Times	Huntington	WV		pre 1989	WVU
Sun	Huntington	WV		1931-1941	Yenser3 [Smith, Alvin D.]
Times-American	Huntington	WV	w	1917-1923	Ba,Ay1921
Tri-State News	Huntington	WV	w	1939-1946	Ba,EP39,40,44
West Virginia Courier	Huntington	WV	w	1905-1908	Ba,Ay1906,1908,Lt1907[Courier]
Institute Monthly	Institute	WV	m	1919-1922	NY19,22
Yellow Jacket	Institute	WV	m	1919-1955	Ay1940,1955,NH42,46,EP46,49,NY46, Dc41,44
McDowell Herald	Keystone	WV	w	1898-1905	Ay1905,WVU
McDowell Times	Keystone	WV	w	1904-1944	Ba,Ay1906,1942,WVU,Lb,Oclc,Lc77, NH42,44,EP38,42,NY22,26,32,Dc41, Yenser6
Pioneer Press	Martinsburg	WV	w	1882-1932	Ba,Ay1888,1919,WVU,Lc77,Lc91,Go, Oclc,WI[e1918],Eur94,NY12,19,22,26,32, Lt1907,Mather
Mountain Eagle	Montgomery	WV		pre 1925	WVU,DANB484
Pioneer	Montgomery	WV	w	1890-1896	Ba,Ay1894,1896,WVU,DANB484
Hardy County News	Moorefield	WV	w	1897-1942	Ba,Ay1940,Lc77

TITLE	CITY	ST.	FREQ.	DATES	SOURCES
West Virginia Tribune	North Fork	WV		pre 1989	WVU
Fair Play	Parkersburg	WV		1908-1909	Ba,Ay1909
Fountain's Digest	Parkersburg	WV	w/m	1914-1927	Ba,Ay1917,1919-1921,1925,NY22
Freeman	Parkersburg	WV	w	1885-1889	Ay1886,1887,Lc72
West Virginia Freeman	Parkersburg	WV	w	1881-1885	Ba,Ay1882,1884,1888,Lc72
Sentinel	Red Star	WV	w	1904-1912	Ba,Ay1912,NY12
West Virginia Beacon Digest	South Charleston	WV	w	1957-1994+	Ga90,94,WVU,BRG,Baid92,API94
West Virginia Enterprise	Terre Alta	WV	w	1883-1884	Ay1884,Lc72
Advocate	Wheeling	WV	w	1922-1938	Ba,Ay1925,NY26,32
People	Wheeling	WV		1885-1886	Mather [Sweeney, William Allison]
Wisconsin Labor Advocate	La Crosse	WI	w	1886-1888	Oclc
Black Voice	Madison	WI		1971	WI
Madison Sun	Madison	WI	sm	1966-1972	Lc72,WI,EP72,Rw,Lb
Madison Times	Madison	WI	w	1990	Oclc
Wisconsin Weekly Blade	Madison	WI	w	1916-1925	Ba,Ay1918,1925,NY19,22,Go,OWI,Lc72
Christian Times	Milwaukee	WI		pre 1993	Mil.PL (see Milwaukee Times)
Deal or Die	Milwaukee	WI		1971	WI
Echo	Milwaukee	WI		1965-1979	WI[1966-1979],Bp
Globe	Milwaukee	WI	w	1945-1953	Ay1950,1953,NH49,WI,EP48,49
Greater Milwaukee Star	Milwaukee	WI	w	1961-1971	Ay1970,1972,EP69,70,71,71
Milwaukee Community Journal	Milwaukee	WI	w/d	1976-1994+	Ga88,94,Oclc,BRG,Baid92,EP77,92, Mil.PL,API90,94,WPN94,SPD87,94
Milwaukee Courier	Milwaukee	WI	w	1963-1994+	Ay1969,1975,Ga87,94,API90,94,Lc91, EP67,93,WPN94,SPD87
Milwaukee Enterprise	Milwaukee	WI	w	1923-1925	Lc72
Milwaukee Enterprise Blade	Milwaukee	WI	w	1925-1932	Lc72,NH49,EP38
Milwaukee Gazette	Milwaukee	WI	w	1960-1966	WI,EP74,SPD67
Milwaukee Soul City Times	Milwaukee	WI	w	1967-1971	EP71,72,EBA,Bp
Milwaukee Star	Milwaukee	WI	w	1979-1994+	Ga88,94,Rw,EP67,93[b1963],Baid92, BRG,Mil.PL[1962-1993],API90,94,Lb, SPD87,94
Milwaukee Star Times	Milwaukee	WI	w	1961-1978	Ay1973,1975,WI,EP72,76,EH[b1971],Bp
Milwaukee Sun	Milwaukee	WI		pre 1972	Lb
Milwaukee Times	Milwaukee	WI	w	1985-1994+	Ga90,94,Mil.PL
National Defender and Sun	Milwaukee	WI	w	1918-1919	Ba,Ay1919
Northwest 76er	Milwaukee	WI	w/m	1990	Oclc
Northwest Enterprise	Milwaukee	WI		1916-1959	Ba
Northwestern Recorder	Milwaukee	WI	w/m	1891-1894	Ba,Br,OWI,Lc72,Lc91,Oclc,WI,Eur94
Post	Milwaukee	WI	w	1915-1919	Ba,Ay1919
Right On	Milwaukee	WI		1970	WI
Sepian	Milwaukee	WI	w	1951-1970	Pr,WI,EP67,SPD67,70
Star	Milwaukee	WI	w	1961-1974	Ay1969,EP67,SPD67,74
Wisconsin Advocate	Milwaukee	WI	w	1898-1915	Ba,Ay1908-1915,Br,OWI,Lc91,Oclc,Lc77, WI,NY12,Lt1907
Wisconsin Afro-American	Milwaukee	WI	w/m	1892-1893	Ba,NWU,OWI,Lc91,Oclc,Lc72

TITLE	CITY	ST.	FREQ.	DATES	SOURCES
Wisconsin Enterprise-Blade	Milwaukee	WI	w	1916-1961	Ba,Ay1935,1961,Br,OWI,WI,NH42,44,46, NY26,32,46,Dc41,44,Yenser6
Wisconsin Weekly Defender	Milwaukee	WI	w	1905-1918	Ba,Ay1914-1918,NY12,Lt1907,OWI, Mather
Communicator News	Racine	WI	w	1984-1992+	EP92,BRG[Milwaukee]
Courier	Racine	WI	w	1971-1979	WI,EP77[b1970],78,79,Lb
Courier	Racine	WI	w	1984-1991+	Oclc,EP91[1985],API90
Racine Community Chronicle	Racine	WI	w	1989-1989	Mil. P.L.
Racine Star News	Racine	WI	w	1972-1976	EP72,73,74,76,EH,Bp
Racine Star Times	Racine	WI	w	1970-1975	EP72,75

Appendix A

SOURCE CODES

AAE — *Afro-American Encyclopedia.* 10 vols. North Miami, Fla.: Educational Book Publishers, Inc., 1974.

AAMC — Chattanooga Afro-American Heritage Museum, 730 M. L. King Boulevard, Chattanooga, TN 37403, (615) 267-1076.

Aba — Abajian, James de T. *Blacks in Selected Newspapers, Censuses and Other Sources: An Index to Names and Subjects.* 3 vols. Boston: G. K. Hall and Co., 1977.

ABSCHL — The American Baptist–Samuel Colgate Historical Library, 1106 South Goodman Street, Rochester, NY 14620-2532, (716) 473-1740.

AHGM — Allen, Desmond Walls. "Black Periodicals Sought." *Arkansas Historical and Genealogical Magazine*, Conway, Ark. (Volume VII, No. 2, March 1994):6.

Alb. PL — Albuquerque Public Library, 501 Copper Avenue NW, Albuquerque, NM 87102, (505) 768-5140.

APIyr — Amalgamated Publishers, Inc. Newspaper Network, 45 West 45th Street, Suite 201, New York, NY 10036; 1990 and 1994 lists.

Asheville — Clarence Vinton, *Asheville Advocate*, 70 Woodfin Place, Asheville, NC 28801, (704) 251-2885.

Ayyear — *N.W. Ayer & Son's Newspaper Annual.* 1880-1909. Used 1905, 1906, 1908, and 1909. *N. W. Ayer & Son's American Newspaper Annual and Directory.* 20 vols. and supplements. Philadelphia: N. W. Ayer & Son, 1910-1929. Used 1911, 1912, 1913, 1914, 1915, 1916, 1917, 1918, 1919, 1920, 1921 and 1921S (Supplement). *N. W. Ayer & Son's Directory of Newspapers & Periodicals.* 40 vols. Philadelphia: N. W. Ayer & Son, 1930-1969. Used 1935-1967, 1969. *Ayer Directory, Newspapers, Magazines and Trade Publications.* Philadelphia: Ayer Press, 1970-1971. Used 1970-1971. *Ayer Directory of Publications.* Philadelphia: Ayer Press, 1972-1982. Used 1972-1982. *The IMS '83 Ayer Directory of Publications; The Professional's Reference of Print Media Published in the United States, Canada, Puerto Rico, Virgin Islands, Bahamas, Bermuda and the Republic of the Philippines.* Fort Washington, Pa.: IMS Press, 1983-1986. Used 1983-1986.

Ba   Barrens, Janelle. "Black Newspapers in the United States, 1829-[sic], compiled in pamphlet form from original charts." [Jefferson City, Mo.]: Lincoln University, 1970.

Baidyear   *Black Americans Information Directory 1990-1991*. Darren L. Smith, ed. Detroit: Gale Research Inc., 1990. *Black Americans Information Directory 1992-1993*. Julia C. Furtaw, ed. Detroit: Gale Research Inc., 1992. *Black Americans Information Directory 1994-1995*. Detroit: Gale Research Inc., 1993.

Bir.CDyear Birmingham City Directory and the year of publication; available at the Birmingham Public Library.

Bir. PL   Birmingham Public Library, Tutwiler Collection of Southern History and Literature, 2100 Park Place, Birmingham, AL 35203, (205) 226-3600; letters May, June and July 1993 from Roger Torbert.

BJ   Daniel, Walter C. *Black Journals of the United States*. Westport, Conn.: Greenwood Press, 1982.

Bl   Blackwell, Gloria. "Black Controlled Media in Atlanta, 1960-1970: The Burden of the Message and the Struggle for Survival." M.A. thesis, Emory University, Atlanta, 1976.

Boris#   Boris, Joseph J. *Who's Who in Colored America: A Biographical Dictionary of Notable Living Persons of Negro Descent*. New York: 1927 and 1928-1929. (Also reviewed 1930-1932, 1938-1940, 1941-1944, 1950 listed under fleming# and yenser#.)

Bp   *The Black Press Periodical Directory 1973*. Black Press Clipping Bureau. Newark, N.J.: Systems Catalog Inc., 1973.

Br   Brown, Warren Henry. *Check List of Negro Newspapers in the United States (1827-1946)*, Jefferson City, Mo.: Lincoln University, Department of Journalism, July 1946. Series No. 2.

BRG   *The Black Resource Guide*. 10th ed. Washington, D.C.: R. Benjamin and Jacqueline L. Johnson, [1992].

Brooks   Brooks, Maxwell R. *The Negro Press Re-Examined, Political Content of Leading Negro Newspapers*. Boston: Christopher Publishing House, 1959.

Bu   *Burrell's 1989 Black Media Directory*. Livingston, N.J.: Burrell, 1989.

Buckley	Buckley, Gail Lumet. *The Hornes: An American Family*. New York: Alfred A. Knopf, Inc., 1986.
Buff.& Erie HS	Buffalo & Erie Co. [New York] Historical Society, 25 Nottingham Court, Buffalo, NY 14216, (716) 873-9644; telephone conversation 6/93.
Cam	Campbell, Georgetta Merritt. *Extant Collections of Early Black Newspapers: A Research Guide to the Black Press, 1880-1915, with an Index to the Boston Guardian, 1902-1904*. Troy, N.Y.: Whitston Publishing Co., 1981.
Cantrell	Cantrell, Kimberly Bess. "A Voice for the Freedman: The Mobile Nationalist, 1865-1869." M.A. thesis, Auburn University, Alabama, 1989.
ChPL	Chicago Public Library, 400 South State Street, Chicago, IL 60605, (312) 747-4300.
Coley	Joseph L. Coley, Editor, *Bakersfield News Observer*, P. O. Box 3624, Bakersfield, CA 93385, (805) 324-9466.
Communicator	*The Communicator Newspaper*, 1228 2nd Avenue, Des Moines, IA 50314, (515) 284-5006.
Craighead	Sandra G. Craighead, 3562 Chelton Road, Cleveland, OH 44120-5023.
Cwg	Grose, Charles William. *Black Newspapers in Texas, 1868-1970*. M.A. thesis, University of Texas at Austin, 1972. Ann Arbor, Mich.: University Microfilms International, 1987.
DANB	Logan, Rayford Whittingham, and Michael R. Winston, eds. *Dictionary of American Negro Biography*. New York: W. W. Norton & Company, 1982.
DCH	Clayton, W. Woodford. *History of Davidson County, Tennessee with Illustrations and Biographical Sketches of its Prominent Men and Pioneers*. Philadelphia: J. W. Lewis & Co., 1880.
Dcyear	United States. Department of Commerce. Bureau of the Census. *Negro Newspapers and Periodicals in the United States: 1940*. Negro Statistical Bulletin No. 1. Washington, D.C.: May 1941. United States. Department of Commerce. Bureau of the Census. *Negro Newspapers and Periodicals in the United States: 1943*. Negro Statistical Bulletin No. 1. Washington, D.C.: August 1944.

EBA	Low, W. Augustus, and Virgil A. Clift, eds. *Encyclopedia of Black America*. New York: McGraw-Hill Book Co., 1981.
EH	*The Ebony Handbook, by the Editors of Ebony*. Chicago: Johnson Pub. Co., 1974.
EPyear	*Editor and Publisher Year Book*. New York: Editor and Publisher, 1932-1993.
Euryear	*Eureka Newspaper Guide 1894 Edition*. Binghamton, N.Y.: Eureka Advertising Agency, 1894.
Fleming	Fleming, James G., and C. E. Burckel, eds. *Who's Who in Colored America: A Biographical Dictionary of Notable Living Persons of Negro Descent*. Yonkers-on-the-Hudson, N.Y.: Christian E. Burckel and Associates, Publishers, 1950. 7th ed.
Gayear	*Gale Directory of Publications*. Detroit: Gale Research Co., 1987-1989. Publisher superseded N. W. Ayer, 1908-1982 and IMS Press, 1983-1986. *Gale Directory of Publications and Broadcast Media*. 3 vols. Detroit: Gale Research Co., 1990-1994.
Go	Gore, George W., Jr. *Negro Journalism: An Essay on the History and Present Conditions of the Negro Press*. Greencastle, Ind.: [Journalism Press], 1922.
GON	Gutgesell, Stephen. *Guide to Ohio Newspapers, 1793-1973: Union Bibliography of Ohio Newspapers Available in Ohio Libraries*. Columbus: Ohio Historical Society, 1974.
Gp	Payne, Gazelia I. "Black Newspapers in North Carolina, a description." M.A. thesis, University of North Carolina at Chapel Hill.
Gr	Gregory, Winifred, ed. *American Newspapers, 1821-1936. A Union List of Files Available in the United States and Canada*. New York: H. W. Wilson, 1937. Bibliographic Society of America, 1937.
GRPL	Grand Rapids Public Library, 60 Library Place NE, Grand Rapids, MI 49503, (616) 456-3360, letter dated 27 July 1992.
Gutg	Gutgesell, Stephen. Ohio Historical Society, 1982 Velma Avenue, Columbus, OH 43211, (614) 297-2300.

HU   Hampton University Library, East Queen Street, Hampton, VA 23668, (804) 727-5371.

IA   Iowa State Historical Department, Division of the State Historical Society, 600 East Locust, Des Moines, IA 50319, (515) 281-3007.

IL   "Newspapers in the Illinois State Historical Library." Illinois State Historical Library, June 1964.

ILNL   Romero, Patricia W. *International Library of Negro Life and History: In Black America 1968: The Year of Awakening*. New York: Publishers Co., Inc., 1969.

Jcw   Wilder, James Chapman. "History of the Alabama Negro Press: Post Reconstruction to 1901." M.A. thesis, University of Alabama, 1964.

JH   *Journalism History*, Northridge, Ca.

JNH   *Journal of Negro History*, Atlanta, Ga.

Jpd   James P. Danky, State Historical Society of Wisconsin, letter 11/92.

JQ   *Journalism Quarterly,* Emory University, Ga. (Vol. XXIV, No. 2, June 1947).

Kfb   Brown, Karen Fitzgerald. *The Black Press of Tennessee, 1865-1980*. Ph.D. dissertation, University of Tennessee, Knoxville, 1982. Ann Arbor, Mich.: University Microfilm International, 1987.

KS   *Kansas Newspapers: A Directory of Newspaper Holdings in Kansas*. Aileen Anderson, ed., comp. Topeka, Kans.: Kansas Library Network Board, 1984.

Lb   La Brie, Henry G., III. *The Black Newspaper in America, A Guide*. 2nd ed. Iowa City: Institute for Communication Studies, University of Iowa, 1972.

Lc73   United States. Library of Congress. Catalog Publications Division. *Newspapers in Microform: United States, 1948-72*. Washington, D.C.: The Library of Congress, 1973.

Lc78   United States. Library of Congress. Catalog Publications Division. *Newspapers in Microform: United States, 1973-1977*. Washington, D.C.: Library of Congress, 1978.

Lc83   United States. Library of Congress. *Newspapers in Microform, 1948-1983.*
                3 vols. Washington, D.C.: Library of Congress, 1984.

Lc91   Pluge, John, Jr. *The Black Press Held by the Library of Congress.*
                Washington, D.C.: Library of Congress, 1991.

Ltyear   Lord and Thomas. *Lord and Thomas' Pocket Directory of the American
                Press...A Complete List of Newspapers, Magazines, Farm Journals, and
                Other Periodicals Published in the United States, Canada, Porto Rico,
                Hawaiian and Philippine Islands.* Chicago: Lord and Thomas, 1907.

MBAL   *Mobile Beacon and Alabama Citizen*, P. O. Box 1407, 2311 Costarides
                Street, Mobile, AL 36633, (205) 479-0629.

Mil.PL   Milwaukee Public Library, 814 West Wisconsin Avenue, Milwaukee, WI
                53233, (414) 278-3000.

Mink   Mink, Arthur. *Title List of Ohio Newspapers.* Columbus, Ohio: Ohio State
                Archaeological and Historical Society, 1945.

MO   Taft, William H., comp. *Missouri Newspapers: When and Where,
                1808-1963.* Columbia, Mo.: State Historical Society of Missouri, 1964.

Mont. Co. PL   Clarksdale-Montgomery Co. Public Library, 329 Main Street, Clarksdale,
                TN 37640, (615) 648-8826.

Mont. HS   Montana Historical Society. *A Union List of Montana Newspapers in
                Montana Repositories.* [Helena, Mont.]: Montana Historical Society, 1987.

Moten   Moten, Rashey Burriel, Jr. "The Negro Press of Kansas." M.A. thesis,
                University of Kansas, Journalism, 1938.

NA   Ploski, Harry A., and James Williams, comp. and ed. *The Negro Almanac:
                A Reference Work on The AFRO-AMERICAN.* New York: John Wiley &
                Sons, 1983.

NC   Jones, Roger C. *Guide to North Carolina Newspapers on Microfilm: North
                Carolina Newspapers Available on Microfilm From the Division of
                Archives and History.* 5th rev. ed. Raleigh: Department of Cultural
                Resources, Division of Archives and History, 1982.

NEW   Williams, Nudie E. *Black Newspapers and the Exodusters of 1879*. Ph.D. dissertation, Oklahoma State University, Stillwater, 1976. Ann Arbor, Mich.: UMI, 1977.

NHyear   Murray, Florence, ed. *Negro Handbook*. New York: Wendell Malliet and Co., and Macmillan Co., 1942, 1944, 1946-1947, 1949.

NJ   Wright, William C., and Paul A. Stellhorn. *Directory of New Jersey Newspapers, 1765-1970*. Trenton: New Jersey Historical Commission, 1977.

NM   Groves, Pearce S., Becky J. Barnett, and Sandra J. Hansen, eds. *New Mexico Newspapers: A Comprehensive Guide to Bibliographical Entries and Locations*. Albuquerque: University of New Mexico Press, 1975.

NUC   United States. Library of Congress. *National Union Catalog pre-1956 Imprints*. 754 vols. London: Munsell Publications, 1961-1981.

NV   Lingenfelter, Richard E., and Karen Rix Gash. *The Newspapers of Nevada: A History and Bibliography, 1854-1979*. Reno, Nev.: University of Nevada Press, 1984.

NWU   Newsome, Steven C. *Northwestern University: The Afro American Newspapers, An Inventory*. Afro American Studies Librarian, March 1976.

NYyear   *Negro Year Book and Annual Encyclopedia of the Negro*. Tuskegee Institute, Alabama: Negro Year Book Publishing Company, 1912-1952.

OCLC   FIRST SEARCH. Online Computer Library Center catalog searched in September 1992 showing all holdings of existing newspapers under the subject heading African American Newspapers.

Oehco   Oehlerts, Donald E. *Guide to Colorado Newspapers, 1859-1984*. 2nd ed. Greeley, Colo.: University of Northern Colorado, 1984.

OWI   Oehlerts, Donald E. *Guide to Wisconsin Newspapers, 1833-1957*. Madison: State Historical Society of Wisconsin, 1958.

PA   Salisbury, Ruth, ed., under the auspices of the Pennsylvania Library Association. *Pennsylvania Newspapers: A Bibliography and Union List*. Pittsburgh: Pennsylvania Library Association, 1969.

Penn   Penn, Irvine Garland. *The Afro-American Press and Its Editors*. New York: Arno Press and The NY Times, 1969 [repr. of Wiley & Co., Springfield, Mass., 1891].

Pr   Pride, Armistead Scott. *Negro Newspapers in the United States, 1966*. [Jefferson City, Mo.: Department of Journalism, Lincoln University, 1966.]

Rh   Rhone, I. H., ed. *The Alabama Negro, 1863-1946*. Mobile, Ala.: Gulf Informer Pub. Co., 1946.

RW   Wolseley, Roland E. *The Black Press, U.S.A*. Ames, Iowa: Iowa State University Press, 1971.

Ryear   *Rowell's American Newspaper Directory Containing a Description of all the Newspapers and Periodicals Published in the United States and Territories, Dominion of Canada and Newfoundland, and of the Towns and Cities in Which They are Published, Together with a Statement or Estimate of the Average Number of Copies Printed by each Publication Catalogued*. New York: G. P. Rowell & Co., 1869-1908.

Saar   Saar, Amanda. *Black Arkansas Newspapers, 1869-1975, A Checklist*. Fayetteville, Ark.: David W. Mullins Library, University of Arkansas, 1976.

SC   Behling, Charles F. "South Carolina Negro Newspapers: Their History, Content and Reception." M.A. thesis, University of South Carolina, 1964.

Sch   [Schomburg, Arthur A.]. *Dictionary Catalog of the Schomburg Collection of Negro Literature and History*. 9 vols. Boston: G. K. Hall and Co., 1983.

Shelby Co. HS   Shelby County Historical Society, P. O. Box 28, Helena, AL 35080.

SI   *Sports Illustrated,* July 1992 issue.

SPDyr   *Standard Periodical Directory*. 16 vols. New York: Oxbridge Communications, Inc., 1967-1994. The 1965 edition did not differentiate African American periodicals.

Th   Thompson, Julius Eric. *The Black Press in Mississippi 1865-1985: A Directory*. West Cornwall, Conn.: Locust Hill Press, 1988.

TNM   Tennessee State Library and Archives. *Tennessee Newspapers: A Cumulative List of Microfilmed Tennessee Newspapers in the Tennessee State Library*. Nashville: Tennessee State Library and Archives, 1978.

TNSLA	Tennessee State Library and Archives, 403 7th Avenue, Nashville, TN 37243-0312, (615) 741-2764, Ann Jones.
Treadway	Ada Treadway, 1237 Beech Street, Waterloo, IA 50703, letter 6/93.
Unct	Connecticut University Library. Special Collections Department. *Alternatives: a Guide to the Newspapers, Magazines, and Newsletters in the Alternative Press Collection in the Special Collections Department of the University of Connecticut Library.* [Storrs]: University of Connecticut, 1976.
Urban Spectrum	*Urban Spectrum,* 710 East 25th Avenue, Denver, CO 80205, (303) 860-9148.
USNP	*United States Newspaper Program National Union List.* Dublin, Ohio: OCLC, 1993. 4th ed. 71 microfiche.
WI	State Historical Society of Wisconsin. *Black Periodicals and Newspapers, a Union List of Holdings in Libraries of the University of Wisconsin and the Library of the State Historical Society of Wisconsin.* 2nd rev. ed. compiled by Neil E. Strache, Maureen E. Hady, James P. Danky, and Nancy J. Diederich. Madison: State Historical Society of Wisconsin, 1979.
WPN	Working Press of the Nation—1969: Newspaper and Allied Services Directory. 45th ed. 4 vols. Chicago: National Research Bureau, Inc., 1994.
WRHS	Western Reserve Historical Society Library, 10825 East Blvd., Cleveland, OH 44106, (216) 721-5722.
WSJ	*Wall Street Journal,* article, 4 Oct 1990, B1.
WVU	West Virginia University, Colson Hall, Morgantown, WV 26506, (304) 293-3536.
Yenser#	Yenser, Thomas. *Who's Who in Colored America: A Biographical Dictionary of Notable Living Persons of Negro Descent.* New York: 1930-1932 3rd ed., 1938-1940 4th ed., 1941-1944 6th ed.

Appendix B

BIBLIOGRAPHY

Abajian, James de T. *Blacks in Selected Newspapers, Censuses and Other Sources: An Index to Names and Subjects.* 3 vols. Boston: G. K. Hall and Co., 1977.

Abajian, James de T. *Blacks in Selected Newspapers, Censuses and Other Sources: An Index to Names and Subjects, Supplement.* 2 vols. Boston: G. K. Hall and Co., 1985.

Abate, Frank R., ed. *Omni Gazetteer of the United States of America.* 11 vols. Detroit: Omnigraphics, Inc., 1991.

Afro-American Encyclopedia. 10 vols. North Miami, Fla.: Educational Book Publishers, Inc., 1974.

Alaska Newspaper Tree: A Guide to the Alaskan Newspaper Holdings of the Elmer E. Rasmuson Library. 2nd ed. [Fairbanks, Alaska]: University of Alaska, Fairbanks, 1980.

Edwin Alden & Bro's. *American Newspaper Catalogue, Including Lists of all Newspapers and Magazines Published in the United States and the Canadas...their Politics, Class or Denomination, Size, and Estimated Circulation. Also special lists of religious, agricultural, the various class publications, and of all newspapers published in foreign languages, and a list...by counties.* Cincinnati and New York: E. Alden & Bro's. Advertising Agency, 1882, 1883.

American Library Directory: a Classified List of Libraries in the United States and Canada with Personnel and Statistical Data. 46th ed. 2 vols. New Providence, N.J.: R. R. Bowker Company, 1993.

N. W. Ayer & Son's American Newspaper Annual and Directory. 20 vols. and supplements. Philadelphia: N. W. Ayer & Son, 1910-1929.

N. W. Ayer & Son's Directory of Newspapers & Periodicals. 40 vols. Philadelphia: N. W. Ayer & Son, 1930-1969.

Ayer Directory, Newspapers, Magazines and Trade Publications. Philadelphia: Ayer Press, 1970-1971.

Ayer Directory of Publications. Philadelphia: Ayer Press, 1972-1982.

Baatz, Wilmer H. *Afro-American Periodicals and Newspapers on Microforms: Microforms Room, Main Library, Indiana University, Bloomington.* [Bloomington]: Indiana University, 1983.

Barrens, Janelle. "Black Newspapers in the United States, 1829-[sic], compiled in pamphlet form from original charts." [Jefferson City, Mo.]: Lincoln University, 1970.

Baugh, Jane Roth. *Union List of Newspaper Holdings in Virginia Private College Libraries.* [Roanoke, Va.]: Hollins College, Fishburn Library, 1988.

Behling, Charles F. "South Carolina Negro Newspapers: Their History, Content and Reception." M.A. thesis, University of South Carolina, 1964.

Belfield, Sherri Denis. "Contemporary Black Newspapers in North Carolina." Honors essay, School of Journalism, University of North Carolina at Chapel Hill, 1989.

Black Americans Information Directory 1990-1991. Darren L. Smith, ed. Detroit: Gale Research Inc., 1990.

Black Americans Information Directory 1992-1993. Julia C. Furtaw, ed. Detroit: Gale Research Inc., 1992.

Black Americans Information Directory 1994-1995. Detroit: Gale Research Inc., 1993.

Black Newspapers Index. Ann Arnbor, Mich.: UMI, 1987-1994.

The Black Press Periodical Directory 1973. Black Press Clipping Bureau. Newark, N.J.: Systems Catalog Inc., 1973.

The Black Resource Guide. 10th ed. Washington, D.C.: R. Benjamin Johnson and Jacqueline L. Johnson, [1992].

Blackwell, Gloria. "Black Controlled Media in Atlanta, 1960-1970: The Burden of the Message and the Struggle for Survival." M.A. thesis, Emory University, Atlanta, 1976.

Boris, Joseph J. *Who's Who in Colored America: A Biographical Dictionary of Notable Living Persons of Negro Descent.* New York: 1927, and 1928-1929. See Yenser and Fleming for 3rd, 5th, 6th, and 7th editions.

Brigham, Clarence Saunders. *History and Bibliography of American Newspapers 1690-1820.* 2 vols. Worcester, Mass.: American Antiquarian Society, 1947.

Brooks, Maxwell R. *The Negro Press Re-Examined, Political Content of Leading Negro Newspapers.* Boston: Christopher Publishing House, 1959.

Brown, Elizabeth Read. *A Union List of Newspapers Published in Michigan Based on the Principal Newspaper Collections in the State with Notes Concerning Papers not Located.* Ann Arbor, Mich.: University of Michigan, Dept. of Library Science, 1954.

Brown, Karen Fitzgerald. *The Black Press of Tennessee, 1865-1980.* Ph.D. dissertation, University of Tennessee, Knoxville, 1982. Ann Arbor, Mich.: University Microfilm International, 1987.

Brown, Warren Henry. *Check List of Negro Newspapers in the United States (1827-1946),* Jefferson City, Mo.: Lincoln University, Department of Journalism, July 1946. Series No. 2.

Buckley, Gail Lumet. *The Hornes: An American Family.* New York: Alfred A. Knopf, Inc., 1986.

Bullock, Penelope Laconia. "The Negro Periodical Press in the United States, 1838-1909." Ph.D. dissertation, University of Michigan, 1971.

Burrell's 1989 Black Media Directory. Livingston, N.J.: Burrell, 1989.

California State Library. *Newspaper Holdings of the California State Library.* Sacramento, Calif.: California State Library Foundation, 1986.

Campbell, Georgetta Merritt. *Extant Collections of Early Black Newspapers: A Research Guide to the Black Press, 1880-1915, with an Index to the Boston Guardian, 1902-1904.* Troy, N.Y.: Whitston Publishing Co., 1981.

Cantrell, Kimberly Bess. "A Voice for the Freedman: The Mobile Nationalist, 1865-1869." M.A. thesis, Auburn University, Alabama, 1989.

Cappon, Lester J. *Virginia Newspapers, 1821-1935: A Bibliography with Historical Introduction and Notes.* New York: Appleton-Century, 1936.

Chambliss, Rollin. "What Negro Newspapers in Georgia Say about Some Social Problems." M.A. thesis, University of Georgia, 1934.

Chapman, Abraham, ed. *Black Voices: An Anthology of Afro-American Literature — Mentor Book.* New York: Penguin, 1968.

The Chicago Manual of Style. 14th ed. Chicago: University of Chicago Press, 1993.

Clayton, W. Woodford. *History of Davidson County, Tennessee with Illustrations and Biographical Sketches of its Prominent Men and Pioneers.* Philadelphia: J. W. Lewis & Co., 1880.

Connecticut University Library. Special Collections Department. *Alternatives: a Guide to the Newspapers, Magazines, and Newsletters in the Alternative Press Collection in the Special Collections Department of the University of Connecticut Library.* [Storrs]: University of Connecticut, 1976.

Cook, C. A. & Co. *C. A. Cook & Co.'s United States Newspaper Directory.* Chicago: C. A. Cook & Co., 1881.

Daniel, Walter C. *Black Journals of the United States.* Westport, Conn.: Greenwood Press, 1982.

Danky, James Philip. *Undergrounds: A Union List of Alternative Periodicals in Libraries of the United States and Canada.* Madison: State Historical Society of Wisconsin, 1974.

Dann, Martin E. *The Black Press, 1827-1890, The Quest for National Identity.* New York: Columbia University Press, 1971.

Davies, Nathaniel. *Afro-American Reference: An Annotated Bibliography.* Westport, Conn.: Greenwood Press, 1985.

Davis, Phyllis. *A Guide to Alaska's Newspapers.* Juneau: Gastineaux Channel Centennial Association and Alaska Division of State Libraries and Museums, 1976.

Davis, Ralph Nelson. "Negro Newspapers in Chicago." M.A. thesis, University of Chicago, 1939. Chicago: 1970.

Delaware University, Newark Library. *Union List of Newspapers in Microform.* Newark, Del.: Delaware University Press, 1964.

Detweiler, Frederick German. *The Negro Press in the United States.* Chicago: University of Chicago Press, 1922.

Diffendal, Anne P. *A Guide of the Newspaper Collection of the State Archives, Nebraska State Historical Society.* Lincoln: [Nebraska State Historical Society], 1977.

Directory of Archives and Manuscript Repositories in the United States. National Historical Publications and Records Commission. 2nd ed. Phoenix: Oryx Press, 1988.

Directory of Historical Organizations in the United States and Canada. 14th ed., Mary Bray Wheeler, ed. Nashville: AASLH Press, 1990.

Directory of the College Student Press in America. 18th ed. New York: Oxbridge Communications, Inc., 1968-1986.

The Ebony Handbook, by the Editors of Ebony. Chicago: Johnson Pub. Co., 1974.

Editor and Publisher Year Book. New York: Editor and Publisher, 1932-1993.

Ellison, Rhoda Coleman. *History and Bibliography of Alabama Newspapers in the 19th Century.* Birmingham: University of Alabama Press, 1954.

Eureka Newspaper Guide 1894 Edition. Binghamton, N.Y.: Eureka Advertising Agency, 1894.

Fenderson, Lewis H. "Development of the Negro Press: 1827-1948." Ph.D. dissertation, University of Pittsburgh, 1948.

Finkle, Lee. *Forum for Protest: The Black Press during World War II.* Rutherford, N.J.: Fairleigh Dickinson University Press, 1975.

Fleming, James G., and C. E. Burckel, eds. *Who's Who in Colored America: A Biographical Dictionary of Notable Living Persons of Negro Descent.* Yonkers-on-the-Hudson, N.Y.: Christian E. Burckel and Associates, Publishers, 1950. 7th ed. See Boris and Yenser for 1st, 2nd, 3rd, 5th, and 6th editions.

Gale Directory of Publications. Detroit: Gale Research Co., 1987-1989. Publication which superseded N. W. Ayer 1908-1982 and IMS Press 1983-1986.

Gale Directory of Publications and Broadcast Media. 3 vols. Detroit: Gale Research Co., 1990-1994.

Gore, George W., Jr. *Negro Journalism: An Essay on the History and Present Conditions of the Negro Press.* Greencastle, Ind.: [Journalism Press], 1922.

Gregory, Winifred, ed. *American Newspapers, 1821-1936. A Union List of Files Available in the United States and Canada.* New York: H. W. Wilson, 1937. Bibliographic Society of America, 1937.

Griesbach, Elizabeth. *Newspaper Holdings in Selected New Jersey Libraries.* Bridgewater, N.J.: The Library, 1987.

Grose, Charles William. *Black Newspapers in Texas, 1868-1970.* M.A. thesis, University of Texas at Austin, 1972. Ann Arbor, Mich.: University Microfilms International, 1987.

Groves, Pearce S., Becky J. Barnett, and Sandra J. Hansen, eds. *New Mexico Newspapers: A Comprehensive Guide to Bibliographical Entries and Locations.* Albuquerque: University of New Mexico Press, 1975.

Gutgesell, Stephen. *Guide to Ohio Newspapers, 1793-1973: Union Bibliography of Ohio Newspapers Available in Ohio Libraries*. Columbus: Ohio Historical Society, 1974.

Haley, James T. *Afro-American Encyclopedia or, The Thoughts, Doings, and Sayings of the Race; Embracing Addresses, Lectures, Biographical Sketches, Sermons, Poems, Names of Universities, Colleges, Seminaries, Newspapers, Books and a History of the Denominations Giving the Numerical Strength of Each*. Nashville: Haley & Florida, 1895.

Higgins, Ruby D., ed. *The Black Student's Guide to College Success*. Westport, Conn.: Greenwood Press, 1993.

Hill, Roy L. *Who's Who in the American Negro Press*. Dallas: Royal Publishing Co., 1960.

Historical Records Survey. Arkansas. *Union List of Arkansas Newspapers, 1819-1942. A Partial Inventory of Arkansas Newspaper Files Available in the Offices of Publishers, Libraries and Private Collections in Arkansas*. Little Rock, Ark: Historical Records Survey, Division of Community Service Programs, Works Projects Administration, 1942.

Historical Records Survey. Mississippi. *Mississippi Newspapers, 1805-1904*. Jackson, Miss.: Works Projects Administration, 1942.

Historical Records Survey. Texas. *Texas Newspapers, 1813-1939. A Union List of Newspaper Files Available in Offices of Publishers, Libraries and a Number of Private Collections*. Houston: San Jacinto Museum of History Association, 1941.

Hogan, Lawrence Daniel. *A Black National News Service: The Associated Negro Press and Claude Barrett, 1919-1945*. Rutherford, N.J.: Fairleigh Dickinson University Press, 1984.

Holmes, Kim. "Activities of the Black Press—1827-1927." Ph.D. dissertation, The George Washington University, 1975.

Hubbard, Harlan Page & Co. *The "Blue Book" of the Leading Newspapers for Leading Advertisers*. New Haven, Conn.: Harlan Page Hubbard, 1882, 1887.

Hubbard's Right Hand Record and Newspaper Directory: Giving in Alphabetical Order, Towns in Each State, with Population, Papers in Each Town...a Complete List of all American Newspapers and all the Leading Newspapers of the World. New Haven, Conn.: Harlan Page Hubbard, 1880.

Hutton, Frank P. "A Description of Black Newspapers in North Carolina." M.A. thesis, University of South Carolina, 1973.

The IMS '83 Ayer Directory of Publications; The Professional's Reference of Print Media Published in the United States, Canada, Puerto Rico, Virgin Islands, Bahamas, Bermuda and the Republic of the Philippines. Fort Washington, Pa.: IMS Press, 1983-1986.

Index to Black Newspapers. Wooster, Ohio: Newspaper Indexing Center, Micro Photo Division of Bell & Howell, Co., 1977-1986.

Inventory of Newspaper Holdings at the State Historical Society of North Dakota. 3 vols. Bismarck, N. Dak.: State Historical Society of North Dakota, 1991.

[Iowa]. *A Bibliography of Iowa Newspapers, 1836-1976.* Iowa City: Iowa State Historical Department, Division of the State Historical Society, 1979.

Irving, Rhoda G. "Advertising in Negro Newspapers." M. A. thesis, Ohio State University, 1935.

Jacobs, Donald M., ed. *Antebellum Black Newspapers: Indices to New York Freedom's Journal (1827-1829), The Rights of All (1829), The Weekly Advocate (1837), and The Colored American (1837-1841).* Westport, Conn.: Greenwood Press, 1976.

Jarboe, Betty M. *Obituaries: A Guide to Sources.* 2nd ed. Boston: G. K. Hall and Co., 1982.

Johnson, James Wesley. "The Associated Negro Press: A Medium of International News and Information, 1919-1967." Ph.D. dissertation, University of Missouri, 1976.

Jones, H. G., and Julius H. Avant. *Union List of North Carolina Newspapers, 1751-1900.* Raleigh, N.C.: State Department of Archives and History, 1963.

Jones, Roger C. *Guide to North Carolina Newspapers on Microfilm: North Carolina Newspapers Available on Microfilm From the Division of Archives and History.* 5th rev. ed. Raleigh, N.C.: Department of Cultural Resources, Division of Archives and History, 1982.

Journalism History. Vol. 1, 1974 to Vol. 20, 1994.

Journalism Quarterly. Vol. I, 1924 to Vol. LXX, 1994.

Journal of Negro History. Vol. I, 1916 to Vol. LXXVII, 1993.

Kansas Newspapers: A Directory of Newspaper Holdings in Kansas. Aileen Anderson, ed., comp. Topeka, Kans.: Kansas Library Network Board, 1984.

Keller, William E. "Newspapers in the Illinois State Historical Library," Illinois Libraries 49, June 1967, pp.439-543.

Kentucky Library Association. *Check List of Kentucky Newspapers Contained in Kentucky Libraries*. Lexington, Ky.: 1935.

Klinefeld, Ann. *Negro Press Digest*. February 7, 1966, March 1968.

La Brie, Henry G., III. *The Black Newspaper in America: A Guide*. Iowa City: Institute for Communication Studies, University of Iowa, 1970.

——. *The Black Newspaper in America, A Guide*. 2nd ed. Iowa City: Institute for Communication Studies, University of Iowa, 1972.

——. *The Black Press: A Bibliography*. Kennebunkport, Maine: Mercer House Press, 1973.

——. *The Black Press in America: A Guide*. 3rd ed. Kennebunkport, Maine: Harvard University, 1973.

——. *A Survey of Black Newspapers in America*. Kennebunkport, Maine: Mercer House Press, 1979.

Lingenfelter, Richard E., and Karen Rix Gash. *The Newspapers of Nevada: A History and Bibliography, 1854-1979*. Reno, Nev.: University of Nevada Press, 1984.

Logan, Rayford Whittingham, and Michael R. Winston, eds. *Dictionary of American Negro Biography*. New York: W. W. Norton & Co., 1982.

Lord and Thomas. *Lord and Thomas' Pocket Directory of the American Press...A Complete List of Newspapers, Magazines, Farm Journals, and Other Periodicals Published in the United States, Canada, Porto Rico, Hawaiian and Philippine Islands*. Chicago: Lord and Thomas, 1907.

Lord and Thomas. *Lord and Thomas and Logan Pocket Directory of the American Press...A Complete List of Newspapers, Magazines, Farm Journals, Religious Papers, Trade and Class Journals, Foreign Language Publications and the Periodicals*. Chicago: Lord and Thomas, 1918, 1920, 1923.

Louisiana Historical Records Survey. *Louisiana Newspapers, 1794-1940, A Union List of Louisiana Newspaper Files Available in Office of Publishers, Libraries and Private Collections in Louisiana*. University, La.: Hill Memorial Library, Louisiana State University, 1941.

Low, W. Augustus, and Virgil A. Clift, eds. *Encyclopedia of Black America*. New York: McGraw-Hill Book Co., 1981.

Luttrell, Estelle. *Newspapers and Periodicals of Arizona, 1859-1911*. University of Arizona Bulletin, 20, July 1949.

Marshall, Albert P., comp. *Guide to Negro Periodical Literature.* 4 vols. Jefferson City, Mo. and Winston-Salem, N.C.: 1941-1946.

Maryland State Department of Education. *A Guide to Newspapers and Newspaper Holdings in Maryland, the Maryland Newspaper Project.* Baltimore: Maryland State Department of Education, Division of Library Development and Services, 1991.

McGhee, Flora Ann Caldwell. "Mississippi Black Newspapers: Their History, Content and Future." Ph.D. dissertation, University of Southern Mississippi, 1985.

McMullan, T. N., ed. *Louisiana Newspapers, 1794-1961: A Union List of Louisiana Newspaper Files Available in Public, College and University Libraries in Louisiana.* Baton Rouge: Louisiana State University and Agricultural and Mechanical Library, 1965.

Mercer, Paul, comp. *Bibliographies and Lists of New York State Newspapers: An Annotated Guide.* Albany, N.Y.: State Library, 1981.

Michigan Newspapers on Microfilm, with a Description of the Michigan Newspapers on Microfilm Project. 4th ed. Lansing: Michigan Bureau of Library Services, 1973.

Miller, John William. *Indiana Newspaper Bibliography: Historical Account of All Indiana Newspapers Published from 1804-1980 and Locational Information for all Available Copies, Both Original and Microfilm.* Indianapolis: Indiana Historical Society, 1982.

Milner, Anita Cheek. *Newspaper Indexes: A Location and Subject Guide for Researchers.* 3 vols. Metuchen, N.J.: The Scarecrow Press, Inc., 1977-1982.

Mink, Arthur. *Title List of Ohio Newspapers.* Columbus, Ohio: Ohio State Archaeological and Historical Society, 1945.

Minnesota University Library, Newspaper and Microform Division. *Newspapers in the University of Minnesota Library: A Complete List of Holdings.* Minneapolis: University of Minnesota Press, 1964.

Montana Historical Society. *A Union List of Montana Newspapers in Montana Repositories.* [Helena, Mont.]: Montana Historical Society, 1987.

Mookini, Esther T. *The Hawaiian Newspapers.* Honolulu: Hawaii Cultural Research Foundation for The Hawaiian Studies Program, University of Hawaii, 1973.

Moses, Bernadine. "A Historical and Analytical View of Black Newspapers in North Carolina." M. A. thesis, University of North Carolina at Chapel Hill.

Moten, Rashey Burriel, Jr. "The Negro Press of Kansas." M.A. thesis, University of Kansas, Journalism, 1938.

Murphy, Virginia B., Daisy Ashford, and Paula Covington, compilers. *Newspaper Resources of Southeast Texas*. Houston: University of Houston Libraries, 1971.

Murray, Florence, ed. *Negro Handbook*. New York: Wendell Malliet and Co., and Macmillan Co., 1942, 1944, 1946-1947, 1949.

National Directory of Community Newspapers. 72nd ed. Minneapolis: American Newspaper Representatives, 1992.

National Directory of Newspapers and Audited Weeklies. Chicago: The National Editorial Association, 1947.

National Geographic Atlas of the World. 5th ed. Washington, D.C.: National Geographic Society, 1981.

National Newspaper Directory and Gazetteer. Boston: Pettingill and Company, 1900, 1902.

Nebraska State Historical Society. *A Guide to the Newspaper Collection of the State Archives, Nebraska State Historical Society*. Lincoln, Neb.: The Society, 1977.

Negro Year Book and Annual Encyclopedia of the Negro. Tuskegee Institute, Alabama: Negro Year Book Publishing Company, 1912-1952.

New Mexico State Library. *New Mexico State Library Newspaper Holdings, 1987*. [Santa Fe, N. Mex.]: Technical Service Bureau, The Library, 1987.

New York Times. *The New York Times Obituaries Index 1858-1968*. New York: The New York Times, 1970.

New York Times. *The New York Times Obituaries Index 1969-1978*. New York: The New York Times, 1980.

Newsome, Steven C. *Northwestern University: The Afro American Newspapers, An Inventory*. Afro American Studies Librarian, March 1976.

Newspapers in the Illinois State Historical Library. Illinois State Historical Library, June 1964.

Newspapers in the Illinois State Historical Library. Springfield, Ill.: Illinois State Library, 1991.

North, Simon Newton Dexter. *History and Present Condition of the Newspaper and Periodical Press of the United States with a Catalogue of the Publications of the Census Year.* Washington, D.C.: Government Publishing Office, 1884.

North Carolina Collection. "Negro Newspapers in North Carolina." Chapel Hill: University of North Carolina, 1969.

Oak, Vishnu Vitthal. *The Negro Newspaper.* Yellow Springs, Ohio: Antioch Press, 1948.

OCLC. FIRST SEARCH. Online Computer Library Center catalog searched in September 1992 showing all holdings of existing newspapers under the subject heading African American Newspapers.

O'Dell, Charles A. *A Columbia, Missouri Black Newspaper: "Professional World" 1901-1903.* Columbia, Mo.: C. A. O'Dell, 1990.

Oehlerts, Donald E. *Guide to Colorado Newspapers, 1859-1963.* Denver: Bibliographical Center for Research, Rocky Mountain Region, 1964.

———. *Guide to Colorado Newspapers, 1859-1984.* 2nd ed. Greeley, Colo.: University of Northern Colorado, 1984.

———. *Guide to Wisconsin Newspapers, 1833-1957.* Madison: State Historical Society of Wisconsin, 1958.

O'Kelly, Charlotte Gwen. "The Black Press and the Black Protest Movement: A Study of the Response of Mass Media to Social Change, 1946-1972." Ph.D. dissertation, The University of Connecticut, 1975.

Orne, Jerrold. *Union List of 64 Domestic Newspapers in Member Institutions of the Association of Southeastern Research Libraries.* [Chapel Hill, N.C.]: ASERL Domestic Newspaper Project, 1971.

Pacific States Newspaper Directory: Containing a Carefully Prepared List of all Newspapers and Periodicals Published in California, Oregon, Washington, Montana, Nevada, Alaska, Utah, Idaho, Arizona, New Mexico, Wyoming, British Columbia, Colorado, Sandwich Islands and Australia. 5th ed. San Francisco: Palmer & Rey Proprietors, Pacific States Advertising Bureau, 1892.

Payne, Gazelia I. "Black Newspapers in North Carolina, a description." M.A. thesis, University of North Carolina at Chapel Hill.

Pearson, Jerry C. "Whatever Happened to Tennessee's Black Newspapers?" A Communications History Report, The University of Tennessee, 1978.

Penn, Irvine Garland. *The Afro-American Press and Its Editors.* New York: Arno Press and The NY Times, 1969 [repr. of Wiley & Co., Springfield, Mass., 1891].

Pettengill, S. M. & Co. *The Advertiser's Hand-book: Comprising a Complete List of all Newspapers, Periodicals, and Magazines Published in the United States and British Possessions...and a History of the Newspaper Press.* New York: S. M. Pettengill & Co., 1870.

——. *A Catalogue of the Newspaper Field at the Centennial Exhibition Fairmount Park, Philadelphia, 1876.* Philadelphia: S. M. Pettengill & Co., [1876].

Pettengill Firm Newspaper Advertising Agency. New York: S. M. Pettengill & Co., 1877, 1879.

Ploski, Harry A., and James Williams, comps. and eds. *The Negro Almanac: A Reference Work on The AFRO-AMERICAN.* New York: John Wiley & Sons, 1983.

Pluge, John, Jr. *The Black Press Held by the Library of Congress.* Washington, D.C.: Library of Congress, 1991.

Preliou, Ilona Maxine. "Factors which contribute to low newspaper subscribership among blacks." M.A.J.C. thesis, University of Florida.

Pride, Armistead Scott. *The Black Press: A Bibliography.* Jefferson City, Mo.: Lincoln University, 1968.

——. *Negro Newspapers in the United States, 1966.* [Jefferson City, Mo.: Department of Journalism, Lincoln University, 1966.]

——. *Negro Newspapers on Microfilm: A Selected List.* Washington, D.C.: Library of Congress, Photoduplication Service, 1953.

——. *A Register and History of Negro Newspapers in the United States: 1827-1950.* Ph.D. dissertation, Northwestern University, 1950. Ann Arbor, Mich.: UMI, n.d.

Rand McNally Road Atlas: United States·Canada·Mexico. 69th ed. U.S.A.: Rand McNally and Company, 1993.

Rathbun, Betty Lou Kilbert. "The Rise of the Modern Negro Press: 1880-1914." Ph.D. dissertation, State University of New York at Buffalo, 1979.

Remington, Edward P. *Edward P. Remington's Annual Newspaper Directory: A List of all Newspapers and Other Periodical Publications of the United States and Canada.* Pittsburgh: E. P. Remington, 1901, 1903, 1907.

Rhone, I. H., ed. *The Alabama Negro, 1863-1946.* Mobile, Ala.: Gulf Informer Pub. Co., 1946.

Richardson, Clement, ed. *The National Cyclopedia of the Colored Race.* Montgomery, Ala.: National Publishing Co., 1919.

Romero, Patricia W. *International Library of Negro Life and History: In Black America 1968: The Year of Awakening.* New York: Publishers Co., Inc., 1969.

Ross, Albert. *Historical Synopsis of the Western Negro Press Association.* Quindaro, Kans.: Western University, 1909.

Rossell, Glenora E. *Pennsylvania Newspapers: A Bibliography and Union List.* 2nd ed. Pittsburgh: Pennsylvania Library Association, 1978.

Rowell's American Newspaper Directory Containing a Description of all the Newspapers and Periodicals Published in the United States and Territories, Dominion of Canada and Newfoundland, and of the Towns and Cities in Which They are Published, Together with a Statement or Estimate of the Average Number of Copies Printed by each Publication Catalogued. New York: G. P. Rowell & Co., 1869-1908.

Rowell, George Presbury & Company. *Centennial Newspaper Exhibition, 1876. A Complete List of American Newspapers. A Statement of the Industries, Characteristics, Population and Location of Towns in Which They are Published; also, A Descriptive Account of the Great Newspapers of the Day.* New York: G. P. Rowell & Co., 1876, 1877, 1881, 1892, 1901, 1904.

Saar, Amanda. *Black Arkansas Newspapers, 1869-1975, A Checklist.* Fayetteville, Ark.: David W. Mullins Library, University of Arkansas, 1976.

Salisbury, Ruth, ed., under the auspices of the Pennsylvania Library Association. *Pennsylvania Newspapers: A Bibliography and Union List.* Pittsburgh: Pennsylvania Library Association, 1969.

Sanders, Charles L., and Linda McLean, eds. *Directory of National Black Organizations.* New York: Afram Associates, 1972.

Sawyer, Frank B. *U. S. Negro Consumer Reference Guide.* New York: World Mutual Exchange, 1960.

——. *Directory of U. S. Negro Newspapers, Magazines and Periodicals and Africa Trade-Travel and Industry Directory of Selected Newspapers and Periodicals*. [New York:] World Mutual Exchange, 1966.

——. *Directory of U. S. Negro Newspapers, Magazines and Periodicals and Africa Trade-Travel and Industry Directory of Selected Newspapers and Periodicals*. Ann Arbor: UMI, 1970.

[Schomburg, Arthur A.]. *Dictionary Catalog of the Schomburg Collection of Negro Literature and History*. 9 vols. Boston: G. K. Hall and Co., 1983.

Sesquicentennial 1827-1977, Black Press Handbook, 1977. Washington, D.C.: National Newspaper Publishers Assoc., 1977.

Slavens, George Everett. "A History of the Missouri Negro Press." Ph.D. dissertation, University of Missouri, 1969.

South Carolina Newspapers on Microfilm. Charleston: South Carolina Library Society, 1956.

Special Libraries Association. *Directory of Newspaper Libraries in the U.S. and Canada*. Project of the Newspaper Division. Grace D. Parch, ed. New York: Special Libraries Association, 1976.

Special Libraries Association. Newspaper Division. *Newspaper Libraries in the U.S. and Canada; a SLA Directory*. 2nd ed., Elizabeth L. Anderson, ed. New York: Special Libraries Association, 1980.

Standard Periodical Directory. New York: Oxbridge Communications, Inc., 1965-1994.

State Historical Society of North Dakota. *The North Dakota Newspapers Inventory*. Bismarck, N.Dak.: State Historical Society of North Dakota, 1992.

State Historical Society of Wisconsin. *Black Periodicals and Newspapers, a Union List of Holdings in Libraries of the University of Wisconsin and the Library of the State Historical Society of Wisconsin*. 2nd rev. ed. compiled by Neil E. Strache, Maureen E. Hady, James P. Danky and Nancy J. Diederich. Madison: State Historical Society of Wisconsin, 1979.

Subscription News Company, Chicago. *American & Foreign Newspapers, Magazines and all Other Periodical Literature: Trade List of the Subscription News Co.* Chicago: The Company, 1893.

Suggs, Henry Lewis, ed. *The Black Press in the South, 1865-1979*. Westport, Conn.: Greenwood Press, 1983.

Taft, William H., comp. *Missouri Newspapers: When and Where, 1808-1963*. Columbia, Mo.: State Historical Society of Missouri, 1964.

Tennessee State Library and Archives. *Tennessee Newspapers: A Cumulative List of Microfilmed Tennessee Newspapers in the Tennessee State Library*. Nashville: Tennessee State Library and Archives, 1978.

Thompson, Julius Eric. *The Black Press in Mississippi 1865-1985: A Directory*. West Cornwall, Conn.: Locust Hill Press, 1988.

Tucker, Susan. *Telling Memories Among Southern Women: Domestic Workers and Their Employers in the Segregated South*. Baton Rouge: Louisiana State University Press, 1988.

United States. Department of Commerce. Bureau of the Census. *Negro Newspapers and Periodicals in the United States 1938*. Washington, D.C.: Bureau of the Census, 1938. C18.193:1/2

——. Department of Commerce. Bureau of the Census. *Negro Newspapers and Periodicals in the United States: 1940*. Negro Statistical Bulletin No. 1. Washington, D.C.: May 1941.

——. Department of Commerce. Bureau of the Census. *Negro Newspapers and Periodicals in the United States: 1943*. Negro Statistical Bulletin No. 1. Washington, D.C.: August 1944.

——. Department of Commerce. Bureau of the Census. *Negro Newspapers and Periodicals in the United States*. Washington, D.C.: Government Printing Office, Bulletin No. 1 [1945]. C3.131:1-5.

——. Library of Congress. *National Union Catalog pre-1956 Imprints*. 754 vols. Washington, D.C.: The Library of Congress, 1961-1981.

——. Library of Congress. *Newspapers in Microform, 1948-1983*. 3 vols. Washington, D.C.: Library of Congress, 1984.

——. Library of Congress. Catalog Publications Division. *Newspapers in Microform: United States, 1948-72*. Washington, D.C.: The Library of Congress, 1973.

——. Library of Congress. Catalog Publications Division. *Newspapers in Microform: United States, 1973-1977*. Washington, D.C.: Library of Congress, 1978.

United States Newspaper Program National Union List. Dublin, Ohio: OCLC, 1993. 4th ed. 71 fiche.

University of Georgia Libraries. *Georgia Newspapers on Microfilm at the University of Georgia Libraries: A Listing (by Date and Reels) of Georgia Newspaper Holdings on Microfilm at the University of Georgia Libraries*. Athens, Ga.: The Libraries, 1987.

University of Idaho Library. *University of Idaho Newspaper Holdings as of December 31, 1979.* [Moscow, Idaho]: University of Idaho Library, 1979.

University of Utah Libraries. *The Utah Newspaper Project: Final Report.* Salt Lake City: University of Utah Libraries, 1987.

Vanden Heuvel, Jon. *Untapped Sources: Americas Newspaper Archives and Histories.* [New York: Columbia University], 1991.

West Virginia University Library. *Newspapers in the West Virginia University Library.* Morgantown, W.Va.: West Virginia University Library, 1964.

West, Earle H., comp. *A Bibliography of Doctoral Research on the Negro, 1933-1966, with supplement 1967-1969.* Washington, D.C.: Howard University and Xerox Microfilms, 1970.

Wescott, Mary, and Allene Ramage. *A Checklist of United States Newspapers.* Part 1. Durham, N.C.: Duke University, 1932.

Who's Who of the Colored Race. Chicago: Half-Century Anniversary of Negro Freedom in the United States, 1915. Detroit: Gale Research Co., 1976 [repr].

Wilder, James Chapman. "History of the Alabama Negro Press: Post Reconstruction to 1901." M.A. thesis, University of Alabama, 1964.

Willey, Malcolm Macdonald. *The Country Newspaper: A Study of Socialization and Newspaper Content.* Chapel Hill: University of North Carolina Press, 1926.

Williams, Nudie E. *Black Newspapers and the Exodusters of 1879.* Ph.D. dissertation, Oklahoma State University, Stillwater, 1976. Ann Arbor, Mich.: UMI, 1977.

Wolseley, Roland E. *The Black Press, U.S.A.* Ames, Iowa: Iowa State University Press, 1971.

Working Press of the Nation—1969: Newspaper and Allied Services Directory. 45th ed. 4 vols. Chicago: National Research Bureau, Inc., 1949-1994.

Wright, William C., and Paul A. Stellhorn. *Directory of New Jersey Newspapers, 1765-1970.* Trenton: New Jersey Historical Commission, 1977.

Yenser, Thomas, ed. *Who's Who in Colored America: A Biographical Dictionary of Notable Living Persons of Negro Descent.* New York: 1930-1932, 1938-1940, and 1941-1944. 3rd, 4th, and 6th eds. See Boris and Fleming for 1st, 2nd, and 7th editions.

TITLE INDEX

Banner and Messenger, Greenville, AL, 4
Banner Enterprise, Raleigh, NC, 98
Banner of Light, Fayetteville, TN, 121
Baptist
    Chattanooga, TN, 120
    New York City, NY, 88
    Richmond, VA, 138
Baptist Advocate
    Opelousas, LA, 62
    Port Gibson, MS, 76
    Spartanburg, SC, 119
Baptist Banner
    Atlanta, GA, 34
    Demopolis, AL, 3
    Mobile, AL, 5
Baptist Beacon, Springfield, OH, 105
Baptist Chronicle, Florence, SC, 118
Baptist College News, Little Rock, AR, 12
Baptist College Searchlight, Muskogee, OK, 108
Baptist Companion
    Portsmouth, VA, 138
    Richmond, VA, 138
Baptist Echo, Mound Bayou, MS, 75
Baptist Family Companion, Knoxville, TN, 121
Baptist Globe, Parsons, KS, 53
Baptist Headlight
    Biloxi, MS, 70
    Carriere, MS, 70
    Houston, TX, 130
    Richmond, VA, 138
    Topeka, KS, 54
Baptist Herald
    Florence, SC, 118
    Keokuk, IA, 51
    Lynchburg, VA, 136
    Memphis, TN, 122
    New York City, NY, 88
    Paducah, KY, 58
    Richmond, VA, 138
    Vicksburg, MS, 77
Baptist Informer
    Muskogee, OK, 108
    Raleigh, NC, 98
    Sumter, SC, 120
Baptist Journal
    Corsicana, TX, 127
    Dallas, TX, 128
    Greenville, MS, 71
    Marshall, TX, 132
    Waco, TX, 134
Baptist Leader
    Anniston, AL, 1
    Birmingham, AL, 1
    Mobile, AL, 5
    Montgomery, AL, 6
    Selma, AL, 7
Baptist Lime Light, Selma, AL, 7
Baptist Messenger
    Baltimore, MD, 63
    Cambridge, MA, 66

Baptist Messenger (cont.)
    Jackson, MS, 73
Baptist Monitor, Bennettsville, SC, 116
Baptist Observer, Chicago, IL, 42
Baptist Organ, Pine Bluff, AR, 14
Baptist Pilot
    Littleton, NC, 98
    Newton, NC, 98
    Waco, TX, 134
    Winton, NC, 101
Baptist Pioneer
    Huntington, WV, 141
    Selma, AL, 7
Baptist Preachers' Union, Greenville, MS, 71
Baptist Progress
    Akron, OH, 101
    Elgin, IL, 47
Baptist Quarterly, Raleigh, NC, 98
Baptist Record
    Jackson, MS, 73
    Kansas City, MO, 79
Baptist Recorder, Chattanooga, TN, 120
Baptist Reporter
    Helena, AR, 10
    Jackson, MS, 73
Baptist Review, Atlanta, GA, 34
Baptist Rival, Ardmore, OK, 106
Baptist Safeguard, Guthrie, OK, 107
Baptist Sentinel
    Lexington, MS, 75
    Raleigh, NC, 98
    Warrenton, NC, 100
Baptist Signal
    Greenville, MS, 71
    Jackson, MS, 73
    Natchez, MS, 76
Baptist Signal Messenger, Natchez, MS, 76
Baptist Standard
    Macon, GA, 39
    Raleigh, NC, 98
Baptist Teacher, Jackson, MS, 73
Baptist Telephone Messenger, Brownwood, TX, 127
Baptist Training Union Leader, Nashville, TN, 124
Baptist Tribune, Charleston, SC, 116
Baptist Trumpet
    Enterprise, MS, 71
    Metropolis City, IL, 48
Baptist Truth
    Cairo, IL, 42
    Macon, GA, 39
    Metropolis City, IL, 48
    Savannah, GA, 40
Baptist Vanguard, Little Rock, AR, 12
Baptist Voice, Princeton, KY, 58
Baptist Watchtower, Evansville, MD, 64
Baptist Women's Era, Selma, AL, 7
Baptist Women's Union
    Greenville, MS, 71

Baptist Women's Union (cont.)
    Mound Bayou, MS, 75
Baptist World, Philadelphia, PA, 111
Barnwell Recorder, Columbia, SC, 117
Bath Times
    Covington, VA, 135
    Hot Springs, VA, 136
Baton Rouge Community Leader, Baton Rouge, LA, 59
Baton Rouge Herald, Baton Rouge, LA, 59
Baton Rouge News Leader, Baton Rouge, LA, 59
Baton Rouge Post, Baton Rouge, LA, 59
Baton Rouge Scotland Press, Scotlandville, LA, 62
Baton Rouge Weekly Press, Baton Rouge, LA, 59
Baxter Vidette, Baxter, AR, 9
Bay Area Report, San Francisco, CA, 20
Bay Cities Informer, Santa Monica, CA, 21
Bay Guardian, San Francisco, CA, 20
Bay State Banner, Boston, MA, 65
Bay Viewer, Berkeley, CA, 15
Bayano Publications, Brooklyn, NY, 86
Bayonet, Boston, MA, 65
Bayou Talk, Moreno Valley, CA, 18
Beacon
    Atlantic City, NJ, 82
    Boley, OK, 106
    Bridgeport, CT, 23
    East St. Louis, IL, 47
    Oakland, CA, 18
Beacon Light
    Chicago, IL, 42
    Greenwood, MS, 72
    Hattiesburg, MS, 72
    Ocala, FL, 31
Beaufort County News, Beaufort, SC, 115
Beauticians Journal and Guide, New York City, NY, 88
Bedford Times Register, Bedford Hts., OH, 101
Bee
    Camden, SC, 116
    Columbia, SC, 117
    Greenville, MS, 71
    Washington, DC, 25
Bee and Leader, Washington, DC, 25
Bee-Free Speech, Chicago, IL, 42
Belmont Courier Bulletin, Menlo Park, CA, 18
Benedict Newsletter, Columbia, SC, 117
Benevolent Banner
    Edwards, MS, 71
    North Topeka, KS, 53
Benevolent Design, Atlanta, GA, 34
Benton County Freedom Train, Ashland, MS, 70
Berkeley Metro Reporter, San Francisco, CA, 20
Berkeley Tri-City Post, Oakland, CA, 18
Beverly Times, Staunton, VA, 139

Blue Grass Bugle, Frankfort, KY, 56
Blue Grass Chronicle, Paris, KY, 58
Blue Ridge Eagle, Cherrylane, NC, 95
Bluefieldian, Bluefield, WV, 141
Bluff City News, Memphis, TN, 122
Bluff City Post, Natchez, MS, 76
Body of Christ, Denver, CO, 22
Boley Elevator, Boley, OK, 106
Boley Informer, Boley, OK, 107
Boley News, Boley, OK, 107
Boley Progress, Boley, OK, 107
Bookertee Searchlight, Bookertee, OK, 107
Boston Banner, South Boston, VA, 139
Boston Chronicle, Boston, MA, 65
Boston Colored Citizen, Boston, MA, 65
Boston Courant, Boston, MA, 65
Boston Greater News, Roxbury, MA, 66
Boston News, Boston, MA, 65
Boston Sun, Boston, MA, 65
Botswana Review, Ivoryton, CT, 23
Bottom Line, Springfield, MA, 66
Bradley District Herald, Fordyce, AR, 10
Bridgeport Inquirer, Hartford, CT, 23
Broad Ax
    Chicago, IL, 42
    Lake Charles, LA, 59
    Salt Lake City, UT, 135
    Wichita, KS, 55
Broad Axe
    Birmingham, AL, 2
    Pittsburgh, PA, 113
    St. Paul, MN, 69
Broadcast
    Macon, GA, 39
    Monroe, LA, 60
    New Orleans, LA, 60
Broadcaster
    Buffalo, NY, 87
    Nashville, TN, 124
Bronze America, Hollywood, CA, 15
Bronze Citizen, Peoria, IL, 48
Bronze Confessions, Miami, FL, 30
Bronze Informer, Peoria, IL, 48
Bronze Raven, Toledo, OH, 105
Bronze Texan News, Fort Worth, TX, 129
Bronze Thrills
    Fort Worth, TX, 129
    North Bergen, NJ, 84
Bronze Woman, Philadelphia, PA, 111
Bronzeman, Chicago, IL, 43
Bronzville News, Los Angeles, CA, 16
Brookhaven Leader, Brookhaven, MS, 70
Brooklyn & Long Island Informer, Jamaica, NY, 88
Brooklyn Monitor, Brooklyn, NY, 86
Brotherhood
    Cincinnati, OH, 101
    Columbus, MS, 71
    Natchez, MS, 76
    Pensacola, FL, 31

Brotherhood Eyes, Dallas, TX, 128
Brother's Optic, Moberly, MO, 80
Broward Times
    Coconut Creek, FL, 28
    Pompano Beach, FL, 32
Brown American, Philadelphia, PA, 111
Brown Book, Nashville, TN, 124
Brownies' Book, New York City, NY, 89
Brownsville News, Flint, MI, 68
Buckeye Review, Youngstown, OH, 106
Buffalo, Fayetteville, NC, 96
Buffalo Spokesman, Buffalo, NY, 87
Buffalo Star, Buffalo, NY, 87
Bugle
    Calvert, TX, 127
    Huntsville, TX, 132
    Navasota, TX, 132
Building Blocks, Washington, DC, 25
Bull Dog Growl, Utica, MS, 77
Bulletin
    Auburn, NY, 86
    Chicago, IL, 43
    Cincinnati, OH, 101
    Dowingtown, PA, 110
    Durham, NC, 96
    Greenville, MS, 71
    Jacksonville, FL, 29
    Louisville, KY, 57
    Memphis, TN, 122
    Nashville, TN, 124
    New Orleans, LA, 60
    New York City, NY, 89
    Tampa, FL, 32
    Washington, DC, 25
    Wilmington, NC, 100
Bulletin Advertiser, Daytona Beach, FL, 28
Bulletin of Medico Chirurgal Society, Washington, DC, 25
Bulletin of National Dental Association, Manassas, VA, 136
Burning Spear
    Gainesville, FL, 28
    Oakland, CA, 18
    St. Petersburg, FL, 32
Business Herald, Donaldsonville, LA, 59
Business Journal, New Orleans, LA, 60
Business World, New York City, NY, 89
Butler County American, Hamilton, OH, 105
Buxton Advocate, Buxton, IA, 51
Buxton Eagle, Oskaloosa, IA, 51
Buxton Gazette, Buxton, IA, 51
Cairo Gazette, Cairo, IL, 42
Calanthian Journal
    Edwards, MS, 71
    Jackson, MS, 73
California Advocate, Fresno, CA, 15
California Cactus, Los Angeles, CA, 16
California Eagle, Los Angeles, CA, 16
California News, Los Angeles, CA, 16
California Times, Sacramento, CA, 19

California Tribune, Los Angeles, CA, 16
California Voice
    Berkeley, CA, 15
    Oakland, CA, 18
    San Francisco, CA, 20
California World, Oakland, CA, 18
Call
    Bell Gardens, CA, 15
    Chicago, IL, 43
    Cleveland, OH, 102
    Miami, FL, 30
    St. Louis, MO, 80
Call and Post
    Akron, OH, 101
    Cincinnati, OH, 101
    Cleveland, OH, 102
    Youngstown, OH, 106
Callaloo, Baltimore, MD, 63
Callaloo: A Black South Journal of Arts and Letters, Lexington, KY, 56
Calvert Eagle, Calvert, TX, 127
Calvin News, New York City, NY, 89
Camden Chronicle, Camden, SC, 116
Camden Daily Courier, Camden, NJ, 83
Camden Jersey Beat, Camden, NJ, 83
Camden News, Camden AR, 9
Camden News, NJ, 83
Camden Union Recorder, Camden, NJ, 83
Camden Weekly, Camden, AR, 9
Campus Core-lator, Berkeley, CA, 15
Campus Digest, Tuskegee, AL, 8
Campus Echo, Durham, NC, 96
Campus Lens, Marshall, TX, 132
Campus Magazine
    Jefferson City, MO, 78
    New York City, NY, 89
Campus Mirror, Atlanta, GA, 34
Canton Citizen, Canton, MS, 70
Cape Fear Journal, Wilmington, NC, 100
Capital, Albany, NY, 85
Capital City Argus, Austin, TX, 126
Capital City Argus and Interracial Review, Austin, TX, 126
Capital City Defender, Nashville, TN, 124
Capital City Post, Tallahassee, FL, 32
Capital City Weekly, Baton Rouge, LA, 59
Capital Outlook, Tallahassee, FL, 32
Capital Plaindealer, Topeka, KS, 54
Capital Times, Washington, DC, 25
Caravan, Philadelphia, PA, 111
Career Focus, Kansas City, MO, 79
Caret
    Newport News, VA, 136
    Tyler, TX, 134
Carib News, New York City, NY, 89
Caribbean Express, New York City, NY, 89
Carolina Citizen
    Greensboro, NC, 97
    Greenville, NC, 97
Carolina Enterprise, Goldsboro, NC, 96

Christian Weekly, Mobile, AL, 5
Chronicle
  Americus, GA, 33
  Charleston, SC, 116
  Chicago, IL, 43
  Evansville, IN, 49
  Florence, SC, 118
  Gaffney, SC, 118
  Jacksonville, FL, 29
  New York City, NY, 89
  Omaha, NE, 82
  Providence, RI, 115
  St. Louis, MO, 80
  Topeka, KS, 54
  Tuscaloosa, AL, 8
  Waynesboro, GA, 41
Chronometer, Americus, GA, 33
Church Advocate
  Baltimore, MD, 63
  Petersburg, VA, 137
Church and School Phalanx, Atlanta, GA, 34
Church and Society World, Atlanta, GA, 34
Church and Southland Advocate, Asheville, NC, 94
Church and State, Langston City, OK, 108
Church Herald
  Charleston, SC, 116
  Troy, AL, 8
Church Journal, MO, 78
Church Observer, Mobile, AL, 5
Church Organ, Chicago, IL, 43
Church Review, Langston City, OK, 108
Church School Herald, Pensacola, FL, 31
Church School Herald-Journal, Charlotte, NC, 95
Church Week, Fort Worth, TX, 129
Church Weekly, Philadelphia, PA, 111
C.I.A.A. Bulletin, Lawrenceville, VA, 136
Cimeter, Muskogee, OK, 108
Cincinnati and Dayton Forum, Dayton, OH, 104
Cincinnati Commercial Guide, Cincinnati, OH, 101
Cincinnati Herald, Cincinnati, OH, 102
Cincinnati Herald of Freedom, Cincinnati, OH, 102
Cincinnati Leader, Cincinnati, OH, 102
Cincinnati News, Cincinnati, OH, 102
Cincinnati News Recorder, Cincinnati, OH, 102
Cincinnati Pilot, Cincinnati, OH, 102
Circuit, Chicago, IL, 43
Citizen
  Benton Harbor, MI, 66
  Berea, KY, 56
  Bessemer, AL, 1
  Boston, MA, 65
  Chattanooga, TN, 120
  Dayton, OH, 104
  Fort Gibson, OK, 107
  Hot Springs, AR, 11
  Houston, TX, 130

Citizen (cont.)
  Louisville, KY, 57
  Nashville, TN, 124
  New York City, NY, 89
  Providence, RI, 115
  Rosedale, MS, 76
  San Francisco, CA, 20
  Selma, AL, 7
  Spokane, WA, 140
  Terre Haute, IN, 51
Citizen Advocate, Norfolk, VA, 137
Citizens Advocate, Los Angeles, CA, 16
Citizens' Appeal, Vicksburg, MS, 77
Citizens Voice, Los Angeles, CA, 16
City Bulletin, Natchez, MS, 76
City Examiner, Nashville, TN, 124
City News
  Boston, MA, 65
  Newark, NJ, 84
  Roxbury, MA, 66
City Paper, Kenly, NC, 98
City Sun, Brooklyn, NY, 86
City Times, Galveston, TX, 130
Claiborne, Port Gibson, MS, 76
Clarion
  Clarksburg, WV, 141
  Evansville, IN, 49
  Morrilton, AR, 13
  Nashville, TN, 124
  Owensboro, KY, 58
  Petersburg, VA, 137
  St. Louis, MO, 80
  Troy, NY, 94
Clarion, Waco, TX, 134
Clarion Post News, Canton, OH, 101
Clark Atlanta University Magazine, Atlanta, GA, 34
Clark University Mentor, Atlanta, GA, 34
Clark University Register, Atlanta, GA, 34
Clarksville Connection, Clarksville, TN, 121
Clarksville Echo, Muskogee Co., OK, 109
Class Magazine, New York City, NY, 89
Claverite, New Orleans, LA, 60
Clearview Patriarch, Clearview, OK, 107
Clearview Tribune, Clearview, OK, 107
Cleveland Guide, Cleveland, OH, 102
Cleveland Herald, Cleveland, OH, 102
Cleveland Metro, Bedford Hts., OH, 101
Clipper
  Alexandria, VA, 135
  Chicago, IL, 43
Close UP Magazine, Jackson, MS, 73
Clubdate Magazine, Cleveland, OH, 102
Coahoma Opportunities Inc. Newsletter, Clarksdale, MS, 70
Coast Appeal, Long Branch, NJ, 83
Coastal Times, Charleston, SC, 116
Coffee Break, Fort Wayne, IN, 49
Coffeyville Globe, Coffeyville, KS, 52
College Advocate, Little Rock, AR, 12

College Arms, Tallahassee, FL, 32
College Journal, Columbia, SC, 117
College Language Association Journal, Atlanta, GA, 34
College Messenger, Little Rock, AR, 12
College Quarterly, Little Rock, AR, 12
College Weekly, New York City, NY, 89
Color, Philadelphia, PA, 111
Color Line, Mount Vernon, NY, 88
Color Magazine, Charleston, WV, 141
Colorado Advance, Colorado Springs, CO, 21
Colorado Advocate, Colorado Springs, CO, 21
Colorado Argus and Weekly Times, Denver, CO, 22
Colorado Black Lifestyle, Denver, CO, 22
Colorado Eagle, Pueblo, CO, 23
Colorado Exponent, Denver, CO, 22
Colorado Journal, Denver, CO, 22
Colorado Springs Gazette, Colorado Springs, CO, 22
Colorado Springs Sun, Colorado Springs, CO, 22
Colorado Statesman, Denver, CO, 22
Colorado Times, Pueblo, CO, 23
Colorado Times Eagle, Pueblo, CO, 23
Colorado Voice, Colorado Springs, CO, 22
Colored Alabamian, Montgomery, AL, 6
Colored Alliance, Austin, TX, 126
Colored Alliance Advocate, Vaiden, MS, 77
Colored American
  Augusta, GA, 36
  Cincinnati, OH, 102
  Galveston, TX, 130
  Helena, AR, 10
  High Point, NC, 98
  New York City, NY, 89
  Tuscaloosa, AL, 8
  Washington, DC, 25
Colored American Appeal, Gretna, LA, 59
Colored American Magazine
  Boston, MA, 65
  New York City, NY, 89
Colored Catholic, Baltimore, MD, 63
Colored Churchman
  Bradford City, VA, 135
  Lawrenceville, VA, 136
  Little Rock, AR, 12
  Luray, VA, 136
  Shenandoah, VA, 139
Colored Citizen
  Bakersfield, CA, 15
  Chattanooga, TN, 120
  Cincinnati, OH, 102
  Helena, MT, 82
  Jackson, MS, 73
  Memphis, TN, 122
  Montgomery, AL, 6
  New York City, NY, 89
  Pensacola, FL, 31
  Pittsburgh, PA, 113

Courier (cont.)
  New York City, NY, 89
  Pensacola, FL, 31
  Racine, WI, 143
  Tampa, FL, 32
  Texarkana, TX, 134
  Tuscaloosa, AL, 8
Courier Digest, Uniontown, PA, 114
CPSB Newsletter, Birmingham, AL, 2
Craftsman, Philadelphia, PA, 111
Craftsman Aero News, Los Angeles, CA, 16
Crenshaw News, Culver City, CA, 15
Creole Magazine, Lafayette, LA, 59
Crescent, New York City, NY, 89
Crescent Magazine, Louisville, KY, 57
Crier, Pittsburgh, PA, 114
Crimson and Gray, Atlanta, GA, 34
Crisis, New York City, NY, 89
Criterion
  Buffalo, NY, 87
  Los Angeles, CA, 16
  Pittsburgh, PA, 114
Critic
  Forsyth, GA, 38
  Macon, GA, 39
  Richmond, MO, 80
  Richmond, VA, 138
  Staunton, VA, 139
Critique, Youngstown, OH, 106
Crow, New Haven, CT, 24
Crusader
  Atlanta, GA, 34
  Baltimore, MD, 63
  Chester, PA, 110
  Gary, IN, 49
  Greenville, SC, 118
  Hyattsville, MD, 64
  New Orleans, LA, 60
  New York City, NY, 89
  Pittsburgh, PA, 114
  Rockford, IL, 48
  Savannah, GA, 40
Crusader Journal, Hot Springs, AR, 11
Crusader Weekly Newsletter, Monroe, NC, 98
Crystal, Hot Springs, AR, 11
Culver City Star, Culver City, CA, 15
Culver City/Westchester Wave, Los
      Angeles, CA, 16
Cumberland Flag
  Huntsville, AL, 4
  Union City, TN, 126
Current, Bayou Goula, LA, 59
Cuttings, Greensboro, NC, 97
Cyclone, Selma, AL, 7
Daily American Citizen, Kansas City, KS, 52
Daily Bulletin
  Chicago, IL, 44
  Dayton, OH, 104
Daily Christian Advocate, Sumter, SC, 120
Daily Christian Index, St. Louis, MO, 80

Daily Citizen
  Kansas City, KS, 52
  New York City, NY, 89
Daily Evening Journal, Washington, IA, 52
Daily Express, Dayton, OH, 104
Daily Guide, St. Paul, MN, 69
Daily Informer, New York City, NY, 89
Daily Metropolitan, Dallas, TX, 128
Daily Monitor, Knoxville, TN, 121
Daily Plaindealer, Kansas City, KS, 52
Daily Promotor, Jacksonville, FL, 29
Daily Record, Wilmington, NC, 100
Daily Searchlight, Muskogee, OK, 108
Daily Spokesman, New Orleans, LA, 60
Daily Standard, Indianapolis, IN, 50
Daily Sun, Washington, DC, 25
Daily World, New York City, NY, 89
Dallas Appeal, Dallas, TX, 128
Dallas Examiner, Dallas, TX, 128
Dallas Express
  Dallas, TX, 128
  Houston, TX, 130
Dallas Informer, Houston, TX, 130
Dallas Leaflet, Dallas, TX, 128
Dallas Post, Selma, AL, 7
Dallas Post Tribune, Dallas, TX, 128
Dallas Weekly, Dallas, TX, 128
Davis' Educational Review, Campti, LA, 59
Dawn
  Baltimore, MD, 63
  Elkton, MD, 64
Dawn Magazine, Washington, DC, 25
Dayton Bulletin, Dayton, OH, 104
Dayton Cincinnati Forum, Dayton, OH, 104
Dayton Defender, Dayton, OH, 104
Dayton Express, Dayton, OH, 104
Dayton Express Urban Weekly, Dayton,
      OH, 104
Dayton Forum, Dayton, OH, 104
Dayton Globe, Dayton, OH, 104
Dayton Standard, Dayton, OH, 104
Dayton Tattler, Dayton, OH, 104
Daytona Industrial Advocate, Daytona, FL, 28
Daytona Times, Daytona Beach, FL, 28
Deal or Die, Milwaukee, WI, 142
Decatur Spot-light, Decatur, IL, 47
Decatur Tribune, Decatur, AL, 3
Declaration, Cincinnati, OH, 102
Decoder, Philadelphia, PA, 111
Deep South Patriot, Louisville, KY, 57
Defender
  Bryn Mawr, PA, 110
  Chattanooga, TN, 120
  East St. Louis, IL, 47
  Eminence, KY, 56
  Fort Worth, TX, 129
  Jacksonville, FL, 29
  Los Angeles, CA, 16
  Louisville, KY, 57
  Mound Bayou, MS, 75

Defender (cont.)
  Nashville, TN, 124
  New Castle, KY, 58
  New York City
    NY (1909-1910), 90
    NY (1930-1931), 90
  Philadelphia, PA, 111
  Sumter, SC, 120
  Timmonsville, SC, 120
  Wilmington, DE, 24
Defender and Baptist Herald, Fort Worth,
      TX, 129
Defiance, Atlanta, GA, 34
DeKalb Weekly, Decatur, GA, 38
Delaware Advocate, Wilmington, DE, 24
Delaware Conference Advocate, Easton,
      MD, 64
Delaware Conference Standard,
      Wilmington, DE, 24
Delaware Defender, Wilmington, DE, 24
Delaware Observer, New Castle, DE, 24
Delaware Reporter, Wilmington, DE, 24
Delaware Spectator, Wilmington, DE, 24
Delaware Star, Wilmington, DE, 24
Delaware Twilight, Wilmington, DE, 24
Delaware Valley Defender, Wilmington,
      DE, 24
Delaware Valley Star, Wilmington, DE, 24
Delta Beacon, Vicksburg, MS, 77
Delta Farmer's Digest, Greenville, MS, 71
Delta Leader
  Greenville, MS, 71
  Jackson, MS, 73
Delta Lighthouse, Greenville, MS, 71
Delta Messenger, Clarksdale, MS, 70
Delta Ministry Report, Greenville, MS, 71
Delta News
  Greenville, MS, 71
  Mobile, AL, 5
Delta Progress
  Mound Bayou, MS, 75
  Shelby, MS, 77
Democrat, Greensboro, NC, 97
Democratic Standard, Leavenworth, KS, 53
Demonstrator, Mound Bayou, MS, 75
Denver Blade, Denver, CO, 22
Denver Challenge, Denver, CO, 22
Denver Chronicle, Denver, CO, 22
Denver Dispatch, Denver, CO, 22
Denver Exponent, Denver, CO, 22
Denver Inquirer, Denver, CO, 22
Denver Star, Denver, CO, 22
Denver Sun, Denver, CO, 22
Denver Weekly News, Denver, CO, 22
Des Moines Register and Leader, Des
      Moines, IA, 51
Despite Everything, New York City, NY, 90
Detroit Advocate, Detroit, MI, 66
Detroit Contender, Detroit, MI, 66
Detroit Courier, Pittsburgh, PA, 114

Gazette (cont.)
  Oklahoma City, OK, 109
  Raleigh, NC, 99
  Savannah, GA, 40
  Syracuse, NY, 94
Gazette and Land Bulletin, Waycross, GA, 41
Gazette News Weekly, Syracuse, NY, 94
Gazetteer and Guide, Buffalo, NY, 87
Gem City Bulletin, Palatka, FL, 31
Genius of Freedom, Albany, NY, 86
*Genocide; Weekly Newsletter and Information
  Sheet*, Cincinnati, OH, 102
Gentlemen of Color, Matteson, IL, 48
Georgia Baptist
  Atlanta, GA, 34
  Augusta, GA, 36
Georgia Broadaxe
  Atlanta, GA, 34
  Macon, GA, 39
Georgia Congregationist, Atlanta, GA, 35
Georgia Courier, Pittsburgh, PA, 114
Georgia Guide, Atlanta, GA, 35
Georgia Insight, Waycross, GA, 41
Georgia Investigator, Americus, GA, 33
Georgia Mail, Waycross, GA, 41
Georgia News Weekly, Atlanta, GA, 35
Georgia Post, Roberta, GA, 40
Georgia Republican
  Augusta, GA, 36
  La Grange, GA, 39
Georgia Sentinel Bulletin, Atlanta, GA, 35
Georgia Speaker, Atlanta, GA, 35
Georgia Times, Savannah, GA, 40
Germ of Truth, Ponce de Leon, FL, 32
Ghetto Speaks Esvid, Detroit, MI, 67
Gibson Report, New York City, NY, 90
Girl's Guide, Oberlin, OH, 105
Gladiator, New York City, NY, 90
Gleanor
  Brunswick, GA, 37
  Knoxville, TN, 122
  Madison, GA, 39
Globe
  Barnesville, GA, 37
  Cleveland, OH, 103
  Jersey City, NJ, 83
  Milwaukee, WI, 142
  New York City, NY, 90
  Savannah, GA, 40
  Washington, DC, 25
Globe Advocate, Houston, TX, 131
Globe and Independent, Nashville, TN, 124
Globe Journal, Hopkinsville, KY, 56
Globe News, St. Paul, MN, 69
Glove Democrat, Hopkinsville, KY, 56
Gold Coast Star News, Riviera Beach, FL, 32
Gold Dollar, Austin, TX, 126
Gold Star News, Deerfield Beach, FL, 28
Gold Torch, Wilberforce, OH, 106
Golden Eagle, Vicksburg, MS, 77

Golden Eaglet, Kansas City, KS, 52
Golden Enterprise, Baltimore, MD, 63
Golden Epoch
  Fort Smith, AR, 10
  Helena, AR, 10
  Winchester, VA, 139
Golden House Digest, Birmingham, AL, 2
Golden Legacy, New York City, NY, 90
Golden Page, Washington, DC, 25
Golden Rule
  Goldsboro, NC, 97
  Greenville, MS, 71
  Greenwood, MS, 72
  New Bern, NC, 98
  Quincy, FL, 32
  Quitman, MS, 76
  Vicksburg, MS, 78
  Wilmington, NC, 100
Good Shepherd's Magazine, Montgomery, AL, 6
Goodwill Ambassador, Detroit, MI, 67
Gospel Banner
  Orangeburg, SC, 119
  St. Matthews, SC, 119
Gospel Messenger, Fort Adams, MS, 71
Gospel Plea, Edwards, MS, 71
Gospel Trumpet, Atlanta, GA, 35
Gracious Living, Cleveland, OH, 103
Grafrica News, East Orange, NJ, 83
Gramblinite, Grambling, LA, 59
Grand Rapids Times, Grand Rapids, MI, 68
Grand Selby Digest, St. Paul, MN, 69
Grapevine
  Chicago, IL, 44
  Fresno, CA, 15
Grapevine Journal, East Lansing, MI, 68
Graphic
  Boston, MA, 65
  Los Angeles, CA, 16
  Philadelphia, PA, 111
Grass Roots News, Washington, DC, 25
Great Circle News, Longview, TX, 132
Great Circle West, Dallas, TX, 128
Greater Boley Area Newsletter, Boley, OK, 107
Greater Milwaukee Star, Milwaukee, WI, 142
Greater News/New Jersey, Newark, NJ, 84
Greene County Democrat, Eutaw, AL, 3
Greensboro Daily News, Greensboro, NC, 97
Greensboro News and Record, Greensboro,
  NC, 97
Greensboro North Carolina Patriot,
  Greensboro, NC, 97
Greensboro Record, Greensboro, NC, 97
Greenville American, Greenville, SC, 118
Greenville Black Star, Columbia, SC, 117
Greenville Gazette [Owl], Greenville, MS, 71
Greenville Leader, Greenville, MS, 71
Grit, Washington, DC, 25
Growl, West Point, MS, 78
Guard
  Pittsburgh, PA, 114

Guard (cont.)
  San Antonio, TX, 133
  Victoria, TX, 134
Guardian
  Attalla, AL, 1
  Boston, MA, 65
  Decatur, AL, 3
  Detroit, MI, 67
Guide
  Baltimore, MD, 63
  Dayton, OH, 104
  Evanston, IL, 47
  Evansville, IN, 49
  Houston, TX, 131
  La Grange, GA, 39
  Natchez, MS, 76
  Statesboro, GA, 41
  Stockton, CA, 21
  Victoria, TX, 134
Guide Post
  Covington, GA, 38
  Madison, GA, 39
Guiding Star, Selma, AL, 7
Guiding Star of Truth, Houston, TX, 131
Gulf Coast Vigilante, Scranton, MS, 77
Gulf Informer, Mobile, AL, 5
Gulfport World, Gulfport, MS, 72
Gum Springs News, Gum Springs, VA, 135
Guthrie Progress, Guthrie, OK, 107
Half Century Magazine, Chicago, IL, 44
Halifax Enterprise, South Boston, VA, 139
Hamitic Palladium, Charleston, SC, 116
Hampton County Elevator, Brunson, SC, 116
*Hampton Institute Journal of Ethnic
  Studies*, Hampton, VA, 135
Hampton Roads Metro Weekender,
  Hampton, VA, 135
Hampton Script, Hampton, VA, 136
Hampton Student, Hampton, VA, 136
Hamtramck-North Detroit Echo
  Detroit, MI, 67
  Hamtramck, MI, 68
Hannibal Register, Hannibal, MO, 78
Happenings, Los Angeles, CA, 16
Happy News, Washington, DC, 25
Harambee
  Bridgeport, CT, 23
  Chattanooga, TN, 120
  Fort Carson, CO, 23
  Las Cruces, NM, 85
  Lawrence, KS, 53
  Los Angeles, CA, 16
  Orange, NJ, 84
  Tougaloo, MS, 77
Harambee Union, Bridgeport, CT, 23
Hard Line, Los Angeles, CA, 16
Hardy County News, Moorefield, WV, 141
Harlem Digest, New York City, NY, 90
Harlem Heights Daily Citizen, New York
  City, NY, 90

Miami Times, Miami, FL, 30
Michigan Age, Ann Arbor, MI, 66
Michigan Chronicle, Detroit, MI, 67
Michigan Citizen, Highland Park, MI, 68
Michigan Independent, Detroit, MI, 67
Michigan Representative, MI, 66
Michigan Scene, Detroit, MI, 67
Michigan Sentinel, Lathrup Village, MI, 68
Michigan State News, Grand Rapids, MI, 68
Michigan World, Detroit, MI, 67
Mid Hudson Herald, Poughkeepsie, NY, 93
Mid South Informer, Walls, MS, 78
Mid State Observer, Nashville, TN, 125
Middle Georgia Index, Eatonton, GA, 38
Midland Express, Boydton, VA, 135
Midland Guide, Cumberland, VA, 135
Mid-South Express, Memphis, TN, 123
Mid-Weekly Progress, Memphis, TN, 123
Midwest Journal, Jefferson City, MO, 78
Mid-Western Post, Indianapolis, IN, 50
Mileston Minute, Holmes Co., MS, 72
Militant
    Detroit, MI, 67
    Los Angeles, CA, 17
    New York City, NY, 91
Milwaukee Community Journal, Milwaukee,
    WI, 142
Milwaukee Courier, Milwaukee, WI, 142
Milwaukee Enterprise, Milwaukee, WI, 142
Milwaukee Enterprise Blade, Milwaukee,
    WI, 142
Milwaukee Gazette, Milwaukee, WI, 142
Milwaukee Soul City Times, Milwaukee,
    WI, 142
Milwaukee Star, Milwaukee, WI, 142
Milwaukee Star Times, Milwaukee, WI, 142
Milwaukee Sun, Milwaukee, WI, 142
Milwaukee Times, Milwaukee, WI, 142
Miner, Hill Top, WV, 141
Ministerial Voice, Muskogee, OK, 108
Minneapolis Messenger, Minneapolis, MN, 69
Minneapolis Observer, Minneapolis, MN, 69
Minneapolis Spokesman, Minneapolis, MN, 69
Minnesota Daily, Minneapolis, MN, 69
Minnesota Messenger, Minneapolis, MN, 69
Minorities and Women in Business,
    Burlington, NC, 95
Minority Bus. Soc. and Cult. Dir., Augusta,
    GA, 37
Minority Business Enterprise, Inglewood, CA, 15
Minority Business Journal, Little Rock, AR, 12
Mirror
    Anniston, AL, 1
    Bessemer, AL, 1
    Birmingham, AL, 2
    Cambridge, MA, 66
    Chicago, IL, 45
    Montgomery, AL, 6
    St. Joseph, MO, 80
    Selma, AL, 7

Mirror of Liberty, New York City, NY, 91
Mirror of the Times, San Francisco, CA, 20
Miss Black America, Philadelphia, PA, 112
Mission, Detroit, MI, 67
Mission Herald
    Louisville, KY, 57
    Philadelphia, PA, 112
Missionary Baptist of OK, OK, 106
Missionary Herald, Birmingham, AL, 2
Missionary Messenger, New Orleans, LA, 61
Missionary Presbyterian, Washington, GA, 41
Missionary Record, Charleston, SC, 116
Missionary Searchlight, Selma, AL, 7
Missionary Seer
    New York City, NY, 91
    Philadelphia, PA, 112
    Washington, DC, 26
Mississippi Baptist, Canton, MS, 70
Mississippi Baptist Herald, Senatobia, MS, 77
Mississippi Brotherhood, Robinsonville, MS, 76
Mississippi Educational Journal, Jackson,
    MS, 74
Mississippi Enterprise
    Chicago, IL, 45
    Jackson, MS, 74
Mississippi Free Press, Jackson, MS, 74
Mississippi Freelance, Greenville, MS, 72
*Mississippi Independent Beauticians Assoc.
    Newsletter*, Jackson, MS, 74
Mississippi Industrial College News, Holly
    Springs, MS, 72
Mississippi Letter, Okolona, MS, 76
Mississippi Memo Digest
    Greenville, MS, 72
    Meridian, MS, 75
Mississippi Mirror, Jackson, MS, 74
Mississippi Monitor, Meridian, MS, 75
Mississippi News, Greenville, MS, 72
Mississippi Newsletter, Tougaloo, MS, 77
Mississippi Old Fellows, Holly Springs,
    MS, 72
Mississippi Republican, Vicksburg, MS, 78
Mississippi Tribune, Vicksburg, MS, 78
Mississippi Weekly, Jackson, MS, 74
Mississippi World, Natchez, MS, 76
Mississippiana, Greenville, MS, 72
Missouri Baptist Together, Jefferson City,
    MO, 78
Missouri Citizen, St. Louis, MO, 80
Missouri Illinois Advance Citizen
    East St. Louis, IL, 47
    St. Louis, MO, 80
Missouri Messenger
    Kansas City, MO, 79
    Macon, MO, 79
Missouri State Post
    Kansas City, KS, 53
    Kansas City, MO, 79
Missouri State Register, Hannibal, MO, 78
Mixer and Server, Boston, MA, 65

Mobile Beacon, Mobile, AL, 5
Mobile Beacon & Alabama Citizen, Mobile, AL, 5
Mobile Nationalist, Mobile, AL, 5
Mobile Weekly Advocate, Mobile, AL, 5
Mobile Weekly Press Forum [Sun], Mobile, AL, 5
Mode, Farnam, NE, 82
Model Cities Action, Trenton, NJ, 85
Model Cities Voice, Perth Amboy, NJ, 84
Moderator, Louisville, KY, 57
Modern Business, New York City, NY, 91
Modern Farmer
    Chicago, IL, 45
    Nashville, TN, 125
Monitor
    Austin, TX, 126
    Beaumont, TX, 127
    Charleston, SC, 116
    Cheraw, SC, 117
    Columbia, SC, 117
    Donaldsonville, LA, 59
    Jackson, MS, 74
    Knoxville, TN, 122
    Malvern, AR, 13
    Montclair, NJ, 83
    Montgomery, AL, 6
    New Orleans, LA, 61
Monmouth Vindicator, Asbury Park, NJ, 82
Monroe Community Leader, Monroe, LA, 60
Monroe Dispatch, Monroe, LA, 60
Montana Plaindealer, Helena, MT, 82
Montgomery Enterprise, Montgomery, AL, 6
Montgomery/Tuskegee Times, Montgomery,
    AL, 6
Monthly Echo, Philadelphia, PA, 112
*Monthly Summary of Events and Trends in
    Race Relations*, Nashville, TN, 125
Moon Illustrated Weekly, Memphis, TN, 123
Morehouse Alumnus, Atlanta, GA, 35
Morehouse College Bulletin, Atlanta, GA, 35
Morgan State College Bulletin, Baltimore, MD, 64
Morgue, Washington, DC, 26
Morning Star, Columbus, MS, 71
Mortician Journal, Atlanta, GA, 35
Mosaic Guide, Little Rock, AR, 12
Moses Bulletin, Baltimore, MD, 64
Mound Bayou News Digest, Mound Bayou,
    MS, 76
Mound Bayou Sentinel, Mound Bayou, MS, 76
Mountain Eagle, Montgomery, WV, 141
Mountain Gleanor
    Asheville, NC, 95
    Raleigh, NC, 99
Mountain Leader, Charleston, WV, 141
Mountain News, Hendersonville, NC, 98
Mountain West Minority Reporter and Sentinel,
    West Valley City, UT, 135
Mouth-Piece
    Sandersville, GA, 40
    Tennille, GA, 41
Mouth-piece, Birmingham, AL, 2

North Star (cont.)
   Rochester, NY, 94
North Star Reporter, Anchorage, AK, 9
Northeast Florida Advocate, Jacksonville,
      FL, 29
Northern Star and Freeman's Advocate,
      Albany, NY, 86
Northwest 76er, Milwaukee, WI, 142
Northwest Bulletin, Seattle, WA, 140
Northwest Clarion, Portland, OR, 110
Northwest Clarion Defender, Portland, OR, 110
Northwest Courier, Tacoma, WA, 140
Northwest Dispatch, Tacoma, WA, 140
Northwest Enterprise
   Milwaukee, WI, 142
   Seattle, WA, 140
Northwest Herald, Seattle, WA, 140
Northwest Journal-Reporter, Tacoma, WA, 141
Northwest Monitor
   Minneapolis, MN, 69
   St. Paul, MN, 69
Northwest News, Detroit, MI, 67
Northwestern Bulletin, St. Paul, MN, 70
Northwestern Bulletin Appeal, St. Paul,
      MN, 70
Northwestern Christian Recorder, Chicago,
      IL, 45
Northwestern Recorder, Milwaukee, WI, 142
Northwestern Vine, Minneapolis, MN, 69
NSBE Bridge, Alexandria, VA, 135
NSBE Journal, New Orleans, LA, 61
NSBE Magazine, Alexandria, VA, 135
N.Y.L.I. Courier, Hempstead, NY, 87
Oahu Papers, Honolulu, HI, 41
Oak Cliff Eagle, Dallas, TX, 128
Oakland Independent, Oakland, CA, 19
Oakland Metro Reporter, San Francisco,
      CA, 21
Oakland New Day Informer, Oakland, CA, 19
Oakland Post, Oakland, CA, 19
Oakland Sunshine, Oakland, CA, 19
Oakland Times-Journal, Oakland, CA, 19
Observer
   Alexandria, LA, 58
   Baton Rouge, LA, 59
   Boston, MA, 65
   Charleston, SC, 116
   Charleston, WV, 141
   Chattanooga, TN, 121
   Chicago, IL, 45
   Denver, CO, 22
   Little Rock, AR, 12
   Macon, MS, 75
   New Orleans, LA, 61
   Portland, OR, 110
   Riverside, CA, 19
   San Francisco, CA, 21
   South Bend, IN, 51
   Stockton, CA, 21
   Toledo, OH, 105

Observer (cont.)
   Trenton, NJ, 85
   Washington, DC, 26
   Waterloo, IA, 52
   Wetumpka, AL, 9
Obsidian, Fredonia, NY, 87
Ocala News, Ocala, FL, 31
Occidental Lighthouse, Oklahoma City, OK, 109
Ocean State Grapevine, Providence, RI, 115
Odd Fellows Budget, Dallas, TX, 128
Odd Fellows Journal
   Montgomery, AL, 6
   Philadelphia, PA, 112
   Washington, DC, 26
Odd Fellows' Journal, Columbia, SC, 117
Odd Fellows' Journal of SC, Abbeville, SC, 115
Odd Fellows' Signal, Cleveland, OH, 103
Odd Fellows' Times, Winston-Salem, NC, 100
Ohio Baptist News, Columbus, OH, 103
Ohio Daily Express, Dayton, OH, 104
Ohio Eagle, Dayton, OH, 104
Ohio Express, Springfield, OH, 105
Ohio Falls Express, Louisville, KY, 58
Ohio Informer, Akron, OH, 101
Ohio Republican, Cincinnati, OH, 102
Ohio Sentinel, Columbus, OH, 103
Ohio Springfield, Springfield, OH, 105
Ohio Standard, Xenia, OH, 106
Ohio Standard and Observer
   Wilberforce, OH, 106
   Xenia, OH, 106
Ohio State Informer, Columbus, OH, 103
Ohio State Journal, Columbus, OH, 103
Ohio State Monitor, Columbus, OH, 103
Ohio State News, Columbus, OH, 104
Ohio State Pioneer, Cleveland, OH, 103
Ohio State Tribune
   Columbus, OH, 104
   Springfield, OH, 105
Ohio Torch, Columbus, OH, 104
Ohio Valley Clarion, Owensboro, KY, 58
Oil City Afro-American, Corsicana, TX, 127
Oklahoma Church and State News,
      Langston City, OK, 108
Oklahoma Constitution, Kingfisher, OK, 107
Oklahoma Defender, Oklahoma City, OK, 109
Oklahoma Dispatch, Oklahoma City, OK, 109
Oklahoma Eagle
   Muskogee, OK, 108
   Tulsa, OK, 109
Oklahoma Enterprise, Guthrie, OK, 107
Oklahoma Freeman, Watonga, OK, 110
Oklahoma Guide
   Guthrie, OK, 107
   Oklahoma City, OK, 109
Oklahoma Hornet, Waukomis?, OK, 110
Oklahoma Independent, Muskogee, OK, 108
Oklahoma Negro News, Bartlesville, OK, 106
Oklahoma Safeguard, Guthrie, OK, 107
Oklahoma School News, Guthrie, OK, 107

Oklahoma Star, Enid, OK, 107
Oklahoma Sun
   Ardmore, OK, 106
   Tulsa, OK, 109
Oklahoma Traveler, Oklahoma City, OK, 109
Oklahoma Tribune, Oklahoma City, OK, 109
Oklahoma Trumpet, Newkirk, OK, 109
Okmulgee Observer, Okmulgee, OK, 109
Old Ironsides' Monthly, Houston, TX, 131
Olio, New Orleans, LA, 61
Omaha Guide, Omaha, NE, 82
Omaha Monitor, Omaha, NE, 82
Omaha Star, Omaha, NE, 82
Omega Bulletin Oracle, Norfolk, VA, 137
On Guard, New York City, NY, 92
On the Ball Magazine, New York City, NY, 92
Onyx News, Columbus, OH, 104
Opinion
   Atlanta, GA, 35
   Boston, MA, 65
   Louisville, KY, 58
Opinion-Enterprise, Marianna, AR, 13
Opportunity, Chicago, IL, 45
Opportunity: Journal of Negro Life, New
      York City, NY, 92
Oracle, Washington, DC, 26
Orange County Star Review, Santa Ana, CA, 21
Orange Star Review, Los Angeles, CA, 17
Orangeburg Black Voice, Columbia, SC, 117
Orangeburg Herald, Orangeburg, SC, 119
Orator, Boston, MA, 65
Organizer, Fort Worth, TX, 129
Orlando Times, Orlando, FL, 31
Our Brother in Black, Muskogee
   OK (1880-1883), 108
   OK (1890-1891), 108
Our Carolina World, Elizabeth City, NC, 96
Our Choking Times, Columbus, OH, 104
Our Colored Missions, New York City, NY, 92
Our Eastern Star
   Fort Smith, AR, 10
   North Little Rock, AR, 13
Our Mail and Express, Red Bank, NJ, 85
Our National Progress, Wilmington, DE, 24
Our Neighbor, Detroit, MI, 67
Our Review, Little Rock, AR, 13
Our Women and Children, Louisville, KY, 58
Our World, New York City, NY, 92
Outlet
   Buffalo, NY, 87
   Los Angeles, CA, 17
Outlook
   Bakersfield, CA, 15
   Leesburg, FL, 30
   Memphis, TN, 123
   Raleigh, NC, 99
   Sacramento, CA, 20
   Winston-Salem, NC, 101
Outlook Magazine, Jackson, MS, 74

Philadelphia Sunday Sun, Philadelphia, PA, 112
Philadelphia Tribune, Philadelphia, PA, 113
Philly Talk, Philadelphia, PA, 113
Phlyon, Atlanta, GA, 35
Phoenix, Savannah, GA, 40
Phoenix Press Weekly, Phoenix, AZ, 9
Photo News, West Palm Beach, FL, 33
Picture News Weekly, Philadelphia, PA, 113
Piedmont, Concord, NC, 96
Piedmont Advocate, Salisbury, NC, 99
Piedmont Index, Concord, NC, 96
Piedmont Indicator, Spartanburg, SC, 120
Piedmont Sun
    Salisbury, NC, 99
    Statesville, NC, 100
Piedmont Voice
    Abbeville, SC, 115
    Greenwood, SC, 119
Pike County News and Record, Troy, AL, 8
Pike County Tribune, McComb, MS, 75
Pilot
    Chicago, IL, 45
    Hartford, CT, 23
    Nashville, TN, 125
    New York City, NY, 92
    Philadelphia, PA, 113
    Portsmouth, OH, 105
    Richmond, VA, 138
    Washington, DC, 26
    Wharton, TX, 134
    Wynne, AR, 14
Pine and Palm
    Boston, MA, 65
    New York City, NY, 92
Pine Bluff Post, Pine Bluff, AR, 14
Pine Bluff Press, Pine Bluff, AR, 14
Pine Bluff Weekly Herald, Pine Bluff, AR, 14
Pine City News, Pine Bluff, AR, 14
Pine Torch
    Brandon, MS, 70
    St. Louis, MO, 80
Pioneer
    Montgomery, WV, 141
    Muskogee, OK, 108
    Toledo, OH, 105
    Waverly, VA, 139
Pioneer Press, Martinsburg, WV, 141
Pittsburg Plain Dealer, Pittsburg, KS, 54
Pittsburgh Courier, Pittsburgh, PA, 114
Pittsburgh News, Pittsburgh, PA, 114
Pittsburgh Renaissance News, Pittsburgh,
    PA, 114
Plain Dealer
    Chicago, IL, 45
    Decatur, AL, 3
    Rochester, PA, 114
Plain Speaker, Orangeburg, SC, 119
Plain Truth of New Orleans, New Orleans,
    LA, 61

Plain Truth: Serving the North End,
    Champaign, IL, 42
Plaindealer
    Cincinnati, OH, 102
    Detroit, MI, 67
    Indianapolis, IN, 50
    Kansas City, KS, 53
    New Haven, CT, 24
    Orangeburg, SC, 119
    Osceola, AR, 14
    Palestine, TX, 133
    Pittsburgh, PA, 114
    Topeka, KS, 54
    Valdosta, GA, 41
    Washington, DC, 26
    Wichita, KS, 55
Plane, Marion, SC, 119
Planet
    Georgetown, SC, 118
    Louisville, KY, 58
    Memphis, TN, 123
    Richmond, VA, 138
Plantation Missionary
    Beloit, AL, 1
    Oberlin, OH, 105
Players, Los Angeles, CA, 17
Pledge, Norwood, LA, 62
Pleiades, Birmingham, AL, 2
Ploughshare, Pittsburgh, PA, 114
Plowman, Columbia, SC, 117
Poetic Journal, Boston, MA, 65
Pointer
    Chauncey, GA, 37
    Patton Junction, AL, 7
    Savannah, GA, 40
Political Digest, Philadelphia, PA, 113
Pomona Clarion, Pomona, CA, 19
Pontiac Agitator, Pontiac, MI, 69
Pontiac Echo, Pontiac, MI, 69
Portland New Age, Portland, OR, 110
Portland Observer, Portland, OR, 110
Portland Skanner, Portland, OR, 110
Post
    Atlanta, GA, 35
    Charlotte, NC, 95
    Chicago, IL, 45
    Greensboro, NC, 97
    Lima, OH, 105
    Milwaukee, WI, 142
    St. Augustine, FL, 32
    Waterloo, IA, 52
    Winston-Salem, NC, 101
Post and National Echo, Alexandria, VA, 135
Post News Sentinel, Seaside, CA, 21
Post Observer, Wichita, KS, 55
Post Tribune, Dallas, TX, 128
Postal Alliance
    Atlanta, GA, 35
    Detroit, MI, 67
    St. Louis, MO, 80

Practical Pointer, Aberdeen, MS, 70
Practical Pride, Aberdeen, MS, 70
Prairie View Standard, Prairie View, TX, 133
Preacher and Teacher
    Dallas, TX, 128
    Kosciusko, MS, 74
Preacher Safeguard, Kosciusko, MS, 74
Preacher's Safeguard, West Point, MS, 78
Precinct Reporter, San Bernardino, CA, 20
Press
    Clarksville, TN, 121
    Helena, AR, 11
    Mobile, AL, 5
    Morgan City, LA, 60
    Port Royal, VA, 138
    Roanoke, VA, 139
    Steelton, PA, 114
    Stockton, CA, 21
    Toledo, OH, 105
Press-Forum Sun, Mobile, AL, 5
Press-Forum Weekly, Mobile, AL, 5
Pride Magazine, Philadelphia, PA, 113
Primary Quarterly, Nashville, TN, 125
Primitive Baptist Herald, Huntsville, AL, 4
Primitive Herald, Tallahassee, FL, 32
Prince Hall Sentinel, New York City, NY, 92
Probe, New York City, NY, 92
Professional World, Columbia, MO, 78
Progress
    Dayton, OH, 104
    Goldsboro, NC, 97
    Hagan, GA, 38
    Helena, AR, 11
    Kingsland, AR, 11
    Laurel, MS, 74
    Omaha, NE, 82
    Quincy, IL, 48
    St. Landry, LA, 62
    Toledo, OH, 105
Progress Messenger, Tacoma, WA, 141
Progress News, Thomasville, GA, 41
Progress Record, Richmond, VA, 138
Progress Reporter, Beaumont, TX, 127
Progressive Afro-American, Pittsburgh, PA, 114
Progressive Age
    Alexandria, LA, 58
    Omaha, NE, 82
    Timpson, TX, 134
Progressive American, New York City, NY, 92
Progressive Banner, Georgiana, AL, 4
Progressive Church Record, Branchville,
    SC, 116
Progressive Citizen, Texarkana, AR, 14
Progressive Educator, Raleigh, NC, 99
Progressive Era
    Athens, GA, 33
    Kankakee, IL, 48
Progressive Herald
    Buffalo, NY, 87
    Seattle, WA, 140

Republican Sun, Providence, RI, 115
Republican Times, Summit, MS, 77
Republican Vindicator, Columbus, OH, 104
Rescue, New Orleans, LA, 61
Responsibility
    Massapequa, NY, 88
    Philadelphia, PA, 113
Review
    Boston, MA, 65
    Chicago, IL, 45
    Indianapolis, IN, 50
    Itta Bena, MS, 73
    Knoxville, TN, 122
    Petersburg, VA, 137
    Philadelphia, PA, 113
    Port Arthur, TX, 133
    Sedalia, MO, 81
Review of Black Political Economics, New
        Brunswick, NJ, 83
Review of Black Political History, New
        York City, NY, 93
Revolution, Chicago, IL, 45
Rhode Island Examiner, Providence, RI, 115
Rhode Island Independent, Providence, RI, 115
Richard Allen Review, Pine Bluff, AR, 14
Richmond Afro American, Richmond, VA, 138
Richmond Colored American, Richmond,
        VA, 138
Richmond Free Press, Richmond, VA, 138
Richmond Metro Reporter, San Francisco,
        CA, 21
Richmond Post, Oakland, CA, 19
Rifle, Columbus, GA, 37
Right House, KY, 56
Right On!
    New York City, NY, 93
    Teaneck, NJ, 85
Right On, Milwaukee, WI, 142
Right Way
    Norfolk, VA, 137
    Terre Haute, IN, 51
Rights and Reviews, New York City, NY, 93
Rights of All, New York City, NY, 93
Ringwood's Home Magazine, Cleveland,
        OH, 103
Rising Sun
    Des Moines, IA, 51
    Everett, WA, 139
    Fayetteville, TN, 121
    Kansas City, MO, 79
    Owensboro, KY, 58
    Pueblo, CO, 23
    Toomsuba, MS, 77
River Rouge and Ecorse Esquire, Detroit,
        MI, 67
Roanoke Daily Press, Roanoke, VA, 139
Roanoke Tribune
    Elizabeth City, NC, 96
    Roanoke, VA, 139

Robbins Journal
    Harvey, IL, 47
    S. Holland, IL, 48
Rochester Sentinel, Rochester, NY, 94
Rochester Voice, Rochester, NY, 94
Rock Hill Black View, Columbia, SC, 118
Rock Island News Times, Rock Island, IL, 48
Rockert, Detroit, MI, 67
Rockford Chronicle, Rockford, IL, 48
Rocky Mount Dispatch, Rocky Mount, NC, 99
Roger Williams Record, Nashville, TN, 125
Rome Enterprise, Rome, GA, 40
Rostrum, Cincinnati, OH, 102
Roxbury Community News, Roxbury, MA, 66
Royal Banner
    New Orleans, LA, 61
    Shreveport, LA, 62
Royal Lion's Tongue, Jacksonville, FL, 29
Royal Messenger
    Chicago, IL, 45
    Forrest City, AR, 10
    Helena, AR, 11
Rumor, New York City, NY, 93
Rural Messenger, Tuskegee, AL, 8
Rust College Sentinel, Holly Springs, MS, 72
Rust Enterprise, Holly Springs, MS, 72
Rustorian, Holly Springs, MS, 72
Rust Enterprise, Holly Springs, MS, 72
Sacramento Observer, Sacramento, CA, 20
Safe Guard-Enterprise, Charlotte, NC, 95
*Sage: A Scholarly Journal on Black
        Women*, Atlanta, GA, 35
St. Augustine's Messenger, Bay Saint Louis,
        MS, 70
St. Elizabeth Chronicle, St. Louis, MO, 80
St. John Herald, Montgomery, AL, 6
St. Joseph Defender, Greenville, AL, 4
St. Louis American, St. Louis, MO, 80
St. Louis Argus, St. Louis, MO, 81
St. Louis Chronicle, St. Louis, MO, 81
St. Louis Crusader, St. Louis, MO, 81
St. Louis Defender, St. Louis, MO, 81
St. Louis Globe-Democrat, St. Louis, MO, 81
St. Louis Independent News, St. Louis, MO, 81
St. Louis Independent-Clarion, St. Louis,
        MO, 81
St. Louis Mirror, St. Louis, MO, 81
St. Louis Monitor, St. Louis, MO, 81
St. Louis New Crusader, St. Louis, MO, 81
St. Louis Palladium, St. Louis, MO, 81
St. Louis Post Dispatch, St. Louis, MO, 81
St. Louis Sentinel, St. Louis, MO, 81
St. Louis Star Sayings, St. Louis, MO, 81
St. Louis Star-Times, St. Louis, MO, 81
St. Louis Tribune, St. Louis, MO, 81
St. Luke Fraternal Bulletin, Richmond, VA, 139
St. Luke Herald, Richmond, VA, 139
St. Mathews Lyceum Gazette, Detroit, MI, 67
St. Paul Bulletin, Lawrenceville, VA, 136
St. Paul Echo, St. Paul, MN, 70

St. Paul Recorder, St. Paul, MN, 70
St. Paul Sun, St. Paul, MN, 70
Salaam, Nyack?, NY, 93
Salem Post, Winston-Salem, NC, 101
Salina Enterprise, Salina, KS, 54
Salt, Springfield, MA, 66
Samaritan Herald, Sumter, SC, 120
Samaritan Herald and Voice of Job,
        Sumter, SC, 120
Samaritan Journal, Salisbury, NC, 99
Samaritan Leader, Sumter, SC, 120
San Antonio Informer
    Houston, TX, 131
    San Antonio, TX, 133
San Antonio Reformer, San Antonio, TX, 133
San Antonio Register, San Antonio, TX, 133
San Carlos Enquirer, Menlo Park, CA, 18
San Diego Monitor, San Diego, CA, 20
San Diego Voice, San Diego, CA, 20
San Diego Voice & Viewpoint, San Diego,
        CA, 20
San Fernando Gazette Express
    Pacoima, CA, 19
    San Fernando, CA, 20
San Fernando News Observer, Bakersfield,
        CA, 15
San Francisco Metro Reporter, San
        Francisco, CA, 21
San Francisco Mundo Hispano, Oakland,
        CA, 19
San Francisco Post
    Oakland, CA, 19
    San Francisco, CA, 21
San Francisco Reporter, San Francisco, CA, 21
San Francisco Sentinel, San Francisco, CA, 21
San Joaquin Metro Reporter, San Francisco,
        CA, 21
San Joaquin Progressor
    San Joaquin, CA, 21
    Stockton, CA, 21
San Jose/Peninsula Metro Reporter, San
        Francisco, CA, 21
Saturday Crusader, New Orleans, LA, 61
Saturday Evening News, Columbus, OH, 104
Saturday Evening Quill, Boston, MA, 65
Saturday Evening Tribune, Muskogee, OK, 108
Saturday News, Hopkinsville, KY, 56
Saturday Times, Hollandale, MS, 72
Savannah Banner, Savannah, GA, 40
Savannah Journal, Savannah, GA, 40
Savannah Tribune, Savannah, GA, 40
Savannah Weekly Echo, Savannah, GA, 40
Savoyager, Chicago, IL, 45
Say, New York City, NY, 93
SBE Journal, Alexandria, VA, 135
Schofield School Bulletin, Aiken, SC, 115
School Herald, Warren, AR, 14
Scimitar
    Ennis, TX, 129
    Memphis, TN, 123

Southern Advocate
  Holly Springs, MS, 72
  Macon, GA, 39
  Mound Bayou, MS, 76
Southern Afro-American
  Dermott, AR, 10
  Tupelo, MS, 77
Southern Age
  Atlanta, GA, 35
  New Orleans, LA, 61
Southern American, Chattanooga, TN, 121
Southern Appeal, Atlanta, GA, 35
Southern Argus
  Baxter Springs, KS, 52
  Fort Scott, KS, 52
  Kansas City, KS, 53
  Kansas City, MO, 79
Southern Broadaxe, Birmingham, AL, 2
Southern Broadcast, Monroe, LA, 60
Southern California Guide, Los Angeles,
    CA, 17
Southern Changes, Atlanta, GA, 36
Southern Christian Recorder
  Atlanta, GA, 36
  Columbus, GA, 37
  Little Rock, AR, 13
  Nashville, TN, 126
  Selma, AL, 7
Southern Courier
  Jacksonville, FL, 29
  Montgomery, AL, 6
Southern Education Report, Nashville, TN, 126
Southern Evangelist, Wilmington, NC, 100
Southern Forge, Lynchburg, VA, 136
Southern Forum, Greenville, MS, 72
Southern Frontier, Atlanta, GA, 36
Southern Gazette, Savannah, GA, 40
Southern Guide
  Columbus, GA, 37
  Houston, TX, 131
Southern Herald, Waco, TX, 134
Southern Illinois Press, East St. Louis, IL, 47
Southern Independent, Selma, AL, 7
Southern Indicator
  Columbia, SC, 118
  Spartanburg, SC, 120
Southern Leader
  Greenville, MS, 72
  Jacksonville, FL, 29
Southern Letter, Tuskegee, AL, 8
Southern Liberator, Forrest City, AR, 10
Southern Life, Atlanta, GA, 36
Southern Mediator
  Jacksonville, AR, 11
  Little Rock, AR, 13
Southern Mediator Journal
  Helena, AR, 11
  Little Rock, AR, 13
Southern Missionary, Lawrenceville, VA, 136
Southern Monitor, Wharton, TX, 134

Southern Negro, Camden, AR, 9
Southern News
  Asheville, NC, 95
  Cave Spring, KY, 56
  Richmond, VA, 139
  Savannah, GA, 40
Southern Newsletter, Louisville, KY, 58
Southern Notes, Utica, MS, 77
Southern Outlook, Eatonton, GA, 38
Southern Patriot
  Louisville, KY, 58
  New Orleans, LA, 61
Southern Planet, Cordele, GA, 38
Southern Ploughman, Columbia, SC, 118
Southern Pride, Horse Creek, AL, 4
Southern Progress, Holly Springs, MS, 72
Southern Racer, Hammond, LA, 59
Southern Recorder, Atlanta, GA, 36
Southern Register, Jackson, MS, 74
Southern Reporter
  Charleston, SC, 117
  Spartanburg, SC, 120
Southern Republican
  New Orleans, LA, 61
  White Springs, FL, 33
Southern Review
  Helena, AR, 11
  Jacksonville, FL, 30
  Montgomery, AL, 6
Southern School News, Nashville, TN, 126
Southern Sentiment, Memphis, TN, 123
Southern Sentinel
  Fitzgerald, GA, 38
  Talladega, AL, 7
Southern Sentinel News, Birmingham, AL, 2
Southern Standard, Macon, GA, 39
Southern Star
  Bethel, AL, 1
  Dothan, AL, 3
  Shreveport, LA, 63
Southern Struggle, Atlanta, GA, 36
Southern Sun
  Columbia, SC, 118
  Sikeston, MO, 81
Southern Tribune
  Petersburg, VA, 137
  Staunton, VA, 139
Southern University Digest, Baton Rouge,
    LA, 59
Southern Voice
  Montgomery, AL, 6
  St. Joseph, LA, 62
Southern Voices, Atlanta, GA, 36
Southern Watchman
  Hamlet, NC, 97
  Mobile, AL, 5
Southern Weekly, Smithfield, NC, 100
Southern Workman, Hampton, VA, 136
Southern World, Atlanta, GA, 36
Southland Herald, Mayesville, SC, 119

Southside Journal, Los Angeles, CA, 17
Southside Virginia Star, Petersburg, VA, 137
Southwest Citizen, Chicago, IL, 46
Southwest Georgian, Albany, GA, 33
Southwest News, Los Angeles, CA, 17
Southwest News Wave, Los Angeles, CA, 17
Southwest Review, Albuquerque, NM, 85
Southwest Topics/Sun Wave, Los Angeles,
    CA, 18
Southwest Wave, Los Angeles, CA, 18
Southwestern Banner, Houston, TX, 131
Southwestern Christian Advocate
  Birmingham, AL, 2
  New Orleans, LA, 61
  Philadelphia, PA, 113
Southwestern Herald, Victoria, TX, 134
Southwestern Journal, Langston City, OK, 108
Southwestern Outlook, Hope, AR, 11
Southwestern Press, Pocahontas, VA, 138
Southwestern Sun, Los Angeles, CA, 18
Southwestern Torch, El Paso, TX, 129
Southwestern World, Muskogee, OK, 108
Southwesterner, Muskogee, OK, 108
Space City, Houston, TX, 131
Space Waye, Norwalk, CT, 24
SPAR Southern Popular Athletic Review,
    Jackson, MS, 74
Sparks Magazine, Birmingham, AL, 2
Speaker
  Eatonville, FL, 28
  Lincoln Heights, OH, 105
  Norfolk, VA, 137
Speakin' Out News
  Decatur, AL, 3
  Huntsville, AL, 4
Speakin' Out Weekly, Decatur, AL, 3
Special Delivery, Waterloo, IA, 52
Spectator
  Buffalo, NY, 87
  Darien, GA, 38
  Galveston, TX, 130
  New Orleans, LA, 61
  Norfolk, VA, 137
  Oxford, MS, 76
  Wilmington, DE, 24
Spectrum, Knoxville, TN, 122
Spelman Messenger, Atlanta, GA, 36
Sphinx It's Journal, Minneapolis, MN, 69
Sphinx Magazine, Memphis, TN, 123
Spirit of Black Springfield, Springfield, IL, 49
Spirit of the Times, New York City, NY, 93
Spirit Publications, Elkhart, IN, 49
Spiritual Sunbeam, Pittsburgh, PA, 114
Spoken Word, New York City, NY, 93
Spokesman
  Baltimore, MD, 64
  Chicago, IL, 46
  Flint, MI, 68
  Ironton, OH, 105
  New Orleans, LA, 62

Bibliographic Checklist of African American Newspapers

Talladega Times, Talladega, AL, 7
Talladegan, Talladega, AL, 7
Tallapoosa News, Alexander City, AL, 1
Tampa Sentinel Bulletin, Tampa, FL, 32
Tan, Chicago, IL, 46
Tan Confessions, Savannah, GA, 40
Tan Pride, Omaha, NE, 82
Tattler
   Muskogee, OK, 108
   New York City, NY, 93
Teacher, Nashville, TN, 126
Teacher and Preacher, Meridian, MS, 75
Telegram
   Atlantic City, NJ, 83
   Charleston, SC, 117
   Detroit, MI, 67
   Jacksonville, FL, 30
   Newark, NJ, 84
   Pittsburgh, PA, 114
   Providence, RI, 115
   Valdosta, GA, 41
   Winston-Salem, NC, 101
Telegraph, Macon, GA, 39
Teller, Los Angeles, CA, 18
Temple Star, Georgiana, AL, 4
Temple University News, Philadelphia, PA, 113
Temple University Weekly, Philadelphia, PA, 113
Tempo, Houston, TX, 131
Tennessean, Nashville, TN, 126
Tennessee Baptist, Nashville, TN, 126
Tennessee Baptist Standard, Brownsville, TN, 120
Tennessee Star, Nashville, TN, 126
Tennessee Valley Reporter, Tuscumbia, AL, 8
Terre Bonne Messenger, Houma, LA, 59
Terre Haute Express, Terre Haute, IN, 51
Test, Galveston, TX, 130
Texarkana Courier, Texarkana, TX, 134
Texarkana Sun, Texarkana, TX, 134
Texas and Louisiana Watchman, Marshall, TX, 132
Texas Baptist Star, Dallas, TX, 128
Texas Blade
   Austin, TX, 127
   Galveston, TX, 130
Texas Christian Recorder, Sealy, TX, 133
Texas Citizen, Houston, TX, 131
Texas Colored Citizen, Luling, TX, 132
Texas Courier, Houston, TX, 131
Texas Examiner, Houston, TX, 131
Texas Freeman, Houston, TX, 131
Texas Guide
   Palestine, TX, 133
   Victoria, TX, 134
Texas Headlight, Austin, TX, 127
Texas Hornet, Forney, TX, 129
Texas Illuminator
   Austin, TX, 127
   San Antonio, TX, 133

Texas Interracial Review
   Austin, TX, 127
   Waco, TX, 134
Texas Messenger, Navasota, TX, 133
Texas News, Seguin, TX, 133
Texas Protest, Dallas, TX, 128
Texas Recorder, Dallas, TX, 128
Texas Reformer
   Denison, TX, 129
   Sherman, TX, 133
Texas Searchlight, Waco, TX, 134
Texas Steer, Tyler, TX, 134
Texas Times, Fort Worth, TX, 130
The Colony Leader, The Colony, TX, 134
Theatrical Newspicture Magazine, Washington, DC, 27
Theological Institute, Atlanta, GA, 36
Third Baptist Church Herald, Topeka, KS, 55
Third World, Washington, DC, 27
Third World Edition, Brooklyn, NY, 86
This Is It, Tampa, FL, 32
Thomasville Progressive News, Thomasville, GA, 41
Thomasville-Tallahassee News, Thomasville, GA, 41
Thoughts on Blackness, Trenton, NJ, 85
Three States, Cairo, IL, 42
Thurson County Dispatch, Tacoma, WA, 141
Tidings, East St. Louis, IL, 47
Tiger's Roar, Savannah, GA, 40
Tilloston Tidings, Austin, TX, 127
Timely Digest Magazine, Minneapolis, MN, 69
Times
   Atlanta, GA, 36
   Benoit, MS, 70
   Boston, MA, 66
   Columbus, GA, 37
   Evergreen, AL, 3
   Fort Worth, TX, 130
   Harrisburg, PA, 111
   Hattiesburg, MS, 72
   Helena, AR, 11
   Jasper, IN, 50
   Memphis, TN, 123
   Milledgeville, GA, 39
   Oakland, CA, 19
   Portland, OR, 110
   Pueblo, CO, 23
   Sedalia, MO, 81
   Stamps, AR, 14
   Statesville, NC, 100
   Terre Haute, IN, 51
   Wichita, KS, 55
Times Forum, Mobile, AL, 5
Times News, Washington, DC, 27
Times Observer, Topeka, KS, 55
Times of Freedom, New York City, NY, 93
Times Plaindealer, Birmingham, AL, 2
Times-American, Huntington, WV, 141
Times-Herald, New Smyrna Beach, FL, 31

Times-Observer
   Kansas City, MO, 79
   St. Joseph, MO, 80
   Topeka, KS, 55
Times-Union, Baltimore, MD, 64
Tips News Illustrated, Houston, TX, 132
Together, Jacksonville, FL, 30
Together: Baptist Educational Center Newsletter, New York City, NY, 93
Together Community Witness Newsletter, Valley Forge, PA, 115
Together; We Shall Overcome, Albany, NY, 86
Togetherness, Jacksonville, FL, 30
Toledo Journal, Toledo, OH, 105
Toledo Sepia City Press, Toledo, OH, 105
Toledo Voice, Toledo, OH, 105
Tonguelet, San Antonio, TX, 133
Topeka Call, Topeka, KS, 55
Topeka Plaindealer, Topeka, KS, 55
Topeka Tribune, Topeka, KS, 55
Topics, Atlantic City, NJ, 83
Torch, Youngstown, OH, 106
Torch Light, Danville, KY, 56
Torchlight
   Bryan, TX, 127
   Chester, SC, 117
   Providence, RI, 115
Torchlight Appeal, Fort Worth, TX, 130
Tougaloo Enterprise, Tougaloo, MS, 77
Tougaloo News, Tougaloo, MS, 77
Tougaloo Quarterly, Tougaloo, MS, 77
Trailer, West Point, GA, 41
Transcript, Evansville, IN, 49
Transition, Detroit, MI, 67
Transition Press, New York City, NY, 93
Trenton Sun, Trenton, NJ, 85
Trenton Tribune, Trenton, NJ, 85
Trestle Boards, Clarksdale, MS, 71
Tri Cities Informer and Call Post, Gadsden, AL, 4
Tri Cities Mirror, Sheffield, AL, 7
Tri City Journal
   Chicago, IL, 46
   Chicago Hts., IL, 46
Tri City News, Toledo, OH, 105
Tri County Bulletin, San Bernardino, CA, 20
Tri County News, Willingboro, NJ, 85
Triangle
   Angola, IN, 49
   Memphis, TN, 123
   Newport, RI, 115
Triangle Advocate, Pittsburgh, PA, 114
Tribunal Aid, High Point, NC, 98
Tribune
   Americus, GA, 33
   Atlanta, GA, 36
   Austin, TX, 127
   Baden, NC, 95
   Baltimore, MD, 64
   Bessemer, AL, 1
   Boley, OK, 107

Weekly Call, Topeka, KS, 55
Weekly Carrier, Fort Wayne, IN, 49
Weekly Challenger, St. Petersburg, FL, 32
Weekly Chronicle, St. Petersburg, FL, 32
Weekly Citizen, Montgomery, AL, 6
Weekly Colored Tidings, Conway, AR, 9
Weekly Colored Times, Conway, AR, 9
Weekly Communicator, Jackson, MS, 74
Weekly Echo, Meridian, MS, 75
Weekly Herald, Jefferson City, MO, 78
Weekly Inquirer, Montclair, NJ, 83
Weekly Journal of Progress, Cuthbert, GA, 38
Weekly Leader, Alexandria, LA, 58
Weekly Louisianian, New Orleans, LA, 62
Weekly Loyal Georgian, Augusta, GA, 37
Weekly Messenger, St. Martinville, LA, 62
Weekly Negro World, Cary, MS, 70
Weekly News
  Columbus, GA, 38
  Decatur, IL, 47
Weekly Observer
  Fern Park, FL, 28
  Myrtle Beach, SC, 119
Weekly Pelican, New Orleans, LA, 62
Weekly Pilot, Birmingham, AL, 3
Weekly Progress, Muskogee, OK, 109
Weekly Prophet, Philadelphia, PA, 113
Weekly Recorder
  Jackson, MS, 74
  Mound Bayou, MS, 76
Weekly Review
  Anniston, AL, 1
  Augusta, GA, 37
  Huntsville, AL, 4
  Lincoln, NE, 82
  Montgomery, AL, 6
  New Albany, IN, 51
  Sioux City, IA, 52
Weekly Sentinel
  Cuthbert, GA, 38
  Mobile, AL, 6
Weekly Star, Mound City, IL, 48
Weid: the Sensibility Review, Homestead, FL, 29
Welcome Friend, St. Louis, MO, 81
Welfarer, New York City, NY, 93
West End News, Cincinnati, OH, 102
West Side Echo, Detroit, MI, 68
West Side Torch, Chicago, IL, 46
West Side Torch Lawndale Edition, Chicago, IL, 46
West Texas Times, Lubbock, TX, 132
West Texas Voice, Galena Park, TX, 130
West Virginia Beacon Digest, South Charleston, WV, 142
West Virginia Clarion, Bluefield, WV, 141
West Virginia Courier, Huntington, WV, 141
West Virginia Digest, Charleston, WV, 141
West Virginia Enterprise
  Charleston, WV, 141

West Virginia Enterprise (cont.)
  Terre Alta, WV, 142
West Virginia Freeman, Parkersburg, WV, 142
West Virginia Tribune, North Fork, WV, 142
West Virginia Weekly, Charleston, WV, 141
Westchester County Press
  Hastings on Hudson, NY, 87
  White Plains, NY, 94
  Yonkers, NY, 94
Westchester Observer, Mount Vernon, NY, 88
Western Advocate
  Compton, CA, 15
  Fort Gibson, OK, 107
Western Age
  Langston City, OK, 108
  Taft, OK, 109
Western American, Oakland, CA, 19
Western Appeal
  Chicago, IL, 46
  St. Paul, MN, 70
  San Francisco, CA, 21
Western Argus, Kansas City, MO, 79
Western Christian Advocate, Longview, TX, 132
Western Christian Recorder
  Kansas City, KS, 53
  Kansas City, MO, 79
  Los Angeles, CA, 18
  Macon, MO, 79
  Nashville, TN, 126
  St. Louis, MO, 81
Western Cyclone, Nicodemus, KS, 53
Western Dispatch
  Los Angeles, CA, 18
  Phoenix, AZ, 9
Western Echo, Bath/Utica, NY, 86
Western Enterprise
  Colorado Springs, CO, 22
  Pittsburgh, PA, 114
Western Florida Bugle, Marianna, FL, 30
Western Guide, Eutaw, AL, 3
Western Herald, Chicago, IL, 46
Western Home, Kingfisher, OK, 107
Western Ideal, Pueblo, CO, 23
Western Index
  Dallas, TX, 129
  Houston, TX, 132
  Topeka, KS, 55
Western Informant, Los Angeles, CA, 18
Western Journal of Black Studies, Pullman, WA, 139
Western Kentucky Progress, Owensboro, KY, 58
Western Messenger
  Jefferson City, MO, 78
  Kansas City, MO, 79
  Macon, MO, 79
  St. Louis, MO, 81
Western News, Los Angeles, CA, 18
Western Opinion, Chicago, IL, 46
Western Optic, Moberly, MO, 80

Western Outlook
  Sacramento, CA, 20
  San Francisco, CA, 21
Western Recorder
  Kansas City, MO, 79
  Topeka, KS, 55
Western Review
  Little Rock, AR, 13
  Sacramento, CA, 20
Western Sentinel, Kansas City, MO, 79
Western Spirit, Paola, KS, 53
Western Star
  Albuquerque, NM, 85
  Fordyce, AR, 10
  Fort Worth, TX, 130
  Houston, TX, 132
  Temple, TX, 133
Western Star of Zion, Dallas, TX, 129
Western Sunrise, Brooklyn, NY, 87
Western Trumpet, Topeka, KS, 55
Western Voice, Las Cruces, NM, 85
Western World
  Ardmore, OK, 106
  Chandler, OK, 107
  Guthrie, OK, 107
  Kingfisher, OK, 108
  Muskogee, OK, 109
  Oklahoma City, OK, 109
  Shawnee, OK, 109
Western World Reporter, Memphis, TN, 123
Westside Gazette, Fort Lauderdale, FL, 28
What's Going On, Los Angeles, CA, 18
What's Happening Now, Fayetteville, NC, 96
Whip, Miami, FL, 31
Whirl-examiner, St. Louis, MO, 81
White Man and the Negro Magazine, Fort Worth, TX, 130
White River Advance, Newport, AR, 13
White River Advocate, Newport, AR, 13
Whole Truth, Memphis, TN, 123
Wichita Globe, Wichita, KS, 55
Wichita Protest, Wichita, KS, 55
Wichita Searchlight, Wichita, KS, 55
Wichita Times, Wichita, KS, 55
Wichita Tribune, Wichita, KS, 55
Wide Awake
  Birmingham, AL, 3
  New Orleans, LA, 62
Wide Awake Bulletin, Birmingham, AL, 3
Wideawake, Gadsden, AL, 4
Wilberforce Student, Wilberforce, OH, 106
Wilberforcian, Wilberforce, OH, 106
Wiley Reporter, Marshall, TX, 132
Wilkinson County Appeal, Woodville, MS, 78
Williamsburg Republican, Kingstree, SC, 119
Wilmington Beacon
  Wilmington, CA, 21
  Wilmington, DE, 24
Wilmington Journal
  Wilmington, DE, 24